READINGS IN SOCIETY AND THOUGHT

IN MODERN AMERICA

Also by HARVEY WISH

Society and Thought in Early America:
A Social and Intellectual History of
the American People Through 1865.
New impression with Revised
Bibliography, 1962.

Society and Thought in Modern America:
A Social and Intellectual History of
the American People from 1865.
Second Edition, 1962.

READINGS IN

SOCIETY AND THOUGHT

IN MODERN AMERICA

HARVEY WISH

Elbert Jay Benton
Distinguished Professor of History
Western Reserve University

DAVID McKAY COMPANY, INC.

NEW YORK

READINGS IN SOCIETY AND
THOUGHT IN MODERN AMERICA

LIBRARY OF CONGRESS CATALOG CARD NUMBER: 66-16644

MANUFACTURED IN THE UNITED STATES OF AMERICA

CONTENTS

INTRODUCTION

To PROVIDE comprehensiveness and direction for this selection of readings in social-intellectual history since 1865, the editor has been guided partly by the themes and organization of his *Society and Thought in Modern America*. Thus the early sections begin with the freedman and the South, the factor of race, and the various ethnic groups, with specific treatment of cultural pluralism and stereotypes. George Fitzhugh of Virginia anticipates Henry Grady's idea of the New South—and both are represented—by envisaging a paternalistic peonage system controlled by planters and merchants; Grady urges Northern businessmen to cooperate economically with the South, but to leave the race question alone. The Louisiana maverick, George Washington Cable, considers himself the spokesman of the liberal "silent South" and candidly reveals the exploitations of the convict lease system and the all-white juries. He reaches, however, only a dwindling audience.

The conservative Fitzhugh–Grady formula has its Negro exponent in Booker T. Washington, who frankly accepting segregation, assumes that if the Negro became economically indispensable to the Southern white, then other social gains might be eventually added. A glimpse of the unreconstructed South and the Klan tradition is afforded by Thomas Dixon's best-selling novel *The Clansman*, which provided the story of the *Birth of a Nation*. The young Dr. W. E. B. Du Bois, not yet converted to his later militant race philosophy, seems to compromise with the conservative Booker T. Washington in terms of a segregated society for the Philadelphia Negro who had failed to win a stake in white society. In a long-forgotten essay, Dr. Franz Boas tells a Negro audience how anthropologists had demolished the myth of Negro inferiority. Finally, Dr. Martin Luther King, Jr., the contemporary exponent of a nonviolent strategy derived from Gandhi and Niebuhr, tells of his intellectual pilgrimage to the Negro Revolution that followed the *Brown* v. *Topeka* case (also included in these selections).

Of the various unifying themes, that of Darwinism is undoubtedly best represented. There are the proliferated religious responses to evolution in Walter Rauschenbusch's emphatic argument for the social gospel and Christian socialism; in Father John Ryan's Catholic Action proposals following Pope Leo XIII's famous encyclical *Rerum Novarum* to halt the estrangement of the workingman from the Church; in the scientific agnosticism of Robert Ingersoll; and in various church leaders.

John Fiske, the historian and philosopher, has been chosen to present the case for the evolutionists like Asa Gray, and the attack on the anti-evolutionist Louis Agassiz, who clung to the traditional version of the origin of species. At some length, William James explains pragmatism and its Darwinian assumptions of a truth discoverable only by experimentation and consequences; and John Dewey offers his famous explanation of pragmatism and Darwinism as marking a revolution in thought that reverses the static classical pattern of 2000 years. Dewey's link of pragmatism and progressive education is most effectively and clearly summarized in his credo, "My Pedagogic Creed," which is completely reproduced.

Along this same line of the Darwinian revolution in thought, there are most of the famous "Reform Darwinists" among the sociologists and related disciplines—Lester F. Ward, who wishes to guide social evolution by an enlightened will, Thorstein Veblen, who hopes to reverse the evolutionary process that produced the leisure class and to make the engineer with an "instinct for workmanship" the leader of society, and Henry George, singletaxer, who is also among the believers in social planning and the intelligent guidance of the course of social evolution. Finally, there are the legal realists and "social jurists" who derive philosophically from the Darwinian revolution—Oliver Wendell Holmes, William O. Douglas, and Earl Warren. Nor are the conservative Spencerians neglected, for William Graham Sumner argues most emphatically for the principles of natural rights and evolving "folkways." H. L. Mencken, the Baltimore iconoclast, and author of many satiric articles on the

fundamentalists of the Bible Belt, who were at war with Darwinism, defines a conservative's idea of liberty.

It seemed most appropriate to relate the great historians to
the Darwinian revolution. Henry Adams tells of his own personal evolution toward scientific materialism in which Darwin
and Helmholtz play a part. Frederick Jackson Turner, who
began his career as a historian when evolutionism was in flower,
uses Darwinism to explain the impact of the moving frontier
upon society. And Charles Beard applies various aspects of pragmatic thought and method, although he tells how he broke with
extreme positivism based on the methods of the natural sciences.
Like the other pragmatists, he retained his suspicion of allegedly absolute truths, objectivity, and the sterility of the traditional quest for certainty.

These illustrations will indicate the patterning attempted in
the selection of these documents. The editor has also sought
to aid the student by offering capsule but interpretive biog-
raphies covering the entire career of each author; and he has
tried to relate the central idea of each selection to this background material. While there will be inevitable omissions of
many individuals deemed important by scholars, this modest-
sized collection should be readable and useful throughout.

READINGS IN SOCIETY AND THOUGHT

IN MODERN AMERICA

Chapter One

THE FREEDMAN AND
THE NEW SOUTH

"THE FREEDMAN
AND HIS FUTURE" *

By George Fitzhugh

George Fitzhugh (1806–81), Port Royal, Virginia, lawyer and proslavery theorist, urges a peonage system to save the helpless freedmen from destructive white competition

In 1869, when *Lippincott's Magazine* published George Fitzhugh's "The Freedman and His Future," the old Virginia lawyer had left his war-damaged plantation home to live at Camp Lee where he would serve as a local legal adviser to a freedman's court. He still retained the same point of view he had held in 1854 when he had published his original *Sociology for the South* to prove that free societies had always failed in history because laissez-faire liberalism ran counter to the fact of human inequality. His *Cannibals All!* (1857) pictured the dire consequences of modern laissez-faire in the then current exploitation of laborers, "slaves without masters," and the poor in starving Ireland. He attacked the harm wrought by Jeffersonian liberalism and such "isms" as religious skepticism, political individualism, feminism, and abolitionism. Fitzhugh insisted that since slavery was normal, necessary, and historical, it must defeat free society; but one of his disturbed readers, Abraham Lincoln, wrote a House-Divided speech to prove that freedom must ultimately triumph everywhere in the world. During the Civil War, pro-Union leaflets cited

* George Fitzhugh, "The Freedman and His Future," *Lippincott's Magazine*, IV (1869), 436–39.

Paternalistic peonage

as representative of Southern thought Fitzhugh's dictum that "Slavery, black or white, is right and necessary."

In "The Freedman and His Future," Fitzhugh revealed that not even the Civil War and Reconstruction had changed his faith in the "slavery principle." He not only pictured ex-slaves and ex-masters as trying to revive the antebellum plantation system, but argued that Negroes could not survive competition with superior whites. Therefore, he urged the creation of a paternalistic peonage system to direct and control former slaves. This idea of peonage was discussed by other Southern planters and was partly exemplified by the new Black Codes, which restrained the Negroes' freedom of movement, and by the system of sharecropping.

*X$ ① Extermination
② Subordination*

1869

IN OUR neighborhood, for the last two years, a force of negroes diminished by more than a third has produced more than a force a third larger before the war. Negroes in the South do not now feign sickness and work lazily, as when slaves. The fear of losing employment is a better stimulant to labor than was the fear of bodily punishment. The falling off of the aggregate crops of the South is sufficiently accounted for by the want of capital to employ labor, without charging the negroes with unwillingness to labor.

After the law prohibiting corporal punishment in the navy was enacted, the old, hard-working, faithful tars, seeing that they were forced to do double work by the worthless and idle, who no longer stood in fear of punishment, took the matter in hand themselves, and gave severer flagellations to the idlers than they had ever received from superior authority.

Thus it will be in the South. Our legislatures will be composed in large part of negroes, and these negroes, seeing that the support of the whole community must fall chiefly on their race, will be most ready to enact vagrant and vagabond laws, which shall compel all the poor to labor, whether they be blacks or whites. The negroes now know that they must ever be the "hewers of wood and drawers of water." Knowing this, they will be far more ready than the whites to punish severely all idleness, because idleness will throw on a few blacks the burden that should be borne equally by all. They will soon perceive, too, that labor alone pays taxes, and that the chief burden of taxation must fall

Labor carries the burden of taxation. Many Negroes are assuming their responsibility

"THE FREEDMAN AND HIS FUTURE" 3.

on them. Lands and houses cannot pay taxes, because they are non-producers. Their owners always reduce the wages of labor and increase rents just in proportion as taxes are increased, and thus transfer the whole burden of taxation to the shoulders of the laboring poor. If they did not thus do, they would be forced to sell their lands and houses to pay the taxes. The negroes, seeing this, will oppose all heavy taxation. Indeed, now that they have given up all hope of "the mule and forty acres of land," we think that they will make quite conservative legislators—at least a few of them, here in Virginia, intermixed with white legislators and held in check by the governor's veto, will do no harm.

I assure you, Mr. Editor, that our negroes will be more profitable to their employers than were slaves to their masters. Besides that we have adopted the high-pressure system of free competitive society and exchanged hickories for hunger, we see the fact every day exhibited around us in the greater productiveness and less expensiveness of free negro labor. Negroes cannot live in the South as they do in the West Indies, on the voluntary fruits of the earth. They must work or starve. Having no lands of their own, and wholly incapable of holding and managing lands if they owned them, they must labor on the lands of the whites, for they are only qualified for farming labor. Even in Barbadoes, the products of the island for some time after emancipation were increased, because there were no waste, unappropriated lands in that island, and the negroes had to work or starve. The failure of the free-labor system in the rest of the West India Islands has been rather owing to the fewness and inefficiency of white employers than to the worthlessness of the negroes. Before our war, a fourth of the slaves were idle, pampered house-servants; a fourth of them were owned by ladies, who indulged them too much and required them to labor too little; and at least another fourth by masters who managed their labor unskillfully and unprofitably; so that not more than one-fourth of the negro slaves were so managed as to make their labor as productive as it should have been. Now there can be no idlers, because idleness brings on starvation. Few have house-servants, because we are too poor to employ them. All must work at productive farm-work, for none but skillful, attentive, industrious farmers can afford to employ negro labor.

So soon as the Southern farmers become able to stock their farms properly, there will arise a demand for all the negro labor of the country, and that labor, being stimulated and impelled by the all-pervading, ever-present, never-ceasing power of hunger, will be more productive than before the war. Let the North be but patient, and leave the management of the negro labor subject to the South, and in a very few years we will send them annually more cotton, sugar, tobacco, wheat, corn, etc., than before the war, and buy more of their manufactures. So long as good lands are abundant, it is idle to talk about the South becoming a manufacturing country. We have not enough labor to cultivate our lands, and that labor of too rude and unskilled a character ever to be adapted to manufacturing.

If, after all, the negroes will not work, we shall be compelled to call in the Chinese. The cotton-fields of the South must be tilled to their utmost capacity for the good of mankind, for even the savage races, who learn nothing else, are fast learning to wear cotton cloth; and cotton-fields cannot be tilled by white labor. But we protest against the cruel and perilous experiment of bringing in Chinese to throttle and strangle out the negroes, until ample time and experience prove that the negroes will not work. We love and admire the amiable, generous, brave, whole-souled negro, and we detest the mean, stingy, cheating, cowardly, treacherous, lying Chinese. The negro is doing very well, as a laborer, at present, and when the late Confederate States are restored to the Union, and all the exciting political issues of the day settled, we have every reason to hope and expect that whites and blacks will get along quite amicably together, and our industrial affairs become more flourishing and profitable than ever before.

No man who knew Virginia before the war, and who will visit it now, will be able to discover the slightest difference in the deportment of the blacks and whites to one another, now and then. He will see the same respectful deference, the same obliging kindness, the same readiness to serve without pay, or the expectation of pay, in all small matters, and the same sense of inferiority, manifested toward the whites by the blacks, now as before the war. He will find, too, the negroes working in the fields for the whites, and working far more faithfully and industriously than when slaves, and laboring for half in wages what they used to get in allowance. Who can tread on the worm, who insult feeble woman, who maltreat the infant, who spurn the sick, the aged, the infirm?—in fine, who is not softened and conciliated by conscious, confessed, unoffending weakness. Sterne beautifully exclaims: *"I am thy servant,* disarms one of the power of a master."* Every word, every gesture, every look of the negro, says in mute eloquence to the white man "I am thy servant."* It would be as easy for the mountains to descend to the plains, for the lakes and seas to dry up, for all nature to change its course, as for the negro to change his deportment toward the white man. He feels his inferiority, and can never divest himself of that feeling. He is kind, generous and obliging, because to be so is part of his amiable nature, which he can never throw off. The negroes are by far the best bred, most polite people in the world. I never saw a vulgar negro, for every one of them knows his place, and behaves as becomes his place. On the other hand, I often meet with assuming, pretentious white men, who are obtrusively and disgustingly vulgar. The white man at the South who is habitually coarse or rude or imperious or insulting in his deportment to negroes is a mere brutal, featherless biped. I have never yet met with the first white man who did thus behave. On the contrary, all white men are more studiously careful to return the negro's polite and respectful salutation with a salutation equally polite and respectful than they are so to return the salutation of white men, because such neglect would wound the black man's feelings, and would probably be attributed to mere inadvertence by the white man. The amicable and kindly relations subsisting between the blacks and whites are owing entirely to the fact that the races are so intermixed and blended together that each negro of necessity becomes dependent on some white man, and may select that man in whom he has most confidence or to whom he is most attached. In time, a relation like that of patron and client in ancient Rome will grow up between whites and blacks. During the whole continuance of the Roman commonwealth this relation was most kindly and faithfully observed. Some legislation is needed to protect children from cruel treatment by their parents and to protect wives from ill-usage by their husbands, but such legislation is seldom called into active exercise.

White colonization is proceeding with rapidity in every corner of the savage world. The civilized and uncivilized races are ever in deadly hostility where they form separate adjoining communities. This hostility is rapidly exterminating the inferior races. Philanthropy has devised or suggested no measures that shall prevent this rapidly-progressing extermination. Blending and

Inferior races will be exterminated.

intermixing the races, with proper social, legal and political regulations, would avert the catastrophe. The whites, however, will not tolerate savages among them unless they can in some way be made useful and profitable. This can only be effected by compelling the savages to serve the whites for a term of years for hire. If I have shown that weakness is power, that it is natural for the feeble and dependent to look up to, obey and love their superiors, and quite as natural for the strong and the wise to protect and care for the feeble, ignorant and dependent, I think I have indicated a possible and peaceful solution of the great social problem of the day. Some will say I propose to reinstate slavery on a broader basis than ever. I propose no such thing, but that government shall discharge its duty by compelling all men who have no visible means of support, to labor. When whites seize upon and appropriate the lands of savages, they deprive them of all means of living. It will be their duty to support them, but they can only do so by compelling them to labor. Savages are all vagrants, but by being compelled to regular labor they would be cured of their vagrancy, and taught much of the useful arts of civilized life. I have no particular partiality for my plan. If any can be suggested equally efficient, and yet milder, I shall prefer it to my own. As to its likeness to slavery, when we analyze the relation between capital and skill and free labor, we shall discover something very like slavery, which yet is not slavery. It would be, in truth, but a necessary apprenticeship—the only feasible means of saving savages from extermination, and at the same time of civilizing them. Even at the South, the prevalent doctrine is, that if savages were sent to common schools, academies, colleges and universities, and educated in all respects like the whites, when they grew up there would be found no difference between the races except in physical appearance. Acting upon this false and cruel doctrine, distinguished politicians and philanthropists are already saying, "We have set the negroes free, furnished them with food and clothing, sent them to common schools, and many to colleges and universities, and given them all the legal and political rights of free citizenship: now, if they cannot get along in the field of free competition, it is their fault, not ours." Now, I verily believe there is not one decently-informed philanthropist in America who does not know that a literary education unfits a full-blooded negro for field-work or other servile offices, prepares him for no other occupation, and thus deprives him of all means

We must save the Negro from extermination → make him a slave again
Assimilation

of support except theft and robbery. The experiment of educating negroes has been assiduously carried on for four thousand years. The Egyptians, in ancient times the most civilized of the white race, have ever been in contact with them; and the Arabs, whose civilization also dates from time immemorial, crossing the narrow straits of Bab-el-Mandeb, have so commingled and crossed blood with them that there are now no really full-blooded, thoroughly black negroes, except on the extreme western coast and in the partially-explored regions about the head of the Nile. In all instances it is found that the brown Mohammedan negroes, crossed with Arabic blood, are superior to the typical, thoroughbred, pure black negroes. But the infusion of white blood has been so small that they have acquired none of the modes or arts of civilized life. They have no houses, no farms, no ploughs, no wagons, no laws, no churches, no public highways, no separate properties, little or no clothing—in fact, none of the institutions that belong to civilized life, and which distinguish civilized men from barbarians. They herd together from necessity, for no African's life would be safe who attempted to live secluded. Their so-called cities, collections of huts, inferior to the residences of the beaver, afford the most conclusive evidence that they are, after four thousand years of association with civilized mankind, very little superior to the other gregarious animals that infest the wilds of Africa. Yet their patronizing friends propose to teach them to read and then start them in life, to make their way in the field of free competition with the civilized whites. But the civilized races will soon occupy all the territories over which savages now roam. They must either subordinate the savages to the whites, preserve their lives, civilize and Christianize them; or, under the banner of "Liberty, Fraternity and Equality," expose them to the war of the wits and of free competition with the whites, and thus cruelly exterminate them.

"THE FREEDMAN'S CASE IN EQUITY" *

By George Washington Cable

George Washington Cable (1844–1925), New Orleans maverick, attacks racial injustice in the courts and schools.

While Southern Local Colorists like Joel Chandler Harris usually avoided realistic aspects of the race question, George Washington Cable focused his rich literary career around this issue. This earnest New Orleans-born Confederate veteran, whose mother and sisters stubbornly refused to join their neighbors in pledging allegiance to the Union conquerors, changed his mind about Southern racial ideas during Reconstruction when he observed white mobs attacking Negro groups. Even his romantic tales, such as the famous *Creole Days* (1879), reflect his strong ethical awareness of racial injustice and other social ills.

In 1885, however, after he moved to Northampton, Massachusetts, he aroused Southern anger by his controversial *The Silent South*, from which the following selection is taken. Southern liberals like Joel Chandler Harris and Henry Grady of the Atlanta *Constitution* were indeed silent to Cable's sweeping proposals to undo the system of Jim Crow at a time when the demagogic Tillmans and Vardamans were in effect encouraging lynchings and attacking the Negro schools.

T HE BELIEF is all too common that the nation, having aimed at a wrong result and missed, has left us of the Southern States to get now such other result as we think best. I say this belief is not universal. There are those among us who see that America has no room for a state of society which makes its lower classes harmless

* From George Washington Cable, *The Silent South* (1879), 16–17, 30–34.

by abridging their liberties, or, as one of the favored class lately said to me, has "got 'em so they don't give no trouble." There is a growing number who see that the one thing we cannot afford to tolerate at large is a class of people less than citizens; and that every interest in the land demands that the freedman be free to become in all things, as far as his own personal gifts will lift and sustain him, the same sort of American citizen he would be if, with the same intellectual and moral calibre, he were white.

Thus we reach the ultimate question of fact. Are the freedman's liberties suffering any real abridgment? The answer is easy. The letter of the laws, with a few exceptions, recognizes him as entitled to every right of an American citizen; and to some it may seem unimportant that there is scarcely one public relation of life in the South where he is (not) arbitrarily and unlawfully compelled to hold toward the white man the attitude of an alien, a menial, and a probable reprobate, by reason of his race and color. One of the marvels of future history will be that it was counted a small matter, by a majority of our nation, for six millions of people within it, made by its own decree a component part of it, to be subjected to a system of oppression so rank that nothing could make it seem small except the fact that they had already been ground under it for a century and a half.

Examine it. It proffers to the freedman a certain security of life and property, and then holds the respect of the community, that dearest of earthly boons, beyond his attainment. It gives him certain guarantees against thieves and robbers, and then holds him under the unearned contumely of the mass of good men and women. It acknowledges in constitutions and statutes his title to an American's freedom and aspirations, and then in daily practice heaps upon him in every public place the most odious distinctions, without giving ear to the humblest plea concerning mental or moral character. It spurns his ambition, tramples upon his languishing self-respect, and indignantly refuses to let him either buy with money, or earn by any excellence of inner life or outward behavior, the most momentary immunity from these public indignities even for his wife and daughters. Need we cram these pages with facts in evidence, as if these were charges denied and requiring to be proven . . . ?

In studying, about a year ago, the practice of letting out public convicts to private lessees to serve out their sentences under private management, I found that it does not belong to all our once

convict – leased – system.

slave States nor to all our once seceded States. Only it is no longer in practice outside of them. Under our present condition in the South, it is beyond possibility that the individual black should behave mischievously without offensively rearousing the old sentiments of the still dominant white man. As we have seen too, the white man virtually monopolizes the jury-box. Add another fact: the Southern States have entered upon a new era of material development. Now, if with these conditions in force the public mind has been captivated by glowing pictures of the remunerative economy of the convict-lease system, and by the seductive spectacle of mines and railways, turnpikes and levees, that everybody wants and nobody wants to pay for, growing apace by convict labor that seems to cost nothing, we may almost assert beforehand that the popular mind will—not so maliciously as unreflectingly—yield to the tremendous temptation to hustle the misbehaving black man into the State prison under extravagant sentence, and sell his labor to the highest bidder who will use him in the construction of public works. For ignorance of the awful condition of these penitentiaries is extreme and general, and the hasty half-conscious assumption naturally is, that the culprit will survive this term of sentence, and its fierce discipline "teach him to behave himself."

But we need not argue from cause to effect only. Nor need I repeat one of the many painful rumors that poured in upon me the moment I began to investigate this point. The official testimony of the prisons themselves is before the world to establish the conjectures that spring from our reasoning. After the erroneous takings of the census of 1880 in South Carolina had been corrected, the population was shown to consist of about twenty blacks to every thirteen whites. One would therefore look for a preponderance of blacks on the prison lists; and inasmuch as they are a people only twenty years ago released from servile captivity, one would not be surprised to see that preponderance large. Yet, when the actual numbers confront us, our speculations are stopped with a rude shock; for what is to account for the fact that in 1881 there were committed to the State prison at Columbia, South Carolina, 406 colored persons and but 25 whites? The proportion of blacks sentenced to the whole black population was one to every 1488; that of the whites to the white population was but one to every 15,644. In Georgia the white inhabitants decidedly outnumber the blacks; yet in the State penitentiary,

October 20, 1880, there were 115 whites and 1071 colored; or if we reject the summary of its tables and refer to the tables themselves (for the one does not agree with the other), there were but 102 whites and 1083 colored. Yet of 52 pardons granted in the two years then closing, 22 were to whites and only 30 to blacks. If this be a dark record, what shall we say of the records of lynch law? But for them there is not room here.

A far pleasanter aspect of our subject shows itself when we turn from courts and prisons to the school-house. And the explanation is simple. Were our educational affairs in the hands of that not high average of the community commonly seen in jury-boxes, with their transient sense of accountability and their crude notions of public interests, there would most likely be no such pleasant contrast. But with us of the South, as elsewhere, there is a fairly honest effort to keep the public-school interests in the hands of the State's most highly trained intelligence. Hence our public educational work is a compromise between the unprogressive prejudices of the general mass of the whites and the progressive intelligence of their best minds. Practically, through the great majority of our higher educational officers, we are fairly converted to the imperative necessity of elevating the colored man intellectually, and are beginning to see very plainly that the whole community is sinned against in every act or attitude of oppression, however gross or however refined.

Yet one thing must be said. I believe it is wise that all have agreed not to handicap education with the race question, but to make a complete surrender of that issue, and let it find adjustment elsewhere first and in the schools last. And yet, in simple truth and justice and in the kindest spirit, we ought to file one exception for that inevitable hour when the whole question must be met. There can be no more real justice in pursuing the freedman's children with humiliating arbitrary distinctions and separations in the school-houses than in putting them upon him in other places. If, growing out of their peculiar mental structure, there are good and just reasons for their isolation, by all means let them be proved and known; but it is simply tyrannous to assume them without proof. I know that just here looms up the huge bugbear of Social Equality. Our eyes are filled with absurd visions of all Shantytown pouring its hordes of unwashed imps into the company and companionship of our own sunny-headed darlings. What utter nonsense! As if our public schools had no gauge of cleanliness, decorum, or moral character! Social Equality! What a godsend it would be if the advocates of the old Southern régime could only see that the color line points straight in the direction of social equality by tending toward the equalization of all whites on one side of the line and of all blacks on the other. We may reach the moon some day, not social equality; but the only class that really effects anything toward it are the makers and holders of arbitrary and artificial social distinctions interfering with society's natural self-distribution. Even the little children everywhere are taught, and begin to learn almost with their A B C, that they will find, and must be guided by, the same variations of the social scale in the public school as out of it; and it is no small mistake to put them or their parents off their guard by this cheap separation on the line of color.

"THE NEW SOUTH" *

By Henry Woodfin Grady

Henry Woodfin Grady (1850–89) defends the new South of industrialization and reformed race relations

Henry W. Grady, champion of an industrialized South, was the son of a Confederate colonel killed during the war, a graduate of the University of Georgia in whose environs he was born, and later a student at the University of Virginia Law School. His reputation came as the editor and part-owner of the Atlanta *Constitution* (whose staff included Joel Chandler Harris, creator of Uncle Remus) and as a vigorous orator who combined hardheaded practicality with traditional Southern sentimentalism. The *Constitution* became the directing beacon of the New South with its progressive merchants and factory owners—misnamed the Bourbons—who were ready to support Negro suffrage if the vote served

* From H. W. Grady, "The New South," Edwin D. Shurter (ed.), *The Complete Orations and Speeches of Henry W. Grady* (New York, 1910), 14–20.

their interests, but who were flatly opposed to Northern interference on race matters.

These were the ideas that Grady presented at a banquet of the
New England Society in New York City on December 21, 1886.
He was to give similar speeches of reconciliation on subsequent
occasions. The informed reader will scarcely recognize Grady's
picture of prevailing race relations as authentic, but such alleged
facts and his bold optimism were calculated to encourage Northern businessmen to regard the New South as an attractive investment. By this time, Northerners had begun to feel serious doubts
about the wisdom of Reconstruction and the then current increase
of lynchings did not inspire any fresh humanitarian impulses.

B UT WHAT is the sum of our work? We have found out that in
the summing up the free negro counts more than he did
as a slave. We have planted the schoolhouse on the hilltop and
made it free to white and black. We have sown towns and cities
in the place of theories, and put business above politics. We
have challenged your spinners in Massachusetts and your iron-
makers in Pennsylvania. We have learned that the $400,000,000
annually received from our cotton crop will make us rich
when the supplies that make it are home-raised. We have reduced the commercial rate of interest from 24 to 6 per cent, and
are floating 4 per cent bonds. We have learned that one Northern
immigrant is worth fifty foreigners, and have smoothed the path
to Southward, wiped out the place where Mason and Dixon's
line used to be, and hung out the latchstring to you and yours.

We have reached the point that marks perfect harmony in every
household, when the husband confesses that the pies which his
wife cooks are as good as those his mother used to bake; and we
admit that the sun shines as brightly and the moon as softly as it
did before the war. We have established thrift in city and country.
We have fallen in love with work. We have restored comfort to
homes from which culture and elegance never departed. We have
let economy take root and spread among us as rank as the crab-
grass which sprung from Sherman's cavalry camps, until we are
ready to lay odds on the Georgia Yankee as he manufactures
relics of the battlefield in a one-story shanty and squeezes pure
olive oil out of his cotton seed, against any downeaster that ever

swapped wooden nutmegs for flannel sausage in the valleys of Vermont. Above all, we know that we have achieved in these "piping times of peace" a fuller independence for the South than that which our fathers sought to win in the forum by their eloquence or compel in the field by their swords.

It is a rare privilege, sir, to have had part, however humble, in this work. Never was nobler duty confided to human hands than the uplifting and upbuilding of the prostrate and bleeding South—misguided, perhaps, but beautiful in her suffering, and honest, brave, and generous always. In the record of her social, industrial, and political illustration we await with confidence the verdict of the world.

But what of the negro? Have we solved the problem he presents or progressed in honor and equity toward solution? Let the record speak to the point. No section shows a more prosperous laboring population than the negroes of the South, none in fuller sympathy with the employing and land-owning class. He shares our school fund, has the fullest protection of our laws, and the friendship of our people. Self-interest, as well as honor, demand that he should have this. Our future, our very existence, depend upon our working out this problem in full and exact justice. We understand that when Lincoln signed the Emancipation Proclamation, your victory was assured, for he then committed you to the cause of human liberty, against which the arms of man cannot prevail—while those of our statesmen who trusted to make slavery the corner stone of the Confederacy doomed us to defeat as far as they could, committing us to a cause that reason could not defend or the sword maintain in sight of advancing civilization.

Had Mr. Toombs said, which he did not say, "that he would call the roll of his slaves at the foot of Bunker Hill," he would have been foolish, for he might have known that whenever slavery became entangled in war it must perish, and that the chattel in human flesh ended forever in New England when your fathers —not to be blamed for parting with what didn't pay—sold their slaves to our fathers—not to be praised for knowing a paying thing when they saw it. The relations of the Southern people with the negro are close and cordial. We remember with what fidelity for four years he guarded our defenseless women and children, whose husbands and fathers were fighting against his freedom. To his eternal credit be it said that whenever he struck a blow for his own liberty, he fought in open battle, and when at last he raised his black and humble hands that the shackles might be struck off, those hands were innocent of wrong against his helpless charges, and worthy to be taken in loving grasp by every man who honors loyalty and devotion. Ruffians have maltreated him, rascals have misled him, philanthropists established a bank for him, but the South, with the North, protests against injustice to this simple and sincere people.

To liberty and enfranchisement is as far as law can carry the negro. The rest must be left to conscience and common sense. It must be left to those among whom his lot is cast, with whom he is indissolubly connected, and whose prosperity depends upon their possessing his intelligent sympathy and confidence. Faith has been kept with him, in spite of calumnious assertions to the contrary by those who assume to speak for us or by frank opponents. Faith will be kept with him in the future, if the South holds her reason and integrity.

But have we kept faith with you? In the fullest sense, yes. When Lee surrendered—I don't say when Johnston surrendered, because I understand he still alludes to the time when he met General Sherman last as the time when he determined to abandon any further prosecution of the struggle—when Lee surrendered, I say, and Johnston quit, the South became, and has since been, loyal to this Union. We fought hard enough to know that we were whipped, and in perfect frankness accept as final the arbitrament of the sword to which we had appealed. The South found her jewel in the toad's head of defeat. The shackles that had held her in narrow limitations fell forever when the shackles of the negro slave were broken. Under the old régime the negroes were slaves to the South; the South was a slave to the system. The old plantation, with its simple police regulations and feudal habit, was the only type possible under slavery. Thus was gathered in the hands of a splendid and chivalric oligarchy the substance that should have been diffused among the people, as the rich blood, under certain artificial conditions, is gathered at the heart, filling that with affluent rapture, but leaving the body chill and colorless.

The old South rested everything on slavery and agriculture, unconscious that these could neither give nor maintain healthy growth. The new South presents a perfect democracy, the oligarchs leading in the popular movement; a social system compact and closely knitted, less splendid on the surface, but stronger at the core; a hundred farms for every plantation, fifty homes for every palace; and a diversified industry that meets the complex needs of this complex age.

The new South is enamored of her new work. Her soul is stirred with the breath of a new life. The light of a grander day is falling fair on her face. She is thrilling with the consciousness of growing power and prosperity. As she stands upright, full-statured and equal among the people of the earth, breathing the keen air and looking out upon the expanded horizon, she understands that her emancipation came because, through the inscrutable wisdom of God, her honest purpose was crossed and her brave armies were beaten.

This is said in no spirit of time-serving or apology. The South has nothing for which to apologize. She believes that the late struggle between the States was war and not rebellion, revolution and not conspiracy, and that her convictions were as honest as yours. I should be unjust to the dauntless spirit of the South and to my own convictions if I did not make this plain in this presence. The South has nothing to take back. . . .

Chapter Two

RACE AND RACISM

"THE ATLANTA EXPOSITION ADDRESS" *

By Booker T. Washington

Booker T. Washington (1856–1915) formulates Negro conservative strategy: patience, loyalty, and apartness in return for jobs

At the Atlanta Exposition of 1895, Booker T. Washington spoke for his race with an authority seldom equaled by any one man. He had come up from slavery through a practical education at Hampton Institute to become the founder and head of the famous Tuskegee Institute. He had himself practiced the counsel that he gave at Atlanta—eschewed agitation, trained Negro craftsmen and teachers for racial institutions, and allied himself with white philanthropists and industrialists who appreciated the fact that the Negro did not join unions and was a dependable worker. But while he stressed industrial education for the masses, he did not neglect Howard University and schools for Negro leaders—"the Talented Tenth," as Dr. W. E. B. Du Bois put it. Washington believed that the Negro would always live in the rural South and that therefore he must not antagonize the whites. Patience, thrift, and hard work seemed to him a better formula than agitation in an era of lynchings and Jim Crow. As in the past, he maintained an alliance between Negroes and the white middle class, which was relatively free from economic competition.

Although the Atlanta Exposition Address has come to be treated as a manifesto for segregation and reaction, it was actually applauded at the time by Dr. Du Bois and other intellectuals as well as the rank and file who were to attack Washington after 1902.

* From Booker T. Washington, *Up From Slavery* (Boston, 1901), 217–37.

ONE-THIRD OF the population of the South is of the Negro race. No enterprise seeking the material, civil, or moral welfare of this section can disregard this element of our population and reach the highest success. I but convey to you, Mr. President and Directors, the sentiment of the masses of my race when I say that in no way have the value and manhood of the American Negro been more fittingly and generously recognized than by the managers of this magnificent exposition at every stage of its progress. It is a recognition that will do more to cement the friendship of the two races than any occurrence since the dawn of our freedom.

Not only this, but the opportunity here afforded will awaken among us a new era of industrial progress. Ignorant and inexperienced, it is not strange that in the first years of our new life we began at the top instead of at the bottom; that a seat in Congress or the state legislature was more sought than real estate or industrial skill; that the political convention or stump speaking had more attractions than starting a daily farm or truck garden.

A ship lost at sea for many days suddenly sighted a friendly vessel. From the mast of the unfortunate vessel was seen a signal, "Water, water; we die of thirst!" The answer from the friendly vessel at once came back, "Cast down your bucket where you are." A second time the signal, "Water, water; send us water!" ran up from the distressed vessel, and was answered, "Cast down your bucket where you are." And a third and fourth signal for water was answered, "Cast down your bucket where you are." The captain of the distressed vessel, at last heeding the injunction, cast down his bucket, and it came up full of fresh, sparkling water from the mouth of the Amazon River. To those of my race who depend on bettering their condition in a foreign land or who underestimate the importance of cultivating friendly relations with the southern white man, who is their next-door neighbor, I would say: "Cast down your bucket where you are"—cast it down in making friends in every manly way of the people of all races by whom we are surrounded.

Cast it down in agriculture, mechanics, in commerce, in domestic service, and in the professions. And in this connection it is well to bear in mind that whatever other sins the South may be called to bear, when it comes to business, pure and simple, it is in the South that the Negro is given a man's chance in the commercial world, and in nothing is this exposition more eloquent than in emphasizing this chance. Our greatest danger is that in the great leap from slavery to freedom we may overlook the fact that the masses of us are to live by the productions of our hands, and fail to keep in mind that we shall prosper in proportion as we learn to dignify and glorify common labor and put brains and skill into the common occupations of life; shall prosper in proportion as we learn to draw the line between the superficial and the substantial, the ornamental gewgaws of life and the useful. No race can prosper till it learns that there is as much dignity in tilling a field as in writing a poem. It is at the bottom of life we must begin, and not at the top. Nor should we permit our grievances to overshadow our opportunities.

To those of the white race who look to the incoming of those of foreign birth and strange tongue and habits for the prosperity of the South, were I permitted I would repeat what I say to my own race, "Cast down your bucket where you are." Cast it down among the eight millions of Negroes whose habits you know, whose fidelity and love you have tested in days when to have proved treacherous meant the ruin of your firesides. Cast down your bucket among these people who have, without strikes and labor wars, tilled your fields, cleared your forests, builded your railroads and cities, and brought forth treasures from the bowels of the earth, and helped make possible this magnificent representation of the progress of the South. Casting down your bucket among my people, helping and encouraging them as you are doing on these grounds, and to education of head, hand, and heart, you will find that they will buy your surplus land, make blossom the waste places in your fields, and run your factories. While doing this, you can be sure in the future, as in the past, that you and your families will be surrounded by the most patient, faithful, lawabiding, and unresentful people that the world has seen. As we have proved our loyalty to you in the past, in nursing your children, watching by the sick-bed of your mothers and fathers, and often following them with tear-dimmed eyes to their graves, so in the future, in our humble way, we shall stand by you with a devotion that no foreigner can approach, ready to lay down our lives, if need be, in defense of yours, interlacing our industrial, commercial, civil, and religious life with yours in a way that shall make the interests of both races one. In all things that are purely social we can be as separate as the fingers, yet one as the hand in all things essential to mutual progress.

There is no defense or security for any of us except in the high-

Plea for negro labor instead of foreign

est intelligence and development of all. If anywhere there are efforts tending to curtail the fullest growth of the Negro, let these efforts be turned into stimulating, encouraging, and making him the most useful and intelligent citizen. Effort or means so invested will pay a thousand per cent interest. These efforts will be twice blessed—"blessing him that gives and him that takes."

There is no escape through law of man or God from the inevitable:—

> The laws of changeless justice bind
> Oppressor with oppressed;
> And close as sin and suffering joined
> We march to fate abreast.

Nearly sixteen millions of hands will aid you in pulling the load upward, or they will pull against you the load downward. We shall constitute one-third and more of the ignorance and crime of the South, or one-third its intelligence and progress; we shall contribute one-third to the business and industrial prosperity of the South, or we shall prove a veritable body of death, stagnating, depressing, retarding every effort to advance the body politic.

Gentlemen of the Exposition, as we present to you our humble effort at an exhibition of our progress, you must not expect overmuch. Starting thirty years ago with ownership here and there in a few quilts and pumpkins and chickens (gathered from miscellaneous sources), remember the path that has led from these to the inventions and production of agricultural implements, buggies, steam-engines, newspapers, books, statuary, carving, paintings, the management of drugstores and banks, has not been trodden without contact with thorns and thistles. While we take pride in what we exhibit as a result of our independent efforts, we do not for a moment forget that our part in this exhibition would fall far short of your expectations but for the constant help that has come to our educational life, not only from the southern states, but especially from northern philanthropists, who have made their gifts a constant stream of blessing and encouragement.

The wisest among my race understand that the agitation of questions of social equality is the extremest folly, and that progress in the enjoyment of all the privileges that will come to us must be the result of severe and constant struggle rather than of artificial forcing. No race that has anything to contribute to the markets of the world is long in any degree ostracized. It is important and right that all privileges of the law be ours, but it is vastly more important that we be prepared for the exercises of these privileges. The opportunity to earn a dollar in a factory just now is worth infinitely more than the opportunity to spend a dollar in an opera house.

In conclusion, may I repeat that nothing in thirty years has given us more hope and encouragement and drawn us so near to you of the white race, as this opportunity offered by the exposition; and here bending, as it were, over the altar that represents the results of the struggles of your race and mine, both starting practically empty-handed three decades ago, I pledge that in your effort to work out the great and intricate problem which God has laid at the doors of the South, you shall have at all times the patient, sympathetic help of my race. Only let this be constantly in mind: that, while from representations in these buildings of the product of field, of forest, of mine, of factory, letters, and art much good will come, yet far above and beyond material benefits will be that higher good, that, let us pray God, will come, in a blotting out of sectional differences and racial animosities and suspicions, in a determination to administer absolute justice, in a willing obedience among all classes to the mandates of law. This, coupled with our material prosperity, will bring into our beloved South a new heaven and a new earth.

"THE BLACK VOTE
OF PHILADELPHIA"*

By William E. B. Du Bois

Dr. William E. B. Du Bois (1868–1963), Negro sociologist and historian, notes the small civic stake of the Philadelphia Negro

Although a rebel against racial injustice, Dr. Du Bois scarcely knew Jim Crow until his early manhood when he took his A.B. degree in the Negro college of Fisk located in Tennessee. This native of Great Barrington, Massachusetts, prided himself upon his mixed ancestry, an asset that may have secured him the opportunity of studying at the University of Berlin, preliminary to taking his Ph.D. at Harvard. Former President Rutherford B. Hayes, head of the Slater Fund for Negroes, was evidently impressed by his application. At Harvard, Du Bois wrote a History thesis, *The Suppression of the African Slave Trade,* which criticized federal officials for collaborating with slave traders in evading the law.

He was teaching Greek and Latin at Wilberforce College when Booker T. Washington delivered his segregationist Atlanta Exposition address; Du Bois then endorsed these views. In 1896, he accepted a research fellowship at the University of Pennsylvania to study the Philadelphia Negro. For a year, he interviewed many hundreds of his race regarding their economic struggle, their health, the schools for his race, pauperism, occupations, the Negro voter, and the restricted contact with whites. In his conclusion to his study, he urged whites to throw off their supremacist attitudes and detachment; to Negroes he spoke of the need for greater efforts to take part in the life of the nation. As yet Du Bois was far from a militant, urging, rather, a loose form of cultural pluralism instead of racial integration.

During 1896–1910, he became more race conscious and impatient with the outbreak of lynchings and disfranchisement. At this time he was a professor of History and Economics at Atlanta University devoted to social research, concentrating especially in mass education, seeing it as a main tool of liberation for the Negro. His well-written, perceptive book, *Souls of Black Folk* (1903), marked the beginning of his war on Booker T. Washington, segregation, and the Tuskegee emphasis upon industrial educa-

* From William E. B. Du Bois, *Charities,* XV (1905–6), 31–35.

tion for the Negro at the expense of a higher liberal arts training for Negro leaders—"the Talented Tenth." Washington represented to him a departure from the historic militancy and agitation for civil rights of Frederick Douglass. In 1905 Du Bois shifted from social research to action by organizing the Niagara Movement for full racial equality in citizenship, education, and jobs. Four years later, he became a founder of the National Association for the Advancement of Colored People, an organization devoted to full American citizenship for Negroes, and became editor of its organ, *The Crisis*.

NAACP
Founder

During World War I, he shared the Negro's disillusionment over the failure to advance democracy and, like Marcus Garvey, grew interested in Africa as a haven, becoming a leader in the Pan-African movement. After visiting the Soviet Union, he showed great interest in the Marxist formulas, although he refused to collaborate with the American Communists who proposed "self-determination in the Black Belt" during the 1930's. He did put forth a semi-Marxist interpretation in *Black Reconstruction* (1935), which stressed the positive achievements of Negro legislators in the so-called Carpetbag Legislatures, opposing the usual "revisionist" portrayal of gross corruption and the "Africanization" of the South. Only in his ninetieth year did Du Bois formally embrace communism and become a citizen of Nkrumah's Ghana. At his death, historians of both races tended to evaluate Dr. Du Bois as a true successor of Frederick Douglass.

THE TYPICAL Philadelphia colored man is a young immigrant from the South, from twenty to forty years of age, who has come to the city to better his fortune, as he conceives fortune. His conception of government, as he comes into a great modern world city, is extremely crude. He knows practically nothing of the actual work of any typical government—local government in the South is a Chinese puzzle to the average citizen; the Negro sees it only in its repressive and harrying functions, and he is allowed to take little or no part in it. The chances are, then, that the young immigrant to Philadelphia has no adequate idea of his duty or privilege as a citizen and has thought little about them, save perhaps in a more or less theoretical way. He comes to find work and freedom—and by freedom he means a chance for expansion, amusement, interest, something to make life larger than it has been on the lonely country plantation, or in the Negro quarter of a southern town. His contact with the new world, then, is as wage-earner and seeker after the goods of life—knowledge and amusement; with this goes the untrammelled right to vote—a right he has never before had, and which his brothers in Philadelphia have not always had.

The laws of 1682 for the new state of Pennsylvania made property holders voters and made the qualifications for freedmen less than those for others. Negro electors undoubtedly helped to adopt the constitution, as the right of suffrage after 1776 was given to "every freeman of the full age of twenty-one years, having resided in this state for the space of one whole year." When the new state constitution of 1790 was framed, it was proposed to limit the suffrage to "free white citizens;" but Albert Gallatin helped to defeat this proposition, and Negroes in the state had the legal right to vote for a half century thereafter. Still public opinion in many cases was against Negroes voting, and in Philadelphia "the colored man could not with safety appear at the polls." One Negro man named Fogg, having been denied the right to vote in Luzerne County, took the case to the courts in 1837. He won in the lower courts but the Supreme Court in a curious decision upheld the exclusion, claiming that a Negro though free could never be a "freeman." The next year the constitutional convention met. The qualifications for suffrage came up and an attempt was made to restrict voting to "free white male" citizens. The amendment was lost by a vote of 61 to 49. This aroused the Negro haters and they began the same sort of campaign of vilification and detraction that the black men of America so often have suffered. Petitions for and against Negro suffrage poured in, but only the latter were printed and published, and Bucks County, where once a Negro nearly had been elected to the legislature, outdid itself in working for exclusion. The result was a protracted fight, and a final adoption of the white suffrage plank by a vote of 77 to 45. The Negroes of Pennsylvania were thus disfranchised for thirty-two years, until the passage of the war amendments.

About 5,500 Negroes were eligible to vote in Philadelphia in 1870. In 1900 there were 20,000 Negro voters and in 1905 there are perhaps 25,000 voters.

Nothing in the Negro immigrant's earning of a living is apt to direct his attention to government unless, of course, he is employed by the city. He is usually employed as servant or laborer by private parties and sees little more of government than when he was in the South. When, after work, and on Sundays and holidays, he starts out for recreation he is apt in the denser parts of the city to run upon two and only two rival claimants for his interest: the church and the club. Parks and out-of-doors sports do not attract him, for he has the country-bred indifference to raw nature and his daily work is largely physical. He is not welcome at the white Young Men's Christian Association, while the Negro branch is a sickly sort of thing constituted largely of prayer meetings and cant. All the ordinary amusements of a great city are either unknown and unappreciated by this newcomer, or he feels by word or glance that he is not wanted. There is left, as I have said, the club and the church. Now the church he knows and knows well: it has been the center of his community from the days his fathers landed in America until now. The chances are, however, that this young man has tired of the monotony of church services and their lack of adaptability to his newer needs and demands; in the South, he has loafed outside the door to laugh and joke and escort his girl home; and he does not take the church seriously—he is rather tired of it.

The Political Club

As he saunters up Lombard street, then, of evenings, he may drop into the church if it is Sunday, and other days he stands lonesomely about, gaping and longing for a fellow soul. But he finds soon that at one place he is welcome and that is at the club. He may be introduced to the club accidentally or by design, through the medium of the saloon or corner pool-room, or by chance companions. At any rate he finds here and there throughout the city ten or fifteen litle groups of good fellows—gay young blades, roystering tellers of doubtful tales, well-dressed connoisseurs of the town's mysteries, and they welcome the newcomer cordially and make him feel at home. No where in Philadelphia is there such a welcome for the friendless, homeless black boy, no where is so much consideration shown for his feelings, his wants, his desire for pleasure. He easily joins therefore the crowd of loafers and idlers and laborers who circle and congregate about these clubs.

What is a "club"? He finds that it is a suite of rooms more or less elaborately furnished where a crowd of men can always be found smoking and talking and drinking. Usually, too, they play cards for small stakes and sometimes gamble with various devices for sums mounting up to $25 or more. Here one may make all kinds of acquaintances from honest laborers to drunken debauchees—and the clubs grade from semi-criminal haunts to respectable well-furnished quarters. Nearly all of them, however, and particularly the lower grades, are above all "political," and they give our young immigrant his first introduction into "politics." He comes to know gradually that these pleasant quarters where his friends meet and enjoy themselves are furnished through "politics"; that if it were not for "politics" they could not have beer to drink or play cards in peace. Moreover, there is poor John So and So arrested last week—he'll get clear by "politics." Is the new Philadelphian willing to help along the folks who are doing these kindnesses to him and his? Why, certainly. And when election day comes he receives a bit of printed paper with unknown names and deposits it in a place indicated.

It may be now that he becomes one of the constituent members of the club, being invited by the president. This president selects his own membership of tried and true men warranted to do as he says: he keeps his hold over them by furnishing them amusement if they are honest laborers, or by giving them money if they are poor laborers out of a job, or loafers, or by protecting them if they fall afoul of the police. The newcomer soon sees that he is in a network of intrigue, influence and bribery. The policeman on his beat, the magistrate, the criminal, the prostitute, the business man, all fit in their little circle in the great "machine," and this is "politics";—of certain questions as to the ownership of gas works, the payment for franchises, the reform of the civil service—of these things he has never heard; he is submerged in a sea of mud and slime called politics which the great and good and wise city of Philadelphia has prepared for him; he has never seen its shores or surface, and of its clearer, sweeter waters he has never heard.

Other Groups

Of the 25,000 Negro voters in Philadelphia from one-half to two-thirds fall into the class I have described. There are, of course, other Negro voters in the city—or rather men eligible to vote. There is, first, the native Philadelphian of Negro descent—

member of an educated and well-to-do group of people. There are the better class of immigrants from the country districts of the state, Maryland, and Virginia. These men come into politics from a different angle. A large number of them, especially of the better class of immigrants, neglect to vote—the campaign of contempt for civic duties and civic privileges has been preached to them assiduously. They have seen those of their number who preached political suicide for the Negro vociferously applauded and they have come to think it a virtue to neglect the exercise of the right of suffrage. Thus the result of the foolish campaign against the Negro in politics has been simply to drive out of political life the very class of Negroes needed most, and to deliver political life and activity into the hands of the political clubs and their ignorant or debased followers.

Then, too, the Negro voter even of the better class feels no civic pride. Philadelphia is not his city; it grants him nothing in particular save what he struggles for in sweat. It shows him no kindness unless he be a criminal or pauper, and under the political organization preceding the recent upheaval, it did not need his vote or seek it. The Negro feels in Philadelphia and in America few promptings of patriotism, and he looks upon all local questions from the standpoint of his social and individual interests. His greatest hardship is difficulty of employment; his characteristic, poverty. This is due to present and past conditions, i. e., prejudice and lack of skill and application. Both these handicaps can be overcome, but it takes hard work. To such a class the direct or indirect bribery of money is a tremendous temptation. Direct distribution of money to Negro voters at the polls is therefore considerable, but this does not touch the upper half or third of the voting population. This part is influenced by the indirect methods of bribery. There are in the employ of the city to-day, approximately:

1 member of the common council.
3 clerks in the city service.
10 or more messengers.
65 policemen.
30 school teachers.

These persons on the whole represent the better class of Negroes and with a few exceptions have given first-class service; but so far as the office-holders themselves are concerned these are the best jobs they could get; probably in no other way could these people get employment that would give them half their present incomes. Their jobs are "in politics," and their holders must and do support the "machine." Moreover, such civic pride as the Negro has is naturally expended on these representatives of his race in public life and they support the party that puts these men in office. Thus office holding is both a direct and indirect bribe to the Negroes and to the better class of them.

The Treatment of the Good-Government Negro

It happens, however, that the political hold of the "machine" in Philadelphia has been so great and far-reaching, their majorities so overwhelming, and the white citizens so supine in their bondage, that the "machine" cares litle for the 25,000 Negro votes and has cut down their patronage lately in some respects; Negroes used to have three counsellors; now they have one, and Boss Durham before his fall said that this "would be the last one." "There are some Negroes in my division," said a ward politician, "and they've been coming to me and telling me what they want, but I tell 'em to go to hell. We don't need their votes." If on finding their support not sought or needed, perhaps the better class do not vote. This makes little difference for the ward bosses having the registration lists vote the names of all who do not appear at the polls. A colored man, headwaiter at a large hotel, went down to the polls; pretty soon he came back. "Did you vote?" he was asked. "No," he said, "I find that I had already voted—I'd like to know which way!"

Suppose now one of the better class of Negroes should determine to go into politics with a view to better conditions. Has this ever happened? Colonel McClure in his *Reminiscences* does not know of any case, but it has been pointed out to him since that he was mistaken. Men of Negro blood like Henry L. Philips, one of the most public-spirited of Philadelphia's citizens, white or black, and Walter P. Hall, a member of the present reform Committee of Seventy, have continually and repeatedly sided with reform movements. And others have, too. Yet it is true that no large mass of colored voters have followed reform movements hitherto. Nor is the reason for this far to seek. Under the machine an honest man interested in politics had no place. A young friend of mine offered his services in his ward. "See the ward Boss" was the answer. And the ward Boss—"What do you want?"

Reformers couldn't offer the negroes jobs for as the "machine."

he said, and he meant: "Do you want protection to run a bawdy house, or to sell liquor without a license or to get somebody out of jail? And if so, are you willing in return to falsify voting lists, round up repeaters, etc." My friend saw nothing attractive in this career and he is consequently "out of politics." When now a reform movement like that of the Municipal League has come, it has invariably made the mistake of supposing that because there are few of the better class of Negroes in politics, there is no better class worth appealing to. Moreover, if a few of the leading Negroes were appealed to what could they say to the masses: could they promise that Negroes would be retained in civil service, or on the police force, or as teachers? No, the reformers were not promising jobs. But this matter was more than the question of a simple job—it was a question of economic opportunity. It was really the same question of earning a living that is the main motive in the political action of the whites. Why are Philadelphia politics dirty? Because the most influential and respected citizens of the town are using public business for private gain. White citizens find that franchises, concessions, and favorable administration furnish them the most money. Negroes, being barred from business, largely find the actual salaries of office not only the greatest attraction, but an actual matter of bread and butter. Thus the Negroes have always been suspicious that the reform movements tended not to their betterment but to their elimination from political life and consequently from the best chance of earning a living. And the attitude of some of the reformers and their contempt for Negroes has not improved this race opinion.

It might be asked—Could not the better element of Negroes outvote the worse element and support an independent movement? This has been tried and the machine beat it. A few years ago a clean young colored lawyer, Harry W. Bass, revolted against the machine and ran for the legislature. He made a good run in the seventh ward, receiving a large vote but not a majority. A little later he ran again and the machine was alarmed. Immediately they nominated another Negro of fairly respectable character on another independent ticket and finally nominated a white candidate on the regular ticket. The result of this three-cornered fight was that Bass received but 400 votes, the white machine candidate was elected, and the other "independent" candidate was given a political job at Harrisburg.

In the present latest upheaval the Negroes are represented on the Committee of Seventy by a business man, Walter P. Hall. In a few of the wards they have organized under the new city party of reform. In the great Negro ward, the seventh, there is one Negro member of the ward committee. While it is uncertain how far the Negro will support reform at present, yet it is certain that an influential part of the better class will co-operate and that there is a great opportunity to give 70,000 Negroes the best chance of education in politics that they have ever had.

The Reconstruction Situation Repeated

What now is the wrong and right of this situation? It is manifestly this: If you wish democratic government to be successful you must strive to inculcate into the humblest citizen a conception of its duties and its rewards. There is no democratic government in Philadelphia, and has not been for a generation. There is an oligarchy of ward politicians and business men using public office for private gain. Into this system a new mass of untrained Negro voters were cast and they followed their leaders, as was perfectly natural. As a mass they went into politics for what they could get out of it and in this respect Lombard and Walnut streets joined hands and made common cause. We have an exact repetition here of the reconstruction difficulties in the South on a smaller scale. The brother thieves of the *Credit-Mobilier,* the Tweed ring, and the other northern tricksters, began the looting of the newly reconstructed southern states. They used the ignorant Negroes for their tools. The result was that the Negroes followed their leaders and stole and looted too. Yet this experience is put into history as a classic example of the unfitness of Negroes to exercise political power. Philadelphia needs to go back to the very a b c of government—to teach its citizens, white or black, the duties and rewards of good citizenship, to open its civil service on equal terms to all and to show the 25,000 Negro voters what government means.

THE CLANSMAN *

By Thomas Dixon, Jr.

Thomas Dixon, Jr. (1864–1946) popularizes racism and inspires a second Klan

About 1915 the technically gifted Hollywood director D. W. Griffith of Kentucky dramatized Thomas Dixon's thoroughly racist novel *The Clansman* (1905) in his film the *Birth of A Nation*. This perennially popular film aroused strong liberal protests and led the NAACP to fight its exhibition for over fifty years. President Woodrow Wilson, although a respected historian and humanitarian, reflected the moviegoers' approval as well as his own Southern background (some of his cabinet members were then ejecting Negroes from the federal service), when he exhibited the picture at the White House, hailing it as a wonderful way to teach history.

Dixon, a North Carolina Baptist minister and lyceum lecturer before he became a novelist, had begun an anti-Negro trilogy in 1902 with *The Leopard's Spots*, which purported to tell "the true story" of the Klan in "one of the most dramatic chapters in the history of the Aryan race." Thaddeus Stevens, as depicted in the following selection, was ready to Africanize the nation and only the popular upsurgence of the Klan saved Southern womanhood from the barbarous freedman—so the theme runs. It seems more than a chance that the *Birth of A Nation* coincided with the advent of the second and perhaps more formidable Klan that reached its peak in the Twenties in a nationwide organization lined up in fascist style against Negroes, Jews, Catholics, radicals, and those presumed to be guilty of immorality.

※᠑

IN QUICK succession every county followed the example of Ulster, and the arms furnished the negroes by the state and National governments were in the hands of the Klan. The League began to collapse in a panic of terror.

* From Thomas Dixon, Jr., *The Clansman* (1905), 341–44.

31.

A gale of chivalrous passion and high action, contagious and intoxicating, swept the white race. The moral, mental, and physical earthquake which followed the first assault on one of their daughters revealed the unity of the racial life of the people. Within the span of a week they had lived a century.

The spirit of the South "like lightning had at last leaped forth, half startled at itself, its feet upon the ashes and the rags," its hands tight-gripped on the throat of tyrant, thug, and thief.

It was the resistless movement of a race, not of any man or leader of men. The secret weapon with which they struck was the most terrible and efficient in human history—these pale hosts of white-and-scarlet horsemen! They struck shrouded in a mantle of darkness and terror. They struck where the power of resistance was weakest and the blow least suspected. Discovery or retaliation was impossible. Not a single disguise was ever penetrated. All was planned and ordered as by destiny. The accused was tried by secret tribunal, sentenced without a hearing, executed in the dead of night without warning, mercy, or appeal. The movements of the Klan were like clockwork, without a word, save the whistle of the Night Hawk, the crack of his revolver, and the hoof-beat of swift horses moving like figures in a dream, and vanishing in mists and shadows.

The old club-footed Puritan,* in his mad scheme of vengeance and party power, had overlooked the Covenanter, the backbone of the South. This man had just begun to fight! His race had defied the Crown of Great Britain a hundred years from the caves and wilds of Scotland and Ireland, taught the English people how to slay a king and build a commonwealth, and, driven into exile into the wilderness of America, led our Revolution, peopled the hills of the South, and conquered the West.

As the young German patriots of 1812 had organized the great struggle for their liberties under the noses of the garrisons of Napoleon, so Ben Cameron had met the leaders of his race in Nashville, Tennessee, within the picket lines of thirty-five thousand hostile troops, and in the ruins of an old homestead discussed and adopted the ritual of the Invisible Empire.

Within a few months this Empire overspread a territory larger than modern Europe. In the approaching election it was reaching

* Editor's note: Thaddeus Stevens, radical leader of the House of Representatives.

out its daring white hands to tear the fruits of victory from twenty million victorious conquerors.

The triumph at which they aimed was one of incredible grandeur. They had risen to snatch power out of defeat and death. Under their clan-leadership the Southern people had suddenly developed the courage of the lion, the cunning of the fox, and the deathless faith of religious enthusiasts.

Society was fused in the white heat of one sublime thought and beat with the pulse of the single will of the Grand Wizard of the Klan at Memphis.

Women and children had eyes and saw not, ears and heard not. Over four hundred thousand disguises for men and horses were made by the women of the South, and not one secret ever passed their lips!

With magnificent audacity, infinite patience, and remorseless zeal, a conquered people were struggling to turn his own weapon against their conqueror, and beat his brains out with the bludgeon he had placed in the hands of their former slaves.

Behind the tragedy of Reconstruction stood the remarkable man whose iron will alone had driven these terrible measures through the chaos of passion, corruption, and bewilderment which followed the first assassination of an American President. As he leaned on his window in this village of the South and watched in speechless rage the struggle at that negro armory, he felt for the first time the foundations sinking beneath his feet. As he saw the black cowards surrender in terror, noted the indifference and cool defiance with which those white horsemen rode and shot, he knew that he had collided with the ultimate force which his whole scheme had overlooked.

He turned on his big club foot from the window, clinched his fist, and muttered:

"But I'll hang that man for this deed if it's the last act of my life!"

The morning brought dismay to the negro, the carpetbagger, and the scalawag of Ulster. A peculiar freak of weather in the early morning added to their terror. The sun rose clear and bright except for a slight fog that floated from the river valley, increasing the roar of the falls. About nine o'clock, a huge black shadow suddenly rushed over Piedmont from the west, and in a moment the town was shrouded in twilight. The cries of birds were hushed, and chickens went to roost as in a total eclipse of the sun. Knots of people gathered on the streets and gazed uneasily at the threatening skies. Hundreds of negroes began to sing and shout and pray, while sensible people feared a cyclone or cloud-burst. A furious downpour of rain was swiftly followed by sunshine, and the negroes rose from their knees, shouting with joy to find the end of the world had after all been postponed.

But that the end of their brief reign in a white man's land had come, but few of them doubted. The events of the night were sufficiently eloquent. The movement of the clouds in sympathy was unnecessary.

"THE REAL RACE PROBLEM" *

By Franz Boas

Franz Boas (1858–1942), anthropologist, explodes the myth of Negro racial inferiority

Born in Westphalia, Germany, of a Jewish family of liberal Forty-eighters, Franz Boas blended the scientific detachment of contemporary German science with a growing desire to enlist science in behalf of persecuted Jews, Negroes, and other minority peoples. Heidelberg and Kiel trained him in geography, mathematics, and physics, but he was won over to anthropology during a meteorological expedition in Baffin Land where he observed the Eskimos. In 1886, he investigated the cultural relationship between Siberian peoples, Eskimos, and American Indians. His Indian linguistic studies became famous. During 1888–92, he taught anthropology at Clark University, became a curator at the American Museum of Natural History, and after 1899 a professor of anthropology at Columbia where he remained until retiring in 1937 as an internationally eminent scholar.

At Columbia, Boas decisively influenced an entire generation of physical and cultural anthropologists. He encouraged accuracy

* Franz Boas, "The Real Race Problem," Address at Second National Negro Conference, May, 1910. Reprinted in *The Crisis*, I (1910), 22–25.

in investigation by teaching meticulous research methods (one of his chief courses was in social statistics). He demolished the social evolutionists who insisted on inevitable stages of culture and led an unremitting war against racism. Boas provided invaluable ammunition to liberals with his *Changes in Bodily Form of Descendants of Immigrants* (1911), which demonstrated that environment could alter such a presumably stable element as head shape. Even more influential was *The Mind of Primitive Man* (1911), which shook the popular belief that the races differed in inherent mental traits. Other books such as *Anthropology and Modern Life* (1928) further proved that race and culture were not organically related. Thus he encouraged the minority groups who fought the discriminatory quota system and the National Origins Clause of the Immigration Law of 1924 and its later applications. (This battle was not won until 1965, long after Boas' death.) During the Nazi era, Boas organized scientists in a war on racial superstition. By this time, his distinguished students like Kroeber, Lowie, Benedict, and Herskovits had done much to liberalize textbook interpretations of race.

The selection below, which was widely republished at the time, was originally an address delivered at the Second National Negro Conference in May, 1910, later published by Dr. W. E. B. Du Bois in *The Crisis*. This emphasis on the Negro was to be taken up by Boas' enthusiastic disciple, Melville J. Herskovits of Northwestern University, the noted Africanist.

THE ESSENTIAL problem before us is founded on the presence of two entirely distinct human types in the same community, and relates to the best possible correlation of the activities of these two types. On the whole, the answer to this problem has been based on the assumption of the superiority of the one type and the inferiority of the other. The first question to be answered by scientific investigation is, in how far the Negro type may be considered the inferior, the white type as the superior.

The Negro Not Inferior

The anthropologist recognizes that the Negro and the white represent the two most divergent types of mankind. The differences in color, form of hair, form of face, are known to all of us. Other differences, better known to anthropologists, are those in the proportions of the limbs and of the trunk of the body, and in the size of the brain.

When we consider inferiority and superiority from a general biological point of view, it must be interpreted as meaning that one type is nearer to certain ancestral forms than another. In this sense, the anthropologist must say that in certain respects the Negro resembles the hypothetical ancestral forms of man more than does the European; while in other respects the European shows greater similarity to the supposed ancestral form. Among the Negro race it is particularly the form of the face that reminds us of the ancestral forms of man/while in regard to the proportions of the body, and particularly the length of the limbs, the Negro is more remote from ancestral forms than is the European.

On the whole, the morphological characteristics of the two races show rather a specialized development in different directions than a higher development in the one race as compared with the other.

Ordinarily, however, the question of inferiority and superiority is formulated in a different manner, based essentially on the capacity of mental achievement; and much stress is laid on two points—the lesser size of the brain of the Negro, and the supposed shortness of the period of development of the Negro child.

Size of Brain

It is true that the average size of the Negro brain is slightly smaller than the average size of the brain of the white race; but it must be borne in mind that a wide range of brain-forms and brain-sizes occur among the white race, beginning with very small brains and extending to very large ones; that the same is true of the Negro race, and that the difference between the averages of the two races is exceedingly small as compared with the range of variability found in either race. Thus it happens that the brain-weights of the bulk of the Negro race and of the bulk of the white race have the same values, with the sole exception that low brain-weights are slightly more frequent among the Negroes, high brain-weights slightly more frequent among the whites.

Elaborate studies of brains of great men, criminals, and normal individuals have proved that the relation between mental ability and brain-weight is rather remote, and that we are not by any means justified in concluding that the larger brain is always the more efficient tool for mental achievement. There is presumably a slight increase of average ability corresponding to a considerable increase in average brain-weight; but this increase is so slight that in a comparison of the mental ability of the Negro race and of the white race, the difference in size of the brain seems quite insignificant.

The second point of which much has been made is the question of the difference in period of development between the two races. It has been claimed that the Negro child develops favorably, but that its development is arrested at an early date. Unfortunately, these statements are not based on careful examination of facts; and while I am unable to refute these views by bringing forward actual anthropometrical statistics bearing upon the subject, I am also not in a position to sustain them by any reliable evidence. The question is an important one, and should receive serious attention.

But even if the observation had been made, its interpretation would not be an easy one without the most painstaking investigation of the social conditions with which the phenomenon is correlated. We know that in the white race the most favorably situated social groups show the most rapid growth in early childhood and an early completion of development; while the poor, who live under more unfavorable social conditions, show a slow and long-continued development, which, however, in its entirety, does not equal the amount of physiological development attained by better-situated individuals of the same race. It appears, there- *Environment* fore, that the simple fact of an early completion of development does not by any means prove mental inferiority, because the better-situated element of our white population furnishes a disproportionately large number of capable and efficient individuals, as compared to the less favorably situated groups.

The whole anatomical and physiological comparison of the Negro and of the white race may be summed up in the statement that certain differences between the two races are so fundamental that they seem to form two quite distinct groups of the human species, the characteristics of which, notwithstanding the great variability of each race, do not overlap; while, in regard to other characteristics, the differences are so slight that the difference between the two races is insignificant, as compared to the range of variability exhibited in each race by itself; and that there are hardly any anatomical or physiological traits developed in such

differences in kind, not value

manner that we are justified in calling one race anatomically or physiologically higher than the other. The existing differences are differences in kind, not in value. This implies that the biological evidence also does not sustain the view, which is so often proposed, that the mental power of the one race is higher than that of the other, although their mental qualities show, presumably, differences analogous to the existing anatomical and physiological differences.

Handicap of Slavery

The objection will be raised that the low stage of culture of the African race in many parts of America, as well as in Africa, shows clearly a lack of mental power, because otherwise the Negro race might have developed a civilization similar to that of Europe. In answer to this objection, we must remember that, on the whole, our conception of African conditions is based altogether too much upon the condition of the uneducated descendant of the American Negro slave. Any one who is familiar with ethnological facts will recognize that the conditions under which the American slave population developed is apt to destroy what little culture may have existed. The complete break with the African past; the imposition of labor, in the results of which the slave had no direct interest; the difficulty of assimilating the elements of civilization by which they were surrounded, all tended equally to reduce to a minimum the amount of independent cultural achievement of the group.

On the other hand, the general impression of African conditions is based altogether too much upon our knowledge of the American Negro. It is not sufficiently well known how highly advanced is the industrial and political organization of aboriginal Africa. Villages that have not been ravaged by Mohammedan or European slave hunters, and which have enjoyed a period of peace, are characterized by high industrial development.

Trade Well Organized

Agriculture flourishes; men and women are engaged in pottery making, weaving, blacksmith work, and metal casting; trade between the different villages is well organized; and in many cases the political organization, owing to the force of character of great men, has led to the establishment of states which cover territories comparable in size only to large sections of our American continent. I think it is not saying too much if I state that among the primitive people of the world, the natives of Central Africa are by far the most advanced, and that the type of their civilization belongs to the same level of culture which was found a few thousand years ago all over the western part of the Old World, including Europe and Western Asia.

If the Africans have not shared in the development which, after many vicissitudes, gradually extended from Egypt and Babylonia over the Mediterranean area, and from there later into Northern Europe, this is due to the fact that Africa occupied a much more remote position in relation to these countries, and that the current of civilization was carried with much greater difficulty through the virgin forests and deserts of Africa than along the shores of the Mediterranean and across the forests and meadow lands of Europe.

Thus it may safely be said that there is no anthropological evidence showing inferiority of the Negro race as compared with the white race, although we may assume that differences in mental characteristics of the two races exist.

Case of the Mulatto

The question that confronts us is not alone the question of the mental aptitude of the full-blood Negro, but also the question of the ability, vigor, and adaptability of the mulatto. In the course of time, since the Negro has been imported into America, a very large amount of influx of white blood has taken place, which has had the result that in those parts of the country where the Negro does not form a very great majority, full-bloods are presumably quite rare. Owing to the peculiar manner of development of this mulatto population, it is very difficult, if not impossible, to trace the exact amount of white blood and of Negro blood in the mixed races; but even a cursory examination of the prevalent types of the colored population shows clearly that the mixture is very extended.

Here the point has often been raised that the mulatto population is inferior to either pure race, or, to use the popular form of expression, that they inherit all the evil characteristics of both parental races, and none of their good qualities. It is obvious that in this exaggerated form the statement is untrue. As a matter of fact, this theory is generally used only so far as it may suit our purposes; and the statement that a mulatto of exceptional ability and strength of character owes his eminence to the white strain in his blood is seriously made without being felt as a contradiction to this theory. Serious attempts have been made to investigate the social and vital characteristics of the mulatto as compared to the Negro race and to the white race; but here again we must recognize with regret that a sound basis for safe conclusions has not been gained yet. It is very difficult to differentiate clearly between those characteristics of the mulatto that are due to the social conditions under which he lives, and those that are due to hereditary causes. In order to determine the actual conditions with any degree of accuracy, extensive investigations would have to be carried through with this specific object in view.

It seems to my mind that the assumption which is generally made is very unlikely, for it ought to be possible to find, either in history or in biology, parallel cases demonstrating the evil effects of intermixture upon mixed types. It seems to my mind that the whole early history of our domesticated animals indicates that mixture has hardly ever had detrimental effect upon the development of varieties. Practically none of our domesticated animals are descendants of a single species. The probable history of our European cattle will illustrate what presumably happened. In all likelihood cattle were first domesticated in Asia and came to Europe in company with a number of tribes that migrated from the East westward. At this period large herds of wild cattle existed in Europe. The herds attracted the wild native bulls, which belonged to a distinct species of cattle, and a gradual mixture of the blood of the domesticated and of the wild cattle took place, which had the effect of modifying the type of the animal that was kept.

Modification in Type

In the same way domesticated cattle would from time to time escape and join the wild herds; so that admixture occurred also in the wild species. This gradual modification of the type of both wild and domesticated animals may be observed even at the present time in Siberia and in Central Asia; and a zoological investigation of our domesticated animals has shown that practically in all cases this has been the development of the existing types. It is a peculiarity incident to domestication that intermixture of distinct types is facilitated. Among wild animals mixture of different species is, on the whole, rare; and mixture of distinct varieties of the same species does not ordinarily occur, because each variety has its own local habitat.

If we want to understand analogous conditions in mankind clearly, we must remember that man, in his bodily form and in his physiological functions, is strictly analogous to domesticated animals. Practically everywhere human culture has advanced so far that the anatomical type of man cannot be compared to that of wild animals, but must be considered as analogous to the type of domesticated animals. This condition has brought it about that intermixture of distinct types has always been easy.

The types of man which were originally strictly localized have not remained so, but extended migrations have been the rule ever since very early times; in fact, as far back as our knowledge of pre-historic archæology carries us. Therefore we find mixtures between distinct types the world over. For our present consideration the mixed types that occur on the borderland of the Negro races seem particularly interesting. I mention among these the Western people of the Polynesian Islands, who are undoubtedly a mixture of negroid types and of another type related to the Malay, a highly gifted people, which, before European contact, had developed a peculiar and interesting culture of their own. More interesting than these are the inhabitants of the southern borderland of the Sahara.

How Populations Were Mixed

In olden times this was the home of the darkest Negro races; but immediately north of them were found people of much lighter complexion, which, in descent, belong to the group of Mediterranean people. They belong to the same group which developed the ancient Egyptian civilization. For long periods these people have made inroads into the Negro territory south of the Sahara, and have established the empire of the Sudan, whose history we can trace about a thousand years back. In this manner a mixed population has developed in many of these regions which has proved exceedingly capable, which has produced a great many men of great power, and which has succeeded in assimilating a considerable amount of Arab culture.

It is quite remarkable to see how, in some of the more remote parts of this country, where intermixture has been very slight, the pure Negro type dominates and has developed exactly the same type of culture which is found in other regions, where the North African type predominates. The development of culture, and the degree of assimilation of foreign elements, depend, in this whole area, not upon the purity of the race, but upon the stability of political conditions, which during long periods have been characterized by an alternation of peaceful development and of warlike conquest.

The history of East Africa, with its extended migrations of people from north to south, is another case illustrating the infusion of foreign blood into the African race without in any way modifying the cultural conditions of the continent, except so far as the introduction of new inventions is concerned.

Mulatto Not Inferior

I think, therefore, that biological analogy as well as historical evidence do not favor the assumption of any material inferiority of the mulatto. The question, however, deserves a painstaking investigation.

The simple facts that Negroes and Europeans live side by side in our country, that the European receives constant large additions from abroad, while the amount of Negro blood receives no additions from outside, must necessarily lead to the result that the relative number of pure Negroes will become less and less in our country. The gradual process of elimination of the full-blooded Negro may be retarded by legislation, but it cannot possibly be avoided.

It seems to my mind that a very serious misunderstanding of the actual conditions of intermixture between Negro and white prevails in many parts of our country. The fear is often expressed that by intermixture between whites and Negroes the whole mass of the white population might be infused with a certain amount of Negro blood. This is not what has actually occurred, but what would result if unions between white women and Negro men were as frequent as unions between Negro men and white women.* As a matter of fact, however, the former type of unions

* Editor's note: Obviously Boas intended to say "white men and Negro women."

—that of the Negro male and of the white female—are exceedingly few in number as compared to the others. It therefore follows that our mulattoes are almost throughout the offspring of Negro mothers and white fathers. Now, we must remember that the total number of children born in the community depends upon the number of mothers, and that the number of children born of the Negro or mulatto women would be approximately the same, no matter whether the fathers are Negroes, mulattoes, or white men. It thus appears that in all cases where mixture between whites and Negroes occurs, as long as this mixture is predominantly a mixture of white fathers and colored mothers, the relative proportion of Negro blood in the following mixed generation becomes less, and that therefore a gradually increasing similarity of the two racial types may develop.

I think we may say with safety that the intensity of racial feeling always depends upon two important causes. The one is the relative number of the two races which come into contact. Where one of the races is overwhelmingly in the majority, and the other race is represented by a few individuals only, intensity of race feeling is generally rather slight; while in all cases where both types are so numerous as to form large social divisions, characterized by habits of their own, and representing a strong economic influence, intense race feelings easily develop. These feelings are strongly emphasized by a second consideration: namely, the amount of difference of type.

This is true, at least, in all countries inhabited by north European, particularly by Teutonic, nations. As long as the general emotional state of our society persists—and there is no reason to assume that our general attitude will change to any appreciable degree within a measurable time—it seems obvious that our race problems will become the less intense, the less the difference in type between the different groups of our people, and the less the isolation of certain social groups. From this point of view, it would seem that one aspect of the solution of the Negro problem lies entirely in the hands of the Negro himself. The less Negro society represents a party with its own aims and its own interest distinct from those of the members of the white race, the more satisfactory will be the relation between the races. On the other hand, it would seem that the inexorable conditions of our life will gradually make toward the disappearance of the most distinctive type of Negro, which will again tend to alleviate the acuteness of race feeling. It may seem like a look into a distant future; but an unbiased examination of conditions as they exist at the present time points to the ultimate result of a levelling of the deep distinctions between the two races and a more and more fruitful co-operation.

"PILGRIMAGE TO NONVIOLENCE" *

By Martin Luther King, Jr.

Martin Luther King, Jr. (1929–   ), explains the origins of his idea of nonviolence

Although Booker T. Washington spoke disparagingly of the untrained fundamentalist Negro preacher, it was a member of the Negro clergy, the well educated Martin Luther King, Jr., who symbolizes the rise of the educated Negro clergy to positions of racial leadership. He is not only the product of his Baptist father's "hard" preaching and vigorous congregational leadership but a scholar who graduated from Morehouse College in Atlanta, Boston University, Crozer Theological Seminary, and who attended other schools as well. He was born and reared in race-conscious Atlanta, became an associate minister in his father's church, and then soared to national prominence as a Negro leader with the Montgomery, Alabama, bus boycott of 1955, which initiated the Negro Revolution. The success of his nonviolent tactics gave the American Negro a unique weapon of liberation that appeared in great contrast to the contemporary violence of guerrilla wars and colonial uprisings.

After converting his congregation as a unit to active membership in the NAACP, he organized the powerful Southern Christian Leadership Conference to demonstrate for antisegregationist causes in general and specifically for voter registration drives in Birmingham, Selma, Montgomery and elsewhere. Conspicuous among the demonstrators were the clergy of both races from virtually every part of the country who joined the secular civil rights

* From Martin Luther King, Jr., *Stride Toward Freedom* (New York: Harper & Row, Publishers, Inc., 1958) 90–92, 97–99. Reprinted by permission of Harper & Row, Publishers, Inc.

supporters. In 1965, King received the Nobel Prize, a fitting international recognition.

In this selection from *Stride Toward Freedom*, the Reverend Martin Luther King traces his intellectual evolution from simple apostolic idealism, which he has never lost, through his examination—and rejection—of Marxism, to his study of Gandhi's pacifism and of Reinhold Niebuhr's philosophy of modified nonviolence.

O FTEN THE question has arisen concerning my own intellectual pilgrimage to nonviolence. In order to get at this question it is necessary to go back to my early teens in Atlanta. I had grown up abhorring not only segregation but also the oppressive and barbarous acts that grew out of it. I had passed spots where Negroes had been savagely lynched, and had watched the Ku Klux Klan on its rides at night. I had seen police brutality with my own eyes, and watched Negroes receive the most tragic injustice in the courts. All of these things had done something to my growing personality. I had come perilously close to resenting all white people.

I had also learned that the inseparable twin of racial injustice was economic injustice. Although I came from a home of economic security and relative comfort, I could never get out of my mind the economic insecurity of many of my playmates and the tragic poverty of those living around me. During my late teens I worked two summers, against my father's wishes—he never wanted my brother and me to work around white people because of the oppressive conditions—in a plant that hired both Negroes and whites. Here I saw economic injustice firsthand, and realized that the poor white was exploited just as much as the Negro. Through these early experiences I grew up deeply conscious of the varieties of injustice in our society.

So when I went to Atlanta's Morehouse College as a freshman in 1944 my concern for racial and economic justice was already substantial. During my student days at Morehouse I read Thoreau's *Essay on Civil Disobedience* for the first time. Fascinated by the idea of refusing to coöperate with an evil system, I was so deeply moved that I reread the work several times. This was my first intellectual contact with the theory of nonviolent resistance.

Not until I entered Crozer Theological Seminary in 1948, however, did I begin a serious intellectual quest for a method to eliminate social evil. Although my major interest was in the fields of theology and philosophy, I spent a great deal of time reading the works of the great social philosophers. I came early to Walter Rauschenbusch's *Christianity and the Social Crisis,* which left an indelible imprint on my thinking by giving me a theological basis for the social concern which had already grown up in me as a result of my early experiences. Of course there were points at which I differed with Rauschenbusch. I felt that he had fallen victim to the nineteenth-century "cult of inevitable progress" which led him to a superficial optimism concerning man's nature. Moreover, he came perilously close to identifying the Kingdom of God with a particular social and economic system—a tendency which should never befall the Church. But in spite of these shortcomings Rauschenbusch had done a great service for the Christian Church by insisting that the gospel deals with the whole man, not only his soul but his body; not only his spiritual well-being but his material well-being. It has been my conviction ever since reading Rauschenbusch that any religion which professes to be concerned about the souls of men and is not concerned about the social and economic conditions that scar the soul, is a spiritually moribund religion only waiting for the day to be buried. It well has been said: "A religion that ends with the individual, ends."

After reading Rauschenbusch, I turned to a serious study of the social and ethical theories of the great philosophers, from Plato and Aristotle down to Rousseau, Hobbes, Bentham, Mill, and Locke. All of these masters stimulated my thinking—such as it was—and, while finding things to question in each of them, I nevertheless learned a great deal from their study.

During the Christmas holidays of 1949 I decided to spend my spare time reading Karl Marx to try to understand the appeal of communism for many people. For the first time I carefully scrutinized *Das Kapital* and *The Communist Manifesto.* I also read some interpretive works on the thinking of Marx and Lenin. In reading such Communist writings I drew certain conclusions that have remained with me as convictions to this day. First I rejected their materialistic interpretation of history. Communism,

[margin note: Secularism & materialism]

avowedly secularistic and materialistic, has no place for God. This I could never accept, for as a Christian I believe that there is a creative personal power in this universe who is the ground and essence of all reality—a power that cannot be explained in materialistic terms. History is ultimately guided by spirit, not matter. Second, I strongly disagreed with communism's ethical relativism. *[margin note: Relativity]* Since for the Communist there is no divine government, no absolute moral order, there are no fixed, immutable principles; consequently almost anything—force, violence, murder, lying—is a justifiable means to the "millennial" end. This type of relativism was abhorrent to me. Constructive ends can never give absolute moral justification to destructive means, because in the final analysis the end is preëxistent in the mean. Third, I opposed communism's political totalitarianism. In communism the individual ends up in subjection to the state. True, the Marxist would argue that the state is an "interim" reality which is to be eliminated when the classless society emerges; but the state is the end. . . . When individuals were in conflict with other individuals; when racial groups and nations were in conflict a more realistic approach seemed necessary. But after reading Gandhi, I saw how utterly mistaken I was.

Gandhi was probably the first person in history to lift the love ethic of Jesus above mere interaction between individuals to a powerful and effective social force on a large scale. Love for Gandhi was a potent instrument for social and collective transformation. It was in this Gandhian emphasis on love and nonviolence that I discovered the method for social reform that I had been seeking for so many months. The intellectual and moral satisfaction that I failed to gain from the utilitarianism of Bentham and Mill, the revolutionary methods of Marx and Lenin, the social-contract theory of Hobbes, the "back to nature" optimism of Rousseau, and the superman philosophy of Nietzsche, I found in the nonviolent resistance philosophy of Gandhi. I came to feel that this was the only morally and practically sound method open to oppressed people in their struggle for freedom.

But my intellectual odyssey to nonviolence did not end here. During my last year in theological school, I began to read the works of Reinhold Niebuhr. The prophetic and realistic elements in Niebuhr's passionate style and profound thought were appealing to me, and I became so enamored of his social ethics that I almost fell into the trap of accepting uncritically everything he wrote.

About this time I read Niebuhr's critique of the pacifist position. Niebuhr had himself once been a member of the pacifist ranks. For several years, he had been national chairman of the Fellowship of Reconciliation. His break with pacifism came in the early thirties, and the first full statement of his criticism of pacifism was in *Moral Man and Immoral Society.* Here he argued that there was no intrinsic moral difference between violent and nonviolent resistance. The social consequences of the two methods were different, he contended, but the differences were in degree rather than kind. Later Niebuhr began emphasizing the irresponsibility of relying on nonviolent resistance when there was no ground for believing that it would be successful in preventing the spread of totalitarian tyranny. It could only be successful, he argued, if the groups against whom the resistance was taking place had some degree of moral conscience, as was the case in Gandhi's struggle against the British. Niebuhr's ultimate rejection of pacifism was based primarily on the doctrine of man. He argued that pacifism failed to do justice to the reformation doctrine of justification by faith, substituting for it a sectarian perfectionism which believes "that divine grace actually lifts man out of the sinful contradictions of history and establishes him above the sins of the world."

At first, Niebuhr's critique of pacifism left me in a state of confusion. As I continued to read, however, I came to see more and more the shortcomings of his position. For instance, many of his statements revealed that he interpreted pacifism as a sort of passive nonresistance to evil expressing naïve trust in the power of love. But this was a serious distortion. My study of Gandhi convinced me that true pacifism is not nonresistance to evil, but nonviolent resistance to evil. Between the two positions, there is a world of difference. Gandhi resisted evil with as much vigor and power as the violent resister, but he resisted with love instead of hate. True pacifism is not unrealistic submission to evil power, as Niebuhr contends. It is rather a courageous confrontation of evil by the power of love, in the faith that it is better to be the recipient of violence than the inflicter of it, since the latter only multiplies the existence of violence and bitterness in the universe, while the former may develop a sense of shame in the opponent, and thereby bring about a transformation and change of heart.

In spite of the fact that I found many things to be desired in Niebuhr's philosophy, there were several points at which he constructively influenced my thinking. Niebuhr's great contribution to contemporary theology is that he has refuted the false optimism characteristic of a great segment of Protestant liberalism, without falling into the anti-rationalism of the continental theologian Karl Barth, or the semi-fundamentalism of other dialectical theologians. Moreover, Niebuhr has extraordinary insight into human nature, especially the behavior of nations and social groups. He is keenly aware of the complexity of human motives and of the relation between morality and power. His theology is a persistent reminder of the reality of sin on every level of man's existence. These elements in Niebuhr's thinking helped me to recognize the illusions of a superficial optimism concerning human nature and the dangers of a false idealism. While I still believed in man's potential for good, Niebuhr made me realize his potential for evil as well. Moreover, Niebuhr helped me to recognize the complexity of man's social involvement and the glaring reality of collective evil.

Many pacifists, I felt, failed to see this. All too many had an unwarranted optimism concerning man and leaned unconsciously toward self-righteousness. It was my revolt against these attitudes under the influence of Niebuhr that accounts for the fact that in spite of my strong leaning toward pacifism, I never joined a pacifist organization. After reading Niebuhr, I tried to arrive at a realistic pacifism. In other words, I came to see the pacifist position not as sinless but as the lesser evil in the circumstances. I felt then, and I feel now, that the pacifist would have a greater appeal if he did not claim to be free from the moral dilemmas that the Christian nonpacifist confronts.

Chapter Three

THE IMMIGRANT, THE INDIAN, CULTURAL PLURALISM, AND STEREOTYPES

A CENTURY OF DISHONOR*
Indian Policy

By Helen Hunt Jackson

Helen Hunt Jackson (1830–85), novelist, awakens the nation's conscience to the betrayal of the Indian

A sensitive daughter of an Amherst classics professor, Helen Hunt Jackson revealed her literary gifts and intense social consciousness after the death of her army husband, Major Hunt. She had become interested in the Indian shortly after settling in California in 1872 and especially after listening to the pleas of two Indians in Boston who spoke out against the lot of the Poncas. Her detailed indictment of Federal Indian policies came in *A Century of Dishonor* (1881), which she hoped would move Congress to action. Those were the years of Indian wars, massacres of the tribesmen, and of Custer's last stand. Mrs. Jackson (she had by this time married a banker and was settled in Colorado Springs) turned to fiction, as Harriet Beecher Stowe had done, to arouse the nation; but *Ramona* (1884) tended to bury its message in its highly romantic story of Anglo-Saxon cruelty to the Indian and

* From Helen Hunt Jackson, *A Century of Dishonor* (1881), 336–42.

the disruption of an idyllic culture. Still, she was a significant force in the movement that produced the various Indian Rights Associations and the passage of the Dawes Act of 1887, which tried to convert tribal culture into the individualistic farmer's society of the white man.

※⁂⁑

THERE ARE within the limits of the United States between two hundred and fifty and three hundred thousand Indians, exclusive of those in Alaska. The names of the different tribes and bands, as entered in the statistical tables of the Indian Office Reports, number nearly three hundred. One of the most careful estimates which have been made of their numbers and localities gives them as follows: "In Minnesota and States east of the Mississippi, about 32,500; in Nebraska, Kansas, and the Indian Territory, 70,650; in the Territories of Dakota, Montana, Wyoming, and Idaho, 65,000; in Nevada and the Territories of Colorado, New Mexico, Utah, and Arizona, 84,000; and on the Pacific slope, 48,000."

Of these, 130,000 are self-supporting on their own reservations, "receiving nothing from the Government except interest on their own moneys, or annuities granted them in consideration of the cession of their lands to the United States." *

This fact alone would seem sufficient to dispose forever of the accusation, so persistently brought against the Indian, that he will not work.

Of the remainder, 84,000 are partially supported by the Government—the interest money due them and their annuities, as provided by treaty, being inadequate to their subsistence on the reservations where they are confined. In many cases, however, these Indians furnish a large part of their support—the White River Utes, for instance, who are reported by the Indian Bureau as getting sixty-six per cent. of their living by "root-digging, hunting, and fishing;" the Squaxin band, in Washington Territory, as earning seventy-five per cent., and the Chippewas of Lake Superior as earning fifty per cent. in the same way. These facts also would seem to dispose of the accusation that the Indian will not work.

* Annual Report of Indian Commissioner for 1872.

There are about 55,000 who never visit an agency, over whom the Government does not pretend to have either control or care. These 55,000 "subsist by hunting, fishing, on roots, nuts, berries, etc., and by begging and stealing;" and this also seems to dispose of the accusation that the Indian will not "work for a living." There remains a small portion, about 31,000, that are entirely subsisted by the Government.

There is not among these three hundred bands of Indians one which has not suffered cruelly at the hands either of the Government or of white settlers. The poorer, the more insignificant, the more helpless the band, the more certain the cruelty and outrage to which they have been subjected. This is especially true of the bands on the Pacific slope. These Indians found themselves of a sudden surrounded by and caught up in the great influx of gold-seeking settlers, as helpless creatures on a shore are caught up in a tidal wave. There was not time for the Government to make treaties; not even time for communities to make laws. The tale of the wrongs, the oppressions, the murders of the Pacific-slope Indians in the last thirty years would be a volume by itself, and is too monstrous to be believed.

It makes little difference, however, where one opens the record of the history of the Indians; every page and every year has its dark stain. The story of one tribe is the story of all, varied only by differences of time and place; but neither time nor place makes any difference in the main facts. Colorado is as greedy and unjust in 1880 as was Georgia in 1830, and Ohio in 1795; and the United States Government breaks promises now as deftly as then, and with an added ingenuity from long practice.

One of its strongest supports in so doing is the wide-spread sentiment among the people of dislike to the Indian, of impatience with his presence as a "barrier to civilization," and distrust of it as a possible danger. The old tales of the frontier life, with its horrors of Indian warfare, have gradually, by two or three generations' telling, produced in the average mind something like an hereditary instinct of unquestioning and unreasoning aversion which it is almost impossible to dislodge or soften.

There are hundreds of pages of unimpeachable testimony on the side of the Indian; but it goes for nothing, is set down as sentimentalism or partisanship, tossed aside and forgotten.

President after president has appointed commission after commission to inquire into and report upon Indian affairs, and to make suggestions as to the best methods of managing them. The reports are filled with eloquent statements of wrongs done to the Indians, of perfidies on the part of the Government; they counsel, as earnestly as words can, a trial of the simple and unperplexing expedients of telling truth, keeping promises, making fair bargains, dealing justly in all ways and all things. These reports are bound up with the Government's Annual Reports, and that is the end of them. It would probably be no exaggeration to say that not one American citizen out of ten thousand ever sees them or knows that they exist, and yet any one of them, circulated throughout the country, read by the right-thinking, right-feeling men and women of this land, would be of itself a "campaign document" that would initiate a revoluton which would not subside until the Indians' wrongs were, so far as is now left possible, righted.

In 1869 President Grant appointed a commission of nine men, representing the influence and philanthropy of six leading States, to visit the different Indian reservations, and to "examine all matters appertaining to Indian affairs."

In the report of this commission are such paragraphs as the following: "To assert that 'the Indian will not work' is as true as it would be to say that the white man will not work.

"Why should the Indian be expected to plant corn, fence lands, build houses, or do anything but get food from day to day, when experience has taught him that the product of his labor will be seized by the white man to-morrow? The most industrious white man would become a drone under similar circumstances. Nevertheless, many of the Indians (the commissioners might more forcibly have said 130,000 of the Indians) are already at work, and furnish ample refutation of the assertion that 'the Indian will not work.' There is no escape from the inexorable logic of facts.

"The history of the Government connections with the Indians is a shameful record of broken treaties and unfulfilled promises. The history of the border white man's connection with the Indians is a sickening record of murder, outrage, robbery, and wrongs committed by the former, as the rule, and occasional savage outbreaks and unspeakably barbarous deeds of retaliation by the latter, as the exception.

"Taught by the Government that they had rights entitled to respect, when those rights have been assailed by the rapacity of the white man, the arm which should have been raised to protect them has ever been ready to sustain the aggressor.

"The testimony of some of the highest military officers of the United State is on record to the effect that, in our Indian wars, almost without exception, the first aggressions have been made by the white man; and the assertion is supported by every civilian of reputation who has studied the subject. In addition to the class of robbers and outlaws who find impunity in their nefarious pursuits on the frontiers, there is a large class of professedly reputable men who use every means in their power to bring on Indian wars for the sake of the profit to be realized from the presence of troops and the expenditure of Government funds in their midst. They proclaim death to the Indians at all times in words and publications, making no distinction between the innocent and the guilty. They irate the lowest class of men to the perpetration of the darkest deeds against their victims, and as judges and jurymen shield them from the justice due to their crimes. Every crime committed by a white man against an Indian is concealed or palliated. Every offence committed by an Indian against a white man is borne on the wings of the post or the telegraph to the remotest corner of the land, clothed with all the horrors which the reality or imagination can throw around it. Against such influences as these the people of the United States need to be warned."

To assume that it would be easy, or by any one sudden stroke of legislative policy possible, to undo the mischief and hurt of the long past, set the Indian policy of the country right for the future, and make the Indians at once safe and happy, is the blunder of a hasty and uninformed judgment. The notion which seems to be growing more prevalent, that simply to make all Indians at once citizens of the United States would be a sovereign and instantaneous panacea for all their ills and all the Government's perplexities, is a very inconsiderate one. To administer complete citizenship of a sudden, all round, to all Indians, barbarous and civilized alike, would be as grotesque a blunder as to dose them all round with any one medicine, irrespective of the symptoms and needs of their diseases. It would kill more than it would cure. Nevertheless, it is true, as was well stated by one of the superintendents of Indian Affairs in 1857, that, "so long as they are not citizens of the United States, their rights of property must remain insecure against invasion. The doors of the federal tribunals being barred against them while wards and dependents, they can only partially exercise the rights of free government, or give to those who make, execute, and construe the few laws they are allowed to enact, dignity sufficient to make them respectable. While they continue individually to gather the crumbs that fall from the table of the United States, idleness, improvidence, and indebtedness will be the rule, and industry, thrift, and freedom from debt the exception. The utter absence of individual title to particular lands deprives every one among them of the chief incentive to labor and exertion—the very mainspring on which the prosperity of a people depends."

All judicious plans and measures for their safety and salvation must embody provisions for their becoming citizens as fast as they are fit, and must protect them till then in every right and particular in which our laws protect other "persons" who are not citizens.

There is a disposition in a certain class of minds to be impatient with any protestation against wrong which is unaccompanied or unprepared with a quick and exact scheme of remedy. This is illogical. When pioneers in a new country find a tract of poisonous and swampy wilderness to be reclaimed, they do not withhold their hands from fire and axe till they see clearly which way roads should run, where good water will spring, and what crops will best grow on the redeemed land. They first clear the swamp. So with this poisonous and baffling part of the domain of our national affairs—let us first "clear the swamp."

However great perplexity and difficulty there may be in the details of any and every plan possible for doing at this late day anything like justice to the Indian, however hard it may be for good statesmen and good men to agree upon the things that ought to be done, there certainly is, or ought to be, no perplexity whatever, no difficulty whatever, in agreeing upon certain things that ought not to be done, and which must cease to be done before the first steps can be taken toward righting the wrongs, curing the ills, and wiping out the disgrace to us of the present condition of our Indians.

Cheating, robbing, breaking promises—these three are clearly things which must cease to be done. One more thing, also, and that is the refusal of the protection of the law to the Indian's rights of property, "of life, liberty, and the pursuit of happiness."

When these four things have ceased to be done, time, statesmanship, philanthropy, and Christianity can slowly and surely do the rest. Till these four things have ceased to be done, statesmanship and philanthropy alike must work in vain, and even Christianity can reap but small harvest.

OBSERVATIONS BY MR. DOOLEY*
Immigration Attitudes, a Humorous View

By Finley Peter Dunne

Finley Peter Dunne (1867–1936) examines anti-immigrant prejudices through the eyes of Messrs. Dooley and Hennessey

Chicago had its witty journalistic interpreter of both the Archer Avenue Irish and the American scene in a son of an Irish carpenter, Finley Peter Dunne, an articulate observer of politics and the Church. Young Dunne rose swiftly in the newspaper world as a reporter and youthful editor of several papers, finally becoming managing editor of the Chicago *Journal* in 1897. By this time he had created the Irish dialect characters of Mr. Dooley, the shrewd bartender, and Mr. Hennessey, his stooge, who commented on the news of the day, usually reflecting the editor's pro-labor, anti-imperialist, and liberal Democratic views. The best dialogues were compiled in *Mr. Dooley in Peace and War* (1898), which poked fun at the bellicosity and vanity of Theodore Roosevelt during the Cuban war. (Roosevelt, who could take a joke on himself, became a good friend of Dunne.) In 1900, Dunne moved to various editorial positions in New York City and associated with Lincoln Steffens and William Allen White as editors of the muckraking *American Magazine.* During 1902–1910 came a series of successful Dooley books, one of which chosen for excerpts here was *Observations by Mr. Dooley* (1902), which offered clever insights into contemporary attitudes toward immigration.

---

* From Finley Peter Dunne, *Observations by Mr. Dooley* (1902), 50–54.

BUT THEY'SE wan question that Congress is goin' to take up that you an' me are intherested in. As a pilgrim father that missed th' first boats, I must raise me claryon voice again' th' invasion iv this fair land be th' paupers an' arnychists iv effete Europe. Ye bet I must—because I'm here first. 'Twas diff'rent whin I was dashed high on th' stern an' rockbound coast. In thim days America was th' refuge iv th' oppressed iv all th' wurruld. They cud come over here an' do a good job iv oppressin' thimsilves. As I told ye I came a little late. Th' Rosenfelts an' th' Lodges bate me be at laste a boat lenth, an' be th' time I got here they was stern an' rockbound thimsilves. So I got a gloryous rayciption as soon as I was towed off th' rocks. Th' stars an' sthripes whispered a welcome in th' breeze an' a shovel was thrust into me hand an' I was pushed into a sthreet excyvatin' as though I'd been born here. Th' pilgrim father who bossed th' job was a fine ol' puritan be th' name iv Doherty, who come over in th' Mayflower about th' time iv th' potato rot in Wexford, an' he made me think they was a hole in th' breakwather iv th' haven iv refuge an' some iv th' wash iv th' seas iv opprission had got through. He was a stern an' rockbound la-ad himsilf, but I was a good hand at loose stones an' wan day—but I'll tell ye about that another time.

"Annyhow, I was rayceived with open arms that sometimes ended in a clinch. I was afraid I wasn't goin' to assimilate with th' airlyer pilgrim fathers an' th' instichoochions iv th' counthry, but I soon found that a long swing iv th' pick made me as good as another man an' it didn't require a gr-reat intellect, or sometimes anny at all, to vote th' dimmycrat ticket, an' before I was here a month, I felt enough like a native born American to burn a witch. Wanst in a while a mob iv intilligint collajeens, whose grandfathers had bate me to th' dock, wud take a shy at me Pathrick's Day procission or burn down wan iv me churches, but they got tired iv that before long; 'twas too much like wurruk.

"But as I tell ye, Hinnissy, 'tis diff'rent now. I don't know why 'tis diff'rent but 'tis diff'rent. 'Tis time we put our back again' th' open dure an' keep out th' savage horde. If that cousin iv ye'ers expects to cross, he'd betther tear f'r th' ship. In a few minyits th' gates 'll be down an' whin th' oppressed wurruld comes hikin' acrost to th' haven iv refuge, they'll do well to put a couplin' pin undher their hats, f'r th' Goddess iv Liberty 'll meet thim at th' dock with an axe in her hand. Congress is goin' to fix it. Me

frind Shaughnessy says so. He was in yisterdah an' says he: ' 'Tis
time we done something to make th' immigration laws sthronger,'
says he. 'Thrue f'r ye, Miles Standish,' says I; 'but what wud ye
do?' 'I'd keep out th' offscourin's iv Europe,' says he. 'Wud ye go
back?' says I. 'Have ye'er joke,' says he. ' 'Tis not so seeryus as it
was befure ye come," says I. 'But what ar-re th' immygrants doin'
that's roonous to us?' I says. 'Well,' says he, 'they're arnychists,' he
says: 'they don't assymilate with th' counthry,' he says. 'Maybe th'
counthry's digestion has gone wrong fr'm too much rich food,'
say I; 'perhaps now if we'd lave off thryin' to digest Rockyfellar
an' thry a simple diet like Schwartzmeister, we wudden't feel th'
effects iv our vittels,' I says. 'Maybe if we'd season th' immygrants
a little or cook thim thurly, they'd go down betther,' I says.

" "They 're arnychists, like Parsons,' he says. 'He wud've been
an immygrant if Texas hadn't been admitted to th' Union,' I says.
'Or Snolgosh,'* he says. 'Has Mitchigan seceded?' I says. 'Or
Gittoo,† he says. 'Who come fr'm th' effete monarchies iv Chicago, west iv Ashland Av'noo,' I says. 'Or what's-his-name, Wilkes
Booth,' he says. 'I don't know what he was—maybe a Boolghar-
yen,' says I. 'Well, annyhow,' says he, 'they're th' scum iv th'
earth.' 'They may be that,' says I; 'but we used to think they was
th' cream iv civilization,' I says. 'They're off th' top annyhow. I
wanst believed 'twas th' best men iv Europe come here, th' la-ads
that was too sthrong and indepindant to be kicked around be a
boorgomasther at home an' wanted to dig out f'r a place where
they cud get a chanst to make their way to th' money. I see their
sons fightin' into politics an' their daughters tachin' young American idee how to shoot too high in th' public school, an' I
thought they was all right. But I see I was wrong. Thim boys out
there towin' wan heavy foot afther th' other to th' rowlin' mills
is all arnychists. There's warrants out f'r all names endin' in
'inski, an' I think I'll board up me windows, f'r,' I says, 'if immygrants is as dangerous to this counthry as ye an' I an' other pilgrim fathers believe they are, they'se enough iv thim sneaked in
already to make us aborigines about as infloointial as the prohibi-
tion vote in th' Twinty-ninth Ward. They'll dash again' our
stern an' rock-bound coast till they bust it,' says I.

" 'But I ain't so much afraid as ye ar-re. I'm not afraid iv me
father an' I'm not afraid iv mesilf. An' I'm not afraid iv Schwartz-

* Editor's note: Czolgosz, assassin of McKinley.
† Editor's note: Guiteau, assassin of Garfield.

meister's father or Hinnery Cabin Lodge's grandfather. We all come over th' same way, an' if me ancestors were not what Hogan calls rigicides, 'twas not because they were not ready an' willin', on'y a king niver come their way. I don't believe in killin' kings, mesilf. I never wud've sawed th' block off that curly-headed potintate that I see in th' pitchers down town, but, be hivins, Presarved Codfish Shaughnessy, if we'd begun a few years ago shuttin' out folks that wudden't mind handin' a bomb to a king, they wudden't be enough people in Mattsachoosetts to make a quorum f'r th' Anti-Impeeryal S'ciety,' says I. 'But what wud ye do with th' offscourin' iv Europe?' says he. 'I'd scour thim some more,' says I.

"An' so th' meetin' iv th' Plymouth Rock Assocyation come to an end. But if ye wud like to get it together, Deacon Hinnissy, to discuss th' immygration question, I'll sind out a hurry call f'r Schwartzmeister an' Mulcahey an' Ignacio Sbarbaro an' Nels Larsen an' Petrus Gooldvink, an' we 'll gather to-night at Fanneilnoviski Hall at th' corner iv Sheridan an' Sigel sthreets. All th' pilgrim fathers is rayquested f'r to bring interpreters."

"Well," said Mr. Hennessy, "divvle th' bit I care, on'y I'm here first, an' I ought to have th' right to keep th' bus fr'm bein' overcrowded."

"Well," said Mr. Dooley, "as a pilgrim father on me gran' nephew's side, I don't know but ye're right. An' they'se wan sure way to keep thim out."

"What's that?" asked Mr. Hennessy.

"Teach thim all about our instichoochions befure they come," said Mr. Dooley.

"DEMOCRACY VERSUS THE MELTING POT"*

Cultural Pluralism

By Horace M. Kallen

Horace M. Kallen (1882–) philosopher, shows that the democratic experience of cultural pluralism is superior to melting pot assimilation

Horace M. Kallen, who has devoted so much of his thinking to the values of cultural pluralism, was himself a Jewish immigrant born in Silesia, Germany, who was brought to the United States in 1887. After taking an A.B. *magna cum laude,* and a Ph.D. at Harvard, he lectured there in philosophy, later taught philosophy and psychology at the University of Wisconsin, and eventually became a professor and dean at the New School of Social Research in New York City where he remained until 1952. From William James, he adopted the "open universe" of pragmatism, democratic reformism, and a lasting appreciation of the human varieties of religious experience inherent in the psychological diversities of man's nature. Like James he was interested in reconciling religious expression with science, and as a self-conscious Jew, he tried to apply these ideas to Judaism and Zionism. Deeply attached to the Jewish heritage and concerned with the survival of the Jew under the pressures of the "melting pot," he became a leading theorist of cultural pluralism and an enthusiastic exponent of the idea of the rich potentialities for human experience inherent in a loose federation of polyglot cultures within America. He was active in the American Jewish Congress, became a director of the Institute of Jewish Affairs, and won national recognition as a witty as well as brilliant debater.

His pioneer essay on cultural pluralism published in *The Nation* on February 25, 1915, and partly reproduced below contains ideas that were to be profoundly and consistently elaborated and extended in his prolific writings. His *Culture and Democracy in the United States* (1924) defined cultural pluralism as "manyness, variety, and differentiation," which can only exist in a free society that permits free exchange of ideas and fosters a liberal education

* Horace M. Kallen, "Democracy Versus the Melting Pot," *The Nation,* Vol. 100 (February 25, 1915), 218–20.

that extends through life. Like John Dewey, he looked at education as a process of critical inquiry that leads to the liberation of men. He eschewed indoctrination, the aristocratic detachment of the ivory tower, and the traditional notion that the sole purpose of the schools was to transmit the cultural heritage intact. This was the argument of *Art and Freedom* (1942). In numerous other books, Kallen dwelt upon the central role of the consumer in a democratic society, discussed (with James Weldon Johnson) the importance of Africa in world democracy, and expressed his lifelong appreciation of the contributions of the various immigrant groups.

WHAT IS the cultural outcome likely to be [for the immigrant], under these conditions [of mass culture]? Surely not the melting-pot. Rather something that has become more and more distinct in the changing State and city life of the last two decades, and which is most articulate and apparent among just those peoples whom Mr. Ross * praises most—the Scandinavians, the Germans, the Irish, the Jews.

It is in the area where Scandinavians are most concentrated that Norwegian is preached on Sunday in more churches than in Norway. That area is Minnesota, not unlike Scandinavia in climate and character. There, if the newspapers are to be trusted, the "foreign language" taught in an increasingly larger number of high schools is Scandinavian. The Constitution of the State resembles in many respects the famous Norwegian Constitution of 1813. The largest city has been chosen as the "spiritual capital," if I may say so, the seat of the Scandinavian "house of life," which the Scandinavian Society in America is reported to be planning to build as a centre from which there is to spread through the land Scandinavian culture and ideals.

The eastern neighbor of Minnesota is Wisconsin, a region of great concentration of Germans. Is it merely a political accident that the centralization of State authority and control has been possible there to a degree heretofore unknown in this country? That the Socialist organization is the most powerful in the land, able under ordinary conditions to have elected the Mayor of a

* Editor's note: Edward A. Ross (sociologist), *The Old World in the New* (New York, 1915).

large city and a Congressman, and kept out of power only by coalition of the other parties? That German is the overwhelmingly predominant "foreign language" in the public schools and in the university? Or that the fragrance of *Deutschthum* pervades the life of the whole State? The earliest German immigrants to America were group conscious to a high degree. They brought with them a cultural tradition and political aspiration. They wanted to found a State. If a State is to be regarded as a mode of life of the mind, they have succeeded. Their language is the predominant "foreign" one throughout the Middle West. The teaching of it is required by law in many places, southern Ohio and Indianapolis, for example. Their national institutions, even to cooking, are as widespread as they are. They are organized into a great national society, the German-American Alliance, which is dedicated to the advancement of German culture and ideals. They encourage and make possible a close and more intimate contact with the fatherland. They endow Germanic museums, they encourage and provide for exchange professorships, erect monuments to German heroes, and disseminate translations of the German classics. And there are, of course, the very excellent German vernacular press, the German theatre, the German club, the German organization of life.

Similar are the Irish, living in strength in Massachusetts and New York. When they began to come to this country they were far less well off and far more passionately self-conscious than the Germans. For numbers of them America was and has remained just a centre from which to plot for the freedom of Ireland. For most it was an opportunity to escape both exploitation and starvation. The way they made was made against both race and religious prejudice: in the course of it they lost much that was attractive as well as much that was unpleasant. But Americanization brought the mass of them also spiritual self-respect, and their growing prosperity both here and in Ireland is what lies behind the more inward phases of Irish Nationalism—the Gaelic movement, the Irish theatre, the Irish Art Society. I omit consideration of such organized bodies as the Ancient Order of Hibernians. All these movements alike indicate the conversion of the negative nationalism of the hatred of England to the positive nationalism of the loving care and development of the cultural values of the Celtic spirit. A significant phase of it is the voting of Irish history into the curriculum of the high schools of Boston. In sum, once the Irish body had been fed and erected, the Irish mind demanded and generated its own peculiar form of self-realization and satisfaction.

And, finally, the Jews. Their attitude towards America is different in a fundamental respect from that of other immigrant nationalities. They do not come to the United States from truly native lands, lands of their proper *natio* and culture. They come from lands of sojourn, where they have been for ages treated as foreigners, at most as semicitizens, subject to disabilities and persecutions. They come with no political aspirations against the peace of other states such as move the Irish, the Poles, the Bohemians. They come with the intention to be completely incorporated into the body-politic of the state. They alone, as Mr. H. G. Wells notes, of all the immigrant peoples have made spontaneously conscious and organized efforts to prepare themselves and their brethren for the responsibilities of American citizenship. There is hardly a considerable municipality in the land, where Jews inhabit, that has not its Hebrew Institute, or its Educational Alliance, or its Young Men's Hebrew Association, or its Community House, especially dedicated to this task. They show the highest percentage of naturalization, according to Mr. Ross's tables, and he concedes that they have benefited politics. Yet of all self-conscious peoples they are the most self-conscious. Of all immigrants they have the oldest civilized tradition, they are longest accustomed to living under law, and are at the outset the most eager and the most successful in eliminating the external differences between themselves and their social environment. Even their religion is flexible and accommodating, as that of the Christian sectaries is not, for change involves no change in doctrine, only in mode of life.

Yet, once the wolf is driven from the door and the Jewish immigrant takes his place in our society a free man and an American, he tends to become all the more a Jew. The cultural unity of his race, history, and background is only continued by the new life under the new conditions. Mr. H. G. Wells calls the Jewish quarter in New York a city within a city, and with more justice than other quarters because, although it is far more in tune with Americanism than the other quarters, it is also far more autonomous in spirit and self-conscious in culture. It has its sectaries, its radicals, its artists, its literati; its press, its literature, its theatre, its Yiddish and its Hebrew, its Talmudical colleges and its

Hebrew schools, its charities and its vanities, and its coördinating organization, the Kehilla, all more or less duplicated wherever Jews congregate in mass. Here not religion alone, but the whole world of radical thinking, carries the mother-tongue and the father-tongue, with all that they imply. Unlike the parochial schools, their separate schools, being national, do not displace the public schools; they supplement the public schools. The Jewish ardor for pure learning is notorious. And, again, as was the case with the Scandinavians, the Germans, the Irish, democracy applied to education has given the Jews their will that Hebrew shall be coördinate with French and German in the regent's examination. On a national scale of organization there is the American Jewish Committee, the Jewish Historical Society, the Jewish Publication Society. Rurally, there is the model Association of Jewish Farmers, with their coöperative organization for agriculture and for agricultural education. In sum, the most eagerly American of the immigrant groups are also the most autonomous and self-conscious in spirit and culture.

Immigrants appear to pass through four phases in the course of being Americanized. In the first phase they exhibit economic eagerness, the greed of the unfed. Since external differences are a handicap in the economic struggle, they "assimilate," seeking thus to facilitate the attainment of economic independence. Once the proletarian level of such independence is reached, the process of assimilation slows down and tends to come to a stop. The immigrant group is still a national group, modified, sometimes improved, by environmental influences, but otherwise a solitary spiritual unit, which is seeking to find its way out on its own social level. This search brings to light permanent group distinctions, and the immigrant, like the Anglo-Saxon American, is thrown back upon himself and his ancestry. Then a process of dissimilation begins. The arts, life, and ideals of the nationality become central and paramount; ethnic and national differences change in status from disadvantages to distinctions. All the while the immigrant has been using the English language and behaving like an American in matters economic and political, and continues to do so. The institutions of the Republic have become the liberating cause and the background for the rise of the cultural consciousness and social autonomy of the immigrant Irishman, German, Scandinavian, Jew, Pole, or Bohemian. On the whole, Americanization has not repressed nationality. Americanization has liberated nationality.

Hence, what troubles Mr. Ross and so many other Anglo-Saxon Americans is not really inequality; what troubles them is *difference*. Only things that are alike in fact and not abstractly, and only men that are alike in origin and in spirit and not abstractly, can be truly "equal" and maintain that inward unanimity of action and outlook which make a national life. The writers of the Declaration of Independence and of the Constitution were not confronted by the practical fact of ethnic dissimilarity among the whites of the country. Their descendants are confronted by it. Its existence, acceptance, and development provide one of the inevitable consequences of the democratic principle on which our theory of government is based, and the result at the present writing is to many worthies very unpleasant. Democratism and the Federal principle have worked together with economic greed and ethnic snobbishness to people the land with all the nationalities of Europe, and to convert the early American nation into the present American state. For in effect we are in the process of becoming a true federal state, such a state as men hope for as the outcome of the European war, a great republic consisting of a federation or commonwealth of nationalities.

Given, in the economic order, the principle of *laissez-faire* applied to a capitalistic society, in contrast with the manorial and guild systems of the past and the Socialist utopias of the future, the economic consequences are the same, whether in America, full of all Europe, or in England, full of the English, Scotch, and Welsh. Given, in the political order, the principle that all men are equal and that each, consequently, under the law at least, shall have the opportunity to make the most of himself, the control of the machinery of government by the plutocracy is a foregone conclusion. *Laissez-faire* and unprecedentedly bountiful natural resources have turned the mind of the state to wealth alone, and in the haste to accumulate wealth considerations of human quality have been neglected and forgotten, the action of government has been remedial rather than constructive, and Mr. Ross's "peasantism," *i. e.*, the growth of an expropriated, degraded industrial class, dependent on the factory rather than on land, has been rapid and vexatious.

The problems which these conditions give rise to are important, but not primarily important. Although they have occupied the minds of all our political theorists, they are problems of means, of instruments, not of ends. They concern the conditions of life, not the *kind of life*, and there appears to have been a general assumption that only one kind of human life is possible in America. But the same democracy which underlies the evils of the economic order underlies also the evils—and the promise—of the ethnic order. Because no individual is merely an individual, the political autonomy of the individual has meant and is beginning to realize in these United States the spiritual autonomy of his group. The process is as yet far from fruition. We are, in fact, at the parting of the ways. A genuine social alternative is before us, either of which parts we may realize if we will. In social construction the will is father to the fact, for the fact is nothing more than the concord or conflict of wills. What do we *will* to make of the United States—a unison, singing the old Anglo-Saxon theme "America," the America of the New England school, or a harmony, in which that theme shall be dominant, perhaps, among others, but one among many, not the only one?

The mind reverts helplessly to the historic attempts at unison in Europe—the heroic failure of the pan-Hellenists, of the Romans, the disintegration and the diversification of the Christian Church, for a time the most successful unison in history; the present-day failures of Germany and of Russia. Here, however, the whole social situation is favorable, as it has never been at any time elsewhere—everything is favorable but the basic law of America itself, and the spirit of American institutions. To achieve unison—it can be achieved—would be to violate these. For the end determines the means, and this end would involve no other means than those used by Germany in Poland, in Schleswig-Holstein, and Alsace-Lorraine; by Russia in the Pale, in Poland, in Finland. Fundamentally it would require the complete nationalization of education, the abolition of every form of parochial and private school, the abolition of instruction in other tongues than English, and the concentration of the teaching of history and literature upon the English tradition. The other institutions of society would require treatment analogous to that administered by Germany to her European acquisitions. And all of this, even if meeting with no resistance, would not completely guarantee the survival as a unison of the older Americanism. For the programme would be applied to diverse ethnic types, and the reconstruction that, with the best will, they might spontaneously make of the tradition would more likely than not be a far cry from the original. It is, already.

The notion that the programme might be realized by radical and even enforced miscegenation, by the creation of the melting-pot by law, and thus by the development of the new "American race," is, as Mr. Ross points out, as mystically optimistic as it is ignorant. In historic times, so far as we know, no new ethnic types have originated, and what we know of breeding gives us no assurance of the disappearance of the old types in favor of the new, only the addition of a new type, if it succeeds in surviving, to the already existing older ones. Biologically, life does not unify; biologically, life diversifies; and it is sheer ignorance to apply social analogies to biological processes. In any event, we know what the qualities and capacities of existing types are; we know how by education to do something towards the repression of what is evil in them and the conservation of what is good. The "American race" is a totally unknown thing; to presume that it will be better because (if we like to persist in the illusion that it is coming) it will be later, is no different from imagining that, because contemporary, Russia is better than ancient Greece. There is nothing more to be said to the pious stupidity that identifies recency with goodness. The unison to be achieved cannot be a unison of ethnic types. It must be, if it is to be at all, a unison of social and historic interests, established by the complete cutting-off of the ancestral memories of our populations, the enforced, exclusive use of the English language and English and American history in the schools and in the daily life.

The attainment of the other alternative, a harmony, also requires concerted public action. But the action would do no violence to our fundamental law and the spirit of our institutions, nor to the qualities of men. It would seek simply to eliminate the waste and the stupidity of our social organization, by way of freeing and strengthening the strong forces actually in operation. Starting with our existing ethnic and cultural groups, it would seek to provide conditions under which each may attain the perfection that is proper to its kind. The provision of such conditions is the primary intent of our fundamental law and the function of our institutions. And the various nationalities which compose our commonwealth must learn first of all this fact, which is perhaps, to most minds, the outstanding ideal content of "Americanism"—that democracy means self-realization through self-control, self-government, and that one is impossible without the other. For the application of this principle, which is realized in a harmony of societies, there are European analogies also. I omit Austria and Turkey, for the union of nationalities is there based more on inadequate force than on consent, and the form of their organization is alien to ours. I think of England and of Switzerland. England is a state of four nationalities—the English, Welsh, Scotch, and Irish (if one considers the Empire, of many more), and while English history is not unmarred by attempts at unison, both the home policy and the imperial policy have, since the Boer War, been realized more and more in the application of the principle of harmony: the strength of the kingdom and the empire have been posited more and more upon the voluntary and autonomous coöperation of the component nationalities. Switzerland is a state of three nationalities, a republic as the United States is, far more democratically governed, concentrated in an area not much different in size, I suspect, from New York city, with a population not far from it in total. Yet Switzerland has the most loyal citizens in Europe. Their language, literary and spiritual traditions are on the one side German, on another Italian, on a third side French. And in terms of social organization, of economic prosperity, of public education, of the general level of culture, Switzerland is the most successful democracy in the world. It conserves and encourages individuality.

The reason lies, I think, in the fact that in Switzerland the conception of "natural rights" operates, consciously or unconsciously, as a generalization from the unalterable data of human nature. What is inalienable in the life of mankind is its intrinsic positive quality—its psychophysical inheritance. Men may change their clothes, their politics, their wives, their religions, their philosophies, to a greater or lesser extent: they cannot change their grandfathers. Jews or Poles or Anglo-Saxons, in order to cease being Jews or Poles or Anglo-Saxons, would have to cease to be. The selfhood which is inalienable in them, and for the realization of which they require "inalienable" liberty, is ancestrally determined, and the happiness which they pursue has its form implied in ancestral endowment. This is what, actually, democracy in operation assumes. There are human capacities which it is the function of the state to liberate and to protect; and the failure of the state as a government means its abolition. Government, the state, under the democratic conception, is merely an instrument, not an end. That it is often an abused instrument, that it is often seized by the powers that prey, that it makes frequent mistakes and considers only secondary ends, surface needs, which vary from moment to moment, is, of course, obvious: hence our social and political chaos. But that it is an instrument, flexibly adjustable to changing life, changing opinion, and needs, our whole electoral organization and party system declare. And as intelligence and wisdom prevail over "politics" and special interests, as the steady and continuous pressure of the inalienable qualities and purposes of human groups more and more dominate the confusion of our common life, the outlines of a possible great and truly democratic commonwealth become discernible.

Its form is that of the Federal republic; its substance a democracy of nationalities, cooperating voluntarily and autonomously in the enterprise of self-realization through the perfection of men according to their kind. The common language of the commonwealth, the language of its great political tradition, is English, but each nationality expresses its emotional and voluntary life in its own language, in its own inevitable æsthetic and intellectual forms. The common life of the commonwealth is politico-economic, and serves as the foundation and background for the realization of the distinctive individuality of each *natio* that composes it. Thus "American civilization" may come to mean the perfection of the coöperative harmonies of "European civilization," the waste, the squalor, and the distress of Europe being eliminated—a multiplicity in a unity, an orchestration of mankind. As in an orchestra, every type of instrument has its specific timbre and tonality, founded in its substance and form; as every type has its appropriate theme and melody in the whole symphony, so in society each ethnic group is the natural instrument, its spirit and culture are its theme and melody, and the harmony and dissonances and discords of them all make the symphony of civilization, with this difference: a musical symphony is written before it is played; in the symphony of civilization the playing is the writing, so that there is nothing so fixed and inevitable about its progressions as in music, so that within the limits set by nature they may vary at will, and the range and variety of the harmonies may become wider and richer and more beautiful.

But the question is, do the dominant classes in America want such a society?

PUBLIC OPINION*
Stereotypes

By Walter Lippmann

*Walter Lippmann (1889–   ) explains the distorting effect of
stereotypes on the nature of public opinion*

Greatest in intellectuality, influence, and prestige among
American journalists is Walter Lippmann, who is also an original
political theorist. His educational opportunities owe much to his
father, a well-to-do New York manufacturer and real estate broker
of German-Jewish ancestry, who made it possible for Lippmann
to enter Harvard from which he graduated in 1910 as a Phi Beta
Kappa. Although he was nominally a college radical as the president of the Harvard Socialist Club, he did not go beyond the
moderate intellectual Fabianism then popular in England. In *A
Preface to Politics* (1913), he greatly modified his socialism and
then dropped it altogether in *Drift and Mastery* (1914). These
liberal writings drew Herbert Croly, the Progressive, to Lippmann
and secured for the young man a stimulating staff position.

During World War I, he served as an assistant to Secretary of
War Baker and then did propaganda work for the army's military
intelligence group, but like many postwar liberals, he felt dis-
illusioned by the Treaty of Versailles. With his insight into the
nature of propaganda, he was ready to analyze "stereotypes"—a
term derived from the printshop—as a prejudiced picture or classification in our minds that substitutes for genuine observation and
thought. This is clearly explained and illustrated in *Public Opinion* (1922)—an extract is given below.

As an editor of the New York *World* (1923–31), he usually opposed the Republican presidential candidates, but he was in truth
an Independent when he became a widely syndicated columnist
for the Republican *Herald-Tribune* thereafter. Sometimes his
errors of judgment were embarrassing indeed, but he never forfeited the respect that he has enjoyed over so many years. His
internationalism kept him close to the foreign policy of the New
Deal. That his thinking was influential in this area was evident
from the impact of his book, *U.S. Foreign Policy: Shield of the*

* From Walter Lippmann, *Public Opinion* (New York: The Macmillan
Company, 1922, 1949), 85–91. Reprinted by permission of The Macmillan Company.

Republic (1943). After World War II, his opinions on the Cold War and its possible mitigation were familiar to the White House, which usually took him quite seriously. His self-styled "conservatism," however, did not mean any real break from the philosophy of the Fair Deal or the New Frontier, for he was ever a strong supporter of civil rights and basically a liberal in the traditional sense. Although his style lacked the light and humorous touch of other major journalists, he made up for this defect by his clarity of thought and solidity. By 1962, according to *Current Biography,* his column was being syndicated through 250 American newspapers and in over twenty-five foreign papers.

I F WE cannot fully understand the acts of other people, until we know what they think they know, then in order to do justice we have to appraise not only the information which has been at their disposal, but the minds through which they have filtered it. For the accepted types, the current patterns, the standard versions, intercept information on its way to consciousness. Americanization, for example, is superficially at least the substitution of American for European stereotypes. Thus the peasant who might see his landlord as if he were the lord of the manor, his employer as he saw the local magnate, is taught by Americanization to see the landlord and employer according to American standards. This constitutes a change of mind, which is, in effect, when the inoculation succeeds, a change of vision. His eye sees differently. One kindly gentlewoman has confessed that the stereotypes are of such overweening importance, that when hers are not indulged, she at least is unable to accept the brotherhood of man and the fatherhood of God: "we are strangely affected by the clothes we wear. Garments create a mental and social atmosphere. What can be hoped for the Americanism of a man who insists on employing a London tailor? One's very food affects his Americanism. What kind of American consciousness can grow in the atmosphere of sauerkraut and Limburger cheese? Or what can you expect of the Americanism of the man whose breath always reeks of garlic?" *

This lady might well have been the patron of a pageant which

* Cited by Mr. Edward Hale Bierstadt, *New Republic,* June 1, 1921, p. 21.

a friend of mine once attended. It was called the Melting Pot, and it was given on the Fourth of July in an automobile town where many foreign-born workers are employed. In the center of the baseball park at second base stood a huge wooden and canvas pot. There were flights of steps up to the rim on two sides. After the audience had settled itself, and the band had played, a procession came through an opening at one side of the field. It was made up of men of all the foreign nationalities employed in the factories. They wore their native costumes, they were singing their national songs; they danced their folk dances, and carried the banners of all Europe. The master of ceremonies was the principal of the grade school dressed as Uncle Sam. He led them to the pot. He directed them up the steps to the rim, and inside. He called them out again on the other side. They came, dressed in derby hats, coats, pants, vest, stiff collar and polka-dot tie, undoubtedly, said my friend, each with an Eversharp pencil in his pocket, and all singing the Star-Spangled Banner.

To the promoters of this pageant, and probably to most of the actors, it seemed as if they had managed to express the most intimate difficulty to friendly association between the older peoples of America and the newer. The contradiction of their stereotypes interfered with the full recognition of their common humanity. The people who change their names know this. They mean to change themselves, and the attitude of strangers toward them.

There is, of course, some connection between the scene outside and the mind through which we watch it, just as there are some long-haired men and short-haired women in radical gatherings. But to the hurried observer a slight connection is enough. If there are two bobbed heads and four beards in the audience, it will be a bobbed and bearded audience to the reporter who knows beforehand that such gatherings are composed of people with these tastes in the management of their hair. There is a connection between our vision and the facts, but it is often a strange connection. A man has rarely looked at a landscape, let us say, except to examine its possibilities for division into building lots, but he has seen a number of landscapes hanging in the parlor. And from them he has learned to think of a landscape as a rosy sunset, or as a country road with a church steeple and a silver moon. One day he goes to the country, and for hours he does not see a single landscape. Then the sun goes down looking rosy. At once he recognizes a landscape and exclaims that it is beautiful. But two days later, when he tries to recall what he saw, the odds are that he will remember chiefly some landscape in a parlor.

Unless he has been drunk or dreaming or insane he did see a sunset, but he saw in it, and above all remembers from it, more of what the oil painting taught him to observe, than what an impressionist painter, for example, or a cultivated Japanese would have seen and taken away with him. And the Japanese and the painter in turn will have seen and remembered more of the form they had learned, unless they happen to be the very rare people who find fresh sight for mankind. In untrained observation we pick recognizable signs out of the environment. The signs stand for ideas, and these ideas we fill out with our stock of images. We do not so much see this man and that sunset; rather we notice that the thing is man or sunset, and then see chiefly what our mind is already full of on those subjects.

There is economy in this. For the attempt to see all things freshly and in detail, rather than as types and generalities, is exhausting, and among busy affairs practically out of the question. In a circle of friends, and in relation to close associates or competitors, there is no shortcut through, and no substitute for, an individualized understanding. Those whom we love and admire most are the men and women whose consciousness is peopled thickly with persons rather than with types, who know us rather than the classification into which we might fit. For even without phrasing it to ourselves, we feel intuitively that all classification is in relation to some purpose not necessarily our own; that between two human beings no association has final dignity in which each does not take the other as an end in himself. There is a taint on any contact between two people which does not affirm as an axiom the personal inviolability of both.

But modern life is hurried and multifarious, above all physical distance separates men who are often in vital contact with each other, such as employer and employee, official and voter. There is neither time nor opportunity for intimate acquaintance. Instead we notice a trait which marks a well known type, and fill in the rest of the picture by means of the stereotypes we carry about in our heads. He is an agitator. That much we notice, or are told. Well, an agitator is this sort of person, and so *he* is this sort of person. He is an intellectual. He is a plutocrat. He is a foreigner.

He is a "South European." He is from Back Bay. He is a Harvard Man. How different from the statement: he is a Yale Man. He is a regular fellow. He is a West Pointer. He is an old army sergeant. He is a Greenwich Villager: what don't we know about him then, and about her? He is an international banker. He is from Main Street.

The subtlest and most pervasive of all influences are those which create and maintain the repertory of stereotypes. We are told about the world before we see it. We imagine most things before we experience them. And those preconceptions, unless education has made us acutely aware, govern deeply the whole process of perception. They mark out certain objects as familiar or strange, emphasizing the difference, so that the slightly familiar is seen as very familiar, and the somewhat strange as sharply alien. They are aroused by small signs, which may vary from a true index to a vague analogy. Aroused, they flood fresh vision with older images, and project into the world what has been resurrected in memory. Were there no practical uniformities in the environment, there would be no economy and only error in the human habit of accepting foresight for sight. But there are uniformities sufficiently accurate, and the need of economizing attention is so inevitable, that the abandonment of all stereotypes for a wholly innocent approach to experience would impoverish human life.

What matters is the character of the stereotypes, and the gullibility with which we employ them. And these in the end depend upon those inclusive patterns which constitute our philosophy of life. If in that philosophy we assume that the world is codified according to a code which we possess, we are likely to make our reports of what is going on describe a world run by our code. But if our philosophy tells us that each man is only a small part of the world, that his intelligence catches at best only phases and aspects in a coarse net of ideas, then, when we use our stereotypes, we tend to know that they are only stereotypes, to hold them lightly, to modify them gladly. We tend, also, to realize more and more clearly when our ideas started, where they started, how they came to us, why we accepted them. All useful history is antiseptic in this fashion. It enables us to know what fairy tale, what school book, what tradition, what novel, play, picture, phrase, planted one preconception in this mind, another in that mind.

Chapter Four

RELIGION:

Christian Socialism,
Catholic Social Action,
Agnosticism,
Fundamentalism

"HAS FREETHOUGHT A CONSTRUCTIVE SIDE?" *

Agnosticism

By Robert Green Ingersoll

Robert Green Ingersoll (1833–99), freethinker, answers the critics of agnosticism

The fact that Robert Ingersoll's father was an orthodox Congregational minister did not inhibit his son's rapid descent to agnosticism. He was born in Dresden, New York, and after several moves was taken to Shawneetown, Illinois, where he became a lawyer. His ability to move juries by his eloquence made him famous, as did his avowed technical skill. (However, his use of this skill in winning an acquittal of a highly suspect client in the Star Route mail fraud cases was perhaps too successful and did not arouse unalloyed admiration.) When the Civil War came, he was an antislavery Democrat; at the end of the war, he emerged a Radical Republican as well as a patriotic Union officer, who had fought in the Tennessee campaigns and who had seen the inside of a Confederate prison.

In Illinois politics, he earned a reputation as an attorney gen-

* From Robert Green Ingersoll, "Has Freethought a Constructive Side?", *The Works of Robert G. Ingersoll,* XI (1908), 437–42.

This all led to his downfall?

eral (1867–69) and enjoyed the honor at the Republican Presidential Convention of 1876 of nominating James G. Blaine, giving that worthy the unforgettable (and later embarrassing) title of "a plumed knight." His "bloody shirt" orations, which helped to elect good Republicans without troubling himself about fundamental issues, could have taken him far up the ladder of national politics. But by now everyone knew that he had made freethinking his religion (he even married a freethinker) and was publishing numerous books such as *Some Mistakes of Moses,* giving lectures on the hypocrisies and cruelties of religion, and telling reporters about the admirable rationalism of Voltaire and Thomas Paine. But even traditionalist farmers came to hear the godless Bob Ingersoll flail the churches. His radicalism never extended to economic matters, and he was uninterested in the successes of the Social Gospel in his day. Yet he inspired such humanistic rebels as Clarence Darrow to fight the obscurantism of fundamentalists who challenged free speech and education.

THE OBJECT of the Freethinker is to ascertain the truth—the conditions of well-being—to the end that this life will be made of value. This is the affirmative, positive, and constructive side.

Without liberty there is no such thing as real happiness. There may be the contentment of the slave—of one who is glad that he has passed the day without a beating—one who is happy because he has had enough to eat—but the highest possible idea of happiness is freedom.

All religious systems enslave the mind. Certain things are demanded—certain things must be believed—certain things must be done—and the man who becomes the subject or servant of this superstition must give up all idea of individuality or hope of intellectual growth and progress.

The religionist informs us that there is somewhere in the universe an orthodox God, who is endeavoring to govern the world, and who for this purpose resorts to famine and flood, to earthquake and pestilence—and who, as a last resort, gets up a revival of religion. That is called "affirmative and positive."

The man of sense knows that no such God exists, and thereupon he affirms that the orthodox doctrine is infinitely absurd. This is called a "negation." But to my mind it is an affirmation, and is a part of the positive side of Freethought.

A man who compels this Deity to abdicate his throne renders a vast and splendid service to the human race.

As long as men believe in tyranny in heaven they will practice tyranny on earth. Most people are exceedingly imitative, and nothing is so gratifying to the average orthodox man as to be like his God.

These same Christians tell us that nearly everybody is to be punished forever, while a few fortunate Christians who were elected and selected billions of ages before the world was created, are to be happy. This they call the "tidings of great joy." The Freethinker denounces this doctrine as infamous beyond the power of words to express. He says, and says clearly, that a God who would create a human being, knowing that that being was to be eternally miserable, must of necessity be an infinite fiend.

The free man, into whose brain the serpent of superstition has not crept, knows that the dogma of eternal pain is an infinite falsehood. He also knows—if the dogma be true—that every decent human being should hate, with every drop of his blood, the creator of the universe. He also knows—if he knows anything—that no decent human being could be happy in heaven with a majority of the human race in hell. He knows that a mother could not enjoy the society of Christ with her children in perdition; and if she could, he knows that such a mother is simply a wild beast. The free man knows that the angelic hosts, under such circumstances, could not enjoy themselves unless they had the hearts of boa-constrictors.

It will thus be seen that there is an affirmative, a positive, a constructive side to Freethought.

What is the positive side?

First: A denial of all orthodox falsehoods—an exposure of all superstitions. This is simply clearing the ground, to the end that seeds of value may be planted. It is necessary, first, to fell the trees, to destroy the poisonous vines, to drive out the wild beasts. Then comes another phase—another kind of work. The Freethinker knows that the universe is natural—that there is no room, even in infinite space, for the miraculous, for the impossible. The Freethinker knows, or feels that he knows, that there is no sovereign of the universe, who, like some petty king or tyrant, delights in showing his authority. He feels that all in the universe are conditioned beings, and that only those are happy who live in accordance with the conditions of happiness, and this fact or

5 things a priest insists on.

truth or philosophy embraces all men and all gods—if there be gods.

The positive side is this: That every good action has good consequences—that it bears good fruit forever—and that every bad action has evil consequences, and bears bad fruit. The Freethinker also asserts that every man must bear the consequences of his actions—that he must reap what he sows, and that he cannot be justified by the goodness of another, or damned for the wickedness of another.

There is still another side, and that is this: The Freethinker knows that all the priests and cardinals and popes know nothing of the supernatural—they know nothing about gods or angels or heavens or hells—nothing about inspired books or Holy Ghosts, or incarnations or atonements. He knows that all this is superstition pure and simple. He knows also that these people—from pope to priest, from bishop to parson, do not the slightest good in this world—that they live upon the labor of others—that they earn nothing themselves—that they contribute nothing toward the happiness, or well-being, or the wealth of mankind. He knows that they trade and traffic in ignorance and fear, that they make merchandise of hope and grief—and he also knows that in every religion the priest insists on five things—First: There is a God. Second: He has made known his will. Third: He has selected me to explain this message. Fourth: We will now take up a collection; and Fifth: Those who fail to subscribe will certainly be damned.

The positive side of Freethought is to find out the truth—the facts of nature—to the end that we may take advantage of those truths, of those facts—for the purpose of feeding and clothing and educating mankind.

In the first place, we wish to find that which will lengthen human life—that which will prevent or kill disease—that which will do away with pain—that which will preserve or give us health.

We also want to go in partnership with these forces of nature, to the end that we may be well fed and clothed—that we may have good houses that protect us from heat and cold. And beyond this—beyond these simple necessities—there are still wants and aspirations, and freethought will give us the highest possible in art—the most wonderful and thrilling in music—the greatest paintings, the most marvelous sculpture—in other words, freethought will develop the brain to its utmost capacity. Freethought is the mother of art and science, of morality and happiness.

It is charged by the worshipers of the Jewish myth, that we destroy, that we do not build.

What have we destroyed? We have destroyed the idea that a monster created and governs this world—the declaration that a God of infinite mercy and compassion upheld slavery and polygamy and commanded the destruction of men, women, and babes. We have destroyed the idea that this monster created a few of his children for eternal joy, and the vast majority for everlasting pain. We have destroyed the infinite absurdity that salvation depends upon belief, that investigation is dangerous, and that the torch of reason lights only the way to hell. We have taken a grinning devil from every grave, and the curse from death—and in the place of these dogmas, of these infamies, we have put that which is natural and that which commends itself to the heart and brain.

Instead of loving God, we love each other. Instead of the religion of the sky—the religion of this world—the religion of the family—the love of husband for wife, of wife for husband—the love of all for children. So that now the real religion is: Let us live for each other; let us live for this world, without regard for the past and without fear for the future. Let us use our faculties and our powers for the benefit of ourselves and others, knowing that if there be another world, the same philosophy that gives us joy here will make us happy there.

Nothing can be more absurd than the idea that we can do something to please or displease an infinite Being. If our thoughts and actions can lessen or increase the happiness of God, then to that extent God is the slave and victim of man.

The energies of the world have been wasted in the service of a phantom—millions of priests have lived on the industry of others and no effort has been spared to prevent the intellectual freedom of mankind.

We know, if we know anything, that supernatural religion has no foundation except falsehood and mistake. To expose these falsehoods—to correct these mistakes—to build the fabric of civilization on the foundation of demonstrated truth—is the task of the Freethinker. To destroy guide-boards that point in the wrong direction—to correct charts that lure to reef and wreck—to drive the fiend of fear from the mind—to protect the cradle from the serpent of superstition and dispel the darkness of ignorance with the sun of science—is the task of the Freethinker.

What constructive work has been done by the church? Christianity gave us a flat world a few thousand years ago—a heaven above it where Jehovah dwells and a hell below it where most people will dwell. Christianity took the ground that a certain belief was necessary to salvation and that this belief was far better and of more importance than the practice of all the virtues. It became the enemy of investigation—the bitter and relentless foe of reason and the liberty of thought. It committed every crime and practiced every cruelty in the propagation of its creed. It drew the sword against the freedom of the world. It established schools and universities for the preservation of ignorance. It claimed to have within its keeping the source and standard of all truth. If the church had succeeded the sciences could not have existed.

Freethought has given us all we have of value. It has been the great constructive force. It is the only discoverer, and every science is its child.

"CATHOLICISM AND APAISM" *

By John Lancaster Spalding

Bishop John Lancaster Spalding (1840–1916), educator, defends American Catholics against "APAism"

Unlike the dominant Irish-American prelates like Archbishop Hughes, Archbishop Ireland, and Monsignor John Ryan, Bishop John L. Spalding of Peoria, Illinois, represented a more indigenous Catholic element. He was a Southerner born in Lebanon, Kentucky, of slaveowning parents and descended from seventeenth-century Maryland settlers. Well educated in liberal arts as well as in theology both in the United States and abroad in Rome

* John L. Spalding, "Catholicism and Apaism," *North American Review*, 159 (1894), 278–87.

and Louvain, he became one of the most distinguished American Catholic educators, theologians, essayists, and administrators. He spoke for Catholics at a time when their rapid growth had aroused such powerful enemies as the American Protective Association (the APA).

Having observed the New York slums, he joined with Archbishop Ireland in sponsoring a western colonization movement for the Irish newcomers, but this failed. As a liberal Catholic, he built a Negro church, assailed the imperialistic spirit of the Spanish-American War, criticized the dominant commercial ethics, urged Catholics to identify themselves with the current secular issues and with the best of cultural life, and accepted the invitation of President Roosevelt during the Coal Strike of 1902 to serve on an investigatory commission. Most important were his contributions to educational theory and his efforts to raise the level of the parochial schools at a time when secularism or Protestant teachings were driving Catholics out of the public schools. He founded a model boys' high school and helped to found the Catholic University of America. Pope Pius X observed, "Few bishops had so great an influence on the life of the people, even outside of religion, and outside the Catholic denomination, as had Bishop Spalding."

Defends Catholics

FACTS ARE stronger than arguments, and it is little better than a waste of words to reply to the charges which are now from many sides brought against Catholics here in the United States. From the earliest colonial period they have been here and have been loyal and devoted citizens. They have taken part in every phase of private and public life. They have mingled with those of other faiths, in the family, in the professions, in the trades, in commerce, in legislative assemblies, and on battlefields where the nation's fate has hung upon the issue. Like other men, they have had their weaknesses and their faults, but among these lack of love for America has had no place. They founded one of the thirteen colonies, and were the first in the New World, the first, indeed, in all the world, to make freedom of conscience an organic part of the constitution of the State. Their action marks an era in the progress of mankind. When the hour came to break the bond which united the colonies with England and which had become a fetter, none more generously than the Catholics hearkened to the trumpet call, and in the darkest days of the struggle

Catholics 1st to grant toleration

Not disloyal!

[handwritten annotation: Cath, arent Dem. because Pope tells them to be.]

Catholics from Europe mingled their blood on our battlefields
with that of our fathers. If long tenure, if fidelity, if honorable
deeds, have aught of efficacy, Catholics have the right to be here,
nor has this right ever become forfeit by any act or attempt of
the Catholic Church in America.

Whatever controversy there may be as to other times and lands,
her course here has been one of honor, of light, of peace, of
beneficence. She has devoted herself to works of religion and humanity. She has done and is doing more for education, for the
orphan, the aged, the sick and the fallen, than any other church.
She has never attempted to dictate to her adherents in civil matters, nor has she sought to control political parties; and if her
followers are to a large extent Democrats rather than Republicans, this is not due to the influence or interference of priests and
bishops, who seldom know or care to what political party the
members of their congregations belong. Catholics, though generally Catholic only in name, have been and are busy, often too
busy, with politics, especially with municipal politics; but this is
a common right of all American citizens, and in centres where
there are great numbers of Catholics, some of them inevitably
will be found among the political schemers, and consequently
will be more or less implicated in the hypocrisy, trickery, and
fraud by which our whole political life is tainted. A bad Catholic
is no better than any other bad man. He is not a Catholic in
truth, but since the Catholic Church, whatever those who do not
know her spirit may think, is patient, broad, and tolerant, she is
slow to expel any one from the fold, loth to pluck up the cockle
lest the wheat also be uprooted. The reckless greed of our great
money getters has led them to induce thousands of the poorest
and most ignorant laborers of Europe to come here to supplant
more intelligent and consequently more costly workers. These
people, many of whom are Catholics, neither understand our
language nor have any right conception of our civil and political
life, and when they are thrown out of work and brought to the
verge of starvation, they sometimes listen to the appeals of An-
archists and resort to violence. The church is not responsible;
her influence, on the contrary, is the only moral and civilizing
force which is brought to bear on these poor people. Far from
desiring this kind of immigration, the American bishops and
priests would be glad to have it cease.

[handwritten annotation: immig. of Catholics]

Towards our fellow-citizens who are not Catholics our behavior is and has been without reproach. We have never sought to excite prejudice against those who differ from us in religious faith: much less have we sought to persecute any man for conscience sake. No body of Catholics in America has ever fostered or in any way encouraged those who wriggle and batten in the filth and animalities of man, and who make a living by going from city to city to appeal to the prurient imaginations and corrupt hearts of the vulgar. If here and there these cowardly attacks have led to violence and riot, the employers of the men whose only argument is outrageous insult are responsible. The Catholic pastors uniformly advise their flocks to keep away from these men and the places in which they hold their meetings. No body of Catholics, in this country, not under the ban of the church, have ever formed themselves into secret oath-bound societies, for good or evil ends. Our bishops and priests have no hidden policy, no deep laid schemes, of any kind. Our life is undisguised, our churches are open to all, our books may be had by every one, in our schools thousands of Protestants are thrown hourly into most intimate contact with our teachers: as servants and partners, as friends and relations, we are intermingled with the whole people. Whoever desires information about us has not far to seek. What then is the cause of the abuse which is heaped upon us, of the distrust of which we seem to be the objects? Why has it been thought necessary to organize secret societies, which have spread rapidly throughout the country, to oppose and hurt us?

These are far-reaching questions, and to answer them satisfactorily in brief space is difficult. At the root of all such outbreaks and movements there lies the traditional Protestant view of the Catholic Church, which, though it has long ceased to have any meaning for enlightened minds, still holds sway over those who are too busy or too ignorant to be able to react against inherited prejudice. They still believe that the Catholic Church is the Scarlet Woman and the Pope the Man of sin; and that Catholics consequently are capable of any crime or baseness which it may occur to any one to impute to them. They believe that Jesuits are cunning hypocrites who are never happy unless they are doing mischief; that nunneries are prisons, or worse; that priests sell permission to commit sin and are ever ready to betray any country they may belong to at the dictate of the Pope. All this, together with whatever else of horrible a perverse or corrupt imagination may be able to conjure up concerning us, the true

prejudice & ignorance.

victims of the Protestant tradition are ready to believe; and, though such retarded minds are become comparatively few, they are still numerous enough to form a nucleus around which may gather all those who, whether honestly or from motives of self-interest, are glad to enter upon an anti-Catholic crusade. The Orange societies constitute a centre of this kind for the Apaists. No more bitter, blind, or fanatical religious spirit exists than theirs. Its prejudice is unrelieved by a suspicion of doubt, its hatred is as genuine as it is unreasoning and unrelenting, and, like a wind-fanned flame, it leaps forth with mad glee whenever there is an opportunity to do harm to Catholics. Here is a force ready at hand, in English-speaking countries, for those who wish to stir up religious strife. What are the causes which have led so many Americans who have no sympathy with Orangeism to form an alliance with the bigots of this sect for the purpose of persecuting Catholics? The rapid and vigorous growth of the Church in America has, I suppose, excited apprehensions of danger among those in whose minds its influence is associated with ignorance, superstition, and corruption. Our success, too, largely due to immigration, may have aroused jealousy as well as fear; and I am the more willing to believe this as I observe, on many sides, that the envious rivalry of Protestant denominations among themselves is a chief cause of their weakness. In thousands of villages where one church and one capable minister would find support, three or four congregations representing different sects are established, and they are all feeble. The result is discouragement and indifference. Among Catholics themselves, in the last few years, a certain spirit of boastfulness became, here and there, manifest. When as yet, leaving aside our accessions from Europe, our losses are greater than our gains, some of us began to proclaim that America was to be made Catholic at no distant day. Though these utterances were merely the expression of zeal, the outburst of a perfervid temper, they aroused unkind thoughts in many whose dislike of us is more genuine than their love of toleration. To make matters worse we began to quarrel among ourselves. National differences of thought, sentiment, and custom, which reach so far and go so deep, threatened to prove stronger than the harmonizing and constructive force of a common religious faith. It happened, as it nearly always does happen when the controversial spirit is let loose, that the real issue came to be not truth and justice, but victory. In the heat of conflict wild words were spoken and overbearing deeds were done. The reporters, who scent a scandal as vultures a carcass, rushed in, and the country was filled with sound and fury. The loyalty of German Catholics was called into question. They were accused of conspiring with a certain Cahensly, a citizen of Prussia, against the interests of this country. Cahensly himself was as powerless as he was unknown, and, if harm he could do, he could do it only by influencing the Pope to do wrong; and the Catholics who made such an outcry against Cahenslyism seemed really to dread lest the Pope should be induced to do a foolish or wicked thing. Their temper was controversial, but the bigots took them seriously. Intelligent people among us know the Pope would not if he could, could not if he would, hurt America; but to multitudes the cry of danger from the Papists is as effective as Dalila's shout to Samson that the Philistines were upon him. The Faribault school compromise, leading at is did to discussions which attracted wide attention, was another cause of alarm. The incident itself was neither novel nor important, and it doubtless would have escaped public notice had not the impression been made that it was the starting of a scheme by which Catholics hoped to get their share of the school fund. It was, in fact, a local affair, as to which there was no preconcerted agreement among the bishops, the far greater number of whom thought such a compromise undesirable, unacceptable even from the Catholic point of view, and all that Rome could be induced to concede was that what had been done at Faribault might be tolerated. Word had gone forth, however, that Faribaultism was a cunningly devised scheme of the Jesuits, by which they expected, while getting financial support for their own schools, to undermine the common schools. The charge was as false as it was ridiculous, but when public suspicion is aroused assertion is as effective as proof.

The Faribault episode, in itself insignificant, became the occasion of sending a papal envoy here, and of establishing a permanent papal delegation in Washington, which, from whatever point it be considered, is an affair of grave moment. From the beginning the American bishops, whenever consulted, strongly opposed the founding of such an institution here. When the question was put to the archbishops at their meeting in New York, in the fall of 1892, it was their almost unanimous opinion that it would be unwise to appoint a delegate for this country, and there seems to be no reason to doubt that the bishops, had the matter been proposed to them, would have taken the same view. The question of a delegation is, of course, not a question of faith, or morals, or discipline, or rule, affecting the whole Church; but one of ecclesiastical policy: and those whose knowledge of the country was most accurate and intimate believed that the establishment of a papal delegation here would be bad policy.

Whether they have been justified by the event, so far as the internal affairs of the church are concerned, it is not necessary here to inquire; but that the Delegate has been and is a source of strength to the Apaists there can be no doubt. With us, as in the Protestant world generally, anti-Catholic prejudice is largely anti-papal prejudice; and when the organs of public opinion were filled with the sayings and doings of "the American Pope," who though a foreigner, with no intention of becoming a citizen, ignorant alike of our language and our traditions, was supposed to have supreme authority in the church in America, fresh fuel was thrown upon the fire of bigotry. The fact that his authority is ecclesiastical merely, and concerns Catholics, not as citizens, but as members of the church, is lost sight of by the multitudes who are persuaded that the papacy is a political power eager to extend its control wherever opportunity may offer. This feeling, which has existed among us from the beginning, led our first bishop, Carroll of Baltimore, who was beyond doubt a devoted churchman and a true patriot, to make an official declaration in 1797, on Washington's birthday, wherein he affirmed that the obedience we owed the Pope is "in things purely spiritual." And such has been our uniform belief and teaching, as whoever takes the trouble to read what those who have the best right to speak for us have written on this subject will see.

Various causes, more or less intimately related to our religious life, having conspired to produce an anti-Catholic outbreak, the movement received added force from sources apparently foreign to the matter. In the long continued struggle between employers and wage-earners, capitalists have come to look upon the labor unions as an obstacle to the successful management of their various businesses, and are therefore anxious to weaken or dissolve these associations. When the Orange spirit began to become more active, it naturally occurred to the managers of railways and other enterprises in which large numbers of men are employed, that religious fanaticism might be made use of to divide the laborers and undermine their unions. For this purpose, then, and not from

unionization
attributed
to Catholics
(by employers)
because
expedient

any hatred of the Catholic religion, for corporations being soulless must be indifferent to religion, the Apaists were encouraged and gained much influence in some of our large carrying and manufacturing concerns. It happened also that the greater number of these fanatics were Republicans, and they became a source of embarrassment to the party. It was impossible to ignore them, and, at first thought, the simplest thing to do seemed to be to connive at them. Very soon, however, they became so strong that connivance ceased to have a meaning, and then, not having the courage or the will to expel them, the party which freed the negro began to encourage the bigots who have gotten up a religious persecution and are striving to deprive Catholics of the rights of freemen. Many Democrats, too, whose hatred of the church is stronger than their love of liberty and fair play, have gone over to the Apaists.

From this brief statement of the causes which have led to the rise and favored the spread of the new knownothingism, I turn to consider some of the charges which the leaders of the crusade advance as a justification of their systematic attack upon American Catholics; and as they are neither new nor true, the discussion of them must necessarily be somewhat uninteresting. There is, first of all, the time-honored objection of a divided and incompatible allegiance—the contention that Catholics, since they owe obedience to the Pope, cannot be loyal subjects of the state. The answer is obvious. Our obedience to the Pope is confined to the domain of religious faith, morals, and discipline; and since the state, with us at least, claims no jurisdiction over such matters, there can be no question of conflict. We have, and none are more thankful for this than the Catholics, a separation of the Church from the State. If it be urged that to draw the line of demarcation is difficult, I reply that in the general course of things this difficulty presents itself hardly at all. That it may arise all confess, but it may arise just as easily for Protestants as for Catholics. All men in our age—and this is one of the most far reaching peculiarities of Christian civilization—hold a double allegiance, and are prepared, if needs be, to appeal from men to God, from laws to conscience, from authority to reason, from numbers to justice. "I will obey all the laws of my country faithfully," say Ruskin, "so far as such laws or commands are consistent with what I suppose to be the law of God; and when they are not or seem in any wise to need change, I will oppose them loyally and delib-

erately, not with malicious, concealed, or disorderly violence."
The Pope has never attempted to interfere in the civil or political
affairs of this country, and were he to attempt to do so his action
would be resented by the Catholics more quickly than by others.
One reason why our representative men have always opposed the
appointment of a papal delegate for the United States was their
unwillingness to give our enemies even a pretext for accusing us, as
citizens, of being under foreign influence. The Pope is our religious, not our civil or political, superior.

Deeds, more than words, prove, and have proven, both our
patriotism and our Catholic faith, and there is no reason why we,
more than others, should make protestation of our loyalty. To
protest is half to confess, as to exhort is to reproach; and to urge
American Catholics to love their country, which is as dear to
them as their heart's blood, is to imply that they fail in this high
duty. Our record for patriotism is without blot or stain, and it is
not necessary for us to hold the flag in our hands when we walk
the streets, to wave it when we speak, to fan ourselves with it
when we are warm, and to wrap it about us when we are cold.
Let us hope, at least, that in speaking of it we shall never stoop
to the vulgar slang of "Old Glory," which is only a lesser desecra-
tion than the shots which riddled it when it floated amid the
battle's smoke upheld by heroic hands.

Another charge, which, like the brook with its senseless prattle,
goes on forever, is that Catholics are foes of the common schools
—as the amiable Episcopal Bishop of Albany puts it, that "they
do not love the public school system nor the theory of universal
education." Were it not that most men become the victims of oft-
repeated assertion, it would be difficult to explain the continuance of this accusation, for our position on the question of
education is at once simple and widely and authoritatively proclaimed. We believe that religion is an essential element of
human nature, and, therefore, of right education; and where it is
possible to do so, we found and maintain schools, in which, along
with other things, we teach also what we believe to be religion.
Inasmuch as this it not done in the common schools, we find the
system defective, but we do not condemn it; for in a country such
as ours no other system of state schools seems to be possible, and
we are openly and without reservation in favor of free schools,
and, consequently, in favor of a school tax. For my own part—and
I think I express the Catholic view—I not only would not, had I

the power, destroy the public-school system, but would leave nothing undone to develop and perfect it. I believe in free schools, in universal education, and, wherever public opinion is sufficiently enlightened, in compulsory school attendance. The objections which the bishops of Wisconsin and of Illinois urged against the Bennet Law and the Edwards Law were based upon the fact that these laws were an infringement on the principle of freedom in matters of education. If here and there individuals have made efforts to get public moneys for parochial schools, the Catholic body is not to be held responsible for their acts.

The attempt to commit the Catholics of the nineteenth century here in America to all the deeds and utterances of those in the middle ages is futile. We do not hold that the Popes have never been in the wrong; nor are we bound, to quote Cardinal Newman, "to defend the policy or the acts of particular popes, whether before or after the great revolt from their authority in the sixteenth century." If the public law of Europe in the eleventh and twelfth centuries permitted them to declare forfeit the authority of tyrannical princes and emperors, it does not follow that they are permitted to do this now. We are Catholics, but we are also men, and though the essential tenets of the faith are immutable we ourselves change with a changing world. We accept with frank sincerity, with cheerful acquiescence, the principles involved in the rule of the people by the people and for the people, and are content to abide the issue. Why, then, in a country in which all have agreed to make freedom of conscience and liberty of worship inalienable rights, in which it is a fundamental principle of public life and rule that no man shall suffer hurt because of his religious faith, is a secret oath-bound society, whose one great aim is to subvert this primary article of our political creed, suffered to exist and encouraged in its nefarious schemes? Why have hundreds of teachers been expelled from their places simply because they were Catholics? Do not Catholics like others pay the school tax? Is not every career open to talent? Why are men hired to go from town to town, not to discuss our doctrines and practices, but to insult, mock, vilify, and calumniate us? No American Catholic certainly can object to the free discussion of his religious beliefs; but abuse, lies, and forgeries, while they can have no tendency to advance the cause of truth, provoke to violence, and where there is liberty there should be protection from such wanton and malicious attacks. Let the fair-minded read any of the numerous Apaist newspapers which are sold on the streets of nearly all our cities and towns, and then ask themselves whether a cause which is upheld by such methods and defended with such weapons is not self-condemned. Their creed is a creed of spite and hatred. Their ways are secret and dark; their arguments are lies and forgeries, and their victims are generally women whose only crime is their intelligence and their religion. In the presence of all this, Bishop Doane, in the spirit of sweetness and light, asks us to take a more conciliatory tone. He would doubtless advise the lamb to conciliate the wolf, for which the only possible conciliation is the having the lamb in its maw. This outburst of anti-Catholic hatred will pass away, of course. The American people love justice and fair play; they live and let live; their very genius is goodwill to men. They are not bigots or fanatics, or persecutors, but in the meanwhile Apaism is hurtful to the best interests of the country, it diverts attention from the momentous problems which are pressing upon us, it separates friend from friend, it sows the seeds of suspicion and distrust, it makes innocent victims, and is doing all that it is possible to do to verify the saying of a well-known Englishman that the only civilized country in which it is less pleasant to live than in the United States is Russia.

But I must make an end. One of the disadvantages under which the magazine writer labors is that when he gets well into his subject, the editor, regardless of Macbeth's curse, is sure to be the first to cry, Hold, enough!

"THE CHURCH AND THE WORKINGMAN" *

By John A. Ryan

Rerum novarum

Father John A. Ryan (1869–1945) asks American Catholics to adopt Pope Leo XIII's plea for involvement in a labor program and not to estrange the workingman

Father John A. Ryan was born of Irish immigrant parents in rural Minnesota and first learned agrarian protest from the Populists of Ignatius Donnelly. He was further influenced by the radicalism of the *Irish World* and the single tax ideas of Henry George; but nothing eclipsed in influence the encyclical *Rerum Novarum* ("On the Condition of Labor") issued by "the Workingman's Pope," Leo XIII, in 1891. John Ryan was to spend a lifetime in teaching and practicing these principles among American Catholics—the idea of a "living family wage," the right to join unions, the need for shorter working hours, and the principle later enunciated in Wilson's Clayton Act that "labor is not a commodity."

labor reformist

John Ryan was ordained a priest in 1898. He studied at the Catholic University where he wrote his dissertation, entitled, fittingly enough, *A Living Wage: Its Ethical and Economic Aspects,* published in 1906. (The same phrase was to appear in the famous Social Creed of 1908 issued by the Methodist Episcopal Church.)

From 1916 to 1937, he held successive professorships at Catholic University in political science, in moral theology and industrial ethics, and in sociology. During much of his life, especially as director of the Social Action Department of the National Catholic Welfare Conference and as a sponsor of such pioneer legislation as Minnesota's minimum wage law, he worked to increase the involvement of his church in labor and welfare issues. As an active progressive, he promoted labor's right to organize, the regulation of monopolies, and the right of the state to intervene for the public interest despite "freedom of contract" technicalities.

A "progressive"

President Franklin D. Roosevelt recognized his national importance by making him a member of the Industrial Appeals Board

---

* John A. Ryan, "The Church and the Workingman," *The Catholic World*, 89 (1909), 776–82.

of the NRA. In 1933, Pope Pius XI, who had elaborated upon the principles of Leo XIII in another encyclical, *Quadragesimo Anno* (1931), rewarded its foremost American exponent with the title of Right Reverend Monsignor. When Father Charles Coughlin began his attack on Roosevelt and his crusades against the conspiracies of the International Bankers, the Jews, and the Communists, Monsignor Ryan denounced the demagoguery of the popular radio priest, characterized his economic panaceas as quackery, and denied that Father Coughlin understood the encyclicals for which he spoke.

In the essay below, the reader will note Father Ryan's effort to reconcile the Church's historic mission of salvation with the need for secular involvement—in order to avoid estranging the American workingman.

"Even though it be only a dream, I like to indulge the thought that some day the Church of the poor will lead them out of bondage, and prove to the unbelieving world its divine mission" (From a private letter of a well-known Catholic social reformer).

THE VIEWPOINT indicated in this sentence is sufficiently frequent among Catholics to justify a brief reconsideration of a somewhat hackneyed topic. Among the Protestant churches that display any considerable amount of vitality, the tendency is rapidly growing toward a conception that identifies religion with humanitarianism, while the majority of non-churchgoers who admit that religion has any useful function probably share the same conception. In such an environment it is not a matter of surprise that many Catholics should exaggerate the social mission of the Church.

The Church is not merely nor mainly a social reform organization, nor is it her primary mission to reorganize society, or to realize the Kingdom of God upon earth. Her primary sphere is the individual soul, her primary object to save souls, that is, to fit them for the Kingdom of God in heaven. Man's true life, the life of the soul, consists in supernatural union with God, which has its beginning during the brief period of his earthly life, but which is to be completed in the eternal existence to come afterward. Compared with this immortal life, such temporary goods as

wealth, liberty, education, or fame, are utterly insignificant. To
make these or any other earthly considerations the supreme aim
would be as foolish as to continue the activities and amusements
of childhood after one had reached maturity. It would be to cling
to the accidental and disregard the essential. Scoffers and sceptics
may contemn this view as "other-worldly," but they cannot deny
that it is the only logical and sane position for men who accept
the Christian teaching on life, death, and immortality. Were the
Church to treat this present life as anything more than a means
to the end, which is immortal life, it would be false to its mission.
It might deserve great praise as a philanthropic association, but
it would have forfeited all right to the name of Christian Church.

Having thus reasserted the obvious truth that the Church's function is the regeneration and improvement of the individual soul
with a view to the life beyond, let us inquire how far this includes
social teaching or social activity. Since the soul cannot live right-
eously except through right conduct, the Church must teach and
enforce the principles of right conduct. Now a very large and very
important part of conduct falls under the heads of charity and
justice. Hence we find that from the beginning the Church propa-
gated these virtues both by word and by action. As regards charity, she taught the brotherhood of man, and strove to make it
real through organizations and institutions. In the early centuries
of the Christian era, the bishops and priests maintained a parochial system of poor relief to which they gave as much active
direction and care as to any of their purely religious functions.
In the Middle Ages the Church promoted and supported the
monastic system with its innumerable institutions for the relief
of all forms of distress. Under her direction and active support
to-day, religious communities maintain hospitals for the sick, and
homes for all kinds of dependents. To take but one instance, the
Church in America collects money for orphan asylums as regularly as for many of her purely religious objects. As regards justice, the Church has always taught the doctrine of individual
dignity, rights, and sacredness, and proclaimed that all men are
essentially equal. Through this teaching the lot of the slave was
humanized, and the institution itself gradually disappeared; serf-
dom was made bearable, and became in time transformed into a
status in which the tiller of the soil enjoyed security of tenure,
protection against the exactions of the lord, and a recognized
place in the social organism. Owing to her doctrine that labor

Labor is honorable

was honorable and was the universal condition and law of life,
the working classes gradually acquired that measure of self-respect and of power which enabled them to set up and maintain
for centuries the industrial democracy that prevailed in the
mediæval towns. Her uniform teaching that the earth was given
by God to all the children of men, and that the individual pro-
prietor was only a steward of his possessions, was preached and
emphasized by the Fathers in language that has brought upon
them the charge of communism. The theological principle that
the starving man who has no other resource may seize what is
necessary from the goods of his neighbor, is merely one particular
conclusion from this general doctrine. She also taught that every
commodity, including labor, had a certain just or fair price from
which men ought not to depart, and that the laborer, like the
member of every other social class, had a right to a decent living
in accordance with the standards of the group to which he belonged. During the centuries preceding the rise of modern capitalism, when the moneylender was the greatest oppressor of the
poor, she forbade the taking of interest. Among her *works* in the
interest of social justice and social welfare, two only will be mentioned here: the achievements of her monks in promoting agriculture and settled life in the midst of the anarchic conditions that
followed the downfall of the Roman Empire, and her encouragement of the Guilds, those splendid organizations which secured
for their members a greater measure of welfare relatively to the
possibilities of the time than any other industrial system that has
ever existed.

usury condemned, not in the interest of social welfare.

To the general proposition that the Church is obliged to inculcate the principles of charity and justice both by precept and by
action, all intelligent persons, whether Catholic or not, will subscribe. Opinions will differ only as to the extent to which she
ought to go in this direction. Let us consider first the problem of
her function as teacher.

The Church cannot be expected to adopt or advocate any particular programme, either partial or comprehensive, of social
reconstruction or social reform. This is as far out of her province
as is the advocacy of definite methods of political organization,
agriculture, manufactures, or finance. Direct participation in matters of this nature would absorb energies that ought to be devoted
to her religious and moral work, and would greatly lessen her
influence over the minds and hearts of men. Her attitude toward

specific measures of social reform can only be that of judge and guide. When necessity warrants it, she pronounces upon their moral character, condemning them if they are bad, encouraging them if they are good. They come within her province only in so far as they involve the principles of morality.

With regard to the moral aspect of existing social and industrial conditions, the Church does lay down sufficiently definite principles. They are almost all contained in the Encyclical, "On the Condition of Labor," issued by Pope Leo XIII. Passing over his declarations on society, the family, Socialism, the State, woman labor, child labor, organization, and arbitration, let us empha- *minimum wage* size his pronouncement that the laborer has a moral claim to a wage that will support himself and his family in reasonable and frugal comfort. Beside this principle let us put the traditional Catholic teaching concerning monopolies, the just price of goods, and fair profits. If these doctrines were enforced throughout the industrial world the social problem would soon be within meas- *monopoly,* urable distance of a satisfactory solution. If all workingmen re- *just price,* ceived living-wages in humane conditions of employment, and if *fair profits.* all capital obtained only moderate and reasonable profits, the serious elements of the problem remaining would soon solve themselves.

But the social principles here referred to are all very general in character. They are of very little practical use unless they are made specific and applied in detail to concrete industrial relations. Does the Church satisfactorily perform this task? Well, it is a task that falls upon the bishops and the priests rather than upon the central authority at Rome. For example, the teaching of Pope Leo about a living-wage, child labor, woman labor, oppressive hours of work, etc., can be properly applied to any region only by the local clergy, who are acquainted with the precise circumstances, and whose duty it is to convert general principles into specific regulations. In this connection another extract from the private letter cited above may be found interesting and suggestive: "If the same fate is not to overcome us that has overtaken— and justly—the Church in Europe, the Catholic Church here will have to see that it cannot commend itself to the masses of the people by begging Dives to be more lavish of his crumbs to Lazarus, or by moral inculcations to employers to deal with their employees in a more Christian manner." There is some exaggeration in both clauses of this sentence. The defection of large numbers of the people from the Church in certain countries of Europe cannot be ascribed to any single cause. Some of its causes antedate the beginnings of the modern social question; others are not social or industrial at all; and still others would have produced a large measure of damaging results despite the most intelligent and most active efforts of the clergy. When due allowance has been made for all these factors it must still be admitted that the losses in question would have been very much smaller, possibly would have been comparatively easy to restore, had the clergy, bishops and priests, realized the significance, extent, and vitality of modern democracy, economic and political, and if they had done their best to permeate it with the Christian principles of social justice. On the other hand, where, as in Germany and Belgium, the clergy have made serious efforts to apply these principles both by teaching and action the movement of anticlericalism has made comparatively little headway. At any rate, the better position of the Church and the superior vitality of religion among the people in these two countries, can be traced quite clearly to the more enlightened attitude of their clergy toward the social problem.

The second clause of the quotation given above underestimates, by implication at least, the value of charity as a remedy for industrial abuses. It cannot, indeed, be too strongly nor too frequently insisted that charity is not a substitute for justice; on the other hand, any solution of the social problem based solely upon conceptions of justice, and not wrought out and continued in the spirit of charity, would be cold, lifeless, and in all probability of short duration. If men endeavor to treat each other merely as equals, ignoring their relation as brothers, they cannot long maintain pure and adequate notions of justice, nor apply the principles of justice fully and fairly to all individuals. The personal and the human element will be wanting. Were employers and employees deliberately and sincerely to attempt to base all their economic relations upon Christian charity, upon the Golden Rule, they would necessarily and automatically place these relations upon a basis of justice. For true and adequate charity includes justice, but justice does not include charity. However, the charity that the writer of the letter condemns is neither true nor adequate; it neither includes justice, nor is of any value in the present situation.

Let it be at once admitted that the clergy of America have done comparatively little to apply the social teachings of the Church, or in particular of the Encyclical "On the Condition of Labor," to our industrial relations. The bishops who have made any pronouncements in the matter could probably be counted on the fingers of one hand, while the priests who have done so are not more numerous proportionally. But there are good reasons for this condition of things. The moral aspects of modern industry are extremely difficult to evaluate correctly; its physical aspects and relations are very complicated and not at all easy of comprehension; and the social problem has only in recent times begun to become acute. Add to these circumstances the fact that the American clergy have for the most part been very busy organizing parishes, building churches and schools, and providing the material equipment of religion generally, and you have a tolerably sufficient explanation of their failure to study the social problem, and expound the social teaching of the Church.

The same conditions account for the comparative inactivity of the American clergy in the matter of social *works*. Up to the present their efforts have been confined to the maintenance of homes for defectives and dependents, and the encouragement of charitable societies. In some of the countries of Europe, particularly Germany and Belgium, and more recently France and Italy, bishops and priests have engaged more or less directly in a great variety of projects for the betterment of social conditions, such as, co-operative societies, rural banks, workingmen's gardens, etc. Obviously activities of this kind are not the primary duty of the clergy, but are undertaken merely as means to the religious and moral improvement of the people. The extent to which any priest or bishop ought to engage in them is a matter of local expediency. So far as general principles are concerned, a priest could with as much propriety assist and direct building societies, co-operative associations of all sorts, settlement houses, consumer's leagues, child labor associations, and a great variety of other social reform activities, as he now assists and directs orphan asylums, parochial schools, St. Vincent de Paul societies, or temperance societies. None of these is a purely religious institution; all of them may be made effective aids to Christian life and Christian faith.

The necessity for both social teaching and social works by our American clergy is very great and very urgent. To this extent the sentence quoted in the body of this paper is not an exaggeration. There is a very real danger that large masses of our workingmen

[handwritten margin note: Church must assume leadership in social reform legislation, otherwise will lose respect.]

will, before many years have gone by, have accepted unchristian views concerning social and industrial institutions, and will have come to look upon the Church as indifferent to human rights and careful only about the rights of property. Let any one who doubts this statement take the trouble to get the confidence and the opinions of a considerable number of intelligent Catholic trade unionists, and to become regular readers of one or two representative labor journals. We are now discussing things as they are, not things as we should like to see them, nor yet things as they were fifteen or twenty-five years ago. Persons who are unable to see the possibility of an estrangement, such as has occurred in Europe, between the people and the clergy in America, forget that modern democracy is twofold, political and economic, and that the latter form has become much the more important. By economic democracy is meant the movement toward a more general and more equitable distribution of economic power and goods and opportunities. At present this economic democracy shows, even in our country, a strong tendency to become secular if not anti-Christian. Here again we are dealing with the actual facts of to-day. Consequently, unless the clergy shall be able and willing to understand, appreciate, and sympathetically direct the aspirations of economic democracy, it will inevitably become more and more unchristian, and pervert all too rapidly a larger and larger proportion of our Catholic population.

[handwritten note: Economic Democracy]

CHRISTIANITY AND THE SOCIAL CRISIS*

By Walter Rauschenbusch

Walter Rauschenbusch (1861–1918) calls for a militant social gospel of Christian socialism

The son of a German minister and biblical scholar who had left for America with the liberal Forty-eighters, Walter Rauschenbusch was born in Rochester, New York, and educated in Germany as well as at the University of Rochester and its theological seminary. As a German-speaking Baptist minister, he worked among German immigrants, especially in the slums of New York City. He read extensively in the social protest literature of Tolstoy, Bellamy, Ruskin, and Marx, though he rejected ideas of class struggle and a materialistic interpretation of history. He studied economics as well as theology at the University of Berlin and observed sympathetically the Fabian socialists in England and the Salvation Army. Before succeeding his father in a theological professorship at Rochester in 1897, he organized the Brotherhood of the Kingdom to promote the ideals of Christian socialism, inspired by apostolic collectivism applied to modern industrial problems. His reputation as the spokesman for a new theology of the social gospel came with the publication of *Christianity and the Social Crisis* (1907), which was translated into Japanese and Chinese as well as European languages. This was followed by other persuasive books that converted many young ministers to the social gospel with its ideal of a Kingdom of Righteousness on earth. Among the new generation in this tradition was Reinhold Niebuhr.

ONE ANSWER to the challenge of the Christian spirit has been the organization of institutional church work. A church perhaps organizes a day-nursery or kindergarten; a playground

* From Walter Rauschenbusch, *Christianity and the Social Crisis* (1907), 304–5, 322–25.

99.

for the children; a meeting-place for young people, or educational facilities for those who are ambitious. It tries to do for people who are living under abnormal conditions what these people under normal conditions ought to do for themselves. This saving helpfulness toward the poor must be distinguished sharply from the money-making efforts of some churches called institutional, which simply run a continuous sacred variety performance.

Confront the Church of Christ with a homeless, playless, joyless, proletarian population, and that is the kind of work to which some Christian spirits will inevitably feel impelled. All honor to them! But it puts a terrible burden on the Church. Institutional work is hard work and costly work. It requires a large plant and an expensive staff. It puts such a strain on the organizing ability and the sympathies of the workers that few can stand it long. The Church by the voluntary gifts and labors of a few here tries to furnish what the entire coöperative community ought to furnish.

Few churches have the resources and leadership to undertake institutional work on a large scale, but most churches in large cities have some institutional features, and all pastors who are at all willing to do it, have institutional work thrust on them. They have to care for the poor. Those of us who passed through the last great industrial depression will never forget the procession of men out of work, out of clothes, out of shoes, and out of hope. They wore down our threshold, and they wore away our hearts. This is the stake of the churches in modern poverty. They are buried at times under a stream of human wreckage. They are turned aside constantly from their more spiritual functions to "serve tables." They have a right, therefore, to inquire who is unloading this burden of poverty and suffering upon them by underpaying, exhausting, and maiming the people. The good Samaritan did not go after the robbers with a shot-gun, but looked after the wounded and helpless man by the wayside. But if hundreds of good Samaritans travelling the same road should find thousands of bruised men groaning to them, they would not be such very good Samaritans if they did not organize a vigilance committee to stop the manufacturing of wounded men. If they did not, presumably the asses who had to lug the wounded to the tavern would have the wisdom to inquire into the causes of their extra work.

· · ·

The Church in past centuries repeatedly lost the respect and

Reverence for Church as the mediator of salvation

affections of the people by its corruptions and the oppression which it sanctioned and intensified, but it was able to regain its hold when it repented and improved. It may be that in coming days the Church in Germany will regain its old influence in the life of the people. But the outlook is not sure. The old mediæval reverence for the Church as the only mediator of salvation is gone, and the people are permanently critical in spirit. Formerly the Church was able to envelop itself in awe by the shimmering mist of idealized history which it spread about its past services. The people are now educated beyond that. So the future is sombre. When a mountain-side is once denuded of vegetation and the roots of the trees no longer lace the soil together and hold the rain, the soil is washed down into the valleys. The rocks are again corroded and might form new soil, but as it is formed, it is again washed away. Because the rocks are bare, they stay bare. From him that hath not is taken even that which he hath.

Now salvation can be found in secular organisation But...

In our own country we are still at the parting of the ways. Our social movement is still in its earliest stages. The bitterness and anger of their fight has not eaten into the heart of the working classes as it has abroad. Many of them are still ready to make their fight in the name of God and Christ, though not of the Church. Populistic conventions used to recite the Lord's Prayer with deep feeling. The Single Tax movement utilized religious ideas freely. A Cooper Union meeting cheered Father McGlynn when he recited the words:"Thy kingdom come! Thy will be done on earth!" Some of the favorite speakers and organizers of the socialists in our country are former Christian ministers, who use their power of ethical and religious appeal. In Labor Lyceums and similar gatherings, ministers are often invited as speakers, though perhaps quite as much in the hope of converting them as with a desire to hear what they have to say. The divorce between the new class movement and the old religion can still be averted.

It is a hopeful fact that in our country the Church is so close to the common people. In many of the largest denominations the churches are organized as pure democracies, and the people own and run them. Our ministry is not an hereditary pundit class, but most ministers have sprung from plain families and have worked for their living before they became ministers. The Church is not connected with the State and is not tainted, as in Europe, with the reputation of being a plain-clothes policeman to club the people into spiritual submission to the ruling powers. The churches of monarchical countries have preached loyalty to the monarchy as an essential part of Christian character. The Church in America believes heartily in political democracy. But a Church which believes in political democracy can easily learn to believe in industrial democracy as soon as it comprehends the connection. It has one foot in the people's camp. The type of Christianity prevailing in America was developed in the Puritan Revolution and has retained the spirit of its origin. It is radical, evangelical, and has the strong bent toward politics which Calvinism has everywhere had. American ministers naturally take a keen interest in public life, and, as well as they know, have tried to bring the religious forces to bear at least on some aspects of public affairs.

As a result of these characteristics, the Christian Church in America is actually deeply affected by sympathy with the social movement. It stands now, at the very beginning of the social movement in America, where the repentant Church of Germany stands after a generation of punishment by atheistic socialism. No other learned profession seems to be so open to socialist ideals as the ministry. Several years ago the *New York Evening Post* began to lament that the Church had gone over to socialism.

Nevertheless the working class have not as yet gained the impression that the Church is a positive reënforcement to them in their struggle. The impression is rather the other way. The eminent ministers whose utterances are most widely disseminated are usually the pastors of wealthy churches, and it is natural that they should echo the views taken by the friends with whom they are in sympathetic intercourse. Even those ministers who are intellectually interested in social problems are not always in sympathy with the immediate conflicts of the working class. They may take a lively interest in municipal reform or public ownership, and yet view dubiously the efforts to create a fighting organization for labor or to end the wages system. We are of a different class and find it hard to sympathize with the class struggle of the wage-workers.

In recent years many ministers have spoken frankly and boldly against the physical violence and brutality in connection with the great strikes, and against the denial of "the right to work." The former protest was made in the name of law and order, the latter in the name of liberty. No one who has ever seen the destruction of property in a riot, or the hounding of scabs by a mob, or the unleashing of the brute passions under the continued strain of a great industrial conflict, can help sympathizing with both contentions. And yet it is probable that when posterity looks back on the struggles of our day, it will judge that the righteous indignation of these protests was directed against a cause that was more righteous still.

Law is unspeakably precious. Order is the daughter of heaven. Yet in practice law and order are on the side of those in possession. The men who are out can get in only through the disturbance of the order now prevailing. Those who in the past cried for law and order at any cost have throttled many a new-born child of justice. The aristocracy and bureaucracy of Russia are all for law and order, for law and order mean the old law and their own order. When the German peasants in 1525, betrayed and murdered by their aristocratic enemies who scorned to keep faith with the _canaille,_ used violence in turn, Luther lost all his former faint sympathy with their fair demands, and called for order at any price. He said they had forfeited all rights, and summoned the forces of order to kill them as one would kill a mad dog. They did it. The princes and barons, assured that they were not only protecting their class interest, but serving God in the bargain, slaughtered probably a hundred thousand, devastated entire districts, broke the backbone of the German peasantry, and retarded the emancipation of a great and worthy class by centuries. It was a very righteous impulse with Luther, and yet we count it one of the darkest stains on his life. That class which he opposed in the blind agony of its emancipation is now rising to intelligence and power, and is forgetting all his great merits for this sin committed against the common people. . . .

Chapter Five

LABOR AND THE ENTREPRENEUR

THE GOSPEL OF WEALTH*

By Andrew Carnegie

Andrew Carnegie (1835–1919), reputedly the richest man in the world, urges the stewardship of wealth ideal

Carnegie belongs to the Horatio Alger rags-to-riches tradition of American business, but is actually untypical of the great entrepreneurs, who were usually of native birth and were descended from old Colonial families who had provided ample schooling and social advantages. Young Carnegie's hard-pressed Scottish parents managed to migrate here in 1848 and to find jobs for father and son. Luck as well as a quick mind attracted the young Andrew, an excellent telegraph operator, to the powerful Thomas A. Scott of the Pennsylvania Railroad, who made him his private secretary. Success came quickly to the young man, for by 1865, after the Civil War had enriched both him and his patron, Carnegie switched from his railroading interests to direct investments in the iron industry, thus reflecting the growing significance of the new Age of Steel. As an iron and steel executive, Carnegie was quick to select talented associates and partners, some of them inventors of key processes, in his determination to eliminate obsolete machinery in the rapidly growing industry. But his labor policies, as the tragic Homestead strike revealed, were not as enlightened as his *Autobiography* suggests.

When Carnegie retired in 1901 and sold out to the United States Steel Corporation for 447 million dollars, he embarked

* From Andrew Carnegie, *The Gospel of Wealth* (London, 1903), 4–7, 15–19.

upon a systematic philanthropy inspired by his "gospel of wealth," his proposal for a kind of biblical stewardship in which the rich man would utilize his great talents to make the best uses of his wealth in the public interest. He had no doubt, as the selection shows, that he was among the fittest in the process of natural selection and that therefore his knowledge should be used to plan the wisest distribution of his money. Like that self-made man, Benjamin Franklin, he was guided by the theory of "self-help" rather than promiscuous giving; both men believed that libraries were the wisest of gifts to enable men to cultivate their self-reliance and individualism through education. Of Carnegie's personal fortune of a quarter of a billion dollars, some 288 million dollars went to American projects and another 62 million dollars were assigned to Britain. Faithful to his precept of avoiding wasteful personal expenditures, he and his family lived moderately—though not ascetically. Carnegie not only built a multitude of libraries here and abroad, assuring himself that local citizens would contribute substantially, but also established the Carnegie Institute of Technology, the Carnegie Foundation—with innumerable philanthropies to education and other areas—the Carnegie Endowment for International Peace, the Hague Peace Palace, the Hero Fund (of which he was especially fond), and aid to pensions for teachers—a pioneer step in a much-needed direction. While critics assailed this as large-scale paternalism, his supporters praised this imaginative application of the gospel of wealth.

THE PRICE which society pays for the law of competition, like the price it pays for cheap comforts and luxuries, is also great; but the advantages of this law are also greater still than its cost—for it is to this law that we owe our wonderful material development, which brings improved conditions in its train. But, whether the law be benign or not, we must say of it, as we say of the change in the conditions of men to which we have referred: It is here; we cannot evade it; no substitutes for it have been found; and while the law may be sometimes hard for the individual, it is best for the race, because it insures the survival of the fittest in every department. We accept and welcome, therefore, as conditions to which we must accommodate ourselves, great inequality of environment; the concentration of business, industrial and commercial, in the hands of a few; and the law of competition between these, as being not only beneficial, but essential to the future progress of the race. Having accepted these, it follows that there must be great scope for the exercise of special ability in the merchant and in the manufacturer who has to conduct affairs upon a great scale. That this talent for organization and management is rare among men is proved by the fact that it invariably secures enormous rewards for its possessor, no matter where or under what laws or conditions. The experienced in affairs always rate the MAN whose services can be obtained as a partner as not only the first consideration, but such as render the question of his capital scarcely worth considering: for able men soon create capital; in the hands of those without the special talent required, capital soon takes wings. Such men become interested in firms or corporations using millions; and, estimating only simple interest to be made upon the capital invested, it is inevitable that their income must exceed their expenditure and that they must, therefore, accumulate wealth. Nor is there any middle ground which such men can occupy, because the great manufacturing or commerical concern which does not earn at least interest upon its capital soon becomes bankrupt. It must either go forward or fall behind; to stand still is impossible. It is a condition essential to its successful operation that it should be thus far profitable, and even that, in addition to interest on capital, it should make profit. It is a law, as certain as any of the others named, that men possessed of this peculiar talent for affairs, under the free play of economic forces must, of necessity, soon be in receipt of more revenue than can be judiciously expended upon themselves; and this law is as beneficial for the race as the others.

Objections to the foundations upon which society is based are not in order, because the condition of the race is better with these than it has been with any other which has been tried. Of the effect of any new substitutes proposed we cannot be sure. The Socialist or Anarchist who seeks to overturn present conditions is to be regarded as attacking the foundation upon which civilization itself rests, for civilization took its start from the day when the capable, industrious workman said to his incompetent and lazy fellow, "If thou dost not sow, thou shalt not reap," and thus ended primitive Communism by separating the drones from the bees. One who studies this subject will soon be brought face to face with the conclusion that upon the sacredness of property civilization itself depends—the right of the laborer to his hundred dollars in the savings-bank, and equally the legal right of the millionaire to his millions. Every man must be allowed "to sit under his own vine and fig-tree, with none to make afraid," if human society is to advance, or even to remain so far advanced as it is. To those who propose to substitute Communism for this intense Individualism, the answer therefore is: The race has tried that. All progress from that barbarous day to the present time has resulted from its displacement. Not evil, but good, has come to the race from the accumulation of wealth by those who have had the ability and energy to produce it. But even if we admit for a moment that it might be better for the race to discard its present foundation, Individualism,—that it is a nobler ideal that man should labor, not for himself alone, but in and for a brother-hood of his fellows, and share with them all in common, realizing Swedenborg's idea of heaven, where, as he says, the angels derive their happiness, not from laboring for self, but for each other,—even admit all this, and a sufficient answer is, This is not evolution, but revolution. It necessitates the changing of human nature itself—a work of eons, even if it were good to change it, which we cannot know.

It is not practicable in our day or in our age. Even if desirable theoretically, it belongs to another and long-succeeding sociological stratum. Our duty is with what is practicable now—with the next step possible in our day and generation. It is criminal to waste our energies in endeavoring to uproot, when all we can profitably accomplish is to bend the universal tree of humanity a little in the direction most favorable to the production of good fruit under existing circumstances. We might as well urge the destruction of the highest existing type of man because he failed to reach our ideal as to favor the destruction of Individualism, Private Property, the Law of Accumulation of Wealth, and the Law of Competition; for these are the highest result of human experience, the soil in which society, so far, has produced the best fruit. Unequally or unjustly, perhaps, as these laws sometimes operate, and imperfect as they appear to the Idealist, they are, nevertheless, like the highest type of man, the best and most valuable of all that humanity has yet accomplished.

.   .   .

. . . [Let us] take [an] instance—that of Mr. Tilden's bequest of five millions of dollars for a free library in the city of New York; but in referring to this one cannot help saying involuntarily: How much better if Mr. Tilden had devoted the last years of his own life to the proper administration of this immense sum; in which case neither legal contest nor any other cause of delay could have interfered with his aims. But let us assume that Mr. Tilden's millions finally become the means of giving to this city a noble public library, where the treasures of the world contained in books will be open to all forever, without money and without price. Considering the good of that part of the race which congregates in and around Manhattan Island, would its permanent benefit have been better promoted had these millions been allowed to circulate in small sums through the hands of the masses? Even the most strenuous advocate of Communism must entertain a doubt upon this subject. Most of those who think will probably entertain no doubt whatever.

Poor and restricted are our opportunities in this life, narrow our horizon, our best work most imperfect; but rich men should be thankful for one inestimable boon. They have it in their power during their lives to busy themselves in organizing benefactions from which the masses of their fellows will derive lasting advantage, and thus dignify their own lives. The highest life is probably to be reached, not by such imitation of the life of Christ as Count Tolstoi gives us, but, while animated by Christ's spirit, by recognizing the changed conditions of this age, and adopting modes of expressing this spirit suitable to the changed conditions under which we live, still laboring for the good of our fellows, which was the essence of his life and teaching, but laboring in a different manner.

This, then, is held to be the duty of the man of wealth: To set an example of modest, unostentatious living, shunning display or extravagance; to provide moderately for the legitimate wants of those dependent upon him; and, after doing so, to consider all surplus revenues which come to him simply as trust funds, which he is called upon to administer, and strictly bound as a matter of duty to administer in the manner which, in his judgment, is best calculated to produce the most beneficial results for the community—the man of wealth thus becoming the mere trustee and agent for his poorer brethren, bringing to their service his superior wisdom, experience, and ability to administer, doing for them better than they would or could do for themselves.

We are met here with the difficulty of determining what are moderate sums to leave to members of the family; what is modest, unostentatious living; what is the test of extravagance. There must be different standards for different conditions. The answer is that it is as impossible to name exact amounts or actions as it is to define good manners, good taste, or the rules of propriety; but, nevertheless, these are verities, well known, although indefinable. Public sentiment is quick to know and to feel what offends these. So in the case of wealth. The rule in regard to good taste in the dress of men or women applies here. Whatever makes one conspicuous offends the canon. If any family be chiefly known for display, for extravagance in home, table, or equipage, for enormous sums ostentatiously spent in any form upon itself—if these be its chief distinctions, we have no difficulty in estimating its nature or culture. So likewise in regard to the use or abuse of its surplus wealth, or to generous, free-handed coöperation in good public uses, or to unabated efforts to accumulate and hoard to the last, or whether they administer or bequeath. The verdict rests with the best and most enlightened public sentiment. The community will surely judge, and its judgments will not often be wrong.

The best uses to which surplus wealth can be put have already been indicated. Those who would administer wisely must, indeed, be wise; for one of the serious obstacles to the improvement of our race is indiscriminate charity. It were better for mankind that the millions of the rich were thrown into the sea than so spent as to encourage the slothful, the drunken, the unworthy. Of every thousand dollars spent in so-called charity to-day, it is probable that nine hundred and fifty dollars is unwisely spent—so spent, indeed, as to produce the very evils which it hopes to mitigate or cure. A well-known writer of philosophic books admitted the other day that he had given a quarter of a dollar to a man who approached him as he was coming to visit the house of his friend. He knew nothing of the habits of this beggar, knew not the use that would be made of this money, although he had every reason to suspect that it would be spent improperly. This man professed to be a disciple of Herbert Spencer; yet the quarter-dollar given that night will probably work more injury than all the money will do good which its thoughtless donor will ever be able to give in true charity. He only gratified his own feelings, saved himself from annoyance— and this was probably one of the most selfish and very worst actions of his life, for in all respects he is most worthy.

In bestowing charity, the main consideration should be to help those who will help themselves; to provide part of the means by which those who desire to improve may do so; to give those who desire to rise the aids by which they may rise; to assist, but rarely or never to do all. Neither the individual nor the race is improved by almsgiving. Those worthy of assistance, except in rare cases, seldom require assistance. The really valuable men of the race never do, except in case of accident or sudden change. Every one has, of course, cases of individuals brought to his own knowledge where temporary assistance can do genuine good, and these he will not overlook. But the amount which can be wisely given by the individual for individuals is necessarily limited by his lack of knowledge of the circumstances connected with each. He is the only true reformer who is as careful and as anxious not to aid the unworthy as he is to aid the worthy, and, perhaps, even more so, for in almsgiving more injury is probably done by rewarding vice than by relieving virtue.

The rich man is thus almost restricted to following the examples of Peter Cooper, Enoch Pratt of Baltimore, Mr. Pratt of Brooklyn, Senator Stanford, and others, who know that the best means of benefiting the community is to place within its reach the ladders upon which the aspiring can rise—free libraries, parks, and means of recreation, by which men are helped in body and mind; works of art, certain to give pleasure and improve the public taste; and public institutions of various kinds, which will improve the general condition of the people; in this manner returning their surplus wealth to the mass of their fellows in the forms best calculated to do them lasting good.

Thus is the problem of rich and poor to be solved. The laws of accumulation will be left free, the laws of distribution free. Individualism will continue, but the millionaire will be but a trustee for the poor, intrusted for a season with a great part of the increased wealth of the community, but administering it for the community far better than it could or would have done for itself. The best minds will thus have reached a stage in the development of the race in which it is clearly seen that there is no mode of disposing of surplus wealth creditable to thoughtful and earnest men into whose hands it flows, save by using it year by year for the general good. This day already dawns. Men may die without incurring the pity of their fellows, still sharers in great business enterprises from which their capital cannot be or has not been withdrawn, and which is left chiefly at death for public uses; yet the day is not far distant when the man who dies leaving behind him millions of available wealth, which was free for him to administer during life, will pass away "unwept, un-honored, and unsung," no matter to what uses he leaves the dross which he cannot take with him. Of such as these the public ver-dict will then be: "The man who dies thus rich dies disgraced."

Such, in my opinion, is the true gospel concerning wealth, obedience to which is destined some day to solve the problem of the rich and the poor, and to bring "Peace on earth, among men good will."

TESTIMONY ON TAYLORIZATION*
Scientific Management

By Louis Brandeis

Louis Brandeis (1856–1941) persuades railroads to try scientific management instead of prolonging inefficiency by securing more rate increases

Louis Brandeis, the son of an idealistic immigrant family of Louisville, Kentucky, brilliantly completed his legal studies at Harvard, practiced law most profitably as a counsel for Boston's major interests, but soon turned to social interests as "the people's lawyer." Like Oliver Wendell Holmes and Roscoe Pound, he was a legal realist interested in analyzing the pragmatic consequences of law upon changing social and economic conditions—another champion of "sociological jurisprudence." Thus he became a social inventor, intent upon preserving the checks of enlightened com-petition upon irrational "Bigness" that menaced efficiency and

* From Louis Brandeis, "Evidence in the Matter of Proposed Advances in Freight Rates," *Senate Hearings,* 61st Cong., 3rd Sess., Vol. 53, 1910–11), 2617–23; testimony given by Brandeis before the Interstate Com-merce Commission.

the public interest. He revived competition among Boston's insurance monopolists who charged high premiums and encouraged lapsed policies among working-class policyholders; this took the economical form of "over the counter" state insurance.

He taught the immigrant garment workers and employees to adopt the new democratic techniques of collective bargaining such as the trade agreement and a system of mediation and arbitration, himself serving as a union and trade lawyer. In the landmark case of *Muller* v. *Oregon* (1908), involving shorter hours for women factory workers, he introduced the Brandeis Brief, which cited fatigue studies to prove the effects of long hours upon the health of women. Thus a shorter day was justified as a valid use of the police power against the individualistic arguments of "freedom of contract."

His attack on concentrated power, "the Money Power," as expressed in his book *Other People's Money* (1914) and his articles on the trusts, influenced Wilson's new Federal Trade Commission and the Clayton Anti-Trust Act. In 1916, the President appointed him to the Supreme Court to join Justice Oliver Wendell Holmes, the other great dissenter, in preserving civil liberty and in checking monopoly during the conservative Twenties.

The widely reported and extensive railroad rate hearings of 1911 gave Brandeis a unique opportunity to publicize the monopoly-fostering effects of allowing perennial rate increases to the carriers. His keen questions shook the railroad executives, for they revealed that their policies were at variance with any objective determination of costs and the public interest. As the selection below indicates, Brandeis presented witnesses and arguments to prove that Frederick W. Taylor's system of scientific management meant the revolutionary application of science to all phases of business and industry. Taylor had measured labor's productivity, tried to eliminate managerial friction with labor by defining a reasonable day's work, assured tremendous savings and profits, and afforded a far better understanding of total operations. Many executives appeared newly convinced, and scientific management soon proved its utility during World War I and afterwards.

Thus again, Brandeis had found wide social applications for his ideal of efficiency in the public interest. His essays, *The Curse of Bigness* (collected in 1934), implied that private monopoly was too deadly a foe of democracy to be tolerated even under the federal regulations urged in Theodore Roosevelt's *New Nationalism;* thus he urged the preventive approach toward "Bigness" stressed in Wilson's *New Freedom* to which he contributed many key ideas. He was no enemy of large scale enterprise as such but of concentrated and unregulated private ownership.

Now, may it please your honors, there precisely is the point at which we take issue, most largely, with the railroads. We say that this situation, this practical declaration of hopelessness which comes from the railroads, this incompetence to deal with the great problem of labor and the great problem of costs, is due to a failure to regard that which the most progressive manufacturers in competitive lines of business have been led to adopt, namely, the science of management.

In saying that the railroads have not adopted the science of managing, I do not wish, in any way, to be deemed as making a charge of incompetence upon railroad management. The railroad managers are, no doubt, taking all the railroads together, subject to the same degrees of competence that are found in private business. Some are extremely competent and some are less so, and some are doubtless incompetent. But what I am proposing, now, is in no sense a personal criticism. What I am proposing is something entirely different from that. Of course the railroads have been subject, and the competence of the managers has been subject to strain even greater than that which exists in private business—strain, in many cases, resulting from the extraordinary size of the unit which they are obliged to administer, the strain resulting, and a very great one, to my mind, incident to the absence of competition, which is an ever great stimulus to most of the private competitive manufacturers, and then an interference, for one reason and another, of the great financial powers who exert a very much greater control over the railroads than they do in ordinary business.

Those are things which put a greater strain upon the competence of the individual man; but it is all that I have no reference to at all. I speak of something which is entirely different, of a new science, which has found its way into private business, and I say it is very new, because it is only a few years, hardly five or six, since that science emerged from that process of gathering together and coordinating principles which had been worked out during the last quarter of a century and reached the form where it may be called a science, and where only within the last three or four years it has attained that introduction into a series of businesses which establishes beyond peradventure that it is applicable alike—a general principle of business.

That science of management, as I shall show you, rests upon principles absolutely opposed to those which exist to-day in the administration of the railroads, and in most private business. Instead of regarding increases of rates with apprehension and regard, it is the fundamental principle evolved and manifested in the business where there is a science of management, that higher wages mean lower costs.

What we ask is that the administration of this commission shall, in the ways that we shall endeavor to point out to you fully, cooperate to reduce costs, instead of combining to increase rates.

What is this science of management? It is a complete reversal, in the first place, of the principles under which work is done. All the work of these employees whose rise in wages is the subject of this universal regard on the part of a railroad, all the work that is done by those men, is done, practically, under a military system—a system where everybody is putting it up to the workman to do work; and he works, more or less, according to the success in the way of force or gentler things to get him to work.

Under the science of management, the process is precisely the opposite. The management, instead of undertaking to order and compel work is aiding that workman to accomplish the results. He is aiding it in this way: By using every effort to make possible the largest accomplishment, invoking science in its highest form to the humblest occupation of the humblest worker. . . .

We shall show you, may it please your honors, that these principles, applicable to all businesses, are applicable practically to all departments of all businesses, and that the estimate which has been made that in the railroad operation of this country an economy of a million dollars a day is possible is an estimate which is by no means extravagant; and you will see as we develop the science and develop its application in varied businesses that that estimate, is, if anything, an underestimate instead of an overestimate.

What more does this involve? What is necessary in order to produce these astounding results? The first thing that is necessary is an analytical study, a scientific study of every operation; that is, everything that man has to do, that the laborer or the mechanic performs; all that is to be studied, with the view to determining whether he is doing that to the best advantage, whether he is getting all that there is out of it, whether his effort is telling. Why is that? For this reason: Because practically every performance of work by the mechanic or by the laborer, as to how he does his work, is practically traditional. A man does it this way—why? Not necessarily because it is the best way, because it is the way the other person did it before he did it; the way he observed some one else doing it; the way he was told to do it, perhaps—possibly in the trade schools of late. But the way of doing things is a way handed down from father to son or passed on from workman to workman.

Now, science, when it comes to that operation, and to every operation of the hand, undertakes to find out whether it is the best way. No presumption is made that it is or that it is not. But when it is attacked by study, by research, as any other proposition is attacked by the research and study of scientists, to see what the facts are.

What does that mean? It means, as in every science, analysis. In the first instance, what we call an "operation," a single operation, is usually made up of a number of operations; that is, of a number of atoms, and each individual step that is taken, the getting ready or picking up the hammer, the picking up of the brick and the putting of it into its place, each operation is subject to the test of science, for the purpose of determining, in the first place, whether there is anything there which is wasteful, either of time or of effort, or whether, possibly, a superior intelligence—or not even, necessarily, a superior intelligence—but a new mind, unaffected by the prejudices of tradition, will find some way of doing this thing without imposing so great a labor upon the man who is doing it.

That analytical study, ordinarily described by the words "time study," is a necessary element, and that results, as in the instance that I referred to, in extraordinary gains, both to the employer and employee. As the employee is obliged to do only that work which is necessary, and the road is made as smooth for him as it is possible for the road to be made for any worker, and he does only that work which is required of a man of his skill, he being aided with helpers, just as he is with the devising of science, he is able to do, not with more effort, but many times with very much less effort, far more in accomplishment—200 and 300 per cent more, in many instances, than he performed before. And the workman, and the employer, and in many instances, we shall be able to show you, the community, get the benefit of that increased performance. The result is higher wages to the workman, less costs, and therefore better profits to the manufacturer, and reduced prices, in many instances, to the consumer—and this reduction in price to the consumer, coincident with the general increase in prices about which we have heard so much, and the increase in the cost of living.

But the laborer's gain is not, as we shall show you, limited merely to dollars. That is a very important, a highly important thing, that wages should be increased. But it is at least as important that the self-respect of the laborer shall increase; that he shall have satisfaction in his work; that he shall have something of the joy of his work which we have. It is an incident, as we shall show you, from a careful study of men working under this system that the workman appreciates it just as much as, perhaps more than, the employer; that instead of having this growing inefficiency of labor, of which we have heard so much, we have a greater efficiency of labor, because we have a greater content, because we have among the laborers, among the mechanics, the same satisfaction in accomplishment, and the same recognition of accomplishment that we have among those who employ mechanics and who employ laborers; that, instead of a feeling of hostility and discontent, we have a feeling of friendliness and content.

We shall show you that, under conditions where ordinarily, labor has been incited, has been led through sympathy with suffering brothers to strike, these men have recognized their treatment and their possibilities and have stood by their work, because it is their work more than the employer's work which this whole science of management develops.

We shall show you also, may it please your honors, that the gain to the manufacturer, the employer, is not confined to mere reduction in operating costs, but that it deals with the very matter about which the railroad heads have been so much troubled—the question of the expenditure of capital for plant, for equipment, and the necessary expenditures for working capital; that in many instances a large part of the gain which has come to capital has come through a great increase in the efficiency of the inanimate as well as the animate part of the system, the plant and the machinery; that they have been able to produce more, and that with the same plant the output has been extraordinarily larger. In brief, it will appear that one of the first incidents in the introduction of scientific management into manufacturing has been the discovery that the manufacturer who was congested before finds himself overequipped.

We believe, and shall show you, that the railroad operation itself affords not a less, but a more favorable field, for the introduction of scientific management than any that now exists; that the very absence of competition among the railroads, and the power which this commission possesses under the law to compel full accounting as to costs, affords the opportunity of greatly advancing and expediting a reduction in costs, in this way: That the costs that we speak of, and the costs that it is important to determine, are the ultimate unit costs in operation. Those costs, in railroads, are wholly unlike the question as to what the average cost of repairing a locomotive or the average cost of keeping a mile of track in good condition may be, or of hauling a ton or a thousand tons of merchandise. Those costs are composite costs. They are very slight guides, if guides at all, to the relative efficiency of operation on the different roads, because they are composite, and affected, as the witnesses have stated, by a large number of different elements. But the original unit costs disclosed by this scientific analysis of operations are costs that as units, as atoms in the operation, are properly comparable. What we shall propose, after the matter has been fully developed before your honors, is that this commission should aid, among other things, this great possible reduction in cost by requiring the ascertainment and the report to this commission of those ultimate unit costs in order, in the first instance, that each railroad may have the opportunity of knowing the lowest cost at which any railroad has performed the particular operation, and thus that each railroad may have the opportunity of reaching the lowest level possible to be reached on the existing state of knowledge. But that will not be the end. That is only the beginning of scientific management. It will afford the necessary starting point for making that careful study of the individual operation which the magnitude of the interests involved, and of the whole country and the whole future demand.

Now, may it please your honors, this introduction of scientific management is, as you will see, obviously not an act, but a process; a process requiring time, and very great time, in its fullness, and very great tact and patience always. It requires time, because it is difficult. It deals with human nature; it deals with existing prejudices that have to be overcome, and that means extraordi-

S. M

nary tact and extraordinary patience and an absolute understanding of what is intended; and, above all, a desire to be
absolutely fair to all concerned. It means that. . . .

"REPORT OF 1905" *
The AFL Philosophy

By Samuel Gompers

*Samuel Gompers (1850–1924), President of the AFL, assails in-
dustrial unionism, labor injunctions, and Chinese immigration*

Born in a London slum of Dutch-Jewish ancestry and appren-
ticed at ten to a cigarmaker—the same occupation as his father's—
Samuel Gompers had little formal education. When the Gompers
family migrated to New York City in 1863, both father and son
worked at cigarmaking. In the then unstable cigarmakers' union,
young Gompers sought actively to remedy its weaknesses, read
books and periodicals on socialism, and met many refugee Marx-
ists, but he decided that class struggle tactics were futile in individualistic America. He helped transform his union into a model
for the strong locals of the American Federation of Labor that
came into existence during 1881–86 with himself as president, a
post that he held until his death in 1924.

He built up a strong system of collective bargaining based on
the strength and self-interest of the craftsman rather than on the
quixotic, idealistic notion of labor solidarity held by such loosely
combined unskilled and skilled unions as the Knights of Labor or
Eugene Debs's American Railway Union. After the Knights went
down to defeat during the Haymarket Riot and the ARU's failure in the Pullman Strike, Gompers became the most powerful
labor leader in the nation. The socialists were anathema to him,
and he made the AFL locals strong by eliminating dual unionism
within each trade and by building up adequate strike funds,
although he usually discouraged strikes. His "pure and simple"
trade unionism held to limited bargaining objectives for higher

* From Samuel Gompers, "Report of 1905," *The American Federationist*
vol. 12 (December, 1905), 940–49.

wages and better conditions and avoided legislative or political actions except for defensive purposes—such as the halting of a "flood" of immigrants or the attempt to eliminate labor injunctions, as did President Wilson's Clayton Act of 1914, which Gompers enthusiastically supported as "the Magna Carta of Labor."

But his regular use of the labor boycott weapon against employers ran afoul of the United States Supreme Court as well as the "open shop" movement sponsored by the National Association of Manufacturers. In the Buck Stove Case, he and his AFL associates narrowly escaped serving prison sentences and managed only by a costly arrangement to save the homes and bank accounts of their members who had been held liable for damages. Still, he greatly stimulated the labor movement, which had seldom attracted more than three per cent of the working force before the turn of the century. By 1917, the AFL registered over two million members. Unlike the radical IWW, Gompers' AFL bolstered capitalism and patriotically supported the war effort of 1918, campaigning for the election and reelection of Wilson and other friends of labor. While the AFL never made a strenuous effort to organize the unskilled and failed to support welfare legislation on the contemporary European scale (Gompers hoped that strong unions could take care of their welfare needs), it did stabilize the long-erratic labor movement that had suffered chronic collapses during hard times and had wasted its resources upon ill-conceived strikes or political panaceas.

It is the older Gompers who is mirrored in *Seventy Years of Life and Labor* (2 vols., 1925), but the evolution of his ideas may best be followed in *The American Federationist* of which he was a very active editor.

The Experience of an "Industrial" Organization

IT WILL be remembered that a few years ago a number of our federal labor unions and laborers' unions, induced by misrepresentations of a few lacking the knowledge of the trade union movement, left the American Federation of Labor and organized what they termed an international laborers' union, with the avowed purpose of bringing into that organization all the laborers of the country, regardless of their occupation or the industry in which they were employed. How utterly absurd were their claim and position they then could not know. If their policy

IWW

Purpose of AFL

could have been brought to any degree of fruition, it would have all the sooner brought about its own destruction. It was a poor imitation of the old and now defunct "Knights of Labor." It would have prevented the organization, which we have accomplished, of a large number of international unions of the so-called unskilled trades and unskilled laborers. The idea entertained by its promoters was so-called industrialism, industrialism carried to its logical conclusion.

It has been the purpose of the American Federation of Labor to encourage, first, organization of workmen into trade unions; second, to bring about international unions of such trades, crafts, and callings, and then to bring about co-operation and amalgamation of kindred trades. Along these lines much good has been accomplished, until we today see the great structure of the organized labor movement of America.

The officers of this international laborers' union at the time of its formation made application for charter, which certainly could not be granted without stultification and general injury to all workmen and the intelligent and orderly growth and development of our movement. We could not grant a charter, or encourage the formation of an organization that would not only destroy itself, but others with it. Its claim to jurisdiction practically covered all callings.

Recently I had correspondence and extensive conference with the new officers of that organization, who recognized the mistake made in its early history and make-up, and the desire was expressed for a common-sense organization, based upon the recognition of true trade union law, policy, and principles. It was frankly admitted that even in the institution of that "industrial" organization, industrialism, as understood both by the founders of that organization and as understood by some recent advocates, is fallacious, injurious, and reactionary. I am in a position to entertain the hope that our fellow workers in that organization will under its new administrative officers work toward a closer unity with the trade union movement, the American Federation of Labor, and efforts to its complete fulfillment should be continued. . . .

The Eight Hour Movement

From the inception of our Federation we have voiced the demand of labor for a shorter workday. In 1884 we called upon and urged all labor to endeavor to establish the eight hour workday, if possible, by agreement with the employers. We have been helpful to many crafts in establishing the eight hour day; the hours of toil for all have been reduced.

With the wonderful improvement in machinery and the application of steam and electric power, our workers are producing wealth surpassing even the imagination, much less the expectation, of a decade or two ago.

Living in a land fertile and bountiful as ours, with its ingenious and industrious people, there can not be any good reason assigned why in our day the toilers should be expected or required to give to labor more than eight hours in a day.

miners plight.

It is untrue to say, as our opponents assert, that wealth production would diminish with the enforcement of eight hours as a normal working day. In the report of the Secretary of Commerce and Labor to the House Committee on Labor is incorporated testimony of employers who for a series of years had tested the practicability of the eight hour day. In no instance where a fair test has been given do employers vary in their favorable attestation of its economy, wisdom, and practicability.

In the construction of the battleship Connecticut under the eight hour plan, and the battleship Louisiana on the ten hour basis, the advantage has been to the former. In the industries in which the eight hour day has been introduced, it has resulted in the greater productivity of labor per man, per day, per year. This has not only been demonstrated in our own country, but in every other wherever it has been introduced. In truth, it is easily demonstrable that a reduction of the hours of labor to eight does not decrease production, but on the contrary increases it; that the power of consumption and use of the products of labor are thereby increased; which in turn will give to industry and production a greater impetus than they can receive in any other way. It out rivals by far the other markets of the world, to which so much attention has been given. Opportunity for leisure and rest after a normal day's work develops a higher physical, intelligent, and moral manhood and makes for the social welfare.

Logic of an 8 hr. day

It is strongly urged upon all fellow-unionists, fellow workers, and friends everywhere to concentrate and devote their energies to the movement for the establishment of the eight hour workday.

I recommend that the general introduction of the eight hour workday be made the chief subject for general discussion in our unions, central bodies, national and international conventions; that employers be approached with a view of their agreement thereto, and should that fail, that preparation in the meantime and thereafter be made to enforce the eight hour day by the demand of the workers. It is our bounden duty by every means within our power to be helpful to our fellow workers in its enforcement. . . .

Chinese Exclusion from All America

Perhaps one of the most momentous questions which will confront the American people, and of which this convention must take cognizance and deal with earnestly, intelligently, and emphatically, is the campaign inaugurated in several quarters for what is called a modification of the law excluding Chinese from entry into the United States or its possessions. Within the past year manifest efforts have been made in this direction, particularly inaugurated and stimulated by antagonistic employers and some of their associations.

Information of an authentic character and from various sources has been communicated to our office showing that a carefully devised policy has been agreed upon and is being carried out. Labor's antagonists realize the fact that American public opinion and sentiment are fully expressed in the existing Chinese exclusion law. They also realize that if the application of the law was sought to be modified so far as it applies to our mainland, it would arouse the opposition of the American people, and the effort is therefore subtly screened by arrangement with the sugar planters of Hawaii, placing them in the position of agitating for a modification of the law so as to permit the immigration of Chinese to that island.

It is seldom that a bold front attack is made in any effort of human activity, and our opponents, through the pretense of the necessity for Chinese laborers to work upon the sugar plantations of Hawaii, entertain the belief that once the law is successfully attacked by so-called modification its entire structure may be eliminated.

An agitation involving the expenditure of vast sums of money has been set on foot by the sugar planters of Hawaii, to which our antagonists on the mainland have largely contributed, all for the purpose of impressing the people of the United States, and particularly the members of Congress, with the supposed necessity for a change in the law so as to allow the immigration of Chinese to the Sandwich islands. Not a fraction of money has been contributed or expended by the government of Hawaii toward the immense amounts that have been and are involved in the appointment of commissions, delegations, in printing reports, and other matter involved in the propagation of thought favorable to Chinese immigration. In their desperation, the sugar planters have endeavored even to suborn some representatives of labor.

There can be no question but that Japanese immigration into Hawaii has had a most baneful influence and result; but it is a queer notion that will seek relief from the evils resulting from Japanese immigration and work by turning to the Chinese, and it shows a perverted conception of real economy, justice, and Americanism.

The information also reaches us that, in carrying out our opponents' policy, the sugar planters have sent an agent to visit various countries for the ostensible purpose of securing immigrants to work on the Hawaiian plantations. The word "ostensible" is used advisedly, for the instructions are given that few, if any, laborers are to be so secured, so that the claim may be made that no workmen can be obtained from either the United States or Europe, thereby making it appear that the only recourse is to the Chinese. A part of the plan of action is to maintain at the capitol in Washington a lobby coming from Hawaii for that purpose.

It will be remembered that for a few years a similar effort was made in the Philippines, and that the conditions were presented in such a light as to make it appear that there was a real necessity for the admission of Chinese to those islands. Since the enactment of our present effective Chinese exclusion law and its complete application to the Philippines and the other insular possessions of, as well as the United States itself, practically a quietus has been given to that agitation and supposed demand for Chinese immigration to the Philippine Islands, but the activity of the pro-Chinese is none the less today than it was some years ago. They have simply changed their plan of campaign from the Philippines to Hawaii.

That there is no dearth of workmen in Hawaii is plainly evident from the figures contained in the census reports and from enumerations of the population made. The difficulty which presents itself is the fact that the sugar planters, when deprived by law from securing Chinese laborers, turned their attention to the Japanese and imported them by shiploads. These are now found to be undesirable and destructive to the interests of labor, business, as well as [other groups].

Bakers' Ten Hour Workday

Much chagrin was felt when the law of the state of New York, providing that workmen employed in bakeries shall not be employed for a longer period than ten hours in any working day, was declared unconstitutional by the Supreme Court of the United States. That law was enacted at the demand of the bakers, organized labor, and the higher public opinion aroused upon the subject.

The law stood the test and was held as constitutional by the highest court in the state of New York. The United States Supreme Court declared it unconstitutional by the narrow margin of a vote of five to four. The minority opinion of the court declared that it is the most far-reaching decision rendered by the court in a hundred years, and that the principles upon which it is based could not and would not have been applied to any other interest.*

The scathing arraignment by the minority opinions of the decision and opinion of the majority of the court is most interesting, and in the not distant future will finally undoubtedly prevail.

It is not amiss, and it is gratifying to say, that what the court declared was unconstitutional in law has been successfully maintained and achieved in fact; and the ten-hour work-day limit is enforced by the organized bakers of New York by agreement with their employers. It is no little satisfaction to be enabled to express my pride in having somewhat aided in securing this result, the court's decision to the contrary notwithstanding.

May we not venture the hope that the bakers, whose occupation is known to be so enervating, will more thoroughly organize, and by application and persistency reduce their daily hours of

* *Lochner versus New York* (1905).

toil to a normal workday of eight hours? Surely, with modern appliances in the trade, long hours of labor can no longer be regarded as necessary or advantageous.

Injunctions, Their Use and Abuse

Despite a number of hearings that were had upon our anti-injunction bill, H. R. 89, introduced in the House by Congressman Grosvener, the Judiciary Committee failed to make a report thereon. In view of the continued use or abuse of the issuance of the writ of injunction in labor disputes, there can be no question but that it is our bounden duty to impress upon Congress the necessity of enacting a bill which shall relieve our fellow workers from the injustice which so many are compelled to endure.

Entirely apart from the unjust course pursued by the courts in issuing the injunctions of which we complain, they can not but have a baneful influence upon all our people, not only in having their lawful rights, one after the other, impaired and invaded, but because of the consequent lack of respect for the law and the courts, which bias and maladministration naturally evolve.

We can not too often repeat our position upon this subject, lest by ignorance or prejudice our attitude is distorted for vicious purposes. There can be no question but that the process of injunctions is a necessary and proper function of equity courts. Their proper application is of incalculable advantage to protect rights when there is no other remedy at law. The use of the injunction in labor disputes can not be defended upon the pretense that there is no other remedy at law for any offense which either workmen or others may commit.

If a workman should commit an offense against the law, or if an organized body be guilty of the same, there is ample provision in the police power and in the law and the courts to apprehend the wrong-doer, confront him with charges subject to trial by a jury of his peers; but workmen may be and often are enjoined from doing the things that they have a perfect, lawful right to do, and yet, when done, they may be guilty of having violated a court's injunction, and they may be, often are, summarily punished by fine or imprisonment, or both, and yet guiltless of any offense against the law.

Aye, men may be charged with an offense of which they may be entirely innocent, punished by the court with imprisonment for violation of the terms of an injunction, and yet when later confronted by a jury, be honorably acquitted. Thus, constitutional guarantees which provide against a man's life or liberty being placed in jeopardy twice upon the same charge are flagrantly violated.

There is no act which is a lawful act that a workman may do from which he should be enjoined from doing by an injunction of a court; there is not an act, if it be an unlawful act, which a court by its injunction may enjoin for which there is not already a law with its provided penalty.

Viewed from any point, the issuance of injunctions, as we have witnessed them in our country, can not be defended in either law or morals.

There is no desire on the part of labor for extra consideration or leniency at the hands of the courts.

We neither request nor desire immunity for any wrongful or unlawful act when committed by a workman.

We have the right, however, to demand to be regarded and treated with absolute equality before the law.

We must and shall be content with nothing less.

Our worst and most bitter antagonists can not dissent from our protest against so vicious a distinction made in injunction cases in the courts by which, upon a one-sided allegation, punishment is meted out to a workman, which is never even made applicable when actions of a similar character are done by another.

This question of the court's abuse of the injunction process is in a most unsatisfactory condition, and will not be settled until settled right. It is the duty and the mission of the organized workers of America to enlighten the public mind, and to press home upon our law-making power the necessity for fairness, for justice, and for the right.

Chapter Six

DARWINISM, PRAGMATISM, AND PROGRESSIVE EDUCATION

"AGASSIZ AND DARWINISM" *

By John Fiske

John Fiske (1842–1901), philosopher and historian, champions evolution against the formidable Louis Agassiz

John Fiske was born in Hartford, Connecticut, of Puritan descent, the son of a lawyer and journalist father and a schoolteacher mother. When his father died, he acquired a wealthy stepfather, a New York lawyer who later became a minister to Russia and a source of much-needed funds for an ever-impecunious scholar. In his youth, Fiske impressed everyone as a prodigy who read voraciously and who easily mastered modern and ancient languages. He did well at Harvard, but his rationalist tendencies, a mixture of Comte's positivism and Darwinian materialism, frightened away the orthodox men who controlled the professorial chair that he always coveted. He traveled and studied abroad, meeting his idols Herbert Spencer, Darwin, and Huxley.

During the Seventies, he expressed his ardent evolutionary ideas in his four-volume *Outlines of Cosmic Philosophy* and his *Darwinism and Other Essays*. He won a reputation as the Huxley of America, an estimate which can be readily inferred from the essay below in which Fiske took on America's most distinguished naturalist, Louis Agassiz.

* John Fiske, "Agassiz and Darwinism," *Popular Science Monthly,* vol. 3 (1873), 692–98.

Always a philosophic optimist, Fiske cheered his audiences with his vigorous presentation of evolution and progress. While Fiske never became either a great philosopher or historian, he was rated very highly in his day, but too much of his time and energy went to his well paid public lectures for women's clubs and too many of these lectures became the stuff out of which his books were made. Modern readers will object to his Anglo-Saxon ethnocentric histories—he was honorary president of the Immigration Restriction League—and to his now-exploded Cavalier myth that attributed this aristocratic origin for Virginia. Yet his synthesis, even allowing for his heavy use of secondary sources, often hit the mark. His thoughtful work, *The Critical Period of American History, 1783–1789* (1889), which interpreted the Constitution as a popularly desired document needed to meet the crises of the Critical Era, has recently won scholarly supporters despite its alleged demolition as a theory by Charles Beard.

Now exploded.

❦

ONE FRIDAY morning, a few weeks ago, as I was looking over the *Nation,* my eye fell upon an advertisement, inserted by the proprietors of the *New-York Tribune,* announcing the final destruction of Darwinism. What especially riveted my attention was the peculiar style of the announcement: "The Darwinian Theory utterly demolished" (or words to that effect) "by AGASSIZ HIMSELF!" Whether from accident or design, the typesetter's choice of Roman capitals was very happy. Upon many readers the effect must have been tremendous; and quite possibly there may be some who, without further investigation, will carry to their dying day the opinion that it is all over with the Darwinian theory, since "Agassiz Himself" has refuted it.

Upon me the effect was such as to make me lay down my paper and ask myself: Can it be that we have, after all, a sort of scientific pope among us? Has it come to this, that the dicta of some one "servant and interpreter of Nature" are to be accepted as final, even against the better judgment of the majority of his compeers? In short, who is Agassiz himself, that he should thus single-handed have demolished the stoutest edifice which observation and deduction have reared since the day when Newton built to such good purpose?

Prof. Agassiz is a naturalist who is justly world-renowned for his achievements. His contributions to geology, to paleontology, and to systematic zoology, have been such as to place him in a very high rank among contemporary naturalists. Not quite in the highest place, I should say; for, apart from all questions of theory, it is probable that Mr. Darwin's gigantic industry, his wonderful thoroughness and accuracy as an observer, and his unrivalled fertility of suggestion, will cause him in the future to be ranked along with Aristotle, Linnæus, and Cuvier; and upon this high level we cannot place Prof. Agassiz. Leaving Mr. Darwin out of the account, we may say that Prof. Agassiz stands in the first rank of contemporary naturalists. But any exceptional supremacy in this first rank can by no means be claimed for him. Both for learning and for sagacity, the names of Gray, Wyman, Huxley, Hooker, Wallace, Lubbock, Lyell, Vogt, Haeckel, and Gegenbaur, are quite as illustrious as the name of Agassiz; and we may note, in passing, that these are the names of men who openly indorse and defend the Darwinian theory.

Possibly, however, there are some who will not be inclined to accept the estimates made in the foregoing paragraph. No doubt there are many people in this country who have long accustomed themselves to regard Prof. Agassiz not simply as one among a dozen or twenty living naturalists of the highest rank, but as occupying a solitary position as the greatest of all living naturalists—as a kind of second Cuvier, for example. There is, to the popular eye, a halo about the name of Agassiz which there is not about the name of Gray; though, if there is any man now living in America, of whom America might justly boast as her chief ornament of pride, so far as science is concerned, that man is unquestionably Prof. Asa Gray. Now, this greater popular fame of Agassiz is due to the fact that he is a European who cast in his lot with us at a time when we were wont to overrate foreign importations of whatever sort. . . . One feels, in reading his writings, that except when he is narrating facts with the pure joyfulness of a specialist exulting in the exposition of his subject (and, when in this mood, he often narrates facts with which his inferences are wholly incompatible), he never makes a point without some regard to its bearings upon theological propositions which his early training has led him to place paramount to all facts of observation whatever. In virtue of this peculiarity of disposition, Prof. Agassiz has become the welcome ally of those zealous but narrowminded theologians, in whom the rapid progress of the Darwinian theory has awakened the easily ex-

plicable but totally groundless fear that the necessary foundations of true religion, or true Christianity, are imperilled. It is
not many years since these very persons regarded Prof. Agassiz
with dread and abhorrence, because of his flat contradiction of
the Bible in his theory of the multiple origin of the human race.
But, now that the doctrine of Evolution has come to be the
unclean thing above all others to be dreaded and abhorred, this
comparatively slight iniquity of Prof. Agassiz has been condoned
or forgotten, and, as the great antagonist of Evolution, he is
welcomed as the defender of the true Church against her foes.

mud slinging

    This preference of theological over scientific considerations
once led Prof. Agassiz (if my memory serves me rightly) to use
language very unbecoming in a professed student of Nature.
Some seven years ago he delivered a course of lectures at the
Cooper Union, and in one of these lectures he observed that he
preferred the theory which makes man out a fallen angel to the
theory which makes him out an improved monkey—a remark
which was quite naturally greeted with laughter and applause.
But the applause was ill-bestowed, for the remark was one of
the most degrading which a scientific lecturer could make. A
scientific inquirer has no business to have "preferences." Such
things are fit only for silly women of society, or for young children who play with facts, instead of making sober use of them.
What matters it whether we are pleased with the notion of a
monkey-ancestry or not? The end of scientific research is the discovery of truth, and not the satisfaction of our whims or fancies,
or even of what we are pleased to call our finer feelings. The
proper reason for refusing to accept any doctrine is, that it is
inconsistent with observed facts, or with some other doctrine
which has been firmly established on a basis of fact. The refusal
to entertain a theory because it seems disagreeable or degrading,
is a mark of intellectual cowardice and insincerity. . . . For
every one of the individuals of which a species is made up, he
will admit the adequacy of the ordinary process of generation;
but for the species as a whole, this process seems to him inadequate, and he flies at once to that refuge of inconsequent and
timid minds—*miracle!*

    This is really just what Prof. Agassiz's theory of the origin of
specific forms amounts to, and this is the reason why, in spite of
grave heresy on minor points, he is now regarded by the evangelical Church as one of its chief champions. Instead of the

natural process of generation—which is the only process by which we have ever known organic beings to be produced—he would fain set up some unknown mysterious process, the nature of which he is careful not to define, but for which he endeavors to persuade us that we have a fair equivalent in sonorous phrases concerning "creative will," "free action of an intelligent mind," and so on. In thus postponing considerations of pure science to considerations of "natural theology," I have no doubt Prof. Agassiz is actuated by a praiseworthy desire to do something for the glory of that Power of which the phenomenal universe is the perpetual but ever-changing manifestation. But how futile is such an attempt as this! How contrary to common-sense it is to say that a species is produced, *not* by the action of blind natural forces, *but* by an intelligent will! For, although this most prominent of all facts seems to be oftenest overlooked by theologians and others whom it most especially concerns, we are all the time, day by day and year by year, in each and every event of our lives, having experience of the workings of that Divine Power which, whether we attribute to it "intelligent will" or not, is unquestionably the one active agent in all the dynamic phenomena of Nature. Little as we know of the intrinsic nature of this Omnipresent Power, which, in our poor human talk, we call God, we do at least know, by daily and hourly experience, what is the character of its working. The whole experience of our lives teaches us that this Power works after a method which, in our scholastic expression, we call the method of cause and effect, or the method of natural law. Traditions of a barbarous and uncultivated age, in which mere grotesque associations of thoughts were mistaken for facts, have told us that this Power has, at various times in the past, worked in a different way—causing effects to appear without cognizable antecedents, even as Aladdin's palace rose in all its wondrous magnificence, without sound of carpenter's hammer or mason's chisel, in a single night. But about such modes of divine action we know nothing whatever from experience; and the awakening of literary criticism, in modern times, has taught us to distrust all such accounts of divine action which conflict with the lessons we learn from what is ever going on round about us. So far as we know aught concerning the works of God, which are being performed in us, through us, and around us, during every moment of that conscious intelligence which enables us to bear witness to them, we know they are works from which the essential relation of a given effect to its adequate cause is never absent. And for this reason, if we view the matter in pure accordance with experience, we are led to maintain that the antagonism or contrariety which seems to exist in Prof. Agassiz's mind between the action of God and the action of natural forces is nothing but a figment of that ancestral imagination from which the lessons which shaped Prof. Agassiz's ways of thinking were derived. So far as experience can tell us any thing, it tells us that divine action *is* the action of natural forces; for, if we refuse to accept this conclusion, what have we to do but retreat to the confession that we have no experience of divine action whatever, and that the works of God have been made manifest only to those who lived in that unknown time when Aladdin's palaces were built, and when species were created, in a single night, without the intervention of any natural process? . . .

Now, when Prof. Agassiz asks us to believe that species have come into existence by means of a special creative fiat, and not through the operation of what are called natural causes, we reply that his request is mere inanity and nonsense. We have no reason to suppose that any creature like a man, or any other vertebrate, or articulate, or mollusk, ever came into existence by any other process than the familiar process of physical generation. To ask us to believe in any other process is to ask us to abandon the experience which we have for the chimeras which we had best not seek to acquire. But Prof. Agassiz does not even suggest any other process for our acceptance. He simply retreats upon his empty phrases, "creative will," the "free workings of an intelligent mind," and so on. Now, in his second course of lectures, I hope he will proceed to tell us, not necessarily how "creative will" actually operated in bringing forth a new species, but how it *may* conceivably have operated, save through the process of physical generation, which we know. In his "Essay on Classification," I remember a passage in which he rightly rejects the notion that any species has arisen from a single pair of parents, and propounds the formula: "Pines have originated in forests, heaths in heather, grasses in prairies, bees in hives, herrings in shoals, buffaloes in herds, men in nations." Now, when Prof. Agassiz asserts that men originated in nations, by some other process than that of physical generation, what does he mean? Does he mean that men dropped down from the sky? Does he mean that the untold millions of organic particles which make up a man all rushed together from the four quarters of the compass, and proceeded, spontaneously or by virtue of some divine sorcery, to aggregate themselves into the infinitely complex organs and tissues of the human body, with all their wondrous and well-defined aptitudes? It is time that this question should be faced, by Prof. Agassiz and those who agree with him, without further shirking. Instead of grandiloquent phrases about the "free action of an intelligent mind," let us have something like a candid suggestion of some process, other than that of physical generation, by which a creature like man can even be imagined to have come into existence. When the time comes for answering this question, we shall find that even Prof. Agassiz is utterly dumb and helpless. The sonorous phrase "special creation," in which he has so long taken refuge, is nothing but a synthesis of vocal sounds which covers and, to some minds, conceals a thoroughly idiotic absence of sense or significance. To say that "Abracadabra is not a genial corkscrew," is to make a statement quite as full of meaning as the statement that species have originated by "special creation."

The purely theological (or theologico-metaphysical and at all events unscientific) character of Prof. Agassiz's objections to the development theory is sufficiently shown by the fact that, in the foregoing paragraphs, I have considered whatever of any account there is in his lectures which can be regarded as an objection. *Arguments* against the development theory such objections cannot be called: they are, at their very best, nothing but *expressions of fear and dislike.* The only remark which I have been able to find, worthy of being dignified as an argument, is the following: "We see that fishes are lowest, that reptiles are higher, that birds have a superior organization to both, and that mammals, with man at their head, are highest. The phases of development which a quadruped undergoes, in his embryonic growth, recall this gradation. He has a fish-like, a reptile-like stage before he shows unmistakable mammal-like features. We do not on this account suppose a quadruped grows out of a fish in our time, for this simple reason, that we live among quadrupeds and fishes, and we know that no such thing takes place. But resemblances of the same kind, separated by geological ages, allow play for the imagination, and for inference unchecked by observation."

I do not believe that Prof. Agassiz's worst enemy—if he ever had an enemy—could have been so hard-hearted as to wish for him the direful catastrophe into which this wonderful piece of argument has plunged him irretrievably. For the question must at once suggest itself to every reader at all familiar with the subject, If Prof. Agassiz supposes that the development theory, as held now-a-days, implies that a quadruped was ever the direct issue of a fish, of what possible value can his opinion be as regards the development theory in any way?

If I may speak frankly, as I have indeed been doing from the outset, I will say that, as regards the Darwinian theory, Prof. Agassiz seems to me to be hopelessly behind the age. I have never yet come across the first indication that he knows what the Darwinian theory is. Against the development theory, as it was taught him by the discussions of forty years ago, he is fond of uttering, I will not say arguments, but expressions of dislike. With the modern development theory, with the circumstances of variation, heredity, and natural selection, he never, in any of his writings, betrays the slightest acquaintance. Against a mere man of straw of his own devising, he industriously hurls anathemas of a quasi-theological character. But any thing like a scientific examination of the character and limits of the agency of natural selection in modifying the appearance and structure of a species, . . . he has never yet brought forth. . . .

"WHAT PRAGMATISM MEANS" *

By William James

William James (1842–1910), philosopher and psychologist, shows why pragmatism offers a theory of truth and an empirical method of attaining it

William James acquired his idealistic bent as a youngster in the stimulating home of his reformist father Henry who brought there Emerson and other highly influential proponents of idealism.

* From William James, "What Pragmatism Means," *Pragmatism* (1907), 45–81 excerpted.

Born in New York City and taken from one school to another (with his brother Henry) in Europe and the United States, James acquired a certain rootlessness as well as a varied education. He chose to study science and completed his M.D. at Harvard, taking time out to join Louis Agassiz' zoological expedition to the Amazon Basin. Possibly his early scientific and materialistic overemphasis led to the deep philosophic doubts and depression that assailed him until he was rescued by reading Renouvier from whom he received a strong grasp on the notion of moral freedom and the will.

As a Harvard instructor in physiology and anatomy during the era of the Darwinian controversy, he taught the philosophy of evolution and related physiology to psychology. Encouraged by President Charles Eliot, he built the first psychological laboratory, probably inspired by Wundt, and trained the first Ph.D. in psychology, G. Stanley Hall. In 1890, he issued his widely read *Principles of Psychology*, which contained discussions of a stream of consciousness, the link between organic reactions and emotions, and some treatment of pragmatism. He dismayed scientists by displaying keen interest in psychical claims and telepathy, a symptom of his "open universe" of the possible.

His *Will to Believe* (1897) used a pragmatic approach to the existence of God and a hereafter. This was elaborated in *The Varieties of Religious Experience* (1902), which showed the psychological adaptations of various kinds of personalities to their own variety of religious truth. His *Moral Equivalent of War* (1910) offered a peaceful substitute for bloodshed in constructive mass labor and reflected his beliefs in anti-imperialism and freedom.

In 1907, James published his lectures on pragmatism from which the selection below is drawn. He shocked many by using the apparently materialistic argument that the test of truth lies in its consequences, its "cash value," and whether it "works." Actually, James was no materialist and certainly no worshiper of what he denounced as "the bitch goddess of success." John Dewey greatly admired James and utilized the pragmatic approach in his own idea of "instrumentalism."

THE PRAGMATIC method is primarily a method of settling metaphysical disputes that otherwise might be interminable. Is the world one or many?—fated or free?—material or spiritual?—here are notions either of which may or may not hold good of the world; and disputes over such notions are unending. The pragmatic method in such cases is to try to interpret each notion by tracing its respective practical consequences. What difference would it practically make to any one if this notion rather than that notion were true? If no practical difference whatever can be traced, then the alternatives mean practically the same thing, and all dispute is idle. . . .

Pragmatism represents a perfectly familiar attitude in philosophy, the empiricist attitude, but it represents it, as it seems to me, both in a more radical and in a less objectionable form than it has ever yet assumed. A pragmatist turns his back resolutely and once for all upon a lot of inveterate habits dear to professional philosophers. He turns away from abstraction and insufficiency, from verbal solutions, from bad *a priori* reasons, from fixed principles, closed systems, and pretended absolutes and origins. He turns towards concreteness and adequacy, towards facts, towards action and towards power. That means the empiricist temper regnant and the rationalist temper sincerely given up. It means the open air and possibilities of nature, as against dogma, artificiality, and the pretence of finality in truth.

At the same time it does not stand for any special results. It is a method only. But the general triumph of that method would mean an enormous change in what I called in my last lecture the 'temperament' of philosophy. Teachers of the ultra-rationalistic type would be frozen out, much as the courtier type is frozen out in republics, as the ultramontane type of priest is frozen out in protestant lands. Science and metaphysics would come much nearer together, would in fact work absolutely hand in hand.

Metaphysics has usually followed a very primitive kind of quest. You know how men have always hankered after unlawful magic, and you know what a great part in magic *words* have always played. If you have his name, or the formula of incantation that binds him, you can control the spirit, genie, afrite, or whatever the power may be. Solomon knew the names of all the spirits, and having their names, he held them subject to his will. So the universe has always appeared to the natural mind as a kind of enigma, of which the key must be sought in the shape of some illuminating or power-bringing word or name. That word names the universe's *principle,* and to possess it is after a fashion to possess the universe itself. 'God,' 'Matter,' 'Reason,' 'the Absolute,' 'Energy,' are so many solving names. You can rest when you have them. You are at the end of your metaphysical quest.

Pragmatic method — constant re-evaluation of words or realities. *very imp.*

But if you follow the pragmatic method, you cannot look on any such word as closing your quest. You must bring out of each word its practical cash-value, set it at work within the stream of your experience. It appears less as a solution, then, than as a program for more work, and more particularly as an indication of the ways in which existing realities may be *changed*.

Theories thus become instruments, not answers to enigmas, in which we can rest. We don't lie back upon them, we move forward, and, on occasion, make nature over again by their aid. Pragmatism unstiffens all our theories, limbers them up and sets each one at work. Being nothing essentially new, it harmonizes with many ancient philosophic tendencies. It agrees with nominalism for instance, in always appealing to particulars; with utilitarianism in emphasizing practical aspects; with positivism in its disdain for verbal solutions, useless questions and metaphysical abstractions.

All these, you see, are *anti-intellectualist* tendencies. Against rationalism as a pretension and a method pragmatism is fully armed and militant. But, at the outset, at least, it stands for no particular results. It has no dogmas, and no doctrines save its method. As the young Italian pragmatist Papini has well said, it lies in the midst of our theories, like a corridor in a hotel. Innumerable chambers open out of it. In one you may find a man writing an atheistic volume; in the next some one on his knees praying for faith and strength; in a third a chemist investigating a body's properties. In a fourth a system of idealistic metaphysics is being excogitated; in a fifth the impossibility of metaphysics is being shown. But they all own the corridor, and all must pass through it if they want a practicable way of getting into or out of their respective rooms.

No particular results then, so far, but only an attitude of orientation, is what the pragmatic method means. *The attitude of looking away from first things, principles, 'categories,' supposed necessities; and of looking towards last things, fruits, consequences, facts.* Deductive Reasoning ?

So much for the pragmatic method! You may say that I have been praising it rather than explaining it to you, but I shall presently explain it abundantly enough by showing how it works on some familiar problems. Meanwhile the word pragmatism has come to be used in a still wider sense, as meaning also a certain *theory of truth*. I mean to give a whole lecture to the statement of that theory, after first paving the way, so I can be very brief now. But brevity is hard to follow, so I ask for your redoubled attention for a quarter of an hour. If much remains obscure, I hope to make it clearer in the later lectures.

One of the most successfully cultivated branches of philosophy in our time is what is called inductive logic, the study of the conditions under which our sciences have evolved. Writers on this subject have begun to show a singular unanimity as to what the laws of nature and elements of fact mean, when formulated by mathematicians, physicists and chemists. When the first mathematical, logical, and natural uniformities, the first *laws,* were discovered, men were so carried away by the clearness, beauty and simplification that resulted, that they believed themselves to have deciphered authentically the eternal thoughts of the Almighty. His mind also thundered and reverberated in syllogisms. He also thought in conic sections, squares and roots and ratios, and geometrized like Euclid. He made Kepler's laws for the planets to follow; he made velocity increase proportionally to the time in falling bodies; he made the law of the sines for light to obey when refracted; he established the classes, orders, families and genera of plants and animals, and fixed the distances between them. He thought the archetypes of all things, and devised their variations; and when we rediscover any one of these his wondrous institutions, we seize his mind in its very literal intention.

But as the sciences have developed farther, the notion has gained ground that most, perhaps all, of our laws are only approximations. The laws themselves, moreover, have grown so numerous that there is no counting them; and so many rival formulations are proposed in all the branches of science that investigators have become accustomed to the notion that no theory is absolutely a transcript of reality, but that any one of them may from some point of view be useful. Their great use is to summarize old facts and to lead to new ones. They are only a man-made language, a conceptual shorthand, as some one calls them, in which we write our reports of nature; and languages, as is well known, tolerate much choice of expression and many dialects. . . .

Riding now on the front of this wave of scientific logic Messrs. Schiller and Dewey appear with their pragmatistic account of what truth everywhere signifies. Everywhere, these teachers say, 'truth' in our ideas and beliefs means the same thing that it means in science. It means, they say, nothing but this, *that ideas (which themselves are but parts of our experience) become true just in so far as they help us to get into satisfactory relation with other parts of our experience,* to summarize them and get about among them by conceptual short-cuts instead of following the interminable succession of particular phenomena. Any idea upon which we can ride, so to speak; any idea that will carry us prosperously from any one part of our experience to any other part, linking things satisfactorily, working securely, simplifying, saving labor; is true for just so much, true in so far forth, true *instrumentally.* This is the 'instrumental' view of truth taught so successfully at Chicago, the view that truth in our ideas means their power to 'work,' promulgated so brilliantly at Oxford.

Messrs. Dewey, Schiller and their allies, in reaching this general conception of all truth, have only followed the example of geologists, biologists and philologists. In the establishment of these other sciences, the successful stroke was always to take some simple process actually observable in operation—as denudation by weather, say, or variation from parental type, or change of dialect by incorporation of new words and pronunciations—and then to generalize it, making it apply to all times, and produce great results by summating its effects through the ages.

The observable process which Schiller and Dewey particularly singled out for generalization is the familiar one by which any individual settles into *new opinions.* The process here is always the same. The individual has a stock of old opinions already, but he meets a new experience that puts them to a strain. Somebody contradicts them; or in a reflective moment he discovers that they contradict each other; or he hears of facts with which they are incompatible; or desires arise in him which they cease to satisfy. The result is an inward trouble to which his mind till then had been a stranger, and from which he seeks to escape by modifying his previous mass of opinions. He saves as much of it as he can, for in this matter of belief we are all extreme conservatives. So he tries to change first this opinion, and then that (for they resist change very variously), until at last some new idea comes up which he can graft upon the ancient stock with a minimum of disturbance of the latter, some idea that mediates between the stock and the new experience and runs them into one another most felicitously and expediently.

This new idea is then adopted as the true one. It preserves the

Everything is Relative

older stock of truths with a minimum of modification, stretching them just enough to make them admit the novelty, but conceiving that in ways as familiar as the case leaves possible. An *outrée* explanation, violating all our preconceptions, would never pass for a true account of a novelty. We should scratch round industriously till we found something less excentric. The most violent revolutions in an individual's beliefs leave most of his old order standing. Time and space, cause and effect, nature and history, and one's own biography remain untouched. New truth is always a go-between, a smoother-over of transitions. It marries old opinion to new fact so as ever to show a minimum of jolt, a maximum of continuity. We hold a theory true just in proportion to its success in solving this 'problem of maxima and minima.' But success in solving this problem is eminently a matter of approximation. We say this theory solves it on the whole more satisfactorily than that theory; but that means more satisfactorily to ourselves, and individuals will emphasize their points of satisfaction differently. To a certain degree, therefore, everything here is plastic.

Old truths are the basis of new truths ; no new thought only re-evaluation

The point I now urge you to observe particularly is the part played by the older truths. Failure to take account of it is the source of much of the unjust criticism levelled against pragmatism. Their influence is absolutely controlling. Loyalty to them is the first principle—in most cases it is the only principle. . . .

You will probably be surprised to learn, then, that Messrs. Schiller's and Dewey's theories have suffered a hailstorm of contempt and ridicule. All rationalism has risen against them. In influential quarters Mr. Schiller, in particular, has been treated like an impudent schoolboy who deserves a spanking. I should not mention this, but for the fact that it throws so much sidelight upon that rationalistic temper to which I have opposed the temper of pragmatism. Pragmatism is uncomfortable away from facts. Rationalism is comfortable only in the presence of abstractions. This pragmatist talk about truths in the plural, about their utility and satisfactoriness, about the success with which they 'work,' etc., suggests to the typical intellectualist mind a sort of coarse lame second-rate makeshift article of truth. Such truths are not real truth. Such tests are merely subjective. As against this, objective truth must be something non-utilitarian, haughty, refined, remote, august, exalted. It must be an absolute correspondence of our thoughts with an equally absolute reality. It must be *compared* — *Prag. doesn't offer the "truth" but only tells why people should follow it & use it,*

what we *ought* to think unconditionally. The conditioned ways in which we *do* think are so much irrelevance and matter for psychology. Down with psychology, up with logic, in all this question!

See the exquisite contrast of the types of mind! The pragmatist clings to facts and concreteness, observes truth at its work in particular cases, and generalizes. Truth, for him, becomes a class-name for all sorts of definite working-values in experience. For the rationalist it remains a pure abstraction, to the bare name of which we must defer. When the pragmatist undertakes to show in detail just *why* we must defer, the rationalist is unable to recognize the concretes from which his own abstraction is taken. He accuses us of *denying* truth; whereas we have only sought to trace exactly why people follow it and always ought to follow it. Your typical ultra-abstractionist fairly shudders at concreteness: other things equal, he positively prefers the pale and spectral. If the two universes were offered, he would always choose the skinny outline rather than the rich thicket of reality. It is so much purer, clearer, nobler. . . .

Men who are strongly of the fact-loving temperament, you may remember me to have said, are liable to be kept at a distance by the small sympathy with facts which that philosophy from the present-day fashion of idealism offers them. It is far too intellectualistic. Old fashioned theism was bad enough, with its notion of God as an exalted monarch, made up of a lot of unintelligible or preposterous 'attributes'; but, so long as it held strongly by the argument from design, it kept some touch with concrete realities. Since, however, darwinism has once for all displaced design from the minds of the 'scientific,' theism has lost that foothold; and some kind of an immanent or pantheistic deity working *in* things rather than above them is, if any, the kind recommended to our contemporary imagination. Aspirants to a philosophic religion turn, as a rule, more hopefully nowadays towards idealistic pantheism than towards the older dualistic theism, in spite of the fact that the latter still counts able defenders. . . .

Prag. brings philo. down to the concrete realities,

Now pragmatism, devoted though she be to facts, has no such materialistic bias as ordinary empiricism labors under. Moreover, she has no objection whatever to the realizing of abstractions, so long as you get about among particulars with their aid and they actually carry you somewhere. Interested in no conclusions but those which our minds and our experiences work out together, she has no *a priori* prejudices against theology. *If theological ideas prove to have a value for concrete life, they will be true, for pragmatism, in the sense of being good for so much. For how much more they are true, will depend entirely on their relations to the other truths that also have to be acknowledged.*

What I said just now about the Absolute, of transcendental idealism, is a case in point. First, I called it majestic and said it yielded religious comfort to a class of minds, and then I accused it of remoteness and sterility. But so far as it affords such comfort, it surely is not sterile; it has that amount of value; it performs a concrete function. As a good pragmatist, I myself ought to call the Absolute true 'in so far forth,' then; and I unhesitatingly now do so.

But what does *true in so far forth* mean in this case? To answer, we need only apply the pragmatic method. What do believers in the Absolute mean by saying that their belief affords them comfort? They mean that since, in the Absolute finite evil is 'overruled' already, we may, therefore, whenever we wish, treat the temporal as if it were potentially the eternal, be sure that we can trust its outcome, and, without sin, dismiss our fear and drop the worry of our finite responsibility. In short, they mean that we have a right ever and anon to take a moral holiday, to let the world wag in its own way, feeling that its issues are in better hands than ours and are none of our business.

The universe is a system of which the individual members may relax their anxieties occasionally, in which the don't-care mood is also right for men, and moral holidays in order,—that, if I mistake not, is part, at least, of what the Absolute is 'known-as,' that is the great difference in our particular experiences which his being true makes, for us, that is his cash-value when he is pragmatically interpreted. Farther than that the ordinary lay-reader in philosophy who thinks favorably of absolute idealism does not venture to sharpen his conceptions. He can use the Absolute for so much, and so much is very precious. He is pained at hearing you speak incredulously of the Absolute, therefore, and disregards your criticisms because they deal with aspects of the conception that he fails to follow.

If the Absolute means this, and means no more than this, who can possibly deny the truth of it? To deny it would be to insist that men should never relax, and that holidays are never in order.

I am well aware how odd it must seem to some of you to hear

me say that an idea is 'true' so long as to believe it is profitable to our lives. That it is *good,* for as much as it profits, you will gladly admit. If what we do by its aid is good, you will allow the idea itself to be good in so far forth, for we are the better for possessing it. But is it not a strange misuse of the word 'truth,' you will say, to call ideas also 'true' for this reason?

To answer this difficulty fully is impossible at this stage of my account. You touch here upon the very central point of Messrs. Schiller's, Dewey's and my own doctrine of truth, which I can not discuss with detail until my sixth lecture. Let me now say only this, that truth is *one species of good,* and not, as is usually supposed, a category distinct from good, and co-ordinate with it. *The true is the name of whatever proves itself to be good in the way of belief, and good, too, for definite, assignable reasons.* Surely you must admit this, that if there were *no* good for life in true ideas, or if the knowledge of them were positively disadvantageous and false ideas the only useful ones, then the current notion that truth is divine and precious, and its pursuit a duty, could never have grown up or become a dogma. In a world like that, our duty would be to *shun* truth, rather. But in this world, just as certain foods are not only agreeable to our taste, but good for our teeth, our stomach, and our tissues; so certain ideas are not only agreeable to think about, or agreeable as supporting other ideas that we are fond of, but they are also helpful in life's practical struggles. If there be any life that it is really better we should lead, and if there be any idea which, if believed in, would help us to lead that life, then it would be really *better for us* to believe in that idea, *unless, indeed, belief in it incidentally clashed with other greater vital benefits.*

'What would be better for us to believe'! This sounds very like a definition of truth. It comes very near to saying 'what we *ought* to believe': and in *that* definition none of you would find any oddity. Ought we ever not to believe what it is *bettter for us* to believe? And can we then keep the notion of what is better for us, and what is true for us, permanently apart?

Pragmatism says no, and I fully agree with her. Probably you also agree, so far as the abstract statement goes, but with a suspicion that if we practically did believe everything that made for good in our own personal lives, we should be found indulging all kinds of fancies about this world's affairs, and all kinds of sentimental superstitions about a world hereafter. Your suspicion here

inseperable

is undoubtedly well founded, and it is evident that something happens when you pass from the abstract to the concrete that complicates the situation.

I said just now that what is better for us to believe is true *unless the belief incidentally clashes with some other vital benefit*. Now in real life what vital benefits is any particular belief of ours most liable to clash with? What indeed except the vital benefits yielded by *other beliefs* when these prove incompatible with the first ones? In other words, the greatest enemy of any one of our truths may be the rest of our truths. Truths have once for all this desperate instinct of self-preservation and of desire to extinguish whatever contradicts them. My belief in the Absolute, based on the good it does me, must run the gauntlet of all my other beliefs. Grant that it may be true in giving me a moral holiday. Nevertheless, as I conceive it,—and let me speak now confidentially, as it were, and merely in my own private person,—it clashes with other truths of mine whose benefits I hate to give up on its account. It happens to be associated with a kind of logic of which I am the enemy, I find that it entangles me in metaphysical paradoxes that are inacceptable, etc., etc. But as I have enough trouble in life already without adding the trouble of carrying these intellectual inconsistencies, I personally just give up the Absolute. I just *take* my moral holidays; or else as a professional philosopher, I try to justify them by some other principle.

If I could restrict my notion of the Absolute to its bare holiday-giving value, it wouldn't clash with my other truths. But we can not easily thus restrict our hypotheses. They carry supernumerary features, and these it is that clash so. My disbelief in the Absolute means then disbelief in those other supernumerary features, for I fully believe in the legitimacy of taking moral holidays.

You see by this what I meant when I called pragmatism a mediator and reconciler and said, borrowing the word from Papini, that she 'unstiffens' our theories. She has in fact no prejudices whatever, no obstructive dogmas, no rigid canons of what shall count as proof. She is completely genial. She will entertain any hypothesis, she will consider any evidence. It follows that in the religious field she is at a great advantage both over positivistic empiricism, with its anti-theological bias, and over religious rationalism, with its exclusive interest in the remote, the noble, the simple, and the abstract in the way of conception.

Papini ?

In short, she widens the field of search for God. Rationalism sticks to logic and the empyrean. Empiricism sticks to the external senses. Pragmatism is willing to take anything, to follow either logic or the senses and to count the humblest and most personal experiences. She will count mystical experiences if they have practical consequences. She will take a God who lives in the very dirt of private fact—if that should seem a likely place to find him.

Her only test of probable truth is what works best in the way of leading us, what fits every part of life best and combines with the collectivity of experience's demands, nothing being omitted. If theological ideas should do this, if the notion of God, in particular, should prove to do it, how could pragmatism possibly deny God's existence? She could see no meaning in treating as 'not true' a notion that was pragmatically so successful. What other kind of truth could there be, for her, than all this agreement with concrete reality?

THE INFLUENCE OF
DARWINISM ON PHILOSOPHY*

By John Dewey

John Dewey (1859–1952) finds that Darwinism overthrew absolutist philosophies and shifted attention to social action

John Dewey, born in Burlington, Vermont, of a grocer who was also a Civil War quartermaster, studied at the University of Vermont where he became interested in Darwinism and Comte's scientific positivism. He completed his graduate work in philosophy at Johns Hopkins University, being especially influenced by Hegelian idealism with its principles of historical continuity and by the laboratory psychology of G. Stanley Hall; he was also influenced by Charles S. Peirce, founder of pragmatism.

During 1884–94, Dewey taught philosophy at the University of Michigan (except for a year at the University of Minnesota) and

* From John Dewey, *The Influence of Darwinism on Philosophy* (Holt, 1910), 9–19.

became deeply interested in educational psychology. His *Applied Psychology* (1889) based the learning process upon the interests and activities of the child and eliminated the practice of mere rote learning. In 1894, President William R. Harper of the University of Chicago invited him to come as chairman of a combined department of philosophy, psychology, and pedagogy; in addition Dewey directed a laboratory elementary school that became famous as the "Dewey School." But, in 1904, he quarreled with Harper and left for Columbia University where he remained until retirement.

His *Democracy and Education* (1916) became the teacher's guide for introducing his democratic variety of progressive education. While rejecting indoctrination, he sought to make the school a miniature society, and environment that would stimulate the child and serve to inculcate in him democratic habits of self-reliance and healthful social attitudes. He revitalized Froebel's "learning by doing" in the progressive Swiss-Prussian tradition of a century before. Like his associate Thorstein Veblen, at Chicago and the New School for Social Research, which he helped found in 1919, he rejected leisure class education and identified himself with the great controversies of his time whether in education, civil rights, socialist panaceas, or the issues of war.

Conservatives disliked Dewey's secularism and his constant concern for social reconstruction. They assailed him for many imaginary crimes (although some may have been committed by enthusiastic but ill-informed disciples), such as "softness" in education, indifference to discipline, the "fads and frills" that burdened taxpayers, the erroneously conceived life-adjustment mission of education, and internationalism. Some attributed to him bad teaching methods that inhibited the learning of reading ("Johnny Can't Read") and other skills. During the conservative 1950's, he became the symbol for many of the alleged defects of American education, but innumerable academicians continued to find in Dewey a limitless source of educational theories.

One of his famous essays given here, "The Influence of Darwinism on Philosophy," taken from a book of that title, explains how Darwin's idea that the organism evolved through chance variations rather than design destroyed the old idealistic philosophy that ignored social action and experimentation. The second essay, "My Pedagogic Creed," is a remarkable condensation of the educational philosophy Dewey held throughout his life, although written at this early date (1897). Note his emphasis upon the social role of the school and the stimulation of real life situations rather than a dependence upon the resources of the teacher alone. Here are his ideas of the "continuing reconstruction of experience" and the belief that since future vocational demands cannot be forecast, training must be very broad and basic indeed.

1

THE EXACT bearings upon philosophy of the new logical out-look are, of course, as yet, uncertain and inchoate. We live in the twilight of intellectual transition. One must add the rashness of the prophet to the stubbornness of the partizan to venture a systematic exposition of the influence upon philosophy of the Darwinian method. At best, we can but inquire as to its general bearing—the effect upon mental temper and complexion, upon that body of half-conscious, half-instinctive intellectual aversions and preferences which determine, after all, our more deliberate intellectual enterprises. In this vague inquiry there happens to exist as a kind of touchstone a problem of long historic currency that has also been much discussed in Darwinian literature. I refer to the old problem of design *versus* chance, mind *versus* matter, as the causal explanation, first or final, of things.

As we have already seen, the classic notion of species carried with it the idea of purpose. In all living forms, a specific type is present directing the earlier stages of growth to the realization of its own perfection. Since this purposive regulative principle is not visible to the senses, it follows that it must be an ideal or rational force. Since, however, the perfect form is gradually approximated through the sensible changes, it also follows that in and through a sensible realm a rational ideal force is working out its own ultimate manifestation. These inferences were extended to nature: (a) She does nothing in vain; but all for an ulterior purpose. (b) Within natural sensible events there is therefore contained a spiritual causal force, which as spiritual escapes perception, but is apprehended by an enlightened reason. (c) The manifestation of this principle brings about a subordination of matter and sense to its own realization, and this ultimate fulfilment is the goal of nature and of man. The design argument thus operated in two directions. Purposefulness accounted for the intelligibility of nature and the possibility of science, while the absolute or cosmic character of this purposefulness gave sanction and worth to the moral and religious endeavors of man. Science was underpinned and morals authorized by one and the same principle, and their mutual agreement was eternally guaranteed.

This philosophy remained, in spite of sceptical and polemic outbursts, the official and the regnant philosophy of Europe for over two thousand years. The expulsion of fixed first and final causes from astronomy, physics, and chemistry had indeed given the doctrine something of a shock. But, on the other hand, increased acquaintance with the details of plant and animal life operated as a counterbalance and perhaps even strengthened the argument from design. The marvelous adaptations of organisms to their environment, of organs to the organism, of unlike parts of a complex organ—like the eye—to the organ itself; the foreshadowing by lower forms of the higher; the preparation in earlier stages of growth for organs that only later had their functioning —these things were increasingly recognized with the progress of botany, zoology, paleontology, and embryology. Together, they added such prestige to the design argument that by the late eighteenth century it was, as approved by the sciences of organic life, the central point of theistic and idealistic philosophy.

The Darwinian principle of natural selection cut straight under this philosophy. If all organic adaptations are due simply to constant variation and the elimination of those variations which are harmful in the struggle for existence that is brought about by excessive reproduction, there is no call for a prior intelligent causal force to plan and preordain them. Hostile critics charged Darwin with materialism and with making chance the cause of the universe.

Some naturalists, like Asa Gray, favored the Darwinian principle and attempted to reconcile it with design. Gray held to what may be called design on the installment plan. If we conceive the "stream of variations" to be itself intended, we may suppose that each successive variation was designed from the first to be selected. In that case, variation, struggle, and selection simply define the mechanism of "secondary causes" through which the "first cause" acts; and the doctrine of design is none the worse off because we know more of its *modus operandi*.

Darwin could not accept this mediating proposal. He admits or rather he asserts that it is "impossible to conceive this immense and wonderful universe including man with his capacity of looking far backwards and far into futurity as the result of blind chance or necessity." [1] But nevertheless he holds that since variations are in useless as well as useful directions, and since the latter are sifted out simply by the stress of the conditions of struggle for existence, the design argument as applied to living beings is unjustifiable; and its lack of support there deprives it of

[1] "Life and Letters," Vol. I., p. 282; cf. 285.

scientific value as applied to nature in general. If the variations of the pigeon, which under artificial selection give the pouter pigeon, are not preordained for the sake of the breeder, by what logic do we argue that variations resulting in natural species are pre-designed? *

2

So much for some of the more obvious facts of the discussion of design *versus* chance, as causal principles of nature and of life as a whole. We brought up this discussion, you recall, as a crucial instance. What does our touchstone indicate as to the bearing of Darwinian ideas upon philosophy? In the first place, the new logic outlaws, flanks, dismisses—what you will—one type of problems and substitutes for it another type. Philosophy forswears inquiry after absolute origins and absolute finalities in order to explore specific values and the specific conditions that generate them.

Darwin concluded that the impossibility of assigning the world to chance as a whole and to design in its parts indicated the insolubility of the question. Two radically different reasons, however, may be given as to why a problem is insoluble. One reason is that the problem is too high for intelligence; the other is that the question in its very asking makes assumptions that render the question meaningless. The latter alternative is unerringly pointed to in the celebrated case of design *versus* chance. Once admit that the sole verifiable or fruitful object of knowledge is the particular set of changes that generate the object of study together with the consequences that then flow from it, and no intelligible question can be asked about what, by assumption, lies outside. To assert—as is often asserted—that specific values of particular truth, social bonds and form of beauty, if they can be shown to be generated by concretely knowable conditions, are meaningless and in vain; to assert that they are justified only when they and their particular causes and effects have all at once been gathered up into some inclusive first cause and some exhaustive final goal, is intellectual atavism. Such argumentation is reversion to the logic that explained the extinction of fire by

---

* "Life and Letters," Vol. II., pp. 146, 170, 245; Vol. I., pp. 283–84. See also the closing portion of his "Variations of Animals and Plants under Domestication."

water through the formal essence of aqueousness and the quenching of thirst by water through the final cause of aqueousness. Whether used in the case of the special event or that of life as a whole, such logic only abstracts some aspect of the existing course of events in order to reduplicate it as a petrified eternal principle by which to explain the very changes of which it is the formalization.

When Henry Sidgwick casually remarked in a letter that as he grew older his interest in what or who made the world was altered into interest in what kind of a world it is anyway, his voicing of a common experience of our own day illustrates also the nature of that intellectual transformation effected by the Darwinian logic. Interest shifts from the wholesale essence back of special changes to the question of how special changes serve and defeat concrete purposes; shifts from an intelligence that shaped things once for all to the particular intelligences which things are even now shaping; shifts from an ultimate goal of good to the direct increments of justice and happiness that intelligent administration of existent conditions may beget and that present carelessness or stupidity will destroy or forego.

In the second place, the classic type of logic inevitably set philosophy upon proving that life *must* have certain qualities and values—no matter how experience presents the matter—because of some remote cause and eventual goal. The duty of wholesale justification inevitably accompanies all thinking that makes the meaning of special occurrences depend upon something that once and for all lies behind them. The habit of derogating from present meanings and uses prevents our looking the facts of experience in the face; it prevents serious acknowledgment of the evils they present and serious concern with the goods they promise but do not as yet fulfil. It turns thought to the business of finding a wholesale transcendent remedy for the one and guarantee for the other. One is reminded of the way many moralists and theologians greeted Herbert Spencer's recognition of an unknowable energy from which welled up the phenomenal physical process without and the conscious operations within. Merely because Spencer labeled his unknowable energy "God," this faded piece of metaphysical goods was greeted as an important and grateful concession to the reality of the spiritual realm. Were it not for the deep hold of the habit of seeking justification for ideal values in the remote and transcendent, surely this reference of them to an unknowable absolute would be despised in comparison with the demonstrations of experience that knowable energies are daily generating about us precious values.

The displacing of this wholesale type of philosophy will doubtless not arrive by sheer logical disproof, but rather by growing recognition of its futility. Were it a thousand times true that opium produces sleep because of its dormitive energy, yet the inducing of sleep in the tired, and the recovery to waking life of the poisoned, would not be thereby one least step forwarded. And were it a thousand times dialectically demonstrated that life as a whole is regulated by a transcendent principle to a final inclusive goal, none the less truth and error, health and disease, good and evil, hope and fear in the concrete, would remain just what and where they now are. To improve our education, to ameliorate our manners, to advance our politics, we must have recourse to specific conditions of generation.

Finally, the new logic introduces responsibility into the intellectual life. To idealize and rationalize the universe at large is after all a confession of inability to master the courses of things that specifically concern us. As long as mankind suffered from this impotency, it naturally shifted a burden of responsibility that it could not carry over to the more competent shoulders of the transcendent cause. But if insight into specific conditions of value and into specific consequences of ideas is possible, philosophy must in time become a method of locating and interpreting the more serious of the conflicts that occur in life, and a method of projecting ways for dealing with them: a method of moral and political diagnosis and prognosis.

The claim to formulate *a priori* the legislative constitution of the universe is by its nature a claim that may lead to elaborate dialectic developments. But it is also one that removes these very conclusions from subjection to experimental test, for, by definition, these results make no differences in the detailed course of events. But a philosophy that humbles its pretensions to the work of projecting hypotheses for the education and conduct of mind, individual and social, is thereby subjected to test by the way in which the ideas it propounds work out in practice. In having modesty forced upon it, philosophy also acquires responsibility.

Doubtless I seem to have violated the implied promise of my earlier remarks and to have turned both prophet and partisan. But in anticipating the direction of the transformations in philosophy to be wrought by the Darwinian genetic and experimental logic, I do not profess to speak for any save those who yield themselves consciously or unconsciously to this logic. No one can fairly deny that at present there are two effects of the Darwinian mode of thinking. On the one hand, there are many making sincere and vital efforts to revise our traditional philosophic conceptions in accordance with its demands. On the other hand, there is as definitely a recrudescence of absolutistic philosophies; an assertion of a type of philosophic knowing distinct from that of the sciences, one which opens to us another kind of reality from that to which the sciences give access; an appeal through experience to something that essentially goes beyond experience. This reaction affects popular creeds and religious movements as well as technical philosophies. The very conquest of the biological sciences by the new ideas has led many to proclaim an explicit and rigid separation of philosophy from science.

Old ideas give way slowly; for they are more than abstract logical forms and categories. They are habits, predispositions, deeply engrained attitudes of aversion and preference. Moreover, the conviction persists—though history shows it to be a hallucination—that all the questions that the human mind has asked are questions that can be answered in terms of the alternatives that the questions themselves present. But in fact intellectual progress usually occurs through sheer abandonment of questions together with both of the alternatives they assume—an abandonment that results from their decreasing vitality and a change of urgent interest. We do not solve them: we get over them. Old questions are solved by disappearing, evaporating, while new questions corresponding to the changed attitude of endeavor and preference take their place. Doubtless the greatest dissolvent in contemporary thought of old questions, the greatest precipitant of new methods, new intentions, new problems, is the one effected by the scientific revolution that found its climax in the "Origin of Species."

"MY PEDAGOGIC CREED" *

By John Dewey

ARTICLE I What Education Is

I believe that all education proceeds by the participation of the individual in the social consciousness of the race. This process begins unconsciously almost at birth, and is continually shaping the individual's powers, saturating his consciousness, forming his habits, training his ideas, and arousing his feelings and emotions. Through this unconscious education the individual gradually comes to share in the intellectual and moral resources which humanity has succeeded in getting together. He becomes an inheritor of the funded capital of civilization. The most formal and technical education in the world cannot safely depart from this general process. It can only organize it or differentiate it in some particular direction.

I believe that the only true education comes through the stimulation of the child's powers by the demands of the social situations in which he finds himself. Through these demands he is stimulated to act as a member of a unity, to emerge from his original narrowness of action and feeling, and to conceive of himself from the standpoint of the welfare of the group to which he belongs. Through the responses which others make to his own activities he comes to know what these mean in social terms. The value which they have is reflected back into them. For instance, through the response which is made to the child's instinctive babblings the child comes to know what those babblings mean; they are transformed into articulate language and thus the child is introduced into the consolidated wealth of ideas and emotions which are now summed up in language.

I believe that this educational process has two sides—one psychological and one sociological; and that neither can be subordinated to the other or neglected without evil results following. Of these two sides, the psychological is the basis. The child's own

* From John Dewey, "My Pedagogic Creed," *The School Journal*, vol. LIV, No. 3 (January 16, 1897), 77–80.

instincts and powers furnish the material and give the starting point for all education. Save as the efforts of the educator connect with some activity which the child is carrying on of his own initiative independent of the educator, education becomes reduced to a pressure from without. It may, indeed, give certain external results, but cannot truly be called educative. Without insight into the psychological structure and activities of the individual, the educative process will, therefore, be haphazard and arbitrary. If it chances to coincide with the child's activity it will get a leverage; if it does not, it will result in friction, or disintegration, or arrest of the child nature.

I believe that knowledge of social conditions, of the present state of civilization, is necessary in order properly to interpret the child's powers. The child has his own instincts and tendencies, but we do not know what these mean until we can translate them into their social equivalents. We must be able to carry them back into a social past and see them as the inheritance of previous race activities. We must also be able to project them into the future to see what their outcome and end will be. In the illustration just used, it is the ability to see in the child's babblings the promise and potency of a future social intercourse and conversation which enables one to deal in the proper way with that instinct.

I believe that the psychological and social sides are organically related and that education cannot be regarded as a compromise between the two, or a superimposition of one upon the other. We are told that the psychological definition of education is barren and formal—that it gives us only the idea of a development of all the mental powers without giving us any idea of the use to which these powers are put. On the other hand, it is urged that the social definition of education, as getting adjusted to civilization, makes of it a forced and external process, and results in subordinating the freedom of the individual to a preconceived social and political status.

I believe that each of these objections is true when urged against one side isolated from the other. In order to know what a power really is we must know what its end, use, or function is; and this we cannot know save as we conceive of the individual as active in social relationships. But, on the other hand, the only possible adjustment which we can give to the child under existing conditions, is that which arises through putting him in com-

With times △ing, educ. can never foresee the future conditions.

plete possession of all his powers. With the advent of democracy and modern industrial conditions, it is impossible to foretell definitely just what civilization will be twenty years from now. Hence it is impossible to prepare the child for any precise set of conditions. To prepare him for the future life means to give him command of himself; it means so to train him that he will have the full and ready use of all his capacities; that his eye and ear and hand may be tools ready to command, that his judgment may be capable of grasping the conditions under which it has to work, and the executive forces be trained to act economically and efficiently. It is impossible to reach this sort of adjustment save as constant regard is had to the individual's own powers, tastes, and interests—say, that is, as education is continually converted into psychological terms.

In sum, I believe that the individual who is to be educated is a social individual and that society is an organic union of individuals. If we eliminate the social factor from the child we are left only with an abstraction; if we eliminate the individual factor from society, we are left only with an inert and lifeless mass. Education, therefore, must begin with a psychological insight into the child's capacities, interests, and habits. It must be controlled at every point by reference to these same considerations. These powers, interests, and habits must be continually interpreted —we must know what they mean. They must be translated into terms of their social equivalents—into terms of what they are capable of in the way of social service.

ARTICLE II *What the School Is*

Progressive educ. should be more relevant.

I believe that the school is primarily a social institution. Education being a social process, the school is simply that form of community life in which all those agencies are concentrated that will be most effective in bringing the child to share in the inherited resources of the race, and to use his own powers for social ends.

I believe that education, therefore, is a process of living and not a preparation for future living.

I believe that the school must represent present life—life as real and vital to the child as that which he carries on in the home, in the neighborhood, or on the playground.

I believe that education which does not occur through forms

Educ.—process of living not a preparation for future living.

of life, or that are worth living for their own sake, is always a poor substitute for the genuine reality and tends to cramp and to deaden.

I believe that the school, as an institution, should simplify existing social life; should reduce it, as it were, to an embryonic form. Existing life is so complex that the child cannot be brought into contact with it without either confusion or distraction; he is either overwhelmed by the multiplicity of activities which are going on, so that he loses his own power of orderly reaction, or he is so stimulated by these various activities that his powers are prematurely called into play and he becomes either unduly specialized or else disintegrated.

I believe that as such simplified social life, the school life should grow gradually out of the home life; that it should take up and continue the activities with which the child is already familiar in the home.

I believe that it should exhibit these activities to the child, and reproduce them in such ways that the child will gradually learn the meaning of them, and be capable of playing his own part in relation to them.

I believe that this is a psychological necessity, because it is the only way of securing continuity in the child's growth, the only way of giving a back-ground of past experience to the new ideas given in school.

I believe that it is also a social necessity because the home is the form of social life in which the child has been nurtured and in connection with which he has had his moral training. It is the business of the school to deepen and extend his sense of the values bound up in his home life.

I believe that much of present education fails because it neglects this fundamental principle of the school as a form of community life. It conceives the school as a place where certain information is to be given, where certain lessons are to be learned, or where certain habits are to be formed. The value of these is conceived as lying largely in the remote future; the child must do these things for the sake of something else he is to do; they are mere preparation. As a result they do not become a part of the life experience of the child and so are not truly educative.

I believe that the moral education centers upon this conception of the school as a mode of social life, that the best and deepest moral training is precisely that which one gets through

If one's purpose is to live in society why not prepare him w/ society; rather than memorization.

"MY PEDAGOGIC CREED" 157.

having to enter into proper relations with others in a unity of work and thought. The present educational systems, so far as they destroy or neglect this unity, render it difficult or impossible to get any genuine, regular moral training.

I believe that the child should be stimulated and controlled in his work through the life of the community.

I believe that under existing conditions far too much of the stimulus and control proceeds from the teacher, because of neglect of the idea of the school as a form of social life.

I believe that the teacher's place and work in the school is to be interpreted from this same basis. The teacher is not in the school to impose certain ideas or to form certain habits in the child, but is there as a member of the community to select the influences which shall affect the child and to assist him in properly responding to these influences.

I believe that the discipline of the school should proceed from the life of the school as a whole and not directly from the teacher. *uniform discipline*

I believe that the teacher's business is simply to determine on the basis of larger experience and riper wisdom, how the discipline of life shall come to the child.

I believe that all questions of the grading of the child and his promotion should be determined by reference to the same standard. Examinations are of use only so far as they test the child's fitness for social life and reveal the place in which he can be of the most service and where he can receive the most help.

ARTICLE III The Subject-Matter of Education

I believe that the social life of the child is the basis of concentration, or correlation, in all his training or growth. The social life gives the unconscious unity and the background of all his efforts and of all his attainments.

I believe that the subject-matter of the school curriculum should mark a gradual differentiation out of the primitive unconscious unity of social life.

I believe that we violate the child's nature and render difficult the best ethical results, by introducing the child too abruptly to a number of special studies, of reading, writing, geography, etc., out of relation to this social life.

I believe, therefore, that the true center of correlation on the

Do your thing

school subjects is not science, nor literature, nor history, nor geography, but the child's own social activities.

I believe that education cannot be unified in the study of science, or so-called nature study, because apart from human activity, nature itself is not a unity; nature in itself is a number of diverse objects in space and time, and to attempt to make it the center of work by itself, is to introduce a principle of radiation rather than one of concentration.

I believe that literature is the reflex expression and interpretation of social experience; that hence it must follow upon and not precede such experience. It, therefore, cannot be made the basis, although it may be made the summary of unification.

History

I believe once more that history is of educative value in so far as it presents phases of social life and growth. It must be controlled by reference to social life. When taken simply as history it is thrown into the distant past and becomes dead and inert. Taken as the record of man's social life and progress it becomes full of meaning. I believe, however, that it cannot be so taken excepting as the child is also introduced directly into social life.

I believe accordingly that the primary basis of education is in the child's powers at work along the same general constructive lines as those which have brought civilization into being.

I believe that the only way to make the child conscious of his social heritage is to enable him to perform those fundamental types of activity which make civilization what it is.

I believe, therefore, in the so-called expressive or constructive activities as the center of correlation.

I believe that this gives the standard for the place of cooking, sewing, manual training, etc., in the school.

I believe that they are not special studies which are to be introduced over and above a lot of others in the way of relaxation or relief, or as additional accomplishments. I believe rather that they represent, as types, fundamental forms of social activity; and that it is possible and desirable that the child's introduction into the more formal subjects of the curriculum be through the medium of these activities.

I believe that the study of science is educational in so far as it brings out the materials and processes which make social life what it is.

I believe that one of the greatest difficulties in the present teaching of science is that the material is presented in purely objective form, or is treated as a new peculiar kind of experience which the child can add to that which he has already had. In reality, science is of value because it gives the ability to interpret and control the experience already had. It should be introduced, not as so much new subject-matter, but as showing the factors already involved in previous experience and as furnishing tools by which that experience can be more easily and effectively regulated.

I believe that at present we lose much of the value of literature and language studies because of our elimination of the social element. Language is almost always treated in the books of pedagogy simply as the expression of thought. It is true that language is a logical instrument, but it is fundamentally and primarily a social instrument. Language is the device for communication; it is the tool through which one individual comes to share the ideas and feelings of others. When treated simply as a way of getting individual information, or as a means of showing off what one has learned, it loses its social motive and end.

I believe that there is, therefore, no succession of studies in the ideal school curriculum. If education is life, all life has, from the outset, a scientific aspect, an aspect of art and culture, and an aspect of communication. It cannot, therefore, be true that the proper studies for one grade are mere reading and writing, and that at a later grade, reading, or literature, or science, may be introduced. The progress is not in the succession of studies but in the development of new attitudes towards, and new interests in, experience.

I believe finally, that education must be conceived as a continuing reconstruction of experience; that the process and the goal of education are one and the same thing.

I believe that to set up any end outside of education, as furnishing its goal and standard, is to deprive the educational process of much of its meaning and tends to make us rely upon false and external stimuli in dealing with the child.

ARTICLE IV The Nature of Method

I believe that the question of method is ultimately reducible to the question of the order of development of the child's powers and interests. The law for presenting and treating material is the law implicit within the child's own nature. Because this is so I believe the following statements are of supreme importance as determining the spirit in which education is carried on:

1. I believe that the active side precedes the passive in the development of the child nature; that expression comes before conscious impression; that the muscular development precedes the sensory; that movements come before conscious sensations; I believe that consciousness is essentially motor or impulsive; that conscious states tend to project themselves in action.

I believe that the neglect of this principle is the cause of a large part of the waste of time and strength in school work. The child is thrown into a passive, receptive, or absorbing attitude. The conditions are such that he is not permitted to follow the law of his nature; the result is friction and waste.

Bad ineffective

I believe that ideas (intellectual and rational processes) also result from action and devolve for the sake of the better control of action. What we term reason is primarily the law of orderly or effective action. To attempt to develop the reasoning powers, the powers of judgment, without reference to the selection and arrangement of means in action, is the fundamental fallacy in our present methods of dealing with this matter. As a result we present the child with arbitrary symbols. Symbols are a necessity in mental development, but they have their place as tools for economizing effort; presented by themselves they are a mass of meaningless and arbitrary ideas imposed from without.

2. I believe that the image is the great instrument of instruction. What a child gets out of any subject presented to him is simply the images which he himself forms with regard to it.

I believe that if nine tenths of the energy at present directed towards making the child learn certain things, were spent in seeing to it that the child was forming proper images, the work of instruction would be indefinitely [infinitely?] facilitated.

I believe that much of the time and attention now given to the preparation and presentation of lessons might be more wisely and profitably expended in training the child's power of imagery and in seeing to it that he was continually forming definite, vivid, and growing images of the various subjects with which he comes in contact in his experience.

3. I believe that interests are the signs and symptoms of growing power. I believe that they represent dawning capacities. Accordingly the constant and careful observation of interests is of the utmost importance for the educator.

I believe that these interests are to be observed as showing the state of development which the child has reached.

I believe that they prophesy the stage upon which he is about to enter.

I believe that only through the continual and sympathetic observation of childhood's interests can the adult enter into the child's life and see what it is ready for, and upon what material it could work most readily and fruitfully.

I believe that these interests are neither to be humored nor repressed. To repress interest is to substitute the adult for the child, and so to weaken intellectual curiosity and alertness, to suppress initiative, and to deaden interest. To humor the interests is to substitute the transient for the permanent. The interest is always the sign of some power below; the important thing is to discover this power. To humor the interest is to fail to penetrate below the surface and its sure result is to substitute caprice and whim for genuine interest.

4. I believe that the emotions are the reflex of actions.

I believe that to endeavor to stimulate or arouse the emotions apart from their corresponding activities, is to introduce an unhealthy and morbid state of mind.

I believe that if we can only secure right habits of action and thought, with reference to the good, the true, and the beautiful, the emotions will for the most part take care of themselves.

I believe that next to deadness and dullness, formalism and routine, our education is threatened with no greater evil than sentimentalism.

I believe that this sentimentalism is the necessary result of the attempt to divorce feeling from action.

ARTICLE V The School and Social Progress

I believe that education is the fundamental method of social progress and reform.

I believe that all reforms which rest simply upon the enactment of law, or the threatening of certain penalties, or upon changes in mechanical or outward arrangements, are transitory and futile.

I believe that education is a regulation of the process of coming to share in the social consciousness; and that the adjustment of

Reforms can't Δ society w/ laws. We must 1st Δ society.

individual activity on the basis of this social consciousness is the only sure method of social reconstruction.

I believe that this conception has due regard for both the individualistic and socialistic ideals. It is duly individual because it recognizes the formation of a certain character as the only genuine basis of right living. It is socialistic because it recognizes that this right character is not to be formed by merely individual precept, example, or exhortation, but rather by the influence of a certain form of institutional or community life upon the individual, and that the social organism through the school, as its organ, may determine ethical results.

I believe that in the ideal school we have the reconciliation of the individualistic and the institutional ideals.

I believe that the community's duty to education is, therefore, its paramount moral duty. By law and punishment, by social agitation and discussion, society can regulate and form itself in a more or less haphazard and chance way. But through education society can formulate its own purposes, can organize its own means and resources, and thus shape itself with definiteness and economy in the direction in which it wishes to move.

I believe that when society once recognizes the possibilities in this direction, and the obligations which these possibilities impose, it is impossible to conceive of the resources of time, attention, and money which will be put at the disposal of the educator.

I believe that it is the business of every one interested in education to insist upon the school as the primary and most effective interest of social progress and reform in order that society may be awakened to realize what the school stands for, and aroused to the necessity of endowing the educator with sufficient equipment properly to perform his task.

I believe that education thus conceived marks the most perfect and intimate union of science and art conceivable in human experience.

I believe that the art of thus giving shape to human powers and adapting them to social service, is the supreme art; one calling into its service the best of artists; that no insight, sympathy, tact, executive power is too great for such service.

I believe that with the growth of psychological service, giving added insight into individual structure and laws of growth; and with growth of social science, adding to our knowledge of the right organization of individuals, all scientific resources can be utilized for the purposes of education.

I believe that when science and art thus join hands the most commanding motive for human action will be reached; the most genuine springs of human conduct aroused and the best service that human nature is capable of guaranteed.

I believe, finally, that the teacher is engaged, not simply in the training of individuals, but in the formation of the proper social life.

I believe that every teacher should realize the dignity of his calling; that he is a social servant set apart for the maintenance of proper social order and the securing of the right social growth.

I believe that in this way the teacher always is the prophet of the true God and the usherer in of the true kingdom of God.

UNIVERSITY OF CHICAGO
JOHN DEWEY
[*signed*]

Chapter Seven

LIBERALS AND CONSERVATIVES FROM THE NINETIES TO THE TWENTIES

TWENTY YEARS AT HULL HOUSE *

By Jane Addams

Jane Addams (1860–1935), founder of Hull House, rejects Tolstoy's primitive Christianity for the organized service ideal of the settlement movement

Perhaps America's greatest woman, Jane Addams, a native of Cedarville, Illinois, and a daughter of an idealistic state senator, struggled against a lifelong physical frailty to advance the nation's welfare. She managed to secure her A.B. at Rockford College in 1882, but her health broke down while she attempted a medical education. In Europe, as the selection below indicates, she found Tolstoy's primitive Christianity impractical and was drawn to the crusade of youth in Toynbee Hall, London, where "residents" learned about poverty at close quarters without acquiring condescension.

In *Twenty Years at Hull House* (1910), she told of the remarkable experiments of her fellow-residents in serving the families of

* From Jane Addams, *Twenty Years at Hull House* (Macmillan, 1910), 66–69, 85–88, 267–71.

the immigrants—"progressive" classes in adult education, a pioneer Little Theater, projects raising the morale of newly arrived women by encouraging their Old World crafts, and social planning that made Hull House a laboratory for child welfare laws. Her dynamic associate, Florence Kelley, became the effective first factory inspector of Illinois after Hull House had lobbied successfully for the law, and another resident, Julia Lathrop, initiated a movement for family adoption of foster children before going on to become the head of the new federal Children's Bureau.

In numerous books and articles as well as in national organizations, Jane Addams advanced the cause of child welfare, a realistic feminism, and world peace. She worked for Roosevelt's Progressive Party in 1912 and acted as a determined mediator during the peace movement preceding America's entrance to World War I. She aided Hoover in the postwar relief drive and supported Wilson's Fourteen Points—some of which she may have originated. Her social analysis was realistic rather than sentimental; she opposed the double standard of morality; and urged that the city child be reared on habits of work rather than outmoded Victorian precepts. For the following generation of social workers, Jane Addams—fittingly rewarded by a Nobel Prize—was indeed an inspiration.

※⁹

THE LONG illness left me in a state of nervous exhaustion with which I struggled for years, traces of it remaining long after Hull-House was opened in 1889. At the best it allowed me but a limited amount of energy, so that doubtless there was much nervous depression at the foundation of the spiritual struggles which this chapter is forced to record. However, it could not have been all due to my health, for as my wise little notebook sententiously remarked, "In his own way each man must struggle, lest the moral law become a far-off abstraction utterly separated from his active life."

It would, of course, be impossible to remember that some of these struggles ever took place at all, were it not for these self-same notebooks, in which, however, I no longer wrote in moments of high resolve, but judging from the internal evidence afforded by the books themselves, only in moments of deep depression when overwhelmed by a sense of failure.

One of the most poignant of these experiences, which occurred during the first few months after our landing upon the other side of the Atlantic, was on a Saturday night, when I received an ineradicable impression of the wretchedness of East London, and also saw for the first time the overcrowded quarters of a great city at midnight. A small party of tourists were taken to the East End by a city missionary to witness the Saturday night sale of decaying vegetables and fruit, which, owing to the Sunday laws in London, could not be sold until Monday, and, as they were beyond safe keeping, were disposed of at auction as late as possible on Saturday night. On Mile End Road, from the top of an omnibus which paused at the end of a dingy street lighted by only occasional flares of gas, we saw two huge masses of ill-clad people clamoring around two hucksters' carts. They were bidding their farthings and ha'pennies for a vegetable held up by the auctioneer, which he at last scornfully flung, with a gibe for its cheapness, to the successful bidder. In the momentary pause only one man detached himself from the groups. He had bidden in a cabbage, and when it struck his hand, he instantly sat down on the curb, tore it with his teeth, and hastily devoured it, unwashed and uncooked as it was. He and his fellows were types of the "submerged tenth," as our missionary guide told us, with some little satisfaction in the then new phrase, and he further added that so many of them could scarcely be seen in one spot save at this Saturday night auction, the desire for cheap food being apparently the one thing which could move them simultaneously. They were huddled into ill-fitting, cast-off clothing, the ragged finery which one sees only in East London. Their pale faces were dominated by that most unlovely of human expressions, the cunning and shrewdness of the bargain-hunter who starves if he cannot make a successful trade, and yet the final impression was not of ragged, tawdry clothing nor of pinched and sallow faces, but of myriads of hands, empty, pathetic, nerveless and workworn, showing white in the uncertain light of the street, and clutching forward for food which was already unfit to eat.

Perhaps nothing is so fraught with significance as the human hand, this oldest tool with which man has dug his way from savagery, and with which he is constantly groping forward. I have never since been able to see a number of hands held upward, even when they are moving rhythmically in a calisthenic exercise, or when they belong to a class of chubby children who wave them in eager response to a teacher's query, without a certain revival of this memory, a clutching at the heart reminiscent of the despair and resentment which seized me then.

For the following weeks I went about London almost furtively, afraid to look down narrow streets and alleys lest they disclose again this hideous human need and suffering. I carried with me for days at a time that curious surprise we experience when we first come back into the streets after days given over to sorrow and death; we are bewildered that the world should be going on as usual and unable to determine which is real, the inner pang or the outward seeming. In time all huge London came to seem unreal save the poverty in its East End. During the following two years on the continent, while I was irresistibly drawn to the poorer quarters of each city, nothing among the beggars of South Italy nor among the saltminers of Austria carried with it the same conviction of human wretchedness which was conveyed by this momentary glimpse of an East London street. It was, of course, a most fragmentary and lurid view of the poverty of East London, and quite unfair. I should have been shown either less or more, for I went away with no notion of the hundreds of men and women who had gallantly identified their fortunes with these empty-handed people, and who, in church and chapel, "relief works," and charities, were at least making an effort towards its mitigation.

Our visit was made in November, 1883, the very year when the *Pall Mall Gazette* exposure started "The Bitter Cry of Outcast London," and the conscience of England was stirred as never before over this joyless city in the East End of its capital. Even then, vigorous and drastic plans were being discussed, and a splendid program of municipal reforms was already dimly outlined. Of all these, however, I had heard nothing but the vaguest rumor. . . .

It is hard to tell just when the very simple plan which afterward developed into the Settlement began to form itself in my mind. It may have been even before I went to Europe for the second time, but I gradually became convinced that it would be a good thing to rent a house in a part of the city where many primitive and actual needs are found, in which young women who had been given over too exclusively to study, might restore a balance of activity along traditional lines and learn of life from life itself; where they might try out some of the things they had been taught and put truth to "the ultimate test of the conduct it dictates or inspires." I do not remember to have mentioned this plan to any one until we reached Madrid in April, 1888. . . .

I had confidence that although life itself might contain many difficulties, the period of mere passive receptivity had come to an end, and I had at last finished with the everlasting "preparation for life," however ill-prepared I might be.

It was not until years afterward that I came upon Tolstoy's phrase "the snare of preparation," which he insists we spread before the feet of young people, hopelessly entangling them in a curious inactivity at the very period of life when they are longing to construct the world anew and to conform it to their own ideals.

We had letters of introduction to Mr. and Mrs. Aylmer Maude of Moscow, since well known as the translators of "Resurrection" and other of Tolstoy's later works, who at that moment were on the eve of leaving Russia in order to form an agricultural colony in South England where they might support themselves by the labor of their hands. We gladly accepted Mr. Maude's offer to take us to Yasnaya Polyana and to introduce us to Count Tolstoy, and never did a disciple journey towards his master with more enthusiasm than did our guide. When, however, Mr. Maude actually presented Miss Smith and myself to Count Tolstoy, knowing well his master's attitude toward philanthropy, he endeavored to make Hull-House appear much more noble and unique than I should have ventured to do.

Tolstoy standing by clad in his peasant garb, listened gravely but, glancing distrustfully at the sleeves of my traveling gown which unfortunately at that season were monstrous in size, he took hold of an edge and pulling out one sleeve to an interminable breadth, said quite simply that "there was enough stuff on one arm to make a frock for a little girl," and asked me directly if I did not find "such a dress" a "barrier to the people." I was too disconcerted to make a very clear explanation, although I tried to say that monstrous as my sleeves were they did not compare in size with those of the working girls in Chicago and that nothing would more effectively separate me from "the people" than a cotton blouse following the simple lines of the human form; even if I had wished to imitate him and "dress as a peasant," it would have been hard to choose which peasant among the thirty-six nationalities we had recently counted in our ward. Fortunately the countess came to my rescue with a recital of her former attempts to clothe hypothetical little girls in yards of material cut from a train and other superfluous parts of her best gown until she had been driven to a firm stand which she advised me to take at once. But neither Countess Tolstoy nor any other friend was on hand to help me out of my predicament later, when I was asked who "fed" me, and how did I obtain "shelter"? Upon my reply that a farm a hundred miles from Chicago supplied me with the necessities of life, I fairly anticipated the next scathing question: "So you are an absentee landlord? Do you think you will help the people more by adding yourself to the crowded city than you would by tilling your own soil?" This new sense of discomfort over a failure to till my own soil was increased when Tolstoy's second daughter appeared at the five-o'clock tea table set under the trees, coming straight from the harvest field where she had been working with a group of peasants since five o'clock in the morning, not pretending to work but really taking the place of a peasant woman who had hurt her foot. She was plainly much exhausted but neither expected nor received sympathy from the members of a family who were quite accustomed to see each other carry out their convictions in spite of discomfort and fatigue. The martyrdom of discomfort, however, was obviously much easier to bear than that to which, even to the eyes of the casual visitor, Count Tolstoy daily subjected himself, for his study in the basement of the conventional dwelling, with it short shelf of battered books and its scythe and spade leaning against the wall, had many times lent itself to that ridicule which is the most difficult form of martyrdom.

That summer evening as we sat in the garden with a group of visitors from Germany, from England and America, who had traveled to the remote Russian village that they might learn of this man, one could not forbear the constant inquiry to one's self, as to why he was so regarded as sage and saint that this party of people should be repeated each day of the year. It seemed to me then that we were all attracted by this sermon of the deed, because Tolstoy had made the one supreme personal effort, one might almost say the one frantic personal effort, to put himself into right relations with the humblest people, with the men who tilled his soil, blacked his boots and cleaned his stables. Doubtless the heaviest burden of our contemporaries is a consciousness of a divergence between our democratic theory on the one hand, that working people have a right to the intellectual resources of society, and the actual fact on the other hand, that thousands of them are so overburdened with toil that there is no leisure nor energy left for the cultivation of the mind. We constantly suffer from the strain and indecision of believing this theory and acting as if we did not believe it, and this man who years before had tried "to get off the backs of the peasants," who had at least simplified his life and worked with his hands, had come to be a prototype to many of his generation.

Doubtless all of the visitors sitting in the Tolstoy garden that evening had excused themselves from laboring with their hands upon the theory that they were doing something more valuable for society in other ways. No one among our contemporaries has dissented from this point of view so violently as Tolstoy himself, and yet no man might so easily have excused himself from hard and rough work on the basis of his genius and of his intellectual contributions to the world. So far, however, from considering his time too valuable to be spent in labor in the field or in making shoes, our great host was too eager to know life to be willing to give up this companionship of mutual labor. One instinctively found reasons why it was easier for a Russian than for the rest of us, to reach this conclusion; the Russian peasants have a proverb which says: "Labor is the house that love lives in," by which they mean that no two people nor group of people, can come into affectionate relations with each other unless they carry on together a mutual task, and when the Russian peasant talks of labor he means labor on the soil, or, to use the phrase of the great peasant, Bondereff, "bread labor." Those monastic orders founded upon agricultural labor, those philosophical experiments like Brook Farm and many another, have attempted to reduce to action this same truth.

"PLUTOCRACY AND PATERNALISM" *

By Lester Frank Ward

Lester Frank Ward (1841–1913), sociologist, urges a welfare state to replace plutocracy

Lester F. Ward was one of ten children of an inventive but impecunious Joliet, Illinois, mechanic father and a talented mother. He was largely self-educated until later on in his life when he earned the degrees of A.B., LL.B., and A.M. at Columbian College (now George Washington University). Meanwhile he had fought and been wounded as a Union soldier, thereafter working as a Treasury clerk at Washington, eventually becoming a geologist and paleontologist for the United States Geological Survey. He showed an increasing interest in evolutionary thought and finally in sociology. In 1883, he published *Dynamic Sociology,* in 1893, *The Psychic Factors of Civilization,* and many more books and articles. As a confirmed religious rationalist (although his grandfather was a minister), he edited *The Iconoclast.* In 1906, when he was almost at a retirement age, he was appointed professor of sociology at Brown University.

Unlike William Graham Sumner and other Spencerian social scientists, he looked upon evolution as a human process that could be guided by the will and intellect rather than merely operate as a passive inevitable development. His writings, as the essay below suggests, urged the need for democratic social planning to achieve human progress. He wished the government to take a central role in this process, sponsoring education on a much larger scale and striving for the abolition of poverty. In recent years, Professor Henry Commager has portrayed Ward as a prophet of the welfare state.

To JUDGE from the tone of the popular press, the country would seem to be between the devil of state interference and the deep sea of gold. The two epithets, "plutocracy" and "pater-

* Lester F. Ward, "Plutocracy and Paternalism," *The Forum,* vol. 20 (1895–96), 300–305.

nalism," so freely applied, are intended to characterize the worst tendencies of the times in these two opposite directions, and are calculated to engender the bitterest feelings in the public mind. If such a thing were possible, it would certainly be useful, standing aloof from the contest, to make a cool, unbiassed analysis of the true meaning of these terms in their relation to the existing state of affairs. While it may be admitted that this is impossible, such an approximation to it as the conditions will allow can certainly do no harm.

On all subjects that interest mankind there are extremes of thought, and these form a sort of penumbra outside the general consensus of opinion among right-minded people. While most persons consider the possession of wealth a rightful condition and a laudable aim of life, there are some who accept Proudhon's dictum, *"la propriété c'est le vol,"* and nearly all shades of opinion between these may be found. The average man desires to see the business interests of society left free and open to equal competition, but there are those who would have the state conduct all industry and make all citizens salaried employees. Between these views there are also many intermediate ones. This condition has always existed very much as it is to-day. On the whole there seems to be little danger that any of the extremes of popular opinion will ever prevail, but at the same time there is always a moderate, often rhythmic, drift in some one direction, so that what were extremes are so no longer, and other unthought-of schemes occupy the van. It is this that constitutes social progress.

Justly or unjustly, society has made wealth a measure of worth. It is easy on general principles to prove that it is not such a measure. Every one is personally cognizant of numerous cases to the contrary. All will admit that, taken in the abstract, the principle is unsound, and yet all act upon it. Not rationally, not perhaps consciously, but still they do it. It is "human nature" to respect those who have, and to care little for those who have not. There is a sort of feeling that if one is destitute there must be a reason for it. It is inevitably ascribed to some personal deficit. In a word, absence of means is, in one form or another, made to stand for absence of merit. Its cause is looked for in character. This is most clearly seen in the marked contrast between the indisposition to help the unsuccessful, and the willingness to help the successful. Aside from the prospect of a *quid pro quo,* no one wants to waste time, energy, or money on what is worthless,—and possession is the primary test of worth.

It would be easy to work out the genesis of this sentiment, and to show how it is the natural result of the universal competition in society, where the fittest to survive is always the one who can gain possession of the greatest amount of this world's goods. It has therefore a rational basis, a substratum of truth on which to rest. We are chiefly concerned with it here as a fact. It is universal. Those who most thoroughly condemn it are influenced by it. The force that works against it in society is not the absence or weakness of the sentiment itself, but another and wholly dissimilar feeling, viz., sympathy. This sentiment is not rational, but illogical, as shown by the fact that men give alms to satisfy temporary want rather than opportunity to supply permanent needs. But of the other sentiment, which may be called "plutolatry,"—the worship of wealth,—even the victims show traces, and in denouncing the rich they unconsciously attribute to them a personal dignity proportional to their wealth.

Thus it comes about that wealth, in the existing state of society, is a tremendous power. It gives not only ease, plenty, luxury, but, what is infinitely more, the respect of all and the envy of the less favored. It gives, in a word, superiority; and the strongest craving of man's nature is, in one way or another, to be set over his fellows. When all this is considered, the futility of the proposal of certain reformers to eradicate the passion for proprietary acquisition becomes apparent. It may be assumed that this passion will continue for an indefinite period to be the ruling element of the industrial state. That it has done and is still doing incalculable service to society few will deny. That it may continue to be useful to the end of our present industrial era will probably be admitted by all but a small class.

If the accumulation of wealth, even for the benefit of individuals, were all that is involved in the term "plutocracy," the indictment would not be serious. If the governing power implied in the last component of the word were nothing more than the normal influence that wealth exerts, no great injury to society could accrue. Even the amassing of colossal fortunes is not an evil in itself, since the very activity which it requires stimulates industry and benefits a large number. There is, it is true, a danger—in the transmission of such fortunes to inactive and non-productive heirs—of creating a non-industrial class in perpetuity;

but this could be remedied, without hardship to any worthy person, by a wise limitation of inheritance.

So much for plutocracy. Let us now turn to the other pole of public opinion and inquire into the meaning of "paternalism." Literally, of course, paternalism in government would be restricted to cases in which the governing power is vested in a single person, who may be regarded as well-disposed and seeking to rule his subjects for their own good, as a father governs his children. But a ruling family, or even a large ruling class, may be supposed to govern from similar motives. In either case the governed are not supposed to have any voice in the matter, but are cared for like children by the assumed wisdom of their rulers. How far from true paternalism is anything that exists in this or any other civilized country to-day may therefore be readily seen. No one will claim that there is any danger, in a representative government with universal suffrage, of any such state being brought about. This shows at the outset that the term is not used in its original and correct sense, but is merely borrowed and applied as a stigma to certain tendencies in republican governments which the users of it do not approve. What are these tendencies? In general it may be said that they are tendencies toward the assumption by the state of functions that are now entrusted to private enterprise.

On the one hand it is logically argued that the indefinite extension of such powers would eventuate in the most extreme socialistic system,—the conduct of all business by the state. On the other hand it is shown with equal logic that the entire relinquishment of the functions which the state has already assumed would be the abolition of government itself. The extremists of one party would land us in socialism; those of the other, in anarchy. But on one side it is said by the more moderate that the true function of government is the protection of society; to which it is replied by the other that such extension of governmental powers is in the interest of protection, viz., protection against the undue rapacity of private enterprise. Here, as almost everywhere else in the realm of polities, it is a question of quantity and not of quality. It is not a difference in principle, but in policy. It is the degree to which the fundamental principle of all government is to be carried out.

If we look for precedents and historical examples we find great diversity. If we take the question of government telegraphy we find that the United States is almost the only country in the civilized world that has not adopted it, while the reports from other countries are practically unanimous in its favor. That such a movement should be called paternalism is therefore quite gratuitous, and must spring from either pecuniary interest or unenlightened prejudice. From this on, up to the question of abolishing the private ownership of land, there is a multitude of problems presenting all shades of difference in the degree to which the principle of state action is to be applied in their solution. They need to be fearlessly investigated, coolly considered, and wisely decided in the true interests of the public. It was not the purpose of this article to discuss any of these questions, but simply to mention them in illustration of the popular use of the term "paternalism." It is clear that that term is employed solely to excite prejudice against the extension of the functions of the state, just as the term "plutocracy" is used to arouse antagonism to the wealthy classes. The words have in these senses no natural meaning, and, with intelligent persons, should have no argumentative weight.

Are there, then, no dangerous or deleterious tendencies in modern society? There certainly are such, and they may be said to be in the direction of both plutocracy and paternalism, giving to these terms not a literal, but a real or scientific meaning, as denoting respectively the too great power of wealth, and the too great solicitude for and fostering of certain interests on the part of government. The first law of economics is that every one may be depended upon at all times to seek his greatest gain. It is both natural and right that the individual should be ever seeking to acquire for himself and his; and this rather irrespective of the rest of the world. It was so in the olden time, when physical strength was almost the only force. It is so to-day, when business shrewdness is practically supreme. Government was instituted to protect the weak from the strong in this universal struggle to possess; or, what is the same thing, to protect society at large. Originally it was occupied solely with abuses caused by brute force. It is still, so far as this primary function of enforcing justice is concerned, practically limited to this class of abuses, relatively trifling as they are. Crime still means this, as it did in the days of King Arthur, and as it does to-day in barbaric countries. Any advantage gained by force is promptly met by the law; but advantage gained by cunning, by superior knowledge,—if it be only of the technicalities of the law,—is not a crime, though its spirit be as bad as that of highway robbery and its consequences a thousand times worse.

From this point of view, then, modern society is suffering from the very opposite of paternalism,—from under-government, from the failure of government to keep pace with the change which civilization has wrought in substituting intellectual for physical qualities as the workers of injustice. Government to-day is powerless to perform its primary and original function of protecting society. There was a time when brigandage stalked abroad throughout Europe and no one was safe in life or property. This was due to lack of adequate government. Man's nature has not changed, but brigandage has succumbed to the strong arm of the law. Human rapacity now works in subtler ways. Plutocracy is the modern brigandage and can be dislodged only by the same power,—the power of the state. All the evils of society are the result of the free flow of natural propensities. The purpose of government is, as far as may be, to prevent this from causing injustice. The physical passions of men are natural and healthy, but they cannot be allowed to go unbridled. Government was established, not to lessen or even to alter them. Exactly the same is needed to be done with the higher acquisitive faculty. It need not be condemned; it cannot be suppressed: but it can and should be directed into harmless ways and restricted to useful purposes. Properly viewed, too, this is to secure its maximum exercise and greatest freedom, for unrestrained license soon leads to conflict, chokes its own free operation, and puts an end to its activity. The true function of government is not to fetter but to liberate the forces of society, not to diminish but to increase their effectiveness. Unbridled competition destroys itself. The only competition that endures is that which goes on under judicious regulation.

If, then, the danger of plutocracy is so largely due to insufficient government, where is the tendency to paternalism in the sense of too much government? This opens up the last and most important aspect of the subject. If there were no influences at work in society but those of unaided nature; if we had a pure physiocracy or government of nature, such as prevails among wild animals, and the weak were thereby sacrificed that the strong might survive to beget the strong, and thus elevate the race along the lines of evolution,—however great the hardship, we might resign ourselves to it as part of the great cosmic scheme. But unforunately this is not the case. Without stopping to show that, from the standpoint of a civilized society, the qualities which best fit men to gain advantage over their fellows are the ones least useful to society at large, it will be sufficient for the present purpose to point out that in the actual state of society it is not even those who, from this biological point of view, are the fittest, that become in fact the recipients of the greatest favors at the hands of society. This is due to the creation, by society itself, of artificial conditions that destroy the balance of forces and completely nullify all the beneficial effects that are secured by the operation of the natural law on the lower plane. Indeed, the effect is reversed, and instead of developing strength, either physical or mental, through activity incident to emulation, it tends to parasitic degeneracy through the pampered idleness of the favored classes.

What, in the last analysis, are these social conditions? They are at bottom integral parts of government. They are embodied in law. Largely they consist of statute law. Where this is wanting they rest on judicial decisions, often immemorial, and belonging to the *lex non scripta*. In a word, they constitute the great system of jurisprudence relating to property and business, gradually built up through the ages to make men secure in their possessions and safe in their business transactions, but which in our day, owing to entirely changed industrial conditions, has become the means of throwing unlimited opportunities in the way of some and of barring out the rest from all opportunities. This system of artificial props, bolsterings, and scaffoldings has grown so perfect as to make exertion needless for the protected class and hopeless for the neglected mass. In a word, it has become the bulwark of monopoly. Says Prof. John R. Commons in his "Distribution of Wealth":

The heads of industries are no longer the independent Napoleons of finance; they find their sphere as high-salaried managers and legal advisers, while the successors of the *entrepreneurs* proper, the original organizers and promoters of enterprises, are simply the commonplace, idle recipients of the permanent profits and the mildly fluctuating temporary profits. . . . Instead of the profits being due to the powerful exertions and abilities of the captains of industry, they are due to certain fixed social relations and rights. The recipients of these incomes may with perfect security become idlers and drones. They abdicate their functions as *entrepreneurs* into the hands of salaried chiefs and advisers. They are no longer performing the services of society which were performed by their ancestors or predecessors, who organized and developed the business to which they have succeeded.

THE THEORY OF
THE LEISURE CLASS*

By Thorstein Veblen

Thorstein Veblen (1857–1929) economist, explains how the leisure class imposes a pecuniary standard of living and unproductive prestige values

One of the most original minds in American economic thought, Thorstein Veblen reflected the outspokenness of the Norwegian immigrants to which his parents belonged. The Wisconsin-born boy was taken with the other children of his family to a farm in Minnesota amid a clannish Norwegian-speaking community (a circumstance that may explain Veblen's rather stiff English style). He was educated at Carleton College, took a Ph.D. in philosophy at Yale, where he studied with William Graham Sumner, and after a delay became a graduate student in economics at Cornell. One of his professors, the orthodox gold-standard theorist J. Lawrence Laughlin, took pleasure in this young man despite his essays on socialism, and when Laughlin became head of the University of Chicago's Economics Department, he took Veblen along as a teaching fellow.

By 1900, Veblen had become an assistant professor, shortly after the appearance of his book, *The Theory of the Leisure Class* (1899), which was crowded with the original ideas that became the basic stock of most of his later books. To conservatives, it seemed like a radical and quixotic attack on the businessman and his alleged corruption of American culture. Increasingly, however, readers came to appreciate his astute applications of cultural anthropology and psychology to economic institutions. He had re-

* From Thorstein Veblen, *The Theory of the Leisure Class* (1899), 102–5, 110–14.

placed the rigid classical approach to problems of consumption and production with a cultural analysis of motivation, a reinterpretation of the concept of "standard of living," and a tracing of the impact of pecuniary values on almost every phase of life, including dress, schools, creative thinking and workmanship, leisure, the relation of economic waste to prestige values, etc.

Veblen's affairs with women drove him out of the University of Chicago and Stanford University. At the University of Missouri, he gave an original course on world civilization, which furnished the substance of *The Instinct of Workmanship* (1904), developing the idea that predatory values inhibited the instinct of workmanship. In 1919, he joined as a staff member James Harvey Robinson, Charles Beard, and John Dewey in founding the experimental institution, the New School for Social Research. In 1918, he had expanded the assumptions of his first volume in *The Higher Learning in America,* which examined business control of the universities in some detail, a title which was frankly borrowed by Robert Maynard Hutchins in 1936 in his hope of freeing the scholar from the pressures of business and industrial firms. (Upton Sinclair apparently drew on Veblen's book when he wrote *The Goose-Step* [1923]). But especially striking among Veblen's work was *The Engineers and the Price System* (1921), which inspired Howard Scott's technocracy movement that hoped to apply Veblen's idea of overthrowing the price or profit system of the leisure class by an elite of engineers.

In 1925, the American Economic Association was ready to forgive Veblen's total lack of orthodoxy by offering him the presidency, but the embittered old man refused the belated offer. More important was the fact that social scientists, especially during the 1930's, were finding new insights in applying the Veblenian concept of prestige values and the pervasive force of pecuniary motives in society; they agreed with many of his observations regarding the evils of absentee ownership in the economy. Stuart Chase, also an unorthodox economist, owed much to Veblen in his analysis of "the tragedy of waste" as an entrepreneurial product. The teaching of economics apparently would never be quite the same as it was before Veblen.

The Pecuniary Standard of Living

FOR THE great body of the people in any modern community, the proximate ground of expenditure in excess of what is required for physical comfort is not a conscious effort to excel in the expensiveness of their visible consumption, so much as it is a desire to live up to the conventional standard of decency in the amount and grade of goods consumed. This desire is not guided by a rigidly invariable standard, which must be lived up to, and beyond which there is no incentive to go. The standard is flexible; and especially it is indefinitely extensible, if only time is allowed for habituation to any increase in pecuniary ability and for acquiring facility in the new and larger scale of expenditure that follows such an increase. It is much more difficult to recede from a scale of expenditure once adopted than it is to extend the accustomed scale in response to an accession of wealth. Many items of customary expenditure prove on analysis to be almost purely wasteful, and they are therefore honorific only, but after they have once been incorporated into the scale of decent consumption, and so have become an integral part of one's scheme of life, it is quite as hard to give up these as it is to give up many items that conduce directly to one's physical comfort, or even that may be necessary to life and health. That is to say, the conspicuously wasteful honorific expenditure that confers spiritual well-being may become more indispensable than much of that expenditure which ministers to the "lower" wants of physical well-being or sustenance only. It is notoriously just as difficult to recede from a "high" standard of living as it is to lower a standard which is already relatively low; although in the former case the difficulty is a moral one, while in the latter it may involve a material deduction from the physical comforts of life.

But while retrogression is difficult, a fresh advance in conspicuous expenditure is relatively easy; indeed, it takes place almost as a matter of course. In the rare cases where it occurs, a failure to increase one's visible consumption when the means for an increase are at hand is felt in popular apprehension to call for explanation, and unworthy motives of miserliness are imputed to those who fall short in this respect. A prompt response to the stimulus, on the other hand, is accepted as the normal effect. This suggests that the standard of expenditure which commonly guides our efforts is not the average, ordinary expenditure already achieved; it is an ideal of consumption that lies just beyond our reach, or to reach which requires some strain. The motive is emulation—the stimulus of an invidious comparison which prompts us to outdo those with whom we are in the habit of classing ourselves. Substantially the same proposition is expressed in the commonplace remark that each class envies and emulates the class next above it in the social scale, while it rarely compares itself with those below or with those who are considerably in advance. That is to say, in other words, our standard of decency in expenditure, as in other ends of emulation, is set by the usage of those next above us in reputability; until, in this way, especially in any community where class distinctions are somewhat vague, all canons of reputability and decency, and all standards of consumption, are traced back by insensible gradations to the usages and habits of thought of the highest social and pecuniary class—the wealthy leisure class.

It is for this class to determine, in general outline, what scheme of life the community shall accept as decent or honorific; and it is their office by precept and example to set forth this scheme of social salvation in its highest, ideal form. But the higher leisure class can exercise this quasi-sacerdotal office only under certain material limitations. The class cannot at discretion effect a sudden revolution or reversal of the popular habits of thought with respect to any of these ceremonial requirements. It takes time for any change to permeate the mass and change the habitual attitude of the people; and especially it takes time to change the habits of those classes that are socially more remote from the radiant body. The process is slower where the mobility of the population is less or where the intervals between the several classes are wider and more abrupt. But if time be allowed, the scope of the discretion of the leisure class as regards questions of form and detail in the community's scheme of life is large; while as regards the substantial principles of reputability, the changes which it can effect lie within a narrow margin of tolerance. Its example and precept carries the force of prescription for all classes below it; but in working out the precepts which are handed down as governing the form and method of reputability —in shaping the usages and the spiritual attitude of the lower classes—this authoritative prescription constantly works under the selective guidance of the canon of conspicuous waste, tempered in varying degree by the instinct of workmanship. To these norms is to be added another broad principle of human nature— the predatory animus—which in point of generality and of psychological content lies between the two just named. The effect of the latter in shaping the accepted scheme of life is yet to be discussed.

The canon of reputability, then, must adapt itself to the economic circumstances, the traditions, and the degree of spiritual maturity of the particular class whose scheme of life it is to regulate. It is especially to be noted that however high its authority and however true to the fundamental requirements of reputability it may have been at its inception, a specific formal observance can under no circumstances maintain itself in force if with the lapse of time or on its transmission to a lower pecuniary class it is found to run counter to the ultimate ground of decency among civilized peoples, namely, serviceability for the purpose of an invidious comparison in pecuniary success.

It is evident that these canons of expenditure have much to say in determining the standard of living for any community and for any class. . . .

With the exception of the instinct of self-preservation, the propensity for emulation is probably the strongest and most alert and persistent of the economic motives proper. In an industrial community this propensity for emulation expresses itself in pecuniary emulation; and this, so far as regards the Western civilised communities of the present, is virtually equivalent to saying that it expresses itself in some form of conspicuous waste. The need of conspicuous waste, therefore, stands ready to absorb any increase in the community's industrial efficiency or output of goods, after the most elementary physical wants have been provided for. Where this result does not follow, under modern conditions, the reason for the discrepancy is commonly to be sought in a rate of increase in the individual's wealth too rapid for the habit of expenditure to keep abreast of it; or it may be that the individual in question defers the conspicuous consumption of the increment to a later date—ordinarily with a view to heightening the spectacular effect of the aggregate expenditure contemplated. As increased industrial efficiency makes it possible to procure the means of livelihood with less labour, the energies of the industrious members of the community are bent to the compassing of a higher result in conspicuous expenditure, rather than slackened to a more comfortable pace. The strain is not lightened as industrial efficiency increases and makes a lighter strain possible, but the increment of output is turned to use to meet this want, which is indefinitely expansible, after the manner commonly imputed in economic theory to higher or spiritual wants. It is owing chiefly to the presence of this element in the standard of living that J.

S. Mill was able to say that "hitherto it is questionable if all the mechanical inventions yet made have lightened the day's toil of any human being."

The accepted standard of expenditure in the community or in the class to which a person belongs largely determines what his standard of living will be. It does this directly by commending itself to his common sense as right and good, through his habitually contemplating it and assimilating the scheme of life in which it belongs; but it does so also indirectly through popular insistence on conformity to the accepted scale of expenditure as a matter of propriety, under pain of disesteem and ostracism. To accept and practise the standard of living which is in vogue is both agreeable and expedient, commonly to the point of being indispensable to personal comfort and to success in life. The standard of living of any class, so far as concerns the element of conspicuous waste, is commonly as high as the earning capacity of the class will permit—with a constant tendency to go higher. The effect upon the serious activities of men is therefore to direct them with great singleness of purpose to the largest possible acquisition of wealth, and to discountenance work that brings no pecuniary gain. At the same time the effect on consumption is to concentrate it upon the lines which are most patent to the observers whose good opinion is sought; while the inclinations and aptitudes whose exercise does not involve a honorific expenditure of time or substance tend to fall into abeyance through disuse.

Through this discrimination in favour of visible consumption it has come about that the domestic life of most classes is relatively shabby, as compared with the éclat of that overt portion of their life that is carried on before the eyes of observers. As a secondary consequence of the same discrimination, people habitually screen their private life from observation. So far as concerns that portion of their consumption that may without blame be carried on in secret, they withdraw from all contact with their neighbours. Hence the exclusiveness of people, as regards their domestic life, in most of the industrially developed communities; and hence, by remoter derivation, the habit of privacy and reserve that is so large a feature in the code of proprieties of the better classes in all communities. The low birthrate of the classes upon whom the requirements of reputable expenditure fall with great urgency is likewise traceable to the exigencies of a standard

Façade

of living based on conspicuous waste. The conspicuous consumption, and the consequent increased expense, required in the reputable maintenance of a child is very considerable and acts as a powerful deterrent. It is probably the most effectual of the Malthusian prudential checks.

The effect of this factor of the standard of living, both in the way of retrenchment in the obscurer elements of consumption that go to physical comfort and maintenance, and also in the paucity or absence of children, is perhaps seen at its best among the classes given to scholarly pursuits. Because of a presumed superiority and scarcity of the gifts and attainments that characterise their life, these classes are by convention subsumed under a higher social grade than their pecuniary grade should warrant. The scale of decent expenditure in their case is pitched correspondingly high, and it consequently leaves an exceptionally narrow margin disposable for the other ends of life. By force of circumstances, their own habitual sense of what is good and right in these matters, as well as the expectations of the community in the way of pecuniary decency among the learned, are excessively high—as measured by the prevalent degree of opulence and earning capacity of the class, relatively to the non-scholarly classes whose social equals they nominally are. In any modern community where there is no priestly monopoly of these occupations, the people of scholarly pursuits are unavoidably thrown into contact with classes that are pecuniarily their superiors. The high standard of pecuniary decency in force among these superior classes is transfused among the scholarly classes with but little mitigation of its rigour; and as a consequence there is no class of the community that spends a larger proportion of its substance in conspicuous waste than these.

"REPLY TO A SOCIALIST" *

By William Graham Sumner

favors unrestricted competition

*William Graham Sumner (1840–1910), pioneer sociologist, up-
holds unrestricted competition against Upton Sinclair's socialism*

Born in Paterson, New Jersey, and reared in Hartford, Connecticut, William G. Sumner was the son of a hard-working and
intelligent father employed in railroad repair shops; in this environment, the boy shared in the Protestant ethic of competition
and success. Young William took his degree at Yale, studied theology abroad, and became an Episcopalian priest in 1869, earning a
reputation as a vigorous preacher and writer on social questions.
But, in 1872, he returned to Yale, this time as a professor of political and social science, serving part of the time as an alderman
and as an active member of the Connecticut school board.

He inspired his students and won lifelong disciples, especially
in his later career as a sociologist. When his enthusiasm for Herbert Spencer's textbook on sociology aroused the objections of
President Noah Porter, he fought publicly and successfully to
keep the book. Like Spencer, he opposed state interference in
industry or welfare, admired the elitism of a strong civil service
system, denounced imperialism and protectionism, and disliked
those reformers who assailed big business or demanded free silver.
He wrote books and many articles on these subjects and expressed
sympathy for "The Forgotten Man" (1883), whom he pictured as
a hard-working citizen who was needlessly taxed by reformers for
welfare schemes.

Sumner tried to create a science of society along Spencerian
lines and based on social evolutionary principles. His most important book, *Folkways* (1907), accounted for ethical beliefs and
customs of a society (mores) as being part of a regional evolutionary development requiring centuries of experience and environmental selection. These mores made anything right or wrong—
a relativist view that delighted rationalists but antagonized tradi-
tionalists or absolutists. Although, as this selection shows, Sumner
denied that he believed in the rightness of the existing order, his
arguments obviously pit the prevailing mores against Upton Sinclair's socialist ideas, which interfered with the natural order of

* From William Graham Sumner, "Reply to a Socialist," *Collier's
Weekly*, October 29, 1904, 123–30.

competition; nothing could change the inborn differences in human capacities.

"ALWAYS DIG out the major premise!" said an experienced teacher of logic and rhetoric. The major premise of Mr. Upton Sinclair is that everybody ought to be happy, and that, if anybody is not so, those who stand near him are under obligations to make him so. He nowhere expresses this. The major premise is always most fallacious when it is suppressed. The statement of the woes of the garment workers is made on the assumption that it carries upon its face some significance. He deduces from the facts two inferences for which he appeals to common consent: (1) that such a state of things ought not to be allowed to continue forever, and (2) that somehow, somewhere, another "system" must be found. The latter inference is one which the socialists always affirm, and they seem to be satisfied that it has some value, both in philosophy and in practical effort. They criticize the "system," by which they mean the social world as it is. They do not perceive that the world of human society is what has resulted from thousands of years of life. It is not a system any more than a man sixty years old is a system. It is a product. To talk of making another system is like talking of making a man of sixty into something else than what his life has made him. As for the inference that some other industrial system must be found, it is as idle as anything which words can express. It leads to nothing and has no significance. The industrial system has changed often and it will change again. Nobody invented former forms. No one can invent others. It will change according to conditions and interests, just as the gilds and manors changed into modern phases. It is frightful to know of the poverty which some people endure. It is also frightful to know of disease, of physical defects, of accidents which cripple the body and wreck life, and of other ills by which human life is encompassed. Such facts appeal to human sympathy, and call for such help and amelioration as human effort can give. It is senseless to enumerate such facts, simply in order to create a state of mind in the hearer, and then to try to make him assent that "the system ought to be changed."

All the hospitals, asylums, almshouses, and other eleemosynary institutions prove that the world is not made right. They prove the existence of people who have not "equal chances" with others. The inmates can not be happy. Generally the institutions also prove the very limited extent to which, with the best intentions and greatest efforts, the more fortunate can do anything to help the matter—that is, to "change the system."

The notion that everybody ought to be happy, and equally happy with all the rest, is the fine flower of the philosophy which has been winning popularity for two hundred years. All the petty demands of natural rights, liberty, equality, etc., are only stepping-stones toward this philosophy, which is really what is wanted. All through human history some have had good fortune and some ill fortune. For some the ills of life have taken all the joy and strength out of existence, while the fortunate have always been there to show how glorious life might be and to furnish dreams of bliss to tantalize those who have failed and suffered. So men have constructed in philosophy theories of universal felicity. They tell us that every one has a natural right to be happy, to be comfortable, to have health, to succeed, to have knowledge, family, political power, and all the rest of the things which anybody can have. They put it all into the major premise. Then they say that we all ought to be equal. That proposition abolishes luck. In making propositions we can imply that all ought to have equally good luck, but, inasmuch as there is no way in which we can turn bad luck into good, or misfortune into good fortune, what the proposition means is that if we can not all have good luck no one shall have it. The unlucky will pull down the lucky. That is all that equality ever can mean. The worst becomes the standard. When we talk of "changing the system," we ought to understand that that means abolishing luck and all the ills of life. We might as well talk of abolishing storms, excessive heat and cold, tornadoes, pestilences, diseases, and other ills. Poverty belongs to the struggle for existence, and we are all born into that struggle. The human race began in utter destitution. It had no physical or metaphysical endowment whatever. The existing "system" is the outcome of the efforts of men for thousands of years to work together, so as to win in the struggle for existence. Probably socialists do not perceive what it means for any man now to turn about and pass his high judgment on the achievements of the human race in the way of civilization, and to propose to change it, by resolution, in about "six years." The result of the long effort has been that we all, in a measure, live above the grade of savages, and that some reach comfort and luxury and mental and moral welfare. Efforts to change the system have not been wanting. They have all led back to savagery. Mr. Sinclair thinks that the French Revolution issued out in liberty. The French Revolution is open to very many different interpretations and constructions; but, on the whole, it left essential interests just about where it found them. A million men lost their lives to get Louis de Bourbon off the throne and Napoleon Bonaparte on it, and by the spoils of Europe to make rich nobles of his generals. That is the most definite and indisputable result of the Revolution. Mr. Sinclair also repeats the familiar warning or threat that those who are not competent to win adequate success in the struggle for existence will "rise." They are going to "shoot," unless we let him and his associates redistribute property. It seems that it would be worth while for them to consider that, by their own hypothesis, those-who-have will possess advantages in "shooting": (1) they will have the guns; (2) they will have the talent on their side because they can pay for it; (3) they can hire an army out of the ranks of their adversaries.

In all this declamation we hear a great deal about votes and political power, "ballots or bullets." Of course this is another outcome of the political and social philosophy of the last two centuries. Mr. Sinclair says that "Democracy is an attitude of soul. It has its basis in the spiritual nature of man, from which it follows that all men are equal, or that, if they are not, they must become so." Then Democracy is a metaphysical religion or mythology. The age is not friendly to metaphysics or mythology, but it falls under the dominion of these old tyrants in its political philosophy. If anybody wants to put his soul in an attitude, he ought to do it. The "system" allows that liberty, and it is far safer than shooting. It is also permitted to believe that, if men are not equal, they will become so. If we wait a while they will all die, and then they will all be equal, although they certainly will not be so before that.

There are plenty of customs and institutions among us which produce evil results. They need reform; and propositions to that end are reasonable and useful. A few years ago we heard of persons who wanted to abolish poverty. They had no plan or scheme by which to do it; in the meantime, however, people were working day by day to overcome poverty as well as they could, each for himself. The talk about abolishing poverty by some resolution or construction has died out. The "industrial system" is just the organized effort which we are all making to overcome poverty. We do not want to change the system unless we can be convinced that we can make a shift which will accomplish that purpose better. Then, be it observed, the system will be changed without waiting for any philosophers to propose it. It is being changed every day, just as quickly as any detail in it can be altered so as to defeat poverty better. This is a world in which the rule is, "Root, hog, or die," and it is also a world in which "the longest pole knocks down the most persimmons." It is the popular experience which has formulated these sayings. How can we make them untrue? They contain immense tragedies. Those who believe that the problems of human pain and ill are waiting for a speculative solution in philosophy or ethics can dream of changing the system; but to everybody else it must seem worse than a waste of time to wrangle about such a thing. It is not a proposition; it does not furnish either a thesis to be tested or a project to be considered.

I am by no means arguing that "everything is for the best in the best of worlds," even in that part of it where the Stars and Stripes still float. I am, on the contrary, one of those who think that there is a great deal to be dissatisfied about. I may be asked what I think would be a remedy for the distress of the garment workers. I answer candidly that I do not know—that is why I have come forward with no proposition. My business now is to show how empty and false Mr. Sinclair's proposition is, and how harmful it would be to heed it. He only adds to our trouble and burden by putting forward erroneous ideas and helping to encourage bad thinking. The plan to rise and shoot has no promise of welfare in it for anybody.

Neither is there any practical sense or tangible project behind the suggestion to redistribute property. Some years ago I heard a socialist orator say that he could get along with any audience except "these measly, mean-spirited workingmen who have saved a few hundred dollars and built a cottage, with a savings bank mortgage, of which they rent the second story and live in the first. They," said he, "will get up and go out, a benchful at a time, when I begin to talk about rent." If he had been open to instruction from facts, he might have learned much from the con-

duct of those measly workingmen. They will fight far more fero-
ciously for their cottages than the millionaires for their palaces.
A redistribution of property means universal war. The final collapse of the French Revolution was due to the proposition to
redistribute property. Property is the opposite of poverty; it is
our bulwark against want and distress, but also against disease
and all other ills, which, if it can not prevent them, it still holds
at a distance. If we weaken the security of property or deprive
people of it, we plunge into distress those who now are above it.

Property is the condition of civilization. It is just as essential
to the state, to religion, and to education as it is to food and
clothing. In the form of capital it is essential to industry, but if
capital were not property it would not do its work in industry.
If we negate or destroy property we arrest the whole life of
civilized society and put men back on the level of beasts. The
family depends on property; the two institutions have been cor-
relative throughout the history of civilization. Property is the
first interest of man in time and in importance. We can conceive
of no time when property was not, and we can conceive of no
social growth in which property was not the prime condition.
The property interest is also the one which moves all men, including the socialists, more quickly and deeply than any other.
Property is that feature of the existing "industrial system" which
would most stubbornly resist change if it was threatened in its
essential character and meaning. There is a disposition now to
apologize for property, even while resisting attack upon it. This
is wrong. Property ought to be defended on account of its reality
and importance, and on account of its rank among the interests
of men.

What the socialists complain of is that we have not yet got the
work of civilization all done and that what has been done does
not produce ideal results. The task is a big one—it may even be
believed that it is infinite, because what we accomplish often only
opens new vistas of trouble. At present we are working on with
all the wisdom we have been able to win, and we hope to gain
more. If the socialists could help by reasonable and practical suggestions, their aid would be welcome. When they propose to redistribute property, or to change the industrial system, they only
disturb the work and introduce confusion and destruction. When
they talk about rising and shooting, as if such acts would not be
unreasonable or beyond possibility, they put themselves at the

limit of the law, and may, before they know it, become favorers
of crime.

"H. L. MENCKEN" *

By H. L. Mencken

Henry L. Mencken (1880–1956) defines the conservative's idea of
liberty

Born in Baltimore and largely self-educated except for studies
in a technical high school, Mencken achieved a scintillating career
as an iconoclastic literary and social critic and even as a respected scholar of the American language. At twenty-five, he had
risen from his early newspaper chores to become editor of the
Baltimore *Evening Herald,* and in 1906 began a long fruitful
association with the Baltimore *Sun,* which lasted until 1941. He
wrote books of poetry, studies of George Bernard Shaw, whom he
often followed rather closely, and one of Friedrich Nietzsche,
whom he believed was the inspiration for his own admiration of
aristocratic elitism and contempt for the "herd." During 1914–23,
he shared the editorship of *The Smart Set* with the equally iconoclastic drama critic George Jean Nathan, with whom he launched
the intellectually influential *American Mercury* in 1924.

Civil libertarians enjoyed Mencken's attack on hypocritical
Comstockery, which was censoring books, plays, and art exhibits.
He convinced many that the Puritans had been blue-nose med-
dlers, witch-burners, and prohibitionists—judgments now rejected
by historians. His generation loved his caustic attack on the fundamentalists of the Bible Belt, who were at war with Darwinism.
An agnostic and economic conservative like Voltaire, he disliked
radicals and reformers; but this side of him was out of joint with
the Great Depression era, and readers became impatient with the
pleasant things he had to say about Mussolini and Hitler while
continuing a lifelong attack on democracy.

His chief critical essays appear in the six series of *Prejudices*
(1919–27) and *Notes on Democracy* (1921). His autobiography

* From H. L. Mencken, "H. L. Mencken," *The Nation,* vol. 117 (December 5, 1923), 647–48.

may be followed in *Happy Days* (1940), *Newspaper Days* (1941), and *Heathen Days* (1943). Authorities praise the scholarship of *The American Language* (1919, frequently revised); most readers enjoy his robust humor even if they reject his critical judgments.

ASK A professional critic to write about himself and you simply ask him to do what he does every day in the practice of his art and mystery. There is, indeed, no criticism that is not a confidence, and there is no confidence that is not self-revelation. When I denounce a book with mocking and contumely, and fall upon the poor author in the brutal, Asiatic manner of a drunken longshoreman, a Ku Kluxer, or a midshipman at Annapolis, I am only saying, in the trade cant, that the fellow disgusts me—that his ideas and his manners are somehow obnoxious to me, as those of a Methodist, a golf-player, or a clog-dancer are obnoxious to me—in brief, that I hold myself to be a great deal better than he is, and am eager to say so. And when, on the other hand, I praise a book in high, astounding terms, and speak of the author as if his life and sufferings were of capital importance to the world, then I am merely saying that I detect something in him, of prejudice, tradition, habit of mind, that is much like something within myself, and that my own life and sufferings are of the utmost importance to me.

That is all there ever is in criticism, once it gets beyond cataloguing. No matter how artfully the critic may try to be impersonal and scientific he is bound to give himself away. In fact, his very effort to be impersonal and scientific is a form of giving himself away, as the writings of my eminent colleague, Prof. Dr. Erskine, well demonstrate. I have never had the honor of being presented to Erskine, but I know quite as well as his grandmother that he is essentially a shy man—that the winds of doctrine alarm him and he has no stomach for rough adventure. Hence his plea for decorum and tradition, i. e., for what has passed the stage of experiment and danger, i. e., for safe harbors and refuges. He can no more get himself out of his criticism than he can get himself out of his skin. Nor can, at the other pole, the critical Bolsheviki of Greenbaum Village—all of them as foreign and as loathsome to Erskine, I daresay, as so many Nietzsches or Beethovens. When these bright young men print profound aesthetic treatises upon the art of Fatty Arbuckle, Gertrude Stein, and the "Parisian Widows" burlesque troupe, they say, of course, nothing that is pertinent to aesthetics, but they do say something extremely amusing about their own tastes, and hence about themselves. More, they say something even more amusing about the seminaries where they were bred to the humanities.

With criticism thus so transparent, so unescapably revelatory, I often marvel that the gentlemen who concern themselves with my own books, often very indignantly, do not penetrate more competently to my essence. Even for a critic I am excessively garrulous and confidential; nevertheless, it is rare for me to encounter a criticism that hits me where I live and have my being. A great deal of ink is wasted trying to discover and denounce my motive in being a critic at all. I am, by one theory, a German spy told off to flay, terrorize, and stampede the Anglo-Saxon. By another I am a secret radical, while professing to admire Coolidge, Judge Gary, and Genghis Khan. By a third, I am a fanatical American chauvinist, bent upon defaming and ruining the motherland. All these notions are nonsense; only the first has even the slightest plausibility. The plain truth is—and how could it be plainer?—that I practice criticism for precisely the same reason that every other critic practices it: because I am a vain fellow, and have a great many ideas on all sorts of subjects, and like to put them into words and harass the human race with them. If I could confine this flow of ideas to one subject I'd be a professor and get some respect. If I could reduce it, say, to one idea a year, I'd be a novelist, a dramatist, or a newspaper editorial writer. But being unable to staunch the flux, and having, as I say, a vast and exigent vanity, I am a critic of books, and through books of *Homo sapiens,* and through *Homo sapiens* of God.

So much for the motive. What, now, of the substance? What is the fundamental faith beneath all the spurting and coruscating of ideas that I have just mentioned? What do I primarily and immovably believe in, as a Puritan believes in hell? I believe in liberty. And when I say liberty, I mean the thing in its widest imaginable sense—liberty up to the extreme limits of the feasible and tolerable. I am against forbidding anybody to do anything, or say anything, or think anything so long as it is at all possible to imagine a habitable world in which he would be free to do, say, and think it. The burden of proof, as I see it, is always upon

opposed to law officers.

the policeman, which is to say, upon the lawmaker, the theologian, the right-thinker. He must prove his case doubly, triply, quadruply, and then he must start all over and prove it again. The eye through which I view him is watery and jaundiced. I do not pretend to be "just" to him—any more than a Christian pretends to be just to the devil. He is the enemy of everything I admire and respect in this world—of everything that makes it various and amusing and charming. He impedes every honest search for the truth. He stands against every sort of good-will and common decency. His ideal is that of an animal trainer, an archbishop, a major general in the army. I am against him until the last galoot's ashore.

This simple and childlike faith in the freedom and dignity of man—here, perhaps, stated with undue rhetoric—should be obvious, I should think, to every critic above the mental backwardness of a Federal judge. Nevertheless, very few of them, anatomizing my books, have ever showed any sign of detecting it. But all the same even the dullest of them has, in his fashion, sensed it; it colors unconsciously all the diatribes about myself that I have ever read. It is responsible for the fact that in England and Germany (and, to the extent that I have ever been heard of at all, in France and Italy) I am regarded as a highly typical American—in truth, as almost the archetype of the American. And it is responsible equally for the fact that here at home I am often denounced as the worst American unhung. The paradox is only apparent. The explanation of it lies in this: that to most Europeans the United States is still regarded naively as the land of liberty *par excellence,* whereas to most Americans the thing itself has long ceased to have any significance, and to large numbers of them, indeed, it has of late taken on an extreme obnoxiousness. I know of no civilized country, indeed, in which liberty is less esteemed than it is in the United States today; certainly there is none in which more persistent efforts are made to limit it and put it down. I am thus, to Americans, a bad American, but to Europeans, still unaware of the practical effects of the Wilson idealism and the Roosevelt saloon-bouncer ethic, I seem to be an eloquent spokesman of the true American tradition. It is a joke, but the joke is not on me.

Liberty, of course, is not for slaves: I do not advocate inflicting it on men against their conscience. On the contrary, I am strongly

in favor of letting them crawl and grovel all they please—before
the Supreme Court of the United States, Gompers, J. P. Morgan,
Henry Cabot Lodge, the Anti-Saloon League, or whatever other
fraud or combination of frauds they choose to venerate. I am
thus unable to make the grade as a Liberal, for Liberalism always
involves freeing human beings against their will—often, indeed,
to their obvious damage, as in the cases of the majority of Negroes
and women. But all human beings are not congenital slaves, even
in America. Here and there one finds a man or a woman with a
great natural passion for liberty—and a hard job getting it. It is,
to me at least, a vast pleasure to go to the rescue of such a victim
of the herd, to give him some aid and comfort in his struggle
against the forces that seek to regiment and throttle him. It is a
double pleasure to succor him when the sort of liberty he strives
for is apparently unintelligible and valueless—for example, liberty to address conventions of the I.W.W., to read the books of
such bad authors as D. H. Lawrence and Petronius Arbiter, to
work twelve hours a day, to rush the can, to carry red flags in
parades, to patronize osteopaths and Christian Science healers, to
belong to the best clubs. Such nonsensical varieties of liberty are
especially sweet to me. I have wrecked my health and dissipated a
fortune defending them—never, so far as I know, successfully.
Why, then, go on? Ask yourself why a grasshopper goes on jump-
ing.

But what has liberty to do with the art of literary criticism, my
principal business in this vale? Nothing—or everything. It seems
to me that it is perfectly possible to write profound and valuable
literary criticism without entering upon the question of freedom
at all, either directly or indirectly. Aesthetic judgments may be
isolated from all other kinds of judgments, and yet remain interesting and important. But this isolation must be performed by
other hands: to me it is as sheer a psychological impossibility as
believing that God condemned forty-two little children to death
for poking fun at Elisha's bald head. When I encounter a new
idea, whether aesthetic, political, theological, or epistemological,
I ask myself, instantly and automatically, what would happen
to its proponent if he should state its exact antithesis. If nothing
would happen to him, then I am willing and eager to listen to
him. But if he would lose anything valuable by a *volte face*—if
stating his idea is profitable to him, if the act secures his roof,

butters his parsnips, gets him a tip—then I hear him with one ear only. He is not a free man. Ergo, he is not a man. For liberty, when one ascends to the levels where ideas swish by and men pursue Truth to grab her by the tail, is the first thing and the last thing. So long as it prevails the show is thrilling and stupendous; the moment it fails the show is a dull and dirty farce.

Chapter Eight

SOCIAL PROTEST:

The Muckrakers, Socialists,
Single Tax, and Progressivism

PROGRESS AND POVERTY *

By Henry George

*Henry George (1839–97), economist, shows how the single tax
would benefit all classes*

The radicalism of Henry George was concerned with one principal idea—the single tax proposal—and reflected his middle-class,
devoutly religious parents of British descent. He was largely self-
educated (aside from attending a private high school and listening
to informal scientific lectures); but he read intensely about contemporary problems and was even considered at one time as a fit
prospect for a professorial post in economics. As a young man he
enjoyed the adventurous life of a sailor and as a ship steward
sailed to San Francisco. At almost the same time, he learned the
typesetting trade that led him into journalism, to engage in editorial work on several newspapers. In San Francisco, Oakland,
and Sacramento, he noted the effects of land speculation on society
and came to attribute the chronic economic depressions to such
speculative activities.

His brochure of 1871, "Our Land and Land Policy," anticipated the main arguments of his classic, *Progress and Poverty*
(1879). Man, he believed, had a natural right to labor on the
land; however, laboring as he did under private ownership and
speculation, he was robbed of part of his reward because of the
unearned economic rent received by the speculator. He proposed
a single tax on this increment in rising land values that would
relieve productive enterprise of the burden of all other taxes. As

* From Henry George, *Progress and Poverty* (1886), 44–53.

the chapter below indicates, he believed that the single tax would specifically benefit every class and eliminate speculation. His observations won the most extravagant praises from Tolstoy, who was much concerned with the Russian agrarian problem, and also from Irish land reformers. His collection of magazine articles in the book *Social Problems* even converted Mayor Tom Johnson of Cleveland, once a cynical businessman, to the path of progressive reform. Newton D. Baker and John Dewey both considered Henry George to be a profound thinker; and the outspoken Catholic reformer, Father Edward McGlynn, was said to have been so influenced by the concept of the single tax that he was excommunicated because of it.

Henry George tried vainly to extend his influence from journalism to politics. Failing in his bid for election to the California legislature, he campaigned unsuccessfully for mayor of New York in 1886, although one of his opponents, young Theodore Roosevelt, ran behind him. He died while attempting a second campaign for the mayoralty. His *Progress and Poverty* became a perennial best seller, selling well into the millions, and most large cities were to witness the blossoming of Henry George Clubs. Even the economists whom George had assailed as reactionary did not dismiss his suggestions regarding the social effects of taxation, and the economics textbooks of the 1960's were apt to give some attention to this original mind.

Of the Effect Upon Individuals and Classes

WHEN IT is first proposed to put all taxes upon the value of land, and thus confiscate rent, all land holders are likely to take the alarm, and there will not be wanting appeals to the fears of small farm and homestead owners, who will be told that this is a proposition to rob them of their hard-earned property. But a moment's reflection will show that this proposition should commend itself to all whose interests as land holders do not largely exceed their interests as laborers or capitalists, or both. And further consideration will show that though the large land holders may lose relatively, yet even in their case there will be an absolute gain. For, the increase in production will be so great that labor and capital will gain very much more than will be lost to private land ownership, while in these gains, and in the greater ones involved in a more healthy social condition, the whole community, including the land owners themselves, will share.

In a preceding chapter I have gone over the question of what is due to the present land holders, and have shown that they have no claim to compensation. But there is still another ground on which we may dismiss all idea of compensation. They will not really be injured.

It is manifest, of course, that the change I propose will greatly benefit all those who live by wages, whether of hand or of head—laborers, operatives, mechanics, clerks, professional men of all sorts. It is manifest, also, that it will benefit all those who live partly by wages and partly by the earnings of their capital—storekeepers, merchants, manufacturers, employing or undertaking producers and exchangers of all sorts—from the peddler or drayman to the railroad or steamship owner—and it is likewise manifest that it will increase the incomes of those whose incomes are drawn from the earnings of capital, or from investments other than in lands, save perhaps the holders of government bonds or other securities bearing fixed rates of interest, which will probably depreciate in selling value, owing to the rise in the general rate of interest, though the income from them will remain the same.

Take, now, the case of the homestead owner—the mechanic, storekeeper, or professional man who has secured himself a house and lot, where he lives, and which he contemplates with satisfaction as a place from which his family cannot be ejected in case of his death. He will not be injured; on the contrary, he will be the gainer. The selling value of his lot will diminish—theoretically it will entirely disappear. But its usefulness to him will not disappear. It will serve his purpose as well as ever. While, as the value of all other lots will diminish or disappear in the same ratio, he retains the same security of always having a lot that he had before. That is to say, he is a loser only as the man who has bought himself a pair of boots may be said to be a loser by a subsequent fall in the price of boots. His boots will be just as useful to him, and the next pair of boots he can get cheaper. So, to the homestead owner, his lot will be as useful, and should he look forward to getting a larger lot, or having his children, as they grow up, get homesteads of their own, he will, even in the matter of lots, be the gainer. And in the present, other things considered, he will be much the gainer. For though he will have more taxes to pay upon his land, he will be released from taxes upon his house and improvements, upon his furniture and personal property, upon all that he and his family eat, drink and wear, while his earnings will be largely increased by the rise of wages, the constant employment, and the increased briskness of trade. His only loss will be, if he wants to sell his lot without getting another, and this will be a small loss compared with the great gain.

And so with the farmer. I speak not now of the farmers who never touch the handles of a plow, who cultivate thousands of acres and enjoy incomes like those of the rich Southern planters before the war; but of the working farmers who constitute such a large class in the United States—men who own small farms, which they cultivate with the aid of their boys, and perhaps some hired help, and who in Europe would be called peasant proprietors. Paradoxical as it may appear to these men until they understand the full bearings of the proposition, of all classes above that of the mere laborer they have most to gain by placing all taxes upon the value of land. That they do not now get as good a living as their hard work ought to give them, they generally feel, though they may not be able to trace the cause. The fact is that taxation, as now levied, falls on them with peculiar severity. They are taxed on all their improvements—houses, barns, fences, crops, stock. The personal property which they have cannot be as readily concealed or undervalued as can the more valuable kinds which are concentrated in the cities. They are not only taxed on personal property and improvements, which the owners of unused land escape, but their land is generally taxed at a higher rate than land held on speculation, simply because it is improved. But further than this, all taxes imposed on commodities, and especially the taxes which, like our protective duties, are imposed with a view of raising the prices of commodities, fall on the farmer without mitigation. For in a country like the United States, which exports agricultural produce, the farmer cannot be protected. Whoever gains, he must lose. Some years ago the Free Trade League of New York published a broadside containing cuts of various articles of necessity marked with the duties imposed by the tariff, and which read something in this wise: "The farmer rises in the morning and draws on his pantaloons taxed 40 per cent. and his boots taxed 30 per cent., striking a light with a match taxed 200 per cent.," and so on, following him through the day and through life, until, killed by taxation, he is lowered into the grave with a rope taxed 45 per cent. This is but a graphic illustration of the manner in which such taxes ultimately fall. The farmer would be a great gainer by the substitution of a single tax upon the value of land for all these taxes, for the taxation of land values would fall with greatest weight, not upon the agricultural districts, where land values are comparatively small, but upon the towns and cities where land values are high; whereas taxes upon personal property and improvements fall as heavily in the country as in the city. And in sparsely settled districts there would be hardly any taxes at all for the farmer to pay. For taxes, being levied upon the value of the bare land, would fall as heavily upon unimproved as upon improved land. Acre for acre, the improved and cultivated farm, with its buildings, fences, orchard, crops, and stock, could be taxed no more than unused land of equal quality. The result would be that speculative values would be kept down, and that cultivated and improved farms would have no taxes to pay until the country around them had been well settled. In fact, paradoxical as it may at first seem to them, the effect of putting all taxation upon the value of land would be to relieve the harder working farmers of all taxation.

But the great gain of the working farmer can be seen only when the effect upon the distribution of population is considered. The destruction of speculative land values would tend to diffuse population where it is too dense to concentrate it where it is too sparse; to substitute for the tenement house, homes surrounded by gardens, and fully to settle agricultural districts before people were driven far from neighbors to look for land. The people of the cities would thus get more of the pure air and sunshine of the country, the people of the country more of the economies and social life of the city. If, as is doubtless the case, the application of machinery tends to large fields, agricultural population will assume the primitive form and cluster in villages. The life of the average farmer is now unnecessarily dreary. He is not only compelled to work early and late, but he is cut off by the sparseness of population from the conveniences, and amusements, the educational facilities, and the social and intellectual opportunities that come with the closer contact of man with man. He would be far better off in all these respects, and his labor would be far more productive, if he and those around him held no more land than they wanted to use.* While his children, as they grew up, would

* Besides the enormous increase in the productive power of labor which would result from the better distribution of population there would be

neither be so impelled to seek the excitement of a city nor would they be driven so far away to seek farms of their own. Their means of living would be in their own hands, and at home.

In short, the working farmer is both a laborer and a capitalist, as well as a land owner, and it is by his labor and capital that his living is made. His loss would be nominal; his gain would be real and great.

In varying degrees is this true of all land holders. Many land holders are laborers of one sort or another. And it would be hard to find a land owner not a laborer, who is not also a capitalist—while the general rule is, that the larger the land owner the greater the capitalist. So true is this that in common thought the characters are confounded. Thus to put all taxes on the value of land, while it would be largely to reduce all great fortunes, would in no case leave the rich man penniless. The Duke of Westminster, who owns a considerable part of the site of London, is probably the richest land owner in the world. To take all his ground rents by taxation would largely reduce his enormous income, but would still leave him his buildings and all the income from them, and doubtless much personal property in various other shapes. He would still have all he could by any possibility enjoy, and a much better state of society in which to enjoy it.

So would the Astors of New York remain very rich. And so, I think, it will be seen throughout—this measure would make no one poorer but such as could be made a great deal poorer without being really hurt. It would cut down great fortunes, but it would impoverish no one.

Wealth would not only be enormously increased; it would be equally distributed. I do not mean that each individual would get the same amount of wealth. That would not be equal distribution, so long as different individuals have different powers and different desires. But I mean that wealth would be distributed in accordance with the degree in which the industry, skill, knowledge, or prudence of each contributed to the common stock. The

---

also a similar economy in the productive power of land. The concentration of population in cities fed by the exhaustive cultivation of large, sparsely populated areas, results in a literal draining into the sea of the elements of fertility. How enormous this waste is may be seen from the calculations that have been made as to the sewage of our cities, and its practical result is to be seen in the diminishing productiveness of agriculture in large sections. In a great part of the United States we are steadily exhausting our lands.

great cause which concentrates wealth in the hands of those who do not produce, and takes it from the hands of those who do, would be gone. The inequalities that continued to exist would be those of nature, not the artificial inequalities produced by the denial of natural law. The non-producer would no longer roll in luxury while the producer got but the barest necessities of animal existence.

The monopoly of the land gone, there need be no fear of large fortunes. For then the riches of any individual must consist of wealth, properly so-called—of wealth, which is the product of labor, and which constantly tends to dissipation, for national debts, I imagine, would not long survive the abolition of the system from which they spring. All fear of great fortunes might be dismissed, for when every one gets what he fairly earns, no one can get more than he fairly earns. How many men are there who fairly earn a million dollars?

LOOKING BACKWARD *

By Edward Bellamy

Edward Bellamy (1850–98), journalist, writes a Utopian romance of national planning and democratic Socialism

Born in Chicopee, Massachusetts, the son of a Baptist minister, and a lifelong resident of western Massachusetts, Bellamy studied law and was admitted to the bar before turning to journalism in Springfield. His first historical novel of social protest was The Duke of Stockbridge, which dealt with Shays's Rebellion. But his reputation came only with Looking Backward (1888). This Utopian romance depicted a Rip Van Winkle of the year 2000, who wakes up to find a socialist society that had abolished money and permitted men to be educated or employed according to preference as well as aptitude. In this world of large-scale enterprise free from waste, men were liberated from recurrent economic

*From Edward Bellamy, Looking Backward (1888), 88–97.

crises, unemployment, and strikes while women enjoyed equality in a society that encouraged eugenics.

Although this Eden may strike some modern readers as uncomfortably confining and pictured in a priggish sentimental manner, the reader of 1888 seemed captivated by both message and spirit. *Looking Backward* sold a million copies, and thousands of readers joined Bellamy or Nationalist (socialist) Clubs in the cause of gradualist socialism. The Nationalist movement made headway in eastern and midwestern politics until the Populist movement absorbed much of it. By the time of the New Deal, Edward Bellamy was once more labeled a prophet of social planning and, in fact, inspired a thoughtful biography by Arthur Morgan of the Tennessee Valley Authority. Franklin Roosevelt found it timely to entitle one of his books, *Looking Forward,* which was no rebuke to Bellamy but rather another contribution to social planning.

. . . "WHO DOES your house-work, then?" I asked.

"There is none to do," said Mrs. Leete, to whom I had addressed this question. "Our washing is all done at public laundries at excessively cheap rates, and our cooking at public kitchens. The making and repairing of all we wear are done outside in public shops. Electricity, of course, takes the place of all fires and lighting. We choose houses no larger than we need, and furnish them so as to involve the minimum of trouble to keep them in order. We have no use for domestic servants."

"The fact," said Dr. Leete, "that you had in the poorer classes a boundless supply of serfs on whom you could impose all sorts of painful and disagreeable tasks, made you indifferent to devices to avoid the necessity for them. But now that we all have to do in turn whatever work is done for society, every individual in the nation has the same interest, and a personal one, in devices for lightening the burden. This fact has given a prodigious impulse to labour-saving inventions in all sorts of industry, of which the combination of the maximum of comfort and minimum of trouble in household arrangements was one of the earliest results.

"In case of special emergencies in the household," pursued Dr. Leete, "such as extensive cleaning or renovation, or sickness in the family, we can always secure assistance from the industrial force."

"But how do you recompense these assistants, since you have no money?"

"We do not pay them, of course, but the nation for them. Their services can be obtained by application at the proper bureau, and their value is pricked off the credit card of the applicant."

"What a paradise for womankind the world must be now!" I exclaimed. "In my day, even wealth and unlimited servants did not enfranchise their possessors from household cares, while the women of the merely well-to-do and poorer classes lived and died martyrs to them."

"Yes," said Mrs. Leete, "I have read something of that; enough to convince me that, badly off as the men, too, were in your day, they were more fortunate than their mothers and wives."

"The broad shoulders of the nation," said Dr. Leete, "bear now like a feather the burden that broke the backs of the women of your day. Their misery came, with all your other miseries, from that incapacity for co-operation which followed from the individualism on which your social system was founded, from your inability to perceive that you can make ten times more profit out of your fellow men by uniting with them than by contending with them. The wonder is, not that you did not live more comfortably, but that you were able to live together at all, who were all confessedly bent on making one another your servants, and securing possession of one another's goods."

"There, there, father, if you are so vehement, Mr. West will think you are scolding him," laughingly interposed Edith.

"When you want a doctor," I asked, "do you simply apply to the proper bureau and take anyone that may be sent?"

"That rule would not work well in the case of physicians," replied Dr. Leete. "The good a physician can do a patient depends largely on his acquaintance with his constitutional tendencies and condition. The patient must be able, therefore, to call in a particular doctor, and he does so just as patients did in your day. The only difference is that, instead of collecting his fee for himself the doctor collects it for the nation by pricking off the amount, according to a regular scale for medical attendance, from the patient's credit card."

"I can imagine," I said, "that if the fee is always the same, and a doctor may not turn away patients, as I suppose he may not, the good doctors are called constantly and the poor doctors left in idleness."

"In the first place, if you will overlook the apparent conceit of the remark from a retired physician," replied Dr. Leete, with a smile, "we have no poor doctors. Anybody who pleases to get a little smattering of medical terms is not now at liberty to practise on the bodies of citizens, as in your day. None but students who have passed the severe tests of the schools, and clearly proved their vocation, are permitted to practise. Then, too, you will observe that there is nowadays no attempt of doctors to build up their practice at the expense of other doctors. There would be no motive for that. For the rest, the doctor has to render regular reports of his work to the medical bureau, and if he is not reasonably well employed, work is found for him."

THE questions which I needed to ask before I could acquire even an outline acquaintance with the institutions of the twentieth century being endless, and Dr. Leete's good nature being equally so, we sat up talking for several hours after the ladies left us. Reminding my host of the point at which our talk had broken off that morning, I expressed my curiosity to learn how the organization of the industrial army was made to afford a sufficient stimulus to diligence in the lack of any anxiety on the worker's part as to his livelihood.

"You must understand in the first place," replied the doctor, "that the supply of incentives to effort is but one of the objects sought in the organization we have adopted for the army. The other, and equally important, is to secure for the file-leaders and captains of the force, and the great officers of the nation, men of proven abilities, who are pledged by their own careers to hold their followers up to the highest standard of performance and permit no lagging. With a view to these two ends the industrial army is organized. First comes the unclassified grade of common labourers, men of all work, to which all recruits during their first three years belong. This grade is a sort of school, and a very strict one, in which the young men are taught habits of obedience, subordination, and devotion to duty. While the miscellaneous nature of the work done by this force prevents the systematic grading of the workers which is afterwards possible, yet individual records are kept, and excellence receives distinction corresponding with the penalties that negligence incurs. It is not, however, policy with us to permit youthful recklessness or indiscretion, when not

deeply culpable, to handicap the future careers of young men,
and all who have passed through the unclassified grade without
serious disgrace have an equal opportunity to choose the life employment they have most liking for. Having selected this, they
enter upon it as apprentices. The length of the apprenticeship
naturally differs in different occupations. At the end of it the
apprentice becomes a full workman, and a member of his trade
or guild. Now not only are the individual records of the apprentices for ability and industry strictly kept, and excellence distinguished by suitable distinctions, but upon the average of his record during apprenticeship the standing given the apprentice
among the full workmen depends.

"While the internal organizations of different industries, mechanical and agricultural, differ according to their peculiar conditions, they agree in a general division of their workers into first,
second, and third grades, according to ability, and these grades
are in many cases sub-divided into first and second classes. According to his standing as an apprentice a young man is assigned his
place as a first, second, or third grade worker. Of course only
young men of unusual ability pass directly from apprenticeship
into the first grade of the workers. The most fall into the lower
grades, working up as they grow more experienced, at the periodi-
cal regradings. These regradings take place in each industry at
intervals corresponding with the length of the apprenticeship
to that industry, so that merit never need wait long to rise, nor
can any rest on past achievements unless they would drop into a
lower rank. One of the notable advantages of a high grading is
the privilege it gives the worker in electing which of the various
branches or process of his industry he will follow as his speciality.
Of course it is not intended that any of these processes shall be
disproportionately arduous, but there is often much difference
between them, and the privilege of election is accordingly highly
prized. So far as possible, indeed, the preferences even of the
poorest workmen, are considered in assigning them their line of
work, because not only their happiness but their usefulness is
thus enhanced. While, however, the wish of the lower grade man
is consulted so far as the exigencies of the service permit, he is
considered only after the upper grade men have been provided
for, and often has to put up with second or third choice, or even
with an arbitrary assignment when help is needed. The privilege
of election attends every regrading, and when a man loses his

grade he also risks having to exchange the sort of work he likes for some other less to his taste. The results of each regrading, giving the standing of every man, in his industry, are gazetted in the public prints, and those who have won promotion since the last regrading receive the nation's thanks and are publicly invested with the badge of their new rank."

"What may this badge be?" I asked.

"Every industry has its emblematic device," replied Dr. Leete, "and this, in the shape of a metallic badge so small that you might not see it unless you knew where to look, is all the insignia which the men of the army wear, except where public convenience demands a distinctive uniform. This badge is the same in form for all grades of industry, but while the badge of the first grade is iron, that of the second grade is silver, and that of the third is gilt.

"Apart from the grand incentive to endeavour afforded by the fact that the high places in the nation are open only to the highest class men, and that rank in the army constitutes the only mode of social distinction for the vast majority who are not aspirants in art, literature, and the professions, various incitements of a minor, but perhaps equally effective, sort are provided in the form of special privileges and immunities in the way of discipline, which the superior class men enjoy. These, while intended to be as little as possible invidious to the less successful, have the effect of keeping constantly before every man's mind the great desirability of attaining the grade next above his own.

"It is obviously important that not only the good but also the indifferent and poor workmen should be able to cherish the ambition of rising. Indeed, the number of the latter being so much greater, it is even more essential that the ranking system should not operate to discourage them than that it should stimulate the others. It is to this end that the grades are divided into classes. The grades as well as the classes being made numerically equal at each regrading, there is not at any time, counting out the officers and the unclassified and apprentice grades, over one-ninth of the industrial army in the lowest class, and most of this number are recent apprentices, all of whom expect to rise. Those who remain during the entire term of service in the lowest class, are but a trifling fraction of the industrial army, and likely to be as deficient in sensibility to their position as in ability to better it.

"It is not even necessary that a worker should win promotion to a higher grade to have at least a taste of glory. While promotion requires a general excellence of record as a worker, honourable mention and various sorts of prizes are awarded for excellence less than sufficient for promotion, and also for special feats and single performances in the various industries. There are many minor distinctions of standing, not only within the grades but within the classes, each of which acts as a spur to the efforts of a group. It is intended that no form of merit shall wholly fail of recognition.

"As for actual neglect of work, positively bad work, or other overt remissness on the part of men incapable of generous motives, the discipline of the industrial army is far too strict to allow anything whatever of the sort. A man able to do duty, and persistently refusing, is sentenced to solitary imprisonment on bread and water till he consents.

"The lowest grade of the officers of the industrial army, that of assistant foremen or lieutenants, is appointed out of men who have held their place for two years in the first class of the first grade. Where this leaves too large a range of choice, only the first group of this class are eligible. No one thus comes to the point of commanding men until he is about thirty years old. After a man becomes an officer, his rating of course no longer depends on the efficiency of his own work, but on that of his men. The foremen are appointed from among the assistant foremen, by the same exercise of discretion limited to a small eligible class. In the appointments to the still higher grades another principle is introduced, which it would take too much time to explain now.

"Of course such a system of grading as I have described would have been impracticable applied to the small industrial concerns of your day, in some of which there were hardly enough employés to have left one apiece for the classes. You must remember that, under the national organization of labour, all industries are carried on by great bodies of men, many of your farms or shops being combined as one. It is also owing solely to the vast scale on which each industry is organized, with co-ordinate establishments in every part of the country, that we are able by exchanges and transfers to fit every man so nearly with the sort of work he can do best.

"And now, Mr. West, I will leave it to you, on the bare outline of its features which I have given, whether those who need special incentives to do their best are likely to lack them under our system. Does it not seem to you that men who found themselves obliged, whether they wished or not, to work, would under such a system be strongly impelled to do their best?"

I replied that it seemed to me the incentives offered were, if any objection were to be made, too strong; that the pace set for the young men was too hot; and such, indeed, I would add with deference, still remains my opinion, now that by longer residence among you I have become better acquainted with the whole subject.

Dr. Leete, however, desired me to reflect, and I am ready to say that it is perhaps a sufficient reply to my objection, that the worker's livelihood is in no way dependent on his ranking, and anxiety for that never embitters his disappointments; that the working hours are short, the vacations regular, and that all emulation ceases at forty-five, with the attainment of middle life.

"There are two or three other points I ought to refer to," he added, "to prevent your getting mistaken impressions. In the first place, you must understand that this system of preferment given the more efficient workers over the less so, in no way contravenes the fundamental idea of our social system, that all who do their best are equally deserving, whether that best be great or small I have shown that the system is arranged to encourage the weaker as well as the stronger with the hope of rising, while the fact that the stronger are selected for the leaders is in no way a reflection upon the weaker, but in the interest of the common weal.

to strive

"Do not imagine, either, because emulation is given free play as an incentive under our system, that we deem it a motive likely to appeal to the nobler sort of men, or worthy of them. Such as these find their motives within, not without, and measure their duty by their own endowments, not by those of others. As long as their achievement is proportioned to their powers, they would consider it preposterous to expect praise or blame because it chanced to be great or small. To such natures emulation appears philosophically absurd, and despicable in a moral aspect by its substitution of envy for admiration, and exultation for regret, in one's attitude toward the successes and the failures of others.

"But all men, even in the last year of the twentieth century, are not of this high order, and the incentives to endeavour requisite for those who are not must be of a sort adapted to their inferior natures. For these, then, emulation of the keenest edge is provided as a constant spur. Those who need this motive will feel it. Those who are above its influence do not need it.

"I should not fail to mention," resumed the doctor, "that for those too deficient in mental or bodily strength to be fairly graded with the main body of workers, we have a separate grade, unconnected with the others,—a sort of invalid corps, the members of which are provided with a light class of tasks fitted to their strength. All our sick in mind and body, all our deaf and dumb, and lame and blind and crippled, and even our insane, belong to this invalid corps, and bear its insignia. The strongest often do nearly a man's work, the feeblest, of course, nothing; but none who can do anything are willing quite to give up. In their lucid intervals, even our insane are eager to do what they can."

"That is a pretty idea of the invalid corps," I said. "Even a barbarian from the nineteenth century can appreciate that. It is a very graceful way of disguising charity, and must be grateful to the feelings of its recipients."

"Charity!" repeated Dr. Leete. "Did you suppose that we consider the incapable class we are talking of objects of charity?"

"Why, naturally," I said, "inasmuch as they are incapable of self-support."

But here the doctor took me up quickly.

"Who is capable of self-support?" he demanded. "There is no such thing in a civilised society as self-support. In a state of society so barbarous as not even to know family co-operation, each individual may possibly support himself, though even then for a part of his life only; but from the moment that men begin to live together, and constitute even the rudest sort of society, self-support becomes impossible. As men grow more civilized, and the subdivision of occupations and services is carried out, a complex mutual dependence becomes the universal rule. Every man, however solitary may seem his occupation, is a member of a vast industrial partnership, as large as the nation, as large as humanity. The necessity of mutual dependence should imply the duty and guarantee of mutual support; and that it did not in your day constituted the essential cruelty and unreason of your system."

"HOW I BECAME A SOCIALIST" *

By Jack London

Jack London (1876–1916), rebel and novelist of adventure, tells of his conversion from rugged individualism to Socialism

As a son of a wandering truck farmer and astrologer, Jack London of San Francisco lived the adventures that he also read about so voraciously. He hobnobbed with rough sailors, robbed oyster beds in the Bay, sailed to Japan, and became the hard-drinking hobo that he describes in *John Barleycorn* (1913). After marching in sympathy with Coxey's Army of the Depression of 1893, he was arrested and turned socialist, as he describes here. Later, for almost a year, he studied at the University of California, showing interest in Spencer and the new sociology, but during 1897–98, he was off for the great adventure in the Klondike gold rush and spent a winter in the Yukon. These experiences became in 1899 the basis of his first short stories in the *Overland Monthly* and the *Atlantic Monthly*. His first and perhaps greatest novel was *The Call of the Wild* (1901), which told of Buck, a domesticated dog who reverts to the savagery of his ancestors to lead a wolf pack. The Darwinian brute is suggested in *The Sea-Wolf* (1904), while other novels seem inspired by Schopenhauer's Will-to-Power, Herbert Spencer's Survival of the Fittest, as well as Nietzsche's Superman—the latter is apparent in *The Iron Heel* (1907). Despite London's ideological confusion (e.g., in 1904, as a correspondent in the Russo-Japanese War, he warned of the Yellow Peril, a curious view for an internationally minded socialist), European left-wing readers liked his socialism while most American readers thoroughly enjoyed his brilliant story-telling ability and his exciting style.

IT IS quite fair to say that I became a Socialist in a fashion somewhat similar to the way in which the Teutonic pagans became Christians—it was hammered into me. Not only was I

* Jack London, "How I Became a Socialist," *War of the Classes* (Macmillan, 1905), 267–78.

not looking for Socialism at the time of my conversion, but I was
fighting it. I was very young and callow, did not know much of
anything, and though I had never even heard of a school called
"Individualism," I sang the pæan of the strong with all my heart.

This was because I was strong myself. By strong I mean that I
had good health and hard muscles, both of which possessions are
easily accounted for. I had lived my childhood on California
ranches, my boyhood hustling newspapers on the streets of a
healthy Western city, and my youth on the ozone-laden waters
of San Francisco Bay and the Pacific Ocean. I loved life in the
open, and I toiled in the open, at the hardest kinds of work.
Learning no trade, but drifting along from job to job, I looked
on the world and called it good, every bit of it. Let me repeat,
this optimism was because I was healthy and strong, bothered
with neither aches nor weaknesses, never turned down by the
boss because I did not look fit, able always to get a job at shovel-
ling coal, sailorizing, or manual labor of some sort. . . .

I hope I have made it clear that I was proud to be one of
Nature's strong-armed noblemen. The dignity of labor was to
me the most impressive thing in the world. Without having read
Carlyle, or Kipling, I formulated a gospel of work which put
theirs in the shade. Work was everything. It was sanctification
and salvation. The pride I took in a hard day's work well done
would be inconceivable to you. It is almost inconceivable to me
as I look back upon it. I was as faithful a wage slave as ever
capitalist exploited. To shirk or malinger on the man who paid
me my wages was a sin, first, against myself, and second, against
him. I considered it a crime second only to treason and just about
as bad.

In short, my joyous individualism was dominated by the orthodox bourgeois ethics. I read the bourgeois papers, listened to the
bourgeois preachers, and shouted at the sonorous platitudes of
the bourgeois politicians. And I doubt not, if other events had
not changed my career, that I should have evolved into a professional strike-breaker, (one of President Eliot's American
heroes), and had my head and my earning power irrevocably
smashed by a club in the hands of some militant trades-unionist.

Just about this time, returning from a seven months' voyage
before the mast, and just turned eighteen, I took it into my head
to go tramping. On rods and blind baggages I fought my way
from the open West, where men bucked big and the job hunted

the man, to the congested labor centres of the East, where men were small potatoes and hunted the job for all they were worth. And on this new *blond-beast* adventure I found myself looking upon life from a new and totally different angle. I had dropped down from the proletariat into what sociologists love to call the "submerged tenth," and I was startled to discover the way in which that submerged tenth was recruited.

I found there all sorts of men, many of whom had once been as good as myself and just as *blond-beastly;* sailor-men, soldier-men, labor-men, all wrenched and distorted and twisted out of shape by toil and hardship and accident, and cast adrift by their masters like so many old horses. I battered on the drag and slammed back gates with them, or shivered with them in box cars and city parks, listening the while to life-histories which began under auspices as fair as mine, with digestions and bodies equal to and better than mine, and which ended there before my eyes in the shambles at the bottom of the Social Pit.

And as I listened my brain began to work. The woman of the streets and the man of the gutter drew very close to me. I saw the picture of the Social Pit as vividly as though it were a concrete thing, and at the bottom of the Pit I saw them, myself above them, not far, and hanging on to the slippery wall by main strength and sweat. And I confess a terror seized me. What when my strength failed? when I should be unable to work shoulder to shoulder with the strong men who were as yet babes unborn? And there and then I swore a great oath. It ran something like this: *All my days I have worked hard with my body, and according to the number of days I have worked, by just that much am I nearer the bottom of the Pit. I shall climb out of the Pit, but not by the muscles of my body shall I climb out. I shall do no more hard work, and may God strike me dead if I do another day's hard work with my body more than I absolutely have to do.* And I have been busy ever since running away from hard work.

Incidentally, while tramping some ten thousand miles through the United States and Canada, I strayed into Niagara Falls, was nabbed by a fee-hunting constable, denied the right to plead guilty or not guilty, sentenced out of hand to thirty days' imprisonment for having no fixed abode and no visible means of support, handcuffed and chained to a bunch of men similarly circumstanced, carted down country to Buffalo, registered at the

Erie County Penitentiary, had my head clipped and my budding mustache shaved, was dressed in convict stripes, compulsorily vaccinated by a medical student who practised on such as we, made to march the lock-step, and put to work under the eyes of guards armed wth Winchester rifles—all for adventuring in *blond-beastly* fashion. Concerning further details deponent sayeth not, though he may hint that some of his plethoric national patriotism simmered down and leaked out of the bottom of his soul somewhere—at least, since that experience he finds that he cares more for men and women and little children than for imaginary geographical lines.

To return to my conversion. I think it is apparent that my rampant individualism was pretty effectively hammered out of me, and something else as effectively hammered in. But, just as I had been an individualist without knowing it, I was now a Socialist without knowing it, withal, an unscientific one. I had been reborn, but not renamed, and I was running around to find out what manner of thing I was. I ran back to California and opened the books. I do not remember which ones I opened first. It is an unimportant detail anyway. I was already It, whatever It was, and by aid of the books I discovered that It was a Socialist. Since that day I have opened many books, but no economic argument, no lucid demonstration of the logic and inevitableness of Socialism affects me as profoundly and convincingly as I was affected on the day when I first saw the walls of the Social Pit rise around me and felt myself slipping down, down, into the shambles at the bottom.

THE SHAME OF THE CITIES *

By Lincoln Steffens

Lincoln Steffens (1866–1936), Prince of Muckrakers, concludes that cities are corrupted by lax public morals rather than by any particular group

Joseph Lincoln Steffens was born in San Francisco, the son of a prosperous businessman, took a bachelor's degree at the University of California (where he displayed an interest in philosophic questions), and also studied at Heidelberg and Munich. In 1892, he began his journalistic career as a reporter for the New York _Evening Post_ and may have been intellectually influenced by his contacts with the socially minded police commissioner, Theodore Roosevelt. After several years as city editor of the New York _Commercial Advertiser,_ he joined the scintillating muckraking staff of _McClure's Magazine,_ working with Ida Tarbell and Ray Stannard Baker.

In 1902, Steffens wrote what he believed was the first "muckraking" article in American journalism, "Tweed Days in St. Louis." Actually, he had a major predecessor in Henry Demarest Lloyd of the Chicago _Tribune,_ who had assailed the Standard Oil monopoly at length in _Wealth Against Commonwealth_ (1894) and in articles dating back to 1882. Steffens went on to write numerous articles on urban corruption, hoping to discover the scientific causes of graft. His rather modest conclusions, as given below, reflect the moralistic thinking of Theodore Roosevelt (whom he quotes approvingly on the causes of corruption) and appear in _The Shame of the Cities_ (1904). By the time he published _The Struggle for Self-Government_ (1906), also based on his newspaper exposés, he had discovered many moral heroes of honest government such as Mayor Tom Johnson of Cleveland and Governor Robert M. La Follette of Wisconsin. Meanwhile, he had left _McClure's_ for the _American Magazine,_ and then moved to _Everybody's,_ each of which was concerned with emphasizing the muckraking theme.

Dissatisfied with the superficial moralistic approach taken by so many reformers, Steffens looked for stronger panaceas in the social gospel, socialism, and the single tax. He visited Communist Russia

* From Lincoln Steffens, _The Shame of the Cities_ (1904), 4–13, which summarizes the author's moralistic philosophy and conclusions regarding city corruption.

in 1917 and 1919 and acquired a decided taste for radical solutions and methods. After an exciting interview with Lenin in 1919, he observed exuberantly, "I have seen the future and it works." For some years he shared the iconoclastic world of the American expatriates in Paris, even seemed greatly impressed by that "strong man," Mussolini, but eventually adopted the Communist credo during the Great Depression. His *Autobiography* (1931) condenses his earlier muckraking books, reflects his growing disillusionment with purely moralistic solutions, and suggests his final pilgrimage to the far left.

❦

EVEN IN government we have given proofs of potential greatness, and our political failures are not complete; they are simply ridiculous. But they are ours. Not alone the triumphs and the statesmen, the defeats and the grafters also represent us, and just as truly. Why not see it so and say it?

Because, I heard, the American people won't "stand for" it. You may blame the politicians, or, indeed, any one class, but not all classes, not the people. Or you may put it on the ignorant foreign immigrant, or any one nationality, but not on all nationalities, not on the American people. But no one class is at fault, nor any one breed, nor any particular interest or group of interests. The misgovernment of the American people is misgovernment by the American people.

When I set out on my travels, an honest New Yorker told me honestly that I would find that the Irish, the Catholic Irish, were at the bottom of it all everywhere. The first city I went to was St. Louis, a German city. The next was Minneapolis, a Scandinavian city, with a leadership of New Englanders. Then came Pittsburgh, Scotch Presbyterian, and that was what my New York friend was. "Ah, but they are all foreign populations," I heard. The next city was Philadelphia, the purest American community of all, and the most hopeless. And after that came Chicago and New York, both mongrel-bred, but the one a triumph of reform, the other the best example of good government that I had seen. The "foreign element" excuse is one of the hypocritical lies that save us from the clear sight of ourselves.

Another such conceit of our egotism is that which deplores our politics and lauds our business. This is the wail of the typical American citizen. Now, the typical American citizen is the business man. The typical business man is a bad citizen; he is busy. If he is a "big business man" and very busy, he does not neglect, he is busy with politics, oh, very busy and very business-like. I found him buying boodlers in St. Louis, defending grafters in Minneapolis, originating corruption in Pittsburg, sharing with bosses in Philadelphia, deploring reform in Chicago, and beating good government with corruption funds in New York. He is a self-righteous fraud, this big business man. He is the chief source of corruption, and it were a boon if he would neglect politics. But he is not the business man that neglects politics; that worthy is the good citizen, the typical business man. He too is busy, he is the one that has no use and therefore no time for politics. When his neglect has permitted bad government to go so far that he can be stirred to action, he is unhappy, and he looks around for a cure that shall be quick, so that he may hurry back to the shop. Naturally, too, when he talks politics, he talks shop. His patent remedy is quack; it is business.

"Give us a business man," he says ("like me," he means). "Let him introduce business methods into politics and government; then I shall be left alone to attend to my business."

There is hardly an office from United States Senator down to Alderman in any part of the country to which the business man has not been elected; yet politics remains corrupt, government pretty bad, and the selfish citizen has to hold himself in readiness like the old volunteer firemen to rush forth at any hour, in any weather, to prevent the fire; and he goes out sometimes and he puts out the fire (after the damage is done) and he goes back to the shop sighing for the business man in politics. The business man has failed in politics as he has in citizenship. Why?

Because politics is business. That's what's the matter with it. That's what's the matter with everything,—art, literature, religion, journalism, law, medicine,—they're all business, and all—as you see them. Make politics a sport, as they do in England, or a profession, as they do in Germany, and we'll have—well, something else than we have now,—if we want it, which is another question. But don't try to reform politics with the banker, the lawyer, and the dry-goods merchant, for these are business men and there are two great hindrances to their achievement of reform: one is that they are different from, but no better than, the politicians; the other is that politics is not "their line." There are exceptions both ways. Many politicians have gone out into business and done well (Tammany ex-mayors, and nearly all the old bosses of Philadelphia are prominent financiers in their cities), and business men have gone into politics and done well (Mark Hanna, for example). They haven't reformed their adopted trades, however, though they have sometimes sharpened them most pointedly. The politician is a business man with a specialty. When a business man of some other line learns the business of politics, he is a politician, and there is not much reform left in him. Consider the United States Senate, and believe me.

The commercial spirit is the spirit of profit, not patriotism; of credit, not honor; of individual gain, not national prosperity; of trade and dickering, not principle. "My business is sacred," says the business man in his heart. "Whatever prospers my business, is good; it must be. Whatever hinders it, is wrong; it must be. A bribe is bad, that is, it is a bad thing to take; but it is not so bad to give one, not if it is necessary to my business." "Business is business" is not a political sentiment, but our politician has caught it. He takes essentially the same view of the bribe, only he saves his self-respect by piling all his contempt upon the bribe-giver, and he has the great advantage of candor. "It is wrong, maybe," he says, "but if a rich merchant can afford to do business with me for the sake of a convenience or to increase his already great wealth, I can afford, for the sake of a living, to meet him half way. I make no pretensions to virtue, not even on Sunday." And as for giving bad government or good, how about the merchant who gives bad goods or good goods, according to the demand?

But there is hope, not alone despair, in the commercialism of our politics. If our political leaders are to be always a lot of political merchants, they will supply any demand we may create. All we have to do is to establish a steady demand for good government. The boss has us split up into parties. To him parties are nothing but means to his corrupt ends. He "bolts" his party, but we must not; the bribe-giver changes his party, from one election to another, from one county to another, from one city to another, but the honest voter must not. Why? Because if the honest voter cared no more for his party than the politician and the grafter, then the honest vote would govern, and that would be bad—for graft. It is idiotic, this devotion to a machine that is used to take our sovereignty from us. If we would leave parties to the politicians, and would vote not for the party, not even for men, but for the city, and the State, and the nation, we should rule parties, and cities, and States, and nation. If we would vote in mass on the more promising ticket, or, if the two are equally bad, would throw out the party that is in, and wait till the next election and then throw out the other party that is in—then, I say, the commercial politician would feel a demand for good government and he would supply it. That process would take a generation or more to complete, for the politicians now really do not know what good government is. But it has taken as long to develop bad government, and the politicians know what that is. If it would not "go," they would offer something else, and, if the demand were steady, they, being so commercial, would "deliver the goods."

But do the people want good government? Tammany says they don't. Are the people honest? Are the people better than Tammany? Are they better than the merchant and the politician? Isn't our corrupt government, after all, representative?

President Roosevelt has been sneered at for going about the country preaching, as a cure for our American evils, good conduct in the individual, simple honesty, courage, and efficiency. "Platitudes!" the sophisticated say. Platitudes? If my observations have been true, the literal adoption of Mr. Roosevelt's reform scheme would result in a revolution, more radical and terrible to existing institutions, from the Congress to the Church, from the bank to the ward organization, than socialism or even than anarchy. Why, that would change all of us—not alone our neighbors, not alone the grafters, but you and me.

No, the contemned methods of our despised politics are the master methods of our braggart business, and the corruption that shocks us in public affairs we practice ourselves in our private concerns. There is no essential difference between the pull that gets your wife into society or a favorable review for your book, and that which gets a heeler into office, a thief out of jail, and a rich man's son on the board of directors of a corporation; none between the corruption of a labor union, a bank, and a political machine; none between a dummy director of a trust and the caucus-bound member of a legislature; none between a labor boss like Sam Parks, a boss of banks like John D. Rockefeller, a boss of railroads like J. P. Morgan, and a political boss like Matthew S. Quay. The boss is not a political, he is an American institution, the product of a freed people that have not the spirit to be free.

And it's all a moral weakness; a weakness right where we think we are strongest. Oh, we are good—on Sunday, and we are "fearfully patriotic" on the Fourth of July. But the bribe we pay to the janitor to prefer our interests to the landlord's, is the little brother of the bribe passed to the alderman to sell a city street, and the father of the air-brake stock assigned to the president of a railroad to have this life-saving invention adopted on his road. And as for graft, railroad passes, saloon and bawdyhouse blackmail, and watered stock, all these belong to the same family. We are pathetically proud of our democratic institutions and our republican form of government, of our grand Constitution and our just laws. We are a free and sovereign people, we govern ourselves and the government is ours. But that is the point. We are responsible, not our leaders, since we follow them. We *let* them divert our loyalty from the United States to some "party"; we *let* them boss the party and turn our municipal democracies into autocracies and our republican nation into a plutocracy. We cheat our government and we let our leaders loot it, and we let them wheedle and bribe our sovereignty from us. True, they pass for us strict laws, but we are content to let them pass also bad laws, giving away public property in exchange; and our good, and often impossible, laws we allow to be used for oppression and blackmail. And what can we say? We break our own laws and rob our own government, the lady at the custom-house, the lyncher with his rope, and the captain of industry with his bribe and his rebate. The spirit of graft and of lawlessness is the American spirit.

And this shall not be said? Not plainly? William Travers Jerome, the fearless District Attorney of New York, says, "You can say anything you think to the American people. If you are honest with yourself you may be honest with them, and they will forgive not only your candor, but your mistakes." This is the opinion, and the experience too, of an honest man and a hopeful democrat. Who says the other things? Who says "Hush," and "What's the use?" and "ALL's well," when all is rotten? It is the grafter; the coward, too, but the grafter inspires the coward. The doctrine of "addition, division, and silence" is the doctrine of graft. "Don't hurt the party," "Spare the fair fame of the city," are boodle yells. The Fourth of July oration is the "front" of graft. There is no patriotism in it, but treason. It is part of the game. The grafters call for cheers for the flag, "prosperity," and "the party," just as a highwayman commands "hands up," and while we are waving and shouting, they float the flag from the nation to the party, turn both into graft factories, and prosperity into a speculative boom to make "weak hands," as the Wall Street phrase has it, hold the watered stock while the strong hands keep the prosperity. "Blame us, blame anybody, but praise the people," this, the politician's advice, is not the counsel of respect for the people, but of contempt. By just such palavering as courtiers play upon the degenerate intellects of weak kings, the bosses, political, financial, and industrial, are befuddling and befooling our sovereign American citizenship; and—likewise— they are corrupting it.

And it is corruptible, this citizenship. "I know what Parks is doing," said a New York union workman, "but what do I care. He has raised my wages. Let him have his graft!" And the Philadelphia merchant says the same thing.

THE JUNGLE *

By Upton Sinclair

Upton Sinclair (1878–   ) writes The Jungle *to expose labor exploitation but inspires a crusade for consumer protection*

Ralph Nader.

The Baltimore-born Upton Sinclair, from an old Colonial family, was reared in New York amid fairly comfortable circumstances as the son of a salesman. A child prodigy, he had read the most difficult classics before he was thirteen and was already a religious skeptic by the time he graduated from City College and began graduate courses at Columbia. He was closely associated with Jack London, the ardent socialist and novelist. In 1906, he published his best seller, *The Jungle*, after spending a week observing the

* From Upton Sinclair, *The Jungle* (1906), 128–33.

shocking conditions in Chicago's Union Stock Yards; but his endeavor to portray labor exploitation among immigrant families was forgotten by most readers, who were even more startled by the description of the filthy conditions in the preparation of meat and its byproducts. For a time, so it was reported, America's meat consumption fell drastically, and Europeans regarded imports with suspicion. Sinclair's revelations of sanitary abuses were confirmed by President Roosevelt's labor commissioners (after the Department of Agriculture had issued a favorable report on the stock yards) and Congress then passed the Meat Inspection Act of 1906, a pioneer landmark (together with the Pure Food and Drug Act of that year) in the history of consumer legislation.

While turning out less-favored novels of protest, Upton Sinclair founded a cooperative community, the Helicon Home Colony of Englewood, New Jersey, attracted the sympathetic Sinclair Lewis, and flirted with the Single Tax movement created by Henry George. Many middle-class readers as well as leftists enjoyed his books—*The Brass Check* (1919), which indicted a kept press, *The Goose-Step* (1923), which pictured the great colleges as pawns of big business, *Boston* (2 vols., 1928), which dramatized the reactionary atmosphere surrounding the execution of Sacco and Vanzetti, and many more. As a resident of California after 1915, he combined literary activities with politics and free speech battles. He attracted national attention in 1934 when he ran for governor of California on the Democratic ticket, but considerably left of the New Deal, on the platform of "End Poverty in California," and "Production for Use, not for Profit." Only the determined efforts of conservatives, the motion picture magnates particularly, defeated EPIC. Films of tramps descending upon California like locusts in the expectation of Sinclair's election apparently frightened many voters. Much more successful with Americans were Sinclair's newer novels, such as the Lanny Budd series, which dwelt upon national and international events, especially Nazism.

EPIC

THE FERTILIZER works of Durham's lay away from the rest of the plant. Few visitors ever saw them, and the few who did would come out looking like Dante, of whom the peasants declared that he had been into hell. To this part of the yards came all the "tankage" and the waste products of all sorts; here they dried out the bones,—and in suffocating cellars where the daylight never came you might see men and women and children bending over whirling machines and sawing bits of bone into all sorts of shapes, breathing their lungs full of the fine dust, and doomed to die, every one of them, within a certain definite time. Here they made the blood into albumen, and made other foul-smelling things into things still more foul-smelling. In the corridors and caverns where it was done you might lose yourself as in the great caves of Kentucky. In the dust and the steam the electric lights would shine like far-off twinkling stars—red and blue-green and purple stars, according to the color of the mist and the brew from which it came. For the odors in these ghastly charnel houses there may be words in Lithuanian, but there are none in English. The person entering would have to summon his courage as for a cold-water plunge. He would go on like a man swimming under water; he would put his handkerchief over his face, and begin to cough and choke; and then, if he were still obstinate, he would find his head beginning to ring, and the veins in his forehead to throb, until finally he would be assailed by an overpowering blast of ammonia fumes, and would turn and run for his life, and come out half-dazed.

On top of this were the rooms where they dried the "tankage," the mass of brown stringy stuff that was left after the waste portions of the carcasses had had the lard and tallow tried out of them. This dried material they would then grind to a fine powder, and after they had mixed it up well with a mysterious but inoffensive brown rock which they brought in and ground up by the hundreds of carloads for that purpose, the substance was ready to be put into bags and sent out to the world as any one of a hundred different brands of standard bone phosphate. And then the farmer in Maine or California or Texas would buy this, at say twenty-five dollars a ton, and plant it with his corn; and for several days after the operation the fields would have a strong odor, and the farmer and his wagon and the very horses that had hauled it would all have it too. In Packingtown the fertilizer is pure, instead of being a flavoring, and instead of a ton or so spread out on several acres under the open sky, there are hundreds and thousands of tons of it in one building, heaped here and there in haystack piles, covering the floor several inches deep, and filling the air with a choking dust that becomes a blinding sandstorm when the wind stirs.

It was to this building that Jurgis came daily, as if dragged by an unseen hand. The month of May was an exceptionally cool one, and his secret prayers were granted; but early in June there came a record-breaking hot spell, and after that there were men wanted in the fertilizer mill.

The boss of the grinding room had come to know Jurgis by this time, and had marked him for a likely man; and so when he came to the door about two o'clock this breathless hot day, he felt a sudden spasm of pain shoot through him—the boss beckoned to him! In ten minutes more Jurgis had pulled off his coat and overshirt, and set his teeth together and gone to work. Here was one more difficulty for him to meet and conquer!

His labor took him about one minute to learn. Before him was one of the vents of the mill in which the fertilizer was being ground—rushing forth in a great brown river, with a spray of the finest dust flung forth in clouds. Jurgis was given a shovel, and along with half a dozen others it was his task to shovel this fertilizer into carts. That others were at work he knew by the sound, and by the fact that he sometimes collided with them; otherwise they might as well not have been there, for in the blinding dust storm a man could not see six feet in front of his face. When he had filled one cart he had to grope around him until another came, and if there was none on hand he continued to grope till one arrived. In five minutes he was, of course, a mass of fertilizer from head to feet; they gave him a sponge to tie over his mouth, so that he could breathe, but the sponge did not prevent his lips and eyelids from caking up with it and his ears from filling solid. He looked like a brown ghost at twilight— from hair to shoes he became the color of the building and of everything in it, and for that matter a hundred yards outside it. The building had to be left open, and when the wind blew Durham and Company lost a great deal of fertilizer.

Working in his shirt sleeves, and with the thermometer at over a hundred, the phosphates soaked in through every pore of Jurgis' skin, and in five minutes he had a headache, and in fifteen was almost dazed. The blood was pounding in his brain like an engine's throbbing; there was a frightful pain in the top of his skull, and he could hardly control his hands. Still, with the memory of his four months' siege behind him, he fought on, in a frenzy of determination; and half an hour later he began to vomit—he vomited until it seemed as if his inwards must be torn into shreds. A man could get used to the fertilizer mill, the boss had said, if he would only make up his mind to it; but Jurgis now began to see that it was a question of making up his stomach.

At the end of that day of horror, he could scarcely stand. He had to catch himself now and then, and lean against a building and get his bearings. Most of the men, when they came out, made straight for a saloon—they seemed to place fertilizer and rattle-snake poison in one class. But Jurgis was too ill to think of drinking—he could only make his way to the street and stagger on to a car. He had a sense of humor, and later on, when he became an old hand, he used to think it fun to board a streetcar and see what happened. Now, however, he was too ill to notice it—how the people in the car began to gasp and sputter, to put their handkerchiefs to their noses, and transfix him with furious glances. Jurgis only knew that a man in front of him immediately got up and gave him a seat; and that half a minute later the two people on each side of him got up; and that in a full minute the crowded car was nearly empty—those passengers who could not get room on the platform having gotten out to walk.

Of course Jurgis had made his home a miniature fertilizer mill a minute after entering. The stuff was half an inch deep in his skin—his whole system was full of it, and it would have taken a week not merely of scrubbing, but of vigorous exercise, to get it out of him. As it was, he could be compared with nothing known to men, save that newest discovery of the savants, a substance which emits energy for an unlimited time, without being itself in the least diminished in power. He smelled so that he made all the food at the table taste, and set the whole family to vomiting; for himself it was three days before he could keep anything upon his stomach—he might wash his hands, and use a knife and fork, but were not his mouth and throat filled with the poison?

And still Jurgis stuck it out! In spite of splitting headaches he would stagger down to the plant and take up his stand once more, and begin to shovel in the blinding clouds of dust. And so at the end of the week he was a fertilizer man for life—he was able to eat again, and though his head never stopped aching, it ceased to be so bad that he could not work.

So there passed another summer. It was a summer of pros-perity, all over the country, and the country ate generously of packing house products, and there was plenty of work for all the family, in spite of the packers' efforts to keep a superfluity of labor. They were again able to pay their debts and to begin to save a little sum; but there were one or two sacrifices they con-

sidered too heavy to be made for long—it was too bad that the
boys should have to sell papers at their age. It was utterly useless
to caution them and plead with them; quite without knowing
it, they were taking on the tone of their new environment. They
were learning to swear in voluble English; they were learning
to pick up cigar stumps and smoke them, to pass hours of their
time gambling with pennies and dice and cigarette cards; they
were learning the location of all the houses of prostitution on
the "Lêvée," and the names of the "madames" who kept them,
and the days when they gave their state banquets, which the
police captains and the big politicians all attended. If a visiting
"country customer" were to ask them, they could show him
which was "Hinkydink's" famous saloon, and could even point
out to him by name the different gamblers and thugs and "hold-
up men" who made the place their headquarters. And worse yet,
the boys were getting out of the habit of coming home at night.
What was the use, they would ask, of wasting time and energy
and a possible carfare riding out to the stockyards every night
when the weather was pleasant and they could crawl under a
truck or into an empty doorway and sleep exactly as well? So
long as they brought home a half dollar for each day, what
mattered it when they brought it? But Jurgis declared that from
this to ceasing to come at all would not be a very long step, and
so it was decided that Vilimas and Nikalojus should return to
school in the fall, and that instead Elzbieta should go out and get
some work, her place at home being taken by her younger
daughter.

Little Kotrina was like most children of the poor, prematurely
made old; she had to take care of her little brother, who was a
cripple, and also of the baby; she had to cook the meals and
wash the dishes and clean house, and have supper ready when
the workers came home in the evening. She was only thirteen,
and small for her age, but she did all this without a murmur;
and her mother went out, and after trudging a couple of days
about the yards, settled down as a servant of a "sausage machine."
Elzbieta was used to working, but she found this change a hard
one, for the reason that she had to stand motionless upon her feet
from seven o'clock in the morning till half-past twelve, and again
from one till half-past five. For the first few days it seemed to her
that she could not stand it—she suffered almost as much as Jurgis
had from the fertilizer, and would come out at sundown with her

head fairly reeling. Besides this, she was working in one of the dark holes, by electric light, and the dampness, too, was deadly—there were always puddles of water on the floor, and a sickening odor of moist flesh in the room. The people who worked here followed the ancient custom of nature, whereby the ptarmigan is the color of dead leaves in the fall and of snow in the winter, and the chameleon, who is black when he lies upon a stump and turns green when he moves to a leaf. The men and women who worked in this department were precisely the color of the "fresh country sausage" they made.

The sausage room was an interesting place to visit, for two or three minutes, and provided that you did not look at the people; the machines were perhaps the most wonderful things in the entire plant. Presumably sausages were once chopped and stuffed by hand, and if so it would be interesting to know how many workers had been displaced by these inventions. On one side of the room were the hoppers, into which men shoveled loads of meat and wheelbarrows full of spices; in these great bowls were whirling knives that made two thousand revolutions a minute, and when the meat was ground fine and adulterated with potato flour, and well mixed with water, it was forced to the stuffing machines on the other side of the room. The latter were tended by women; there was a sort of spout, like the nozzle of a hose, and one of the women would take a long string of "casing" and put the end over the nozzle and then work the whole thing on, as one works on the finger of a tight glove. This string would be twenty or thirty feet long, but the woman would have it all on in a jiffy; and when she had several on, she would press a lever, and a stream of sausage meat would be shot out, taking the casing with it as it came. Thus one might stand and see appear, miraculously born from the machine, a wriggling snake of sausage of incredible length. In front was a big pan which caught these creatures, and two more women who seized them as fast as they appeared and twisted them into links. This was for the uninitiated the most perplexing work of all; for all that the woman had to give was a single turn of the wrist; and in some way she contrived to give it so that instead of an endless chain of sausages, one after another, there grew under her hands a bunch of strings, all dangling from a single center. It was quite like the feat of a prestidigitator—for the woman worked so fast that the eye could literally not follow her, and there was only a mist of motion, and tangle after tangle of sausages appearing. In the midst of the mist, however, the visitor would suddenly notice the tense set face, with the two wrinkles graven in the forehead, and the ghastly pallor of the cheeks; and then he would suddenly recollect that it was time he was going on. The woman did not go on; she stayed right there—hour after hour, day after day, year after year, twisting sausage links and racing with death. It was piecework, and she was apt to have a family to keep alive; and stern and ruthless economic laws had arranged it that she could only do this by working just as she did, with all her soul upon her work, and with never an instant for a glance at the well-dressed ladies and gentlemen who came to stare at her, as at some wild beast in a menagerie.

THE PROMISE OF
AMERICAN LIFE *

By Herbert David Croly

Herbert David Croly (1869–1930) hails Theodore Roosevelt as an enlightened Hamiltonian nationalist and reformer who made the State the instrument of the Progressive Movement

Herbert D. Croly studied philosophy with William James at Harvard and edited for some years the notable *Architectural Record*. In 1909, he published *The Promise of American Life*, which, despite its turgid style and limited popular appeal, influenced progressive thought. As the following selection indicates, he discovered Roosevelt and his New Nationalism before the apostle of the Square Deal knew him. Roosevelt had broken with the conservative wing of the Republican party under Taft, criticized trust-busting as ineffective, and turned toward a philosophy of strong state control and reform leadership particularly in the regulation of large corporations. He appeared to be the kind of Hamiltonian that Croly desired to revive the historic mission of

* From Herbert David Croly, *The Promise of American Life* (1909), 167–71.

the Republicans to achieve national responsibility as they had done in the antislavery movement.

Croly supported—and presumably influenced—both Roosevelt's New Nationalism, which recognized that Bigness was here to stay but which believed that it could be directed toward beneficent ends by the state and Wilson's New Freedom which stressed the antimonopoly tradition. His national influence among liberals grew immensely when he founded in 1914 *The New Republic,* aided by endowments from Willard Straight, the subject of his biography published that same year. He tried to make it the spokesman of the Progressive movement, backed Wilson on foreign policy until Croly decided to fight the Versailles Treaty, and supported La Follette's Progressive party in 1924.

Theodore Roosevelt as a Reformer

I T IS fortunate, consequently, that one reformer can be named whose work has tended to give reform the dignity of a constructive mission. Mr. Theodore Roosevelt's behavior at least is not dictated by negative conception of reform. During the course of an extremely active and varied political career he has, indeed, been all kinds of a reformer. His first appearance in public life, as a member of the Legislature of New York, coincided with an outbreak of dissatisfaction over the charter of New York City; and Mr. Roosevelt's name was identified with the bills which began the revision of that very much revised instrument. Somewhat later, as one of the Federal Commissioners, Mr. Roosevelt made a most useful contribution to the more effective enforcement of the Civil Service Law. Still later, as Police Commissioner of New York City, he had his experience of reform by means of unregenerate instruments and administrative lies. Then, as Governor of the State of New York, he was instrumental in securing the passage of a law taxing franchises as real property and thus faced for the first time and in a preliminary way the many-headed problem of the trusts. Finally, when an accident placed him in the Presidential chair, he consistently used the power of the Federal government and his own influence and popularity for the purpose of regulating the corporations in what he believed to be the public interest. No other American has had anything like so varied and so intimate an acquaintance with the practical work of reform as has Mr. Roosevelt; and when, after more than twenty years of such experience, he adds to the work of administrative reform the additional task of political and economic reconstruction, his originality cannot be considered the result of innocence. Mr. Roosevelt's reconstructive policy does not go very far in purpose or achievement, but limited as it is, it does tend to give the agitation for reform the benefit of a much more positive significance and a much more dignified task.

Mr. Roosevelt has imparted a higher and more positive significance to reform, because throughout his career he has consistently stood for an idea, from which the idea of reform cannot be separated—namely, the national idea. He has, indeed, been even more of a nationalist than he has a reformer. His most important literary work was a history of the beginning of American national expansion. He has treated all public questions from a vigorous, even from an extreme, national standpoint. No American politician was more eager to assert the national interest against an actual or a possible foreign enemy; and not even William R. Hearst was more resolute to involve his country in a war with Spain. Fortunately, however, his aggressive nationalism did not, like that of so many other statesmen, faint from exhaustion as soon as there were no more foreign enemies to defy. He was the first political leader of the American people to identify the national principle with an ideal of reform. He was the first to realize that an American statesman could no longer really represent the national interest without becoming a reformer. Mr. Grover Cleveland showed a glimmering of the necessity of this affiliation; but he could not carry it far, because, as a sincere traditional Democrat, he could not reach a clear understanding of the meaning either of reform or of nationality. Mr. Roosevelt, however, divined that an American statesman who eschewed or evaded the work of reform came inevitably to represent either special and local interests or else a merely Bourbon political tradition, and in this way was disqualified for genuinely national service. He divined that the national principle involved a continual process of internal reformation; and that the reforming idea implied the necessity of more efficient national organization. Consequently, when he became President of the United States and the official representative of the national interest of the country, he attained finally his proper sphere of action. He immediately began the salutary and indispensable work of nationalizing the reform movement.

The nationalization of reform endowed the movement with new vitality and meaning. What Mr. Roosevelt really did was to revive the Hamiltonian ideal of constructive national legislation. During the whole of the nineteenth century that ideal, while by no means dead, was disabled by associations and conditions from active and efficient service. Not until the end of the Spanish War was a condition of public feeling created, which made it possible to revive Hamiltonianism. That war and its resulting policy of extra-territorial expansion, so far from hindering the process of domestic amelioration, availed, from the sheer force of the national aspirations it aroused, to give a tremendous impulse to the work of national reform. It made Americans more sensitive to a national idea and more conscious of their national responsibilities, and it indirectly helped to place in the Presidential chair the man who, as I have said, represented both the national idea and the spirit of reform. The sincere and intelligent combination of those two ideas is bound to issue in the Hamiltonian practice of constructive national legislation.

Of course Theodore Roosevelt is Hamiltonian with a difference. Hamilton's fatal error consisted in his attempt to make the Federal organization not merely the effective engine of the national interest, but also a bulwark against the rising tide of democracy. The new Federalism or rather new Nationalism is not in any way inimical to democracy. On the contrary, not only does Mr. Roosevelt believe himself to be an unimpeachable democrat in theory, but he has given his fellow-countrymen a useful example of the way in which a college-bred and a well-to-do man can become by somewhat forcible means a good practical democrat. The whole tendency of his programme is to give a democratic meaning and purpose to the Hamiltonian tradition and method. He proposes to use the power and the resources of the Federal government for the purpose of making his countrymen a more complete democracy in organization and practice; but he does not make these proposals, as Mr. Bryan does, gingerly and with a bad conscience. He makes them with a frank and full confidence in an efficient national organization as the necessary agent of the national interest and purpose. He has completely abandoned that part of the traditional democratic creed which tends to regard the assumption by the government of responsibility, and its endowment with power adequate to the responsibility as inherently dangerous and undemocratic. He realizes that any efficiency of organization and delegation of power which is necessary to the promotion of the American national interest must be helpful to democracy. More than any other American political leader, except Lincoln, his devotion both to the national and to the democratic ideas is thorough-going and absolute.

As the founder of a new national democracy, then, his influence and his work have tended to emancipate American democracy from its Jeffersonian bondage. They have tended to give a new meaning to popular government by endowing it with larger powers, more positive responsibilities, and a better faith in human excellence. Jefferson believed theoretically in human goodness, but in actual practice his faith in human nature was exceedingly restricted. Just as the older aristocratic theory had been to justify hereditary political leadership by considering the ordinary man as necessarily irresponsible and incapable, so the early French democrats, and Jefferson after them, made faith in the people equivalent to a profound suspicion of responsible official leadership. Exceptional power merely offered exceptional opportunities for abuse. He refused, as far as he could, to endow special men, even when chosen by the people, with any opportunity to promote the public welfare proportionate to their abilities. So far as his influence has prevailed the government of the country was organized on the basis of a cordial distrust of the man of exceptional competence, training, or independence as a public official. To the present day this distrust remains the sign by which the demoralizing influence of the Jeffersonian democratic creed is most plainly to be traced. So far as it continues to be influential it destroys one necessary condition of responsible and efficient government, and it is bound to paralyze any attempt to make the national organization adequate to the promotion of the national interest. Mr. Roosevelt has exhibited his genuinely national spirit in nothing so clearly as in his endeavor to give to men of special ability, training, and eminence a better opportunity to serve the public. He has not only appointed such men to office, but he has tried to supply them with an administrative machinery which would enable them to use their abilities to the best public advantage; and he has thereby shown a faith in human nature far more edifying and far more genuinely democratic than that of Jefferson or Jackson.

Mr. Roosevelt, however, has still another title to distinction among the brethren of reform. He has not only nationalized the movement, and pointed it in the direction of a better conception of democracy, but he has rallied to its banner the ostensible, if not the very enthusiastic, support of the Republican party. He has restored that party to some sense of its historic position and purpose. As the party which before the War had insisted on making the nation answerable for the solution of the slavery problem, it has inherited the tradition of national responsibility for the national good; but it was rapidly losing all sense of its historic mission, and, like the Whigs, was constantly using its principle and its prestige as a cloak for the aggrandizement of special interests. At its worst it had, indeed, earned some claim on the allegiance of patriotic Americans by its defense of the fiscal system of the country against Mr. Bryan's well-meant but dangerous attack, and by its acceptance after the Spanish War of the responsibilities of extra-territorial expansion; but there was grave danger that its alliance with the "vested" interests would make it unfaithful to its past as the party of responsible national action. It escaped such a fate only by an extremely narrow margin; and the fact that it did escape is due chiefly to the personal influence of Theodore Roosevelt. The Republican party is still very far from being a wholly sincere agent of the national reform interest. Its official leadership is opposed to reform; and it cannot be made to take a single step in advance except under compulsion. But Mr. Roosevelt probably prevented it from drifting into the position of an anti-reform party—which if it had happened would have meant its ruin, and would have damaged the cause of national reform. A Republican party which was untrue to the principle of national responsibility would have no reason for existence; and the Democratic party, as we have seen, cannot become the party of national responsibility without being faithless to its own creed.

Chapter Nine

THE
GREAT HISTORIANS:

Henry Adams, F. J. Turner, and Charles Beard

"THE ABYSS OF IGNORANCE" *

By Henry Adams

Henry Adams (1838–1918) seeks metaphysical unity amid the multiplicity of his times

This great-grandson of President John Adams, the grandson of John Quincy Adams and of Peter Brooks, the richest man in Boston, and the son of Lincoln's outstanding minister to England, Charles Francis Adams, apparently reveled in his social inheritance, even if he spoke of his failures in *The Education of Henry Adams* (1918). His stimulating home offered him an education which he did not find at Harvard, and his father gave him new opportunities in Germany, where he studied civil law, and in England, where he acted as his father's secretary and also embarked upon a career in journalism. Back home, he wrote articles assailing Grantism and Jay Gould's crooked gold speculations, which were part of the Gilded Age that Adams detested. In 1870, Harvard gave him a teaching post in medieval history, where he proceeded to introduce the novel seminar method of Leopold von Ranke, the father of "scientific history"—the system that made critical use of documents, although it rejected the deliberate application of natural science analogies to history. Adams and his seminar students wrote *Essays in Anglo-Saxon Law* (1876). Be-

* From Henry Adams, *The Education of Henry Adams* (Boston: Houghton Mifflin Company, 1918), chap. 29, 426–32. Reprinted by permission of Houghton Mifflin Company.

fore quitting Harvard (his fortune did not require that he pursue the arduous task of teaching), he had begun to offer American history courses and within a decade or so he embarked upon his monumental *History . . . of the Jefferson and Madison Administrations* (1889–91). While he appeared to be revenging the old Adamses for the deeds of the Republicans, his judgments sustained the test of longevity. The younger historians of the 1960's continue to teach the Adams version of the nationalistic causes for the War of 1812, and they appreciate the expertness of Adams in handling diplomatic history as well as his treatment of the actual fighting. Some have discovered great talents in his handling of social-cultural history, brief though that section happens to be.

But after the *History* came Adams' fruitless search for a positivist philosophy of history that would offer predictability like physics or biology. His unique book, *Mont-Saint-Michel and Chartres* (1904) aroused the enthusiasm of Gothic-style architects like Ralph Adams Cram and the medievalists; it also showed that Adams was seeking a philosophy of history inspired by natural science, especially by the Second Law of Thermodynamics, for he spoke of the Virgin as well as the modern dynamo as central sources of energy. *The Education of Henry Adams* (1918), which gains literary effectiveness from his use of the third person, tells of his itinerary from Lyell and Darwin to Helmholtz and the contemporaries, ever seeking a modern metaphysic and the capture of mathematical physics for the service of history.

The selection below relates Adams' lifelong search for a philosophic unity that could explain and comprise the multiplicity of energy and movement in the twentieth century.

⚡

. . . LIFE AT last managed of its own accord to settle itself into a working arrangement. After so many years of effort to find one's drift, the drift found the seeker, and slowly swept him forward and back, with a steady progress oceanwards. Such lessons as summer taught, winter tested, and one had only to watch the apparent movement of the stars in order to guess one's declination. The process is possible only for men who have exhausted auto-motion. Adams never knew why, knowing nothing of Faraday, he began to mimic Faraday's trick of seeing lines of force all about him, where he had always seen lines of will. Perhaps the effect of knowing no mathematics is to leave the mind to imagine figures—images—phantoms; one's mind is a watery mirror at best;

but, once conceived, the image became rapidly simple, and the lines of force presented themselves as lines of attraction. Repulsions counted only as battle of attractions. By this path, the mind stepped into the mechanical theory of the universe before knowing it, and entered a distinct new phase of education.

This was the work of the dynamo and the Virgin of Chartres. Like his masters, since thought began, he was handicapped by the eternal mystery of Force—the sink of all science. For thousands of years in history, he found that Force had been felt as occult attraction—love of God and lust for power in a future life. After 1500, when this attraction began to decline, philosophers fell back on some *vis a tergo*—instinct of danger from behind, like Darwin's survival of the fittest; and one of the greatest minds, between Descartes and Newton—Pascal—saw the master-motor of man in *ennui*, which was also scientific: "I have often said that all the troubles of man come from his not knowing how to sit still." Mere restlessness forces action. "So passes the whole of life. We combat obstacles in order to get repose, and, when got, the repose is insupportable; for we think either of the troubles we have, or of those that threaten us; and even if we felt safe on every side, *ennui* would of its own accord spring up from the depths of the heart where it is rooted by nature, and would fill the mind with its venom."

> "If goodness lead him not, yet weariness
> May toss him to My breast."

Ennui, like Natural Selection, accounted for change, but failed to account for direction of change. For that, an attractive force was essential; a force from outside; a shaping influence. Pascal and all the old philosophies called this outside force God or Gods. Caring but little for the name, and fixed only on tracing the Force, Adams had gone straight to the Virgin at Chartres, and asked her to show him God, face to face, as she did for St. Bernard. She replied, kindly as ever, as though she were still the young mother of to-day, with a sort of patient pity for masculine dulness: "My dear outcast, what is it you seek? This is the Church of Christ! If you seek him through me, you are welcome, sinner or saint; but he and I are one. We are Love! We have little or nothing to do with God's other energies which are infinite, and concern us the less because our interest is only in man, and the infinite is not knowable to man. Yet if you are troubled by your ignorance, you see how I am surrounded by the masters of the schools! Ask them!"

The answer sounded singularly like the usual answer of British science which had repeated since Bacon that one must not try to know the unknowable, though one was quite powerless to ignore it; but the Virgin carried more conviction, for her feminine lack of interest in all perfections except her own was honester than the formal phrase of science; since nothing was easier than to follow her advice, and turn to Thomas Aquinas, who, unlike modern physicists, answered at once and plainly: "To me," said St. Thomas, "Christ and the Mother are one Force—Love—simple, single and sufficient for all human wants; but Love is a human interest which acts even on man so partially that you and I, as philosophers, need expect no share in it. Therefore we turn to Christ and the Schools who represent all other Force. We deal with Multiplicity and call it God. After the Virgin has redeemed by her personal Force as Love all that is redeemable in man, the Schools embrace the rest, and give it Form, Unity, and Motive."

This chart of Force was more easily studied than any other possible scheme, for one had but to do what the Church was always promising to do—abolish in one flash of lightning not only man, but also the Church itself, the earth, the other planets, and the sun, in order to clear the air; without affecting mediæval science. The student felt warranted in doing what the Church threatened—abolishing his solar system altogether—in order to look at God as actual; continuous movement, universal cause, and interchangeable force. This was pantheism, but the Schools were pantheist; at least as pantheistic as the *Energetik* of the Germans; and their duty was the ultimate energy, whose thought and act were one.

Rid of man and his mind, the universe of Thomas Aquinas seemed rather more scientific than that of Haeckel or Ernst Mach. Contradiction for contradiction, Attraction for attraction, Energy for energy, St. Thomas's idea of God had merits. Modern science offered not a vestige of proof, or a theory of connection between its forces, or any scheme of reconciliation between thought and mechanics; while St. Thomas at least linked together the joints of his machine. As far as a superficial student could follow, the thirteenth century supposed mind to be a mode of force directly derived from the intelligent prime motor, and the cause of all form and sequence in the universe—therefore the only proof of unity. Without thought in the unit, there could be no unity; without unity no orderly sequence or ordered society. Thought alone was Form. Mind and Unity flourished or perished together.

This education startled even a man who had dabbled in fifty educations all over the world; for, if he were obliged to insist on a Universe, he seemed driven to the Church. Modern science guaranteed no unity. The student seemed to feel himself, like all his predecessors, caught, trapped, meshed in this eternal drag-net of religion.

In practice the student escapes this dilemma in two ways: the first is that of ignoring it, as one escapes most dilemmas; the second is that the Church rejects pantheism as worse than atheism, and will have nothing to do with the pantheist at any price. In wandering through the forests of ignorance, one necessarily fell upon the famous old bear that scared children at play; but, even had the animal shown more logic than its victim, one had learned from Socrates to distrust, above all other traps, the trap of logic—the mirror of the mind. Yet the search for a unit of force led into catacombs of thought where hundreds of thousands of educations had found their end. Generation after generation of painful and honest-minded scholars had been content to stay in these labyrinths forever, pursuing ignorance in silence, in company with the most famous teachers of all time. Not one of them had ever found a logical highroad of escape.

Adams cared little whether he escaped or not, but he felt clear that he could not stop there, even to enjoy the society of Spinoza and Thomas Aquinas. True, the Church alone had asserted unity with any conviction, and the historian alone knew what oceans of blood and treasure the assertion had cost; but the only honest alternative to affirming unity was to deny it; and the denial would require a new education. At sixty-five years old a new education promised hardly more than the old.

Possibly the modern legislator or magistrate might no longer know enough to treat as the Church did the man who denied unity, unless the denial took the form of a bomb; but no teacher would know how to explain what he thought he meant by denying unity. Society would certainly punish the denial if ever any one learned enough to understand it. Philosophers, as a rule, cared little what principles society affirmed or denied, since the philosopher commonly held that though he might sometimes be right by good luck on some one point, no complex of individual opinions could possibly be anything but wrong; yet, supposing society to be ignored, the philosopher was no further forward. Nihilism had no bottom. For thousands of years every philosopher had stood on the shore of this sunless sea, diving for pearls and never finding them. All had seen that, since they could not find bottom, they must assume it. The Church claimed to have found it, but, since 1450, motives for agreeing on some new assumption of Unity, broader and deeper than that of the Church, had doubled in force until even the universities and schools, like the Church and State, seemed about to be driven into an attempt to educate, though specially forbidden to do it.

Like most of his generation, Adams had taken the word of science that the new unit was as good as found. It would not be an intelligence—probably not even a consciousness—but it would serve. He passed sixty years waiting for it, and at the end of that time, on reviewing the ground, he was led to think that the final synthesis of science and its ultimate triumph was the kinetic theory of gases; which seemed to cover all motion in space, and to furnish the measure of time. So far as he understood it, the theory asserted that any portion of space is occupied by molecules of gas, flying in right lines at velocities varying up to a mile in a second, and colliding with each other at intervals varying up to 17,750,000 times in a second. To this analysis—if one understood it right—all matter whatever was reducible, and the only difference of opinion in science regarded the doubt whether a still deeper analysis would reduce the atom of gas to pure motion.

Thus, unless one mistook the meaning of motion, which might well be, the scientific synthesis commonly called Unity was the scientific analysis commonly called Multiplicity. The two things were the same, all forms being shifting phases of motion. Granting this ocean of colliding atoms, the last hope of humanity, what happened if one dropped the sounder into the abyss—let it go—frankly gave up Unity altogether? What was Unity? Why was one to be forced to affirm it?

Here everybody flatly refused help. Science seemed content with its old phrase of "larger synthesis," which was well enough for science, but meant chaos for man. One would have been glad to stop and ask no more, but the anarchist bomb bade one go on, and the bomb is a powerful persuader. One could not stop, even to enjoy the charms of a perfect gas colliding seventeen million times in a second, much like an automobile in Paris. Science itself had been crowded so close to the edge of the abyss that its attempts to escape were as metaphysical as the leap, while an ignorant old man felt no motive for trying to escape, seeing that the only escape possible lay in the form of *vis a tergo* commonly called Death. He got out his Descartes again; dipped into his Hume and Berkeley; wrestled anew with his Kant; pondered solemnly over his Hegel and Schopenhauer and Hartmann; strayed gaily away with his Greeks—all merely to ask what Unity meant, and what happened when one denied it.

Apparently one never denied it. Every philosopher, whether sane or insane, naturally affirmed it. The utmost flight of anarchy seemed to have stopped with the assertion of two principles, and even these fitted into each other, like good and evil, light and darkness. Pessimism itself, black as it might be painted, had been content to turn the universe of contradictions into the human thought as one Will, and treat it as representation. Metaphysics insisted on treating the universe as one thought or treating thought as one universe; and philosophers agreed, like kinetic gas, that the universe could be known only as motion of mind, and therefore as unity. One could know it only as one's self; it was psychology.

Of all forms of pessimism, the metaphysical form was, for a historian, the least enticing. Of all studies, the one he would rather have avoided was that of his own mind. He knew no tragedy so heartrending as introspection, and the more, because—as Mephistopheles said of Marguerite—he was not the first. Nearly all the highest intelligence known to history had drowned itself in the reflection of its own thought, and the bovine survivors had rudely told the truth about it, without affecting the intelligent. One's own time had not been exempt. Even since 1870 friends by scores had fallen victims to it. Within five-and-twenty years, a new library had grown out of it. Harvard College was a focus of the study; France supported hospitals for it; England published magazines of it. Nothing was easier than to take one's mind in one's hand, and ask one's psychological friends what they made of it, and the more because it mattered so little to either party, since their minds, whatever they were, had pretty nearly ceased to reflect, and let them do what they liked with the small remnant, they could scarcely do anything very new with it. All one asked was to learn what they hoped to do. . . .

"THE SIGNIFICANCE OF THE FRONTIER IN AMERICAN HISTORY" *

By Frederick Jackson Turner

Frederick Jackson Turner (1861–1932), Wisconsin historian, shows how America's growth was shaped by the frontier

Trained at the University of Wisconsin, where frontier traditions were fresh, and at the Johns Hopkins University, where Germanic origins were stressed, Professor Turner of Wisconsin (and later Harvard) chose to devote the rest of his life to a study of the influences of the western frontier upon American history. The famous essay given here in full reflects his Darwinistic idea that the frontier "section" is an evolving cultural area and that the frontier itself is a process rather than a fixed line. He explains historical change through physiography, Indian and ethnic groups, and the idea that American democracy and national traits came out of the wilderness with its cheap lands and elements of struggle. This rather deterministic approach accounts for the fact that historians like Turner and Charles Beard, however brilliant and suggestive, were unable to understand slavery as a moral issue. Turner's idea of a closed frontier, presented during the panic year of 1893, seemed pessimistic, but his later essays show his belief in the growing necessity of social planning rather than a frontier dependence upon rugged individualism. In fact, the contributors to Franklin D. Roosevelt's Commonwealth Club address of 1932, A. A. Berle, Jr., particularly, were to cite Turner's closed frontier theory as a justification for the New Deal's planning

* Frederick J. Turner, "The Significance of the Frontier in American History," *Annual Report of the American Historical Association* (Washington, 1894), 199–227.

ideal, necessitated by the seeming evidence that our economy had "matured" and that our future task was scientific administration rather than expansion. There is no question that Turner's theories, despite the current criticism, stimulated the teaching and writing of American history as no other historian had done.

IN A recent bulletin of the Superintendent of the Census for 1890 appear these significant words: "Up to and including 1880 the country had a frontier of settlement, but at present the unsettled area has been so broken into by isolated bodies of settlement that there can hardly be said to be a frontier line. In the discussion of its extent, its westward movement, etc., it can not, therefore, any longer have a place in the census reports." This brief official statement marks the closing of a great historic movement. Up to our own day American history has been in a large degree the history of the colonization of the Great West. The existence of an area of free land, its continuous recession, and the advance of American settlement westward, explain American development.

Behind institutions, behind constitutional forms and modifications, lie the vital forces that call these organs into life and shape them to meet changing conditions. The peculiarity of American institutions is, the fact that they have been compelled to adapt themselves to the changes of an expanding people—to the changes involved in crossing a continent, in winning a wilderness, and in developing at each area of this progress out of the primitive economic and political conditions of the frontier into the complexity of city life. Said Calhoun in 1817, "We are great, and rapidly— I was about to say fearfully—growing!" So saying, he touched the distinguishing feature of American life. All peoples show development; the germ theory of politics has been sufficiently emphasized. In the case of most nations, however, the development has occurred in a limited area; and if the nation has expanded, it has met other growing peoples whom it has conquered. But in the case of the United States we have a different phenomenon. Limiting our attention to the Atlantic coast, we have the familiar phenomenon of the evolution of institutions in a limited area, such as the rise of representative government; the differentiation of simple colonial governments into complex organs; the progress from primitive industrial society, without division of labor, up to manufacturing civilization. But we have in addition to this a recurrence of the process of evolution in each western area reached in the process of expansion. Thus American development has exhibited not merely advance along a single line, but a return to primitive conditions on a continually advancing frontier line, and a new development for that area. American social development has been continually beginning over again on the frontier. This perennial rebirth, this fluidity of American life, this expansion westward with its new opportunities, its continuous touch with the simplicity of primitive society, furnish the forces dominating American character. The true point of view in the history of this nation is not the Atlantic coast, it is the great West. Even the slavery struggle, which is made so exclusive an object of attention by writers life Prof. von Holst, occupies its important place in American history because of its relation to westward expansion.

In this advance, the frontier is the outer edge of the wave—the meeting point between savagery and civilization. Much has been written about the frontier from the point of view of border warfare and the chase, but as a field for the serious study of the economist and the historian it has been neglected.

The American frontier is sharply distinguished from the European frontier—a fortified boundary line running through dense populations. The most significant thing about the American frontier is, that it lies at the hither edge of free land. In the census reports it is treated as the margin of that settlement which has a density of two or more to the square mile. The term is an elastic one, and for our purposes does not need sharp definition. We shall consider the whole frontier belt, including the Indian country and the outer margin of the "settled area" of the census reports. This paper will make no attempt to treat the subject exhaustively; its aim is simply to call attention to the frontier as a fertile field for investigation, and to suggest some of the problems which arise in connection with it.

In the settlement of America we have to observe how European life entered the continent, and how America modified and developed that life and reacted on Europe. Our early history is the study of European germs developing in an American environment. Too exclusive attention has been paid by institutional students to the Germanic origins, too little to the American factors. The frontier is the line of most rapid and effective Americanization. The wilderness masters the colonist. It finds him a European in dress, industries, tools, modes of travel, and thought. It takes him from the railroad car and puts him in the birch canoe. It strips off the garments of civilization and arrays him in the hunting shirt and the moccasin. It puts him in the log cabin of the Cherokee and Iroquois and runs an Indian palisade around him. Before long he has gone to planting Indian corn and plowing with a sharp stick; he shouts the war cry and takes the scalp in orthodox Indian fashion. In short, at the frontier the environment is at first too strong for the man. He must accept the conditions which it furnishes, or perish, and so he fits himself into the Indian clearings and follows the Indian trails. Little by little he transforms the wilderness, but the outcome is not the old Europe, not simply the development of Germanic germs, any more than the first phenomenon was a case of reversion to the Germanic mark. The fact is, that here is a new product that is American. At first, the frontier was the Atlantic coast. It was the frontier of Europe in a very real sense. Moving westward, the frontier became more and more American. As successive terminal moraines result from successive glaciations, so each frontier leaves its traces behind it, and when it becomes a settled area the region still partakes of the frontier characteristics. Thus the advance of the frontier has meant a steady movement away from the influence of Europe, a steady growth of independence on American lines. And to study this advance, the men who grew up under these conditions, and the political, economic, and social results of it, is to study the really American part of our history.

Stages of Frontier Advance

In the course of the seventeenth century the frontier was advanced up the Atlantic river courses, just beyond the "fall line," and the tidewater region became the settled area. In the first half of the eighteenth century another advance occurred. Traders followed the Delaware and Shawnese Indians to the Ohio as early as the end of the first quarter of the century. Gov. Spotswood, of Virginia, made an expedition in 1714 across the Blue Ridge. The end of the first quarter of the century saw the advance of the Scotch-Irish and the Palatine Germans up the

Shenandoah Valley into the western part of Virginia, and along the Piedmont region of the Carolinas. The Germans in New York pushed the frontier of settlement up the Mohawk to German Flats. In Pennsylvania the town of Bedford indicates the line of settlement. Settlements had begun on New River, a branch of the Kanawha, and on the sources of the Yadkin and French Broad. The King attempted to arrest the advance by his proclamation of 1763, forbidding settlements beyond the sources of the rivers flowing into the Atlantic; but in vain. In the period of the Revolution the frontier crossed the Alleghanies into Kentucky and Tennessee, and the upper waters of the Ohio were settled. When the first census was taken in 1790, the continuous settled area was bounded by a line which ran near the coast of Maine, and included New England except a portion of Vermont and New Hampshire, New York along the Hudson and up the Mohawk about Schenectady, eastern and southern Pennsylvania, Virginia well across the Shenandoah Valley, and the Carolinas and eastern Georgia. Beyond this region of continuous settlement were the small settled areas of Kentucky and Tennessee, and the Ohio, with the mountains intervening between them and the Atlantic area, thus giving a new and important character to the frontier. The isolation of the region increased its peculiarly American tendencies, and the need of transportation facilities to connect it with the East called out important schemes of internal improvement, which will be noted farther on. The "West," as a self-conscious section, began to evolve.

From decade to decade distinct advances of the frontier occurred. By the census of 1820 the settled area included Ohio, southern Indiana and Illinois, southeastern Missouri, and about one-half of Louisiana. This settled area had surrounded Indian areas, and the management of these tribes became an object of political concern. The frontier region of the time lay along the Great Lakes, where Astor's American Fur Company operated in the Indian trade, and beyond the Mississippi, where Indian traders extended their activity even to the Rocky Mountains; Florida also furnished frontier conditions. The Mississippi River region was the scene of typical frontier settlements.

The rising steam navigation on western waters, the opening of the Erie Canal, and the westward extension of cotton culture added five frontier states to the Union in this period. Grund, writing in 1856, declares: "It appears then that the universal disposition of Americans to emigrate to the western wilderness, in order to enlarge their dominion over inanimate nature, is the actual result of an expansive power which is inherent in them, and which by continually agitating all classes of society is constantly throwing a large portion of the whole population on the extreme confines of the State, in order to gain space for its development. Hardly is a new State or Territory formed before the same principle manifests itself again and gives rise to a further emigration; and so is it destined to go on until a physical barrier must finally obstruct its progress."

In the middle of this century the line indicated by the present eastern boundary of Indian Territory, Nebraska, and Kansas marked the frontier of the Indian country. Minnesota and Wisconsin still exhibited frontier conditions, but the distinctive frontier of the period is found in California, where the gold discoveries had sent a sudden tide of adventurous miners, and in Oregon, and the settlements in Utah. As the frontier had leaped over the Alleghanies, so now it skipped the Great Plains and the Rocky Mountains; and in the same way that the advance of the frontiersmen beyond the Alleghanies had caused the rise of important questions of transportation and internal improvement, so now the settlers beyond the Rocky Mountains needed means of communication with the East, and in the furnishing of these arose the settlement of the Great Plains and the development of still another kind of frontier life. Railroads, fostered by land grants, sent an increasing tide of immigrants into the far West. The United States Army fought a series of Indian wars in Minnesota, Dakota, and the Indian Territory.

By 1880 the settled area had been pushed into northern Michigan, Wisconsin, and Minnesota, along Dakota rivers, and in the Black Hills region, and was ascending the rivers of Kansas and Nebraska. The development of mines in Colorado had drawn isolated frontier settlements into that region, and Montana and Idaho were receiving settlers. The frontier was found in these mining camps and the ranches of the Great Plains. The superintendent of the census for 1890 reports, as previously stated, that the settlements of the West lie so scattered over the region that there can no longer be said to be a frontier line.

In these successive frontiers we find natural boundary lines which have served to mark and to affect the characteristics of the frontiers, namely: The "fall line"; the Alleghany Mountains; the

Mississippi; the Missouri, where its direction approximates north and south; the line of the arid lands, approximately the ninety-ninth meridian; and the Rocky Mountains. The fall line marked the frontier of the seventeenth century; the Alleghanies that of the eighteenth; the Mississippi that of the first quarter of the nineteenth; the Missouri that of the middle of this century (omitting the California movement); and the belt of the Rocky Mountains and the arid tract, the present frontier. Each was won by a series of Indian wars.

The Frontier Furnishes a Field for Comparative Study of Social Development

At the Atlantic frontier one can study the germs of processes repeated at each successive frontier. We have the complex European life sharply precipitated by the wilderness into the simplicity of primitive conditions. The first frontier had to meet its Indian question, its question of the disposition of the public domain, of the means of intercourse with older settlements, of the extension of political organization, of religious and educational activity. And the settlement of these and similar questions for one frontier served as a guide for the next. The American student needs not to go to the "prim little townships of Sleswick" for illustrations of the law of continuity and development. For example, he may study the origin of our land policies in the colonial land policy: he may see how the system grew by adapting the statutes to the customs of the successive frontiers. He may see how the mining experience in the lead regions of Wisconsin, Illinois, and Iowa was applied to the mining laws of the Rockies, and how our Indian policy has been a series of experimentations on successive frontiers. Each tier of new States has found in the older ones material for its constitutions. Each frontier has made similar contributions to American character, as will be discussed farther on.

But with all these similarities there are essential differences, due to the place element and the time element. It is evident that the farming frontier of the Mississippi Valley presents different conditions from the mining frontier of the Rocky Mountains. The frontier reached by the Pacific Railroad, surveyed into rectangles, guarded by the United States Army, and recruited by the daily immigrant ship, moves forward at a swifter pace and in a different way than the frontier reached by the birch canoe or the pack horse. The geologist traces patiently the shores of ancient seas, maps their areas, and compares the older and the newer. It would be a work worth the historian's labors to mark these various frontiers and in detail compare one with another. Not only would there result a more adequate conception of American development and characteristics, but invaluable additions would be made to the history of society.

Loria, the Italian economist, has urged the study of colonial life as an aid in understanding the stages of European development, affirming that colonial settlement is for economic science what the mountain is for geology, bringing to light primitive stratifications. "America," he says, "has the key to the historical enigma which Europe has sought for centuries in vain, and the land which has no history reveals luminously the course of universal history." There is much truth in this. The United States lies like a huge page in the history of society. Line by line as we read this continental page from west to east we find the record of social evolution. It begins with the Indian and the hunter; it goes on to tell of the disintegration of savagery by the entrance of the trader, the pathfinder of civilization; we read the annals of the pastoral stage in ranch life; the exploitation of the soil by the raising of unrotated crops of corn and wheat in sparsely settled farming communities; the intensive culture of the denser farm settlement; and finally the manufacturing organization with city and factory system. This page is familiar to the student of census statistics, but how little of it has been used by our historians. Particularly in eastern States this page is a palimpsest. What is now a manufacturing State was in an earlier decade an area of intensive farming. Earlier yet it had been a wheat area, and still earlier the "range" had attracted the cattle-herder. Thus Wisconsin, now developing manufacture, is a State with varied agricultural interests. But earlier it was given over to almost exclusive grain-raising, like North Dakota at the present time.

Each of these areas has had an influence in our economic and political history; the evolution of each into a higher stage has worked political transformations. But what constitutional historian has made any adequate attempt to interpret political facts by the light of these social areas and changes?

The Atlantic frontier was compounded of fisherman, fur-trader, miner, cattle-raiser, and farmer. Excepting the fisherman, each type of industry was on the march toward the West, impelled by an irresistible attraction. Each passed in successive waves across the continent. Stand at Cumberland Gap and watch the procession of civilization, marching single file—the buffalo following the trail to the salt springs, the Indian, the fur-trader and hunter, the cattle-raiser, the pioneer farmer—and the frontier has passed by. Stand at South Pass in the Rockies a century later and see the same procession with wider intervals between. The unequal rate of advance compels us to distinguish the frontier into the trader's frontier, the rancher's frontier, or the miner's frontier, and the farmer's frontier. When the mines and the cow pens were still near the fall line the traders' pack trains were tinkling across the Alleghanies, and the French on the Great Lakes were fortifying their posts, alarmed by the British trader's birch canoe. When the trappers scaled the Rockies, the farmer was still near the mouth of the Missouri.

The Indian Trader's Frontier

Why was it that the Indian trader passed so rapidly across the continent? What effects followed from the trader's frontier? The trade was coeval with American discovery. The Norsemen, Vespuccius, Verrazani, Hudson, John Smith, all trafficked for furs. The Plymouth pilgrims settled in Indian cornfields, and their first return cargo was of beaver and lumber. The records of the various New England colonies show how steadily exploration was carried into the wilderness by this trade. What is true for New England is, as would be expected, even plainer for the rest of the colonies. All along the coast from Maine to Georgia the Indian trade opened up the river courses. Steadily the trader passed westward, utilizing the older lines of French trade. The Ohio, the Great Lakes, the Mississippi, the Missouri, and the Platte, the lines of western advance, were ascended by traders. They found the passes in the Rocky Mountains and guided Lewis and Clarke, Fremont, and Bidwell. The explanation of the rapidity of this advance is connected with the effects of the trader on the Indian. The trading post left the unarmed tribes at the mercy of those that had purchased fire-arms—a truth which the Iroquois Indians wrote in blood, and so the remote and unvisited tribes gave eager welcome to the trader. "The savages," wrote La Salle, "take better care of us French than of their own children; from us only can they get guns and goods." This accounts for the trader's power and the rapidity of his advance. Thus the disintegrating forces of civilization entered the wilderness. Every river valley and Indian trail became a fissure in Indian society, and so that society became honeycombed. Long before the pioneer farmer appeared on the scene, primitive Indian life had passed away. The farmers met Indians armed with guns. The trading frontier, while steadily undermining Indian power by making the tribes ultimately dependent on the whites, yet, through its sale of guns, gave to the Indians increased power of resistance to the farming frontier. French colonization was dominated by its trading frontier; English colonization by its farming frontier. There was an antagonism between the two frontiers as between the two nations. Said Duquesne to the Iroquois, "Are you ignorant of the difference between the king of England and the king of France? Go see the forts that our king has established and you will see that you can still hunt under their very walls. They have been placed for your advantage in places which you frequent. The English, on the contrary, are no sooner in possession of a place than the game is driven away. The forest falls before them as they advance, and the soil is laid bare so that you can scarce find the wherewithal to erect a shelter for the night."

And yet, in spite of this opposition of the interests of the trader and the farmer, the Indian trade pioneered the way for civilization. The buffalo trail became the Indian trail, and this became the trader's "trace"; the trails widened into roads, and the roads into turnpikes, and these in turn were transformed into railroads. The same origin can be shown for the railroads of the South, the far West, and the Dominion of Canada. The trading posts reached by these trails were on the sites of Indian villages which had been placed in positions suggested by nature; and these trading posts, situated so as to command the water systems of the country, have grown into such cities as Albany, Pittsburgh, Detroit, Chicago, St. Louis, Council Bluffs, and Kansas City. Thus civilization in America has followed the arteries made by geology, pouring an ever richer tide through them, until at last the slender paths of aboriginal intercourse have been broadened and interwoven into the complex mazes of modern commercial lines; the wilderness has been interpenetrated by lines of civilization growing ever more numerous. It is like the steady growth of a complex nervous system for the originally simple, inert continent. If one would understand why we are to-day one nation, rather than a collection of isolated states, he must study this economic and social consolidation of the country. In this progress from savage conditions lie topics for the evolutionist.

The effect of the Indian frontier as a consolidating agent in our history is important. From the close of the seventeenth century various intercolonial congresses have been called to treat with Indians and establish common measures of defense. Particularism was strongest in colonies with no Indian frontier. This frontier stretched along the western border like a cord of union. The Indian was a common danger, demanding united action. Most celebrated of these conferences was the Albany congress of 1754, called to treat with the Six Nations, and to consider plans of union. Even a cursory reading of the plan proposed by the congress reveals the importance of the frontier. The powers of the general council and the officers were, chiefly, the determination of peace and war with the Indians, the regulation of Indian trade, the purchase of Indian lands, and the creation and government of new settlements as a security against the Indians. It is evident that the unifying tendencies of the Revolutionary period were facilitated by the previous cooperation in the regulation of the frontier. In this connection may be mentioned the importance of the frontier, from that day to this, as a military training school, keeping alive the power of resistance to aggression, and developing the stalwart and rugged qualities of the frontiersman.

The Rancher's Frontier

It would not be possible in the limits of this paper to trace the other frontiers across the continent. Travelers of the eighteenth century found the "cowpens" among the canebrakes and peavine pastures of the South, and the "cow drivers" took their droves to Charleston, Philadelphia, and New York. Travelers at the close of the War of 1812 met droves of more than a thousand cattle and swine from the interior of Ohio going to Pennsylvania to fatten for the Philadelphia market. The ranges of the Great Plains, with ranch and cowboy and nomadic life, are things of yesterday and of to-day. The experience of the Carolina cowpens guided the ranchers of Texas. One element favoring the rapid extension of the rancher's frontier is the fact that in a remote country lacking transportation facilities the product must be in small bulk, or must be able to transport itself, and the cattle raiser could easily drive his product to market. The effect of these great ranches on the subsequent agrarian history of the localities in which they existed should be studied.

The Farmer's Frontier

The maps of the census reports show an uneven advance of the farmer's frontier, with tongues of settlement pushed forward and with indentations of wilderness. In part this is due to Indian resistance, in part to the location of river valleys and passes, in part to the unequal force of the centers of frontier attraction. Among the important centers of attraction may be mentioned the following: fertile and favorably situated soils, salt springs, mines, and army posts.

Army Posts

The frontier army post, serving to protect the settlers from the Indians, has also acted as a wedge to open the Indian country, and has been a nucleus for settlement. In this connection mention should also be made of the Government military and exploring expeditions in determining the lines of settlement. But all the more important expeditions were greatly indebted to the earliest pathmakers, the Indian guides, the traders and trappers, and the French voyageurs, who were inevitable parts of governmental expeditions from the days of Lewis and Clarke. Each expedition was an epitome of the previous factors in western advance.

Salt Springs

In an interesting monograph, Victor Hehn has traced the effect of salt upon early European development, and has pointed out how it affected the lines of settlement and the form of administration. A similar study might be made for the salt springs of the United States. The early settlers were tied to the coast by the need of salt, without which they could not preserve their meats or live in comfort. Writing in 1752, Bishop Spangenburg says of a colony for which he was seeking lands in North Carolina, "They will require salt & other necessaries which they can neither manufacture nor raise. Either they must go to Charleston, which is 300 miles distant * * * Or else they must go to Boling's Point in V^a on a branch of the James & is also 300 miles from here * * * Or else they must go down the Roanoke—I know not how many miles—where salt is brought up from the Cape Fear." This may serve as a typical illustration. An annual pilgrimage to the coast for salt thus became essential. Taking flocks or furs and ginseng root, the early settlers sent their pack trains after seeding time each year to the coast. This proved to be an important educational influence, since it was almost the only way in which the pioneer learned what was going on in the East. But when discovery was made of the salt springs of the Kanawha, and the Holston, and Kentucky, and central New York, the West began to be freed from dependence on the coast. It was in part the effect of finding these salt springs that enabled settlement to cross the mountains.

From the time the mountains rose between the pioneer and the seaboard, a new order of Americanism arose. The West and the East began to get out of touch of each other. The settlements from the sea to the mountains kept connection with the rear and had a certain solidarity. But the over-mountain men grew more and more independent. The East took a narrow view of American advance, and nearly lost these men. Kentucky and Tennessee history bears abundant witness to the truth of this statement. The East began to try to hedge and limit westward expansion. Though Webster could declare that there were no Alleghanies in his politics, yet in politics in general they were a very solid factor.

Land

The exploitation of the beasts took hunter and trader to the west, the exploitation of the grasses took the rancher west, and the exploitation of the virgin soil of the river valleys and prairies attracted the farmer. Good soils have been the most continuous attraction to the farmer's frontier. The land hunger of the Virginians drew them down the rivers into Carolina, in early colonial days; the search for soils took the Massachusetts men to

Pennsylvania and to New York. As the eastern lands were taken up migration flowed across them to the west. Daniel Boone, the great backwoodsman, who combined the occupations of hunter, trader, cattle-raiser, farmer, and surveyor—learning, probably from the traders, of the fertility of the lands on the upper Yadkin, where the traders were wont to rest as they took their way to the Indians, left his Pennsylvania home with his father, and passed down the Great Valley road to that stream. Learning from a trader whose posts were on the Red River in Kentucky of its game and rich pastures, he pioneered the way for the farmers to that region. Thence he passed to the frontier of Missouri, where his settlement was long a landmark on the frontier. Here again he helped to open the way for civilization, finding salt licks, and trails, and land. His son was among the earliest trappers in the passes of the Rocky Mountains, and his party are said to have been the first to camp on the present site of Denver. His grandson, Col. A. J. Boone, of Colorado, was a power among the Indians of the Rocky Mountains, and was appointed an agent by the Government. Kit Carson's mother was a Boone. Thus this family epitomizes the backwoodsman's advance across the continent.

The farmer's advance came in a distinct series of waves. In Peck's New Guide to the West, published in Boston in 1837, occurs this suggestive passage:

Generally, in all the western settlements, three classes, like the waves of the ocean, have rolled one after the other. First comes the pioneer, who depends for the subsistence of his family chiefly upon the natural growth of vegetation, called the "range," and the proceeds of hunting. His implements of agriculture are rude, chiefly of his own make, and his efforts directed mainly to a crop of corn and a "truck patch." The last is a rude garden for growing cabbage, beans, corn for roasting ears, cucumbers, and potatoes. A log cabin, and, occasionally, a stable and corn-crib, and a field of a dozen acres, the timber girdled or "deadened," and fenced, are enough for his occupancy. It is quite immaterial whether he ever becomes the owner of the soil. He is the occupant for the time being, pays no rent, and feels as independent as the "lord of the manor." With a horse, cow, and one or two breeders of swine, he strikes into the woods with his family, and becomes the founder of a new county, or perhaps state. He builds his cabin, gathers around him a few other families of similar tastes and habits, and occupies till the range is somewhat subdued, and hunting a little precarious, or, which is more frequently the case, till the neighbors crowd around, roads, bridges, and fields annoy him, and he lacks elbow room. The preemption law enables him to dispose of his cabin and cornfield to the next class of emigrants; and, to employ his own figures, he "breaks for the high timber," "clears out for the New Purchase," or migrates to Arkansas or Texas, to work the same process over.

The next class of emigrants purchase the lands, add field to field, clear out the roads, throw rough bridges over the streams, put up hewn log houses with glass windows and brick or stone chimneys, occasionally plant orchards, build mills, schoolhouses, court-houses, etc., and exhibit the picture and forms of plain, frugal, civilized life.

Another wave rolls on. The men of capital and enterprise come. The settler is ready to sell out and take the advantage of the rise in property, push farther into the interior and become, himself, a man of capital and enterprise in turn. The small village rises to a spacious town or city; substantial edifices of brick, extensive fields, orchards, gardens, colleges, and churches are seen. Broadcloths, silks, leghorns, crapes, and all the refinements, luxuries, elegancies, frivolities, and fashions are in vogue. Thus wave after wave is rolling westward; the real Eldorado is still farther on.

A portion of the two first classes remain stationary amidst the general movement, improve their habits and condition, and rise in the scale of society.

The writer has traveled much amongst the first class, the real pioneers. He has lived many years in connection with the second grade; and now the third wave is sweeping over large districts of Indiana, Illinois, and Missouri. Migration has become almost a habit in the West. Hundreds of men can be found, not over 50 years of age, who have settled for the fourth, fifth, or sixth time on a new spot. To sell out and remove only a few hundred miles makes up a portion of the variety of backwoods life and manners.

Omitting those of the pioneer farmers who move from the love of adventure, the advance of the more steady farmer is easy to understand. Obviously the immigrant was attracted by the cheap lands of the frontier, and even the native farmer felt their influence strongly. Year by year the farmers who lived on soil whose returns were diminished by unrotated crops were offered the virgin soil of the frontier at nominal prices. Their growing families demanded more lands, and these were dear. The competition of the unexhausted, cheap, and easily tilled prairie lands compelled the farmer either to go west and continue the exhaustion of the soil on a new frontier, or to adopt intensive culture. Thus the census of 1890 shows, in the Northwest, many counties in which there is an absolute or a relative decrease of population. These States have been sending farmers to advance the frontier on the plains, and have themselves begun to turn to intensive farming and to manufacture. A decade before this, Ohio had shown the same transition stage. Thus the demand for land and the love of wilderness freedom drew the frontier ever onward.

Having now roughly outlined the various kinds of frontiers, and their modes of advance, chiefly from the point of view of the frontier itself, we may next inquire what were the influences on the East and on the Old World. A rapid enumeration of some of the more noteworthy effects is all that I have time for.

Composite Nationality

First, we note that the frontier promoted the formation of a composite nationality for the American people. The coast was preponderantly English, but the later tides of continental immigration flowed across to the free lands. This was the case from the early colonial days. The Scotch Irish and the Palatine Germans, or "Pennsylvania Dutch," furnished the dominant element in the stock of the colonial frontier. With these peoples were also the freed indented servants, or redemptioners, who at the expiration of their time of service passed to the frontier. Governor Spotswood of Virginia writes in 1717, "The inhabitants of our frontiers are composed generally of such as have been transported hither as servants, and, being out of their time, settle themselves where land is to be taken up and that will produce the necessarys of life with little labour." Very generally these redemptioners were of non-English stock. In the crucible of the frontier the immigrants were Americanized, liberated, and fused into a mixed race, English in neither nationality nor characteristics. The process has gone on from the early days to our own. Burke and other writers in the middle of the eighteenth century believed that Pennsylvania was "threatened with the danger of being wholly foreign in language, manners, and perhaps even inclinations." The German and Scotch-Irish elements in the frontier of the South were only less great. In the middle of the present century the German element in Wisconsin was already so considerable that leading publicists looked to the creation of a German state out of the commonwealth by concentrating their colonization. Such examples teach us to beware of misinterpreting the fact that there is a common English speech in America into a belief that the stock is also English.

Industrial Independence

In another way the advance of the frontier decreased our dependence on England. The coast, particularly of the South, lacked diversified industries, and was dependent on England for the bulk of its supplies. In the South there was even a dependence on the Northern colonies for articles of food. Governor Glenn, of South Carolina, writes in the middle of the eighteenth century: "Our trade with New York and Philadelphia was of this sort, draining us of all the little money and bills we could gather from other places for their bread, flour, beer, hams, bacon, and other things of their produce, all which, except beer, our new townships begin to supply us with, which are settled with very industrious and thriving Germans. This no doubt diminishes the number of shipping and the appearance of our trade, but it is far from being a detriment to us." Before long the frontier created a demand for merchants. As it retreated from the coast it became less and less possible for England to bring her supplies directly to the consumer's wharfs, and carry away staple crops, and staple crops began to give way to diversified agriculture for a time. The effect of this phase of the frontier action upon the northern section is perceived when we realize how the advance of the frontier aroused seaboard cities like Boston, New York, and Baltimore, to engage in rivalry for what Washington called "the extensive and valuable trade of a rising empire."

Effects on National Legislation

The legislation which most developed the powers of the National Government, and played the largest part in its activity, was conditioned on the frontier. Writers have discussed the subjects of tariff, land, and internal improvement, as subsidiary to the slavery question. But when American history comes to be rightly viewed it will be seen that the slavery question is an incident. In the period from the end of the first half of the present century to the close of the civil war slavery rose to primary, but far from exclusive, importance. But this does not justify Dr. von Holst (to take an example) in treating our constitutional history in its formative period down to 1828 in a single volume, giving six volumes chiefly to the history of slavery from 1828 to 1861, under the title "Constitutional History of the United States." The growth of nationalism and the evolution of American political institutions were dependent on the advance of the frontier. Even so recent a writer as Rhodes, in his "History of the United States Since the Compromise of 1850," has treated the legislation called out by the western advance as incidental to the slavery struggle.

This is a wrong perspective. The pioneer needed the goods of the coast, and so the grand series of internal improvement and railroad legislation began, with potent nationalizing effects. Over internal improvements occurred great debates, in which grave constitutional questions were discussed. Sectional groupings appear in the votes, profoundly significant for the historian. Loose construction increased as the nation marched westward. But the West was not content with bringing the farm to the factory. Under the lead of Clay—"Harry of the West"—protective tariffs were passed, with the cry of bringing the factory to the farm. The disposition of the public lands was a third important subject of national legislation influenced by the frontier.

The Public Domain

The public domain has been a force of profound importance in the nationalization and development of the Government. The effects of the struggle of the landed and the landless States, and of the ordinance of 1787, need no discussion. Administratively the frontier called out some of the highest and most vitalizing activities of the General Government. The purchase of Louisiana was perhaps the constitutional turning point in the history of the Republic, inasmuch as it afforded both a new area for national legislation and the occasion of the downfall of the policy of strict construction. But the purchase of Louisiana was called out by frontier needs and demands. As frontier States accrued to the Union the national power grew. In a speech on the dedication of the Calhoun monument Mr. Lamar explained: "In 1789 the States were the creators of the Federal Government; in 1861 the Federal Government was the creator of a large majority of the States."

When we consider the public domain from the point of view of the sale and disposal of the public lands we are again brought face to face with the frontier. The policy of the United States in dealing with its lands is in sharp contrast with the European system of scientific administration. Efforts to make this domain a source of revenue, and to withhold it from emigrants in order that settlement might be compact, were in vain. The jealousy and the fears of the East were powerless in the face of the demands of the frontiersmen. John Quincy Adams was obliged to confess: "My own system of administration, which was to make the national domain the inexhaustible fund for progressive and unceasing internal improvement, has failed." The reason is obvious; a system of administration was not what the West demanded; it wanted land. Adams states the situation as follows: "The slaveholders of the South have bought the cooperation of the western country by the bribe of the western lands, abandoning to the new Western States their own proportion of the public property and aiding them in the design of grasping all the lands into their own hands. Thomas H. Benton was the author of this system, which he brought forward as a substitute for the American system of Mr. Clay, and to supplant him as the leading statesman of the West. Mr. Clay, by his tariff compromise with Mr. Calhoun, abandoned his own American system. At the same time he brought forward a plan for distributing among all the States of the Union the proceeds of the sales of the public lands. His bill for that purpose passed both Houses of Congress, but was vetoed by President Jackson, who, in his annual message of December, 1832, formally recommended that all public lands should be gratuitously given away to individual adventurers and to the States in which the lands are situated.

"No subject," said Henry Clay, "which has presented itself to the present, or perhaps any preceding, Congress, is of greater magnitude than that of the public lands." When we consider the far-reaching effects of the Government's land policy upon political, economic, and social aspects of American life, we are disposed to agree with him. But this legislation was framed under frontier influences, and under the lead of Western statesmen like Benton and Jackson. Said Senator Scott of Indiana in 1841: "I consider the preemption law merely declaratory of the custom or common law of the settlers."

National Tendencies of the Frontier

It is safe to say that the legislation with regard to land, tariff, and internal improvements—the American system of the nationalizing Whig party—was conditioned on frontier ideas and needs. But it was not merely in legislative action that the frontier worked against the sectionalism of the coast. The economic and social characteristics of the frontier worked against sectionalism. The men of the frontier had closer resemblances to the Middle region than to either of the other sections. Pennsylvania had been the seed-plot of frontier emigration, and, although she passed on her settlers along the Great Valley into the west of Virginia and the Carolinas, yet the industrial society of these Southern frontiersmen was always more like that of the Middle region than like that of the tide-water portion of the South, which later came to spread its industrial type throughout the South.

The Middle region, entered by New York harbor, was an open door to all Europe. The tide-water part of the South represented typical Englishmen, modified by a warm climate and servile labor, and living in baronial fashion on great plantations; New England stood for a special English movement—Puritanism. The Middle region was less English than the other sections. It had a wide mixture of nationalities, a varied society, the mixed town and county system of local government, a varied economic life, many religious sects. In short, it was a region mediating between New England and the South, and the East and the West. It represented that composite nationality which the contemporary United States exhibits, that juxtaposition of non-English groups, occupying a valley or a little settlement, and presenting reflections of the map of Europe in their variety. It was democratic and nonsectional, if not national; "easy, tolerant, and contented"; rooted strongly in material prosperity. It was typical of the modern United States. It was least sectional, not only because it lay between North and South, but also because with no barriers to shut out its frontiers from its settled region, and with a system of connecting waterways, the Middle region mediated between East and West as well as between North and South. Thus it became the typically American region. Even the New Englander, who was shut out from the frontier by the Middle region, tarrying in New York or Pennsylvania on his westward march, lost the acuteness of his sectionalism on the way.

The spread of cotton culture into the interior of the South finally broke down the contrast between the "tide-water" region and the rest of the State, and based Southern interests on slavery. Before this process revealed its results the western portion of the South, which was akin to Pennsylvania in stock, society, and industry, showed tendencies to fall away from the faith of the fathers into internal improvement legislation and nationalism. In the Virginia convention of 1829–'30, called to revise the constitution, Mr. Leigh, of Chesterfield, one of the tide-water counties, declared:

One of the main causes of discontent which led to this convention, that which had the strongest influence in overcoming our veneration for the work of our fathers, which taught us to contemn the sentiments of Henry and Mason and Pendleton, which weaned us from our reverence for the constituted authorities of the State, was an overweening passion for internal improvement. I say this with perfect knowledge, for it has been avowed to me by gentlemen from the West over and over again. And let me tell the gentleman from Albemarle (Mr. Gordon) that it has been another principal object of those who set this ball of revolution in motion, to overturn the doctrine of State rights, of which Virginia has been the very pillar, and to remove the barrier she has interposed to the interference of the Federal Government in that same work of internal improvement, by so reorganizing the legislature that Virginia, too, may be hitched to the Federal car.

It was this nationalizing tendency of the West that transformed the democracy of Jefferson into the national republicanism of Monroe and the democracy of Andrew Jackson. The West of the war of 1812, the West of Clay, and Benton, and Harrison, and Andrew Jackson, shut off by the Middle States and the mountains from the coast sections, had a solidarity of its own with national tendencies. On the tide of the Father of Waters, North and South met and mingled into a nation. Interstate migration went steadily on—a process of cross-fertilization of ideas and institutions. The fierce struggle of the sections over slavery on the western frontier does not diminish the truth of this statement; it proves the truth of it. Slavery was a sectional trait that would not down, but in the West it could not remain sectional. It was the greatest of frontiersmen who declared: "I believe this Government can not endure permanently half slave and half free. It will become all of one thing or all of the other." Nothing works for nationalism like intercourse within the nation. Mobility of population is death to localism, and the western frontier worked irresistibly in unsettling population. The effects reached back from the frontier and affected profoundly the Atlantic coast and even the Old World.

Growth of Democracy

But the most important effect of the frontier has been in the promotion of democracy here and in Europe. As has been indicated, the frontier is productive of individualism. Complex society is precipitated by the wilderness into a kind of primitive organization based on the family. The tendency is anti-social. It produces antipathy to control, and particularly to any direct control. The tax-gatherer is viewed as a representative of oppression. Prof. Osgood, in an able article, has pointed out that the frontier conditions prevalent in the colonies are important factors in the explanation of the American Revolution, where individual liberty was sometimes confused with absence of all effective government. The same conditions aid in explaining the difficulty of instituting a strong government in the period of the confederacy. The frontier individualism has from the beginning promoted democracy.

The frontier States that came into the Union in the first quarter of a century of its existence came in with democratic suffrage provisions, and had reactive effects of the highest importance upon the older States whose peoples were being attracted there. An extension of the franchise became essential. It was *western* New York that forced an extension of suffrage in the constitutional convention of that State in 1821; and it was *western* Virginia that compelled the tide-water region to put a more liberal suffrage provision in the constitution framed in 1830, and to give to the frontier region a more nearly proportionate representation with the tide-water aristocracy. The rise of democracy as an effective force in the nation came in with western preponderance under Jackson and William Henry Harrison, and it meant the triumph of the frontier—with all of its good and with all of its evil elements. An interesting illustration of the tone of frontier democracy in 1830 comes from the same debates in the Virginia convention already referred to. A representative from western Virginia declared:

But, sir, it is not the increase of population in the West which this gentleman ought to fear. It is the energy which the mountain breeze and western habits impart to those emigrants. They are regenerated, politically I mean, sir. They soon become *working politicians;* and the difference, sir, between a *talking* and a *working* politician is immense. The Old Dominion has long been celebrated for producing great orators; the ablest metaphysicians in policy; men that can split hairs in all abstruse questions of political economy. But at home, or when they return from Congress, they have negroes to fan them asleep. But a Pennsylvania, a New York, an Ohio, and a western Virginia statesman, though far inferior in logic, metaphysics, and rhetoric to an old Virginia statesman, has this advantage, that when he returns home he takes off his coat and takes hold of the plow. This gives him bone and muscle, sir, and preserves his republican principles pure and uncontaminated.

So long as free land exists, the opportunity for a competency exists, and economic power secures political power. But the democracy born of free land, strong in selfishness and individualism, intolerant of administrative experience and education, and pressing individual liberty beyond its proper bounds, has its dangers as well as its benefits. Individualism in America has allowed a laxity in regard to governmental affairs which has rendered possible the spoils system and all the manifest evils that follow from the lack of a highly developed civic spirit. In this connection may be noted also the influence of frontier conditions in permitting lax business honor, inflated paper currency and wild-cat banking. The colonial and revolutionary frontier was the region whence emanated many of the worst forms of an evil currency. The West in the war of 1812 repeated the phenomenon on the frontier of that day, while the speculation and wild-cat banking of the period of the crisis of 1837 occurred on the new frontier belt of the next tier of States. Thus each one of the periods of lax financial integrity coincides with periods when a new set of frontier communities had arisen, and coincides in area with these successive frontiers, for the most part. The recent Populist agitation is a case in point. Many a State that now declines any connection with the tenets of the Populists, itself adhered to such ideas in an earlier stage of the development of the State. A primitive society can hardly be expected to show the intelligent appreciation of the complexity of business interests in a developed society. The continual recurrence of these areas of paper-money agitation is another evidence that the frontier can be isolated and studied as a factor in American history of the highest importance.

Attempts to Check and Regulate the Frontier

The East has always feared the result of an unregulated advance of the frontier, and has tried to check and guide it. The English authorities would have checked settlement at the headwaters of the Atlantic tributaries and allowed the "savages to enjoy their deserts in quiet lest the peltry trade should decrease." This called out Burke's splendid protest:

If you stopped your grants, what would be the consequence? The people would occupy without grants. They have already so occupied in many places. You can not station garrisons in every part of these deserts. If you drive the people from one place, they will carry on their annual tillage and remove with their flocks and herds to another. Many of the people in the back settlements are already little attached to particular situations. Already they have topped the Appalachian mountains. From thence they behold before them an immense plain, one vast, rich, level meadow; a square of five hundred miles. Over this they would wander without a possibility of restraint; they would change their manners with their habits of life; would soon forget a government by which they were disowned; would become hordes of English Tartars; and, pouring down upon your unfortified frontiers a fierce and irresistible cavalry, become masters of your governors, and your counselors, your collectors and comptrollers, and of all the slaves that adhered to them. Such would, and in no long time must, be the effect of attempting to forbid as a crime and to suppress as an evil the command and blessing of Providence, "Increase and multiply." Such would be the happy result of an endeavor to keep as a lair of wild beasts that earth which God, by an express charter, has given to the children of men.

But the English Government was not alone in its desire to limit the advance of the frontier and guide its destinies. Tidewater Virginia and South Carolina gerrymandered those colonies to insure the dominance of the coast in their legislatures. Washington desired to settle a State at a time in the Northwest; Jefferson would reserve from settlement the territory of his Louisiana purchase north of the thirty-second parallel, in order to offer it to the Indians in exchange for their settlements east of the Mississippi. "When we shall be full on this side," he writes, "we may lay off a range of States on the western bank from the head to the mouth, and so range after range, advancing compactly as we multiply." Madison went so far as to argue to the French minister that the United States had no interest in seeing population extend itself on the right bank of the Mississippi, but should rather fear it. When the Oregon question was under debate, in 1824, Smyth, of Virginia, would draw an unchangeable line for the limits of the United States at the outer limit of two tiers of States beyond the Mississippi, complaining that the seaboard States were being drained of the flower of their population by the bringing of too much land into market. Even Thomas Benton, the man of widest views of the destiny of the West, at this stage of his career declared that along the ridge of the Rocky mountains "the western limits of the Republic should be drawn, and the statue of the fabled god Terminus should be raised upon its highest peak, never to be thrown down." But the attempts to limit the boundaries, to restrict land sales and settlement and to deprive the West of its share of political power were all in vain. Steadily the frontier of settlement advanced and carried with it individualism, democracy, and nationalism, and powerfully affected the East and the Old World.

Missionary Activity

The most effective efforts of the East to regulate the frontier came through its educational and religious activity, exerted by interstate migration and by organized societies. Speaking in 1835, Dr. Lyman Beecher declared: "It is equally plain that the religious and political destiny of our nation is to be decided in the West," and he pointed out that the population of the West "is assembled from all the States of the Union and from all the nations of Europe, and is rushing in like the waters of the flood, demanding for its moral preservation the immediate and universal action of those institutions which discipline the mind and arm the conscience and the heart. And so various are the opinions and habits, and so recent and imperfect is the acquaintance, and so sparse are the settlements of the West, that no homogeneous public sentiment can be formed to legislate immediately into being the requisite institutions. And yet they are all needed immediately in their utmost perfection and power. A nation is being 'born in a day.' * * * But what will become of the West if her prosperity rushes up to such a majesty of power, while those great institutions linger which are necessary to form the mind and the conscience and the heart of that vast world. It must not be permitted. * * * Let no man at the East quiet himself and dream of liberty, whatever may become of the West. * * * Her destiny is our destiny."

With the appeal to the conscience of New England, he adds appeals to her fears lest other religious sects anticipate her own. The New England preacher and school-teacher left their mark on the West. The dread of Western emancipation from New England's political and economic control was paralleled by her fears lest the West cut loose from her religion. Commenting in 1850 on reports that settlement was rapidly extending northward in Wisconsin, the editor of the Home Missionary writes: "We scarcely know whether to rejoice or mourn over this extension of our settlements. While we sympathize in whatever tends to increase the physical resources and prosperity of our country, we can not forget that with all these dispersions into remote and still remoter corners of the land the supply of the means of grace is becoming relatively less and less." Acting in accordance with such ideas, home missions were established and Western colleges were erected. As seaboard cities like Philadelphia, New York, and Baltimore strove for the mastery of Western trade, so the various denominations strove for the possession of the West. Thus an intellectual stream from New England sources fertilized the West. Other sections sent their missionaries; but the real struggle was between sects. The contest for power and the expansive tendency furnished to the various sects by the existence of a moving frontier must have had important results on the character of religious organization in the United States. The multiplication of rival churches in the little frontier towns had deep and lasting social effects. The religious aspects of the frontier make a chapter in our history which needs study.

Intellectual Traits

From the conditions of frontier life came intellectual traits of profound importance. The works of travelers along each frontier from colonial days onward describe certain common traits, and these traits have, while softening down, still persisted as survivals in the place of their origin, even when a higher social organization succeeded. The result is that to the frontier the American intellect owes its striking characteristics. That coarseness and strength combined with acuteness and inquisitiveness; that practical, inventive turn of mind, quick to find expedients; that masterful grasp of material things, lacking in the artistic but powerful to effect great ends; that restless, nervous energy; that dominant individualism, working for good and for evil, and withal that buoyancy and exuberance which comes with freedom —these are traits of the frontier, or traits called out elsewhere because of the existence of the frontier. Since the days when the fleet of Columbus sailed into the waters of the New World, America has been another name for opportunity, and the people of the United States have taken their tone from the incessant expansion which has not only been open but has even been forced upon them. He would be a rash prophet who should assert that the expansive character of American life has now entirely ceased. Movement has been its dominant fact, and, unless this training has no effect upon a people, the American energy will continually demand a wider field for its exercise. But never again will such gifts of free land offer themselves. For a moment, at the frontier, the bonds of custom are broken and unrestraint is triumphant. There is not *tabula rasa*. The stubborn American environment is there with its imperious summons to accept its conditions; the inherited ways of doing things are also there; and yet, in spite of environment, and in spite of custom, each frontier did indeed furnish a new field of opportunity, a gate of escape from the bondage of the past; and freshness, and confidence, and scorn of older society, impatience of its restraints and its ideas, and indifference to its lessons, have accompanied the frontier. What the Mediterranean Sea was to the Greeks, breaking the bond of custom, offering new experiences, calling out new institutions and activities, that, and more, the ever retreating frontier has been to the United States directly, and to the nations of Europe more remotely. And now, four centuries from the discovery of America, at the end of a hundred years of life under the Constitution, the frontier has gone, and with its going has closed the first period of American history.

"WRITTEN HISTORY AS AN ACT OF FAITH" *

By Charles Beard

Charles Beard (1874–1948), historian, rejects any historical objectivity that aspires to the certainty and methods of the natural sciences

Charles Beard, an Indiana-born son of a small-town banker, enjoyed an education at De Pauw College, studies and observations abroad, finally obtaining a Ph.D. in history at Columbia. He broke away from his family's conservative Republicanism to embrace the social action ideas of the welfare state that he learned in Bismarck's Germany and that he had observed in the idealistic Oxford students who came as "residents" to the slum-surrounded Toynbee Hall with its pioneer settlement movement. He was definitely committed to the idea of social action as he worked with the British Labour Party and its meliorist program.

As a historian and political scientist at Columbia (1907–17), he learned and practiced the progressive New History ideas of James Harvey Robinson and, in 1919, helped him to found the experimental New School for Social Research. His lifelong adherence to the New History is suggested in the essay below, "Written History as an Act of Faith," in which he rejects the alleged mechanical "objectivity" of Leopold von Ranke as unnaturally "value-free" and seemingly detached while actually serving the cause of reaction. When he wrote the classic, *An Economic Interpretation of the Constitution* in 1913, too many readers assumed that this was a muckrakish exposé to show that the Founding Fathers wished to raise the value of their federal securities by replacing the Articles of Confederation with the Constitution that protected creditor interests. Actually, Beard was praising the hardheaded realism of the Founders who succeeded in creating a lasting document by basing it squarely upon enlightened self-interest.

As he said many time later, he was definitely concerned with economic interpretations of history, a theory derived not from Marx but from James Madison, especially as he presented his idea

* Charles Beard, "Written History as an Act of Faith" (Presidential Address delivered before the American Historical Association, December 28, 1933), *American Historical Review* 39 (1934), 219–29. Reprinted by permission of the American Historical Association, Washington, D.C.

in the famous argument in the Tenth Number of the *Federalist Papers*. Yet Beard's best-known work, *The Rise of American Civilization*, obviously borrows the class conflict structure of a Marxist historian, Algie Simons. There is not only F. J. Turner's emphasis (which Simons also borrowed) on the conflict of interests between creditors and debtors, but also causal relationships implied between land speculators and outright conspirators. Beard saw the Civil War as a conflict between planters and industrialists and—like Turner—forgot that slavery contained a moral issue. He interpreted the Fourteenth Amendment as a conspiratorial victory for corporate power and privilege rather than as a gain for the preservation of human rights.

He wrote substantial best sellers that circled the globe, and his numerous articles for *The New Republic* regarding the Nye Investigation of 1934 convinced many intellectuals that the United States had entered World War I because of the pressures of bankers and munition makers. His isolationism even penetrated postwar historiography when he wrote that Roosevelt had maneuvered the Japanese to strike the first blow at Pearl Harbor.

Much more important was the influence of his books and articles upon the nature and philosophy of history, especially in his addresses on "That Noble Dream" and "Written History as an Act of Faith." Although he professed to discard historical relativity as a self-cancellative philosophy, his emphasis upon changing "frames of reference" upon which historians must lean and his attack on objectivity led historians to classify him as an extreme relativist. However, as the essay below shows, he went no further than the democratic pragmatists in the tradition of John Dewey to point out the illusiveness of the quest for certainty.

✶✶✶

HISTORY HAS been called a science, an art, an illustration of theology, a phase of philosophy, a branch of literature. It is none of these things, nor all of them combined. On the contrary, science, art, theology, and literature are themselves merely phases of history as past actuality and their particular forms at given periods and places are to be explained, if explained at all, by history as knowledge and thought. The philosopher, possessing little or no acquaintance with history, sometimes pretends to expound the inner secret of history,* but the historian turns upon him and expounds the secret of the philosopher, as far as

* For a beautiful example, see the passages on America in the introduction to Hegel's *Philosophy of History*.

it may be expounded at all, by placing him in relation to the movement of ideas and interests in which he stands or floats, by giving to his scheme of thought its appropriate relativity. So it is with systems of science, art, theology, and literature. All the light on these subjects that can be discovered by the human mind comes from history as past actuality.

What, then, is this manifestation of omniscience called history? It is, as Croce says, contemporary thought about the past. History as past actuality includes, to be sure, all that has been done, said, felt, and thought by human beings on this planet since humanity began its long career. History as record embraces the monuments, documents, and symbols which provide such knowledge as we have or can find respecting past actuality. But it is history as thought, not as actuality, record, or specific knowledge, that is really meant when the term history is used in its widest and most general significance. It is thought about past actuality, instructed and delimited by history as record and knowledge—record and knowledge authenticated by criticism and ordered with the help of the scientific method. This is the final, positive, inescapable definition. It contains all the exactness that is possible and all the bewildering problems inherent in the nature of thought and the relation of the thinker to the thing thought about.

Although this definition of history may appear, at first glance, distressing to those who have been writing lightly about "the science of history" and "the scientific method" in historical research and construction, it is in fact in accordance with the most profound contemporary thought about history, represented by Croce, Riezler, Karl Mannheim, Mueller-Armack, and Heussi, for example. It is in keeping also with the obvious and commonplace. Has it not been said for a century or more that each historian who writes history is a product of his age, and that his work reflects the spirit of the times, of a nation, race, group, class, or section? No contemporary student of history really believes that Bossuet, Gibbon, Mommsen, or Bancroft could be duplicated to-day. Every student of history knows that his colleagues have been influenced in their selection and ordering of materials by their biases, prejudices, beliefs, affections, general upbringing, and experience, particularly social and economic; and if he has a sense of propriety, to say nothing of humor, he applies the canon to himself, leaving no exceptions to the rule.

The pallor of waning time, if not of death, rests upon the latest volume of history, fresh from the roaring press.

Why do we believe this to be true? The answer is that every written history—of a village, town, county, state, nation, race, group, class, idea, or the wide world—is a selection and arrangement of facts, of recorded fragments of past actuality. And the selection and arrangement of facts—a combined and complex intellectual operation—is an act of choice, conviction, and interpretation respecting values, is an act of thought. Facts, multitudinous and beyond calculation, are known, but they do not select themselves or force themselves automatically into any fixed scheme of arrangement in the mind of the historian. They are selected and ordered by him as he thinks. True enough, where the records pertaining to a small segment of history are few and presumably all known, the historian may produce a fragment having an aspect of completeness, as, for example, some pieces by Fustel de Coulanges; but the completeness is one of documentation, not of history. True enough also, many historians are pleased to say of their writings that their facts are selected and ordered only with reference to inner necessities, but none who takes this position will allow the same exactitude and certainty to the works of others, except when the predilections of the latter conform to his own pattern.

Contemporary thought about history, therefore, repudiates the conception dominant among the schoolmen during the latter part of the nineteenth century and the opening years of the twentieth century—the conception that it is possible to describe the past as it actually was, somewhat as the engineer describes a single machine. The formula itself was a passing phase of thought about the past. Its author, Ranke, a German conservative, writing after the storm and stress of the French Revolution, was weary of history written for, or permeated by, the purposes of revolutionary propaganda. He wanted peace. The ruling classes in Germany, with which he was affiliated, having secured a breathing spell in the settlement of 1815, wanted peace to consolidate their position. Written history that was cold, factual, and apparently undisturbed by the passions of the time served best the cause of those who did not want to be disturbed. Later the formula was fitted into the great conception of natural science—cold neutrality over against the materials and forces of the physical world. Truths of nature, ran the theory, are to be discovered by maintaining the most severe objectivity; therefore the truth of history may be revealed by the same spirit and method. The reasoning seemed perfect to those for whom it was satisfactory. But the movement of ideas and interests continued, and bondage to conservative and scientific thought was broken by criticism and events. As Croce and Heussi have demonstrated, so-called neutral or scientific history reached a crisis in its thought before the twentieth century had advanced far on the way.

This crisis in historical thought sprang from internal criticism —from conflicts of thought within historiography itself—and from the movement of history as actuality; for historians are always engaged, more or less, in thinking about their own work and are disturbed, like their fellow citizens, by crises and revolutions occurring in the world about them. As an outcome of this crisis in historiography, the assumption that the actuality of history is identical with or closely akin to that of the physical world, and the assumption that any historian can be a disembodied spirit as coldly neutral to human affairs as the engineer to an automobile have both been challenged and rejected. Thus, owing to internal criticism and the movement of external events, the Ranke formula of history has been discarded and laid away in the museum of antiquities. It has ceased to satisfy the human spirit in its historical needs. Once more, historians recognize formally the obvious, long known informally, namely, that any written history inevitably reflects the thought of the author in his time and cultural setting.

That this crisis in thought presents a distressing dilemma to many historians is beyond question. It is almost a confession of inexpiable sin to admit in academic circles that one is not a man of science working in a scientific manner with things open to deterministic and inexorable treatment, to admit that one is more or less a guesser in this vale of tears. But the only escape from the dust and storm of the present conflict, and from the hazards of taking thought, now before the historian, is silence or refuge in some minute particularity of history as actuality. He may edit documents, although there are perils in the choice of documents to be edited, and in any case the choice of documents will bear some reference to an interpretation of values and importance—subjective considerations. To avoid this difficulty, the historian may confine his attention to some very remote and microscopic area of time and place, such as the price of cotton in Alabama between 1850 and 1860, or the length of wigs in the reign of Charles II, on the pleasing but false assumption that he is really describing an isolated particularity as it actually was, an isolated area having no wide-reaching ramifications of relations. But even then the historian would be a strange creature if he never asked himself why he regarded these matters as worthy of his labor and love, or why society provides a living for him during his excursions and explorations.

The other alternative before the student of history as immense actuality is to face boldly, in the spirit of Cato's soliloquy, the wreck of matter and the crush of worlds—the dissolution of that solid assurance which rested on the formula bequeathed by Ranke and embroidered by a thousand hands during the intervening years. And when he confronts without avoidance contemporary thought about the nature of written history, what commands does he hear?

The supreme command is that he must cast off his servitude to the assumptions of natural science and return to his own subject matter—to history as actuality. The hour for this final declaration of independence has arrived: the contingency is here and thought resolves it. Natural science is only one small subdivision of history as actuality with which history as thought is concerned. Its dominance in the thought of the Western World for a brief period can be explained, if at all, by history; perhaps in part by reference to the great conflict that raged between the theologians and scientists after the dawn of the sixteenth century—an intellectual conflict associated with the economic conflict between landed aristocracies, lay and clerical, on the one side, and the rising bourgeois on the other.

The intellectual formulas borrowed from natural science, which have cramped and distorted the operations of history as thought, have taken two forms: physical and biological. The first of these rests upon what may be called, for convenience, the assumption of causation: everything that happens in the world of human affairs is determined by antecedent occurrences, and events of history are the illustrations or data of laws to be discovered, laws such as are found in hydraulics. It is true that no historian has ever been able to array the fullness of history as actuality in any such deterministic order; Karl Marx has gone further than any other. But under the hypothesis that it is possible, historians have been arranging events in neat little chains of causation which explain, to their satisfaction, why succeeding events happen; and they have attributed any shortcomings in result to the inadequacy of their known data, not to the falsity of the assumption on which they have been operating. Undiscouraged by their inability to bring all history within a single law, such as the law of gravitation, they have gone on working in the belief that the Newtonian trick will be turned some time, if the scientific method is applied long and rigorously enough and facts are heaped up high enough, as the succeeding grists of doctors of philosophy are ground out by the universities, turned loose on "research projects", and amply supplied by funds.

Growing rightly suspicious of this procedure in physico-historiography, a number of historians, still bent on servitude to natural science, turned from physics to biology. The difficulties and failures involved in all efforts to arrange the occurrences of history in a neat system of historical mechanics were evident to them. But on the other side, the achievements of the Darwinians were impressive. If the totality of history could not be brought into a deterministic system without doing violence to historical knowledge, perhaps the biological analogy of the organism could be applied. And this was done, apparently without any realization of the fact that thinking by analogy is a form of primitive animism. So under the biological analogy, history was conceived as a succession of cultural organisms rising, growing, competing, and declining. To this fantastic morphological assumption Spengler chained his powerful mind. Thus freed from self-imposed slavery to physics, the historian passed to self-imposed subservience to biology. Painfully aware of the perplexities encountered as long as he stuck to his own business, the historian sought escape by employing the method and thought of others whose operations he did not understand and could not control, on the simple, almost childlike, faith that the biologist, if not the physicist, really knew what he was about and could furnish the clue to the mystery.

But the shadow of the organismic conception of history had scarcely fallen on the turbulent actuality of history when it was scrutinized by historians who were thinking in terms of their own subject as distinguished from the terms of a mere subdivision of history. By an inescapable demonstration Kurt Riezler has made it clear that the organismic theory of history is really the old determinism of physics covered with murky words. The rise, growth, competition, and decline of cultural organisms is meaningless unless fitted into some overarching hypothesis—either the hypothesis of the divine drama or the hypothesis of causation in the deterministic sense. Is each cultural organism in history, each national or racial culture, an isolated particularity governed by its own mystical or physical laws? Knowledge of history as actuality forbids any such conclusion. If, in sheer desperation, the historian clings to the biological analogy, which school is he to follow—the mechanistic or the vitalistic? In either case he is caught in the deterministic sequence, if he thinks long enough and hard enough.

Hence the fate of the scientific school of historiography turns finally upon the applicability of the deterministic sequence to the totality of history as actuality. Natural science in a strict sense, as distinguished from mere knowledge of facts, can discover system and law only where occurrences are in reality arranged objectively in deterministic sequences. It can describe these sequences and draw from them laws, so-called. From a given number of the occurrences in any such sequence, science can predict what will happen when the remainder appear.

With respect to certain areas of human occurrences, something akin to deterministic sequences is found by the historian, but the perdurance of any sequence depends upon the perdurance in time of surrounding circumstances which cannot be brought within any scheme of deterministic relevancies. Certainly all the occurrences of history as actuality cannot be so ordered; most of them are unknown and owing to the paucity of records must forever remain unknown.

If a science of history were achieved, it would, like the science of celestial mechanics, make possible the calculable prediction of the future in history. It would bring the totality of historical occurrences within a single field and reveal the unfolding future to its last end, including all the apparent choices made and to be made. It would be omniscience. The creator of it would possess the attributes ascribed by the theologians to God. The future once revealed, humanity would have nothing to do except to await its doom.

To state the case is to dispose of it. The occurrences of history—the unfolding of ideas and interests in time-motion—are not identical in nature with the data of physics, and hence in their totality they are beyond the reach of that necessary instrument of natural science—mathematics—which cannot assign meaningful values to the imponderables, immeasurables, and contingencies of history as actuality.

Having broken the tyranny of physics and biology, contemporary thought in historiography turns its engines of verification upon the formula of historical relativity—the formula that makes all written history merely relative to time and circumstance, a passing shadow, an illusion. Contemporary criticism shows that the apostle of relativity is destined to be destroyed by the child of his own brain. If all historical conceptions are merely relative to passing events, to transitory phases of ideas and interests, then the conception of relativity is itself relative. When absolutes in history are rejected the absolutism of relativity is also rejected. So we must inquire: To what spirit of the times, to the ideas and interests of what class, group, nation, race, or region does the conception of relativity correspond? As the actuality of history moves forward into the future, the conception of relativity will also pass, as previous conceptions and interpretations of events have passed. Hence, according to the very doctrine of relativity, the skeptic of relativity will disappear in due course, beneath the ever-tossing waves of changing relativities. If he does not suffer this fate soon, the apostle of relativity will surely be executed by his own logic. Every conception of history, he says, is relative to time and circumstances. But by his own reasoning he is then compelled to ask: To what are these particular times and circumstances relative? And he must go on with receding sets of times and circumstances until he confronts an absolute: the totality of history as actuality which embraces all times and circumstances and all relativities.

Contemporary historical thought is, accordingly, returning upon itself and its subject matter. The historian is casting off his servitude to physics and biology, as he formerly cast off the shackles of theology and its metaphysics. He likewise sees the doctrine of relativity crumble in the cold light of historical knowledge. When he accepts none of the assumptions made by theology, physics, and biology, as applied to history, when he passes out from under the fleeting shadow of relativity, he confronts the absolute in his field—the absolute totality of all historical occurrences past, present, and becoming to the end of all things. Then he finds it necessary to bring the occurrences of history as actuality under one or another of the broad conceptions.

The first is that history as total actuality is chaos, perhaps with little islands of congruous relativities floating on the surface, and that the human mind cannot bring them objectively into any all-embracing order or subjectively into any consistent system. The second is that history as actuality is a part of some order of nature and revolves in cycles eternally—spring, summer, autumn, and winter, democracy, aristocracy, and monarchy, or their variants, as imagined by Spengler. The third is that history as actuality is moving in some direction away from the low level of primitive beginnings, on an upward gradient toward a more ideal order—as imagined by Condorcet, Adam Smith, Karl Marx, or Herbert Spencer.

Abundant evidence can be marshaled, has been marshaled, in support of each of these conceptions of history as actuality, but all the available evidence will not fit any one of them. The hypothesis of chaos admits of no ordering at all; hence those who operate under it cannot write history, although they may comment *on* history. The second admits of an ordering of events only by arbitrarily leaving out of account all the contradictions in the evidence. The third admits of an ordering of events, also by leaving contradictions out of consideration. The historian who writes history, therefore, consciously or unconsciously performs an act of faith, as to order and movement, for certainty as to order and movement is denied to him by knowledge of the actuality with which he is concerned. He is thus in the position of a statesman dealing with public affairs; in writing he acts and in acting he makes choices, large or small, timid or bold, with respect to some conception of the nature of things. And the degree of his influence and immortality will depend upon the length and correctness of his forecast—upon the verdict of history yet to come. His faith is at bottom a conviction that something true can be known about the movement of history and his conviction is a subjective decision, not a purely objective discovery.

But members of the passing generation will ask: Has our work done in the scientific spirit been useless? Must we abandon the scientific method? The answer is an emphatic negative. During the past fifty years historical scholarship, carried on with judicial calm, has brought achievements of value beyond calculation. Particular phases of history once dark and confused have been illuminated by research, authentication, scrutiny, and the ordering of immediate relevancies. Nor is the empirical or scientific method to be abandoned. It is the only method that can be employed in obtaining accurate knowledge of historical facts, personalities, situations, and movements. It alone can disclose conditions that made possible what happened. It has a value in itself—a value high in the hierarchy of values indispensable to the life of a democracy. The inquiring spirit of science, using the scientific method, is the chief safeguard against the tyranny of authority, bureaucracy, and brute power. It can reveal by investigation necessities and possibilities in any social scene and also offerings with respect to desirabilities to be achieved within the limits of the possible.

The scientific method is, therefore, a precious and indispensable instrument of the human mind; without it society would sink down into primitive animism and barbarism. It is when this method, a child of the human brain, is exalted into a master and a tyrant that historical thought must enter a caveat. So the historian is bound by his craft to recognize the nature and limitations of the scientific method and to dispel the illusion that it can produce a science of history embracing the fullness of history, or of any large phase, as past actuality.

This means no abandonment of the tireless inquiry into objective realities, especially economic realities and relations; not enough emphasis has been laid upon the conditioning and determining influences of biological and economic necessities or upon researches designed to disclose them in their deepest and widest ramifications. This means no abandonment of the inquiry into the forms and development of ideas as conditioning and determining influences; not enough emphasis has been laid on this phase of history by American scholars.

But the upshot to which this argument is directed is more fundamental than any aspect of historical method.

It is that any selection and arrangement of facts pertaining to any large area of history, either local or world, race or class, is controlled inexorably by the frame of reference in the mind of the selector and arranger. This frame of reference includes things deemed necessary, things deemed possible, and things deemed desirable. It may be large, informed by deep knowledge, and illuminated by wide experience; or it may be small, uninformed, and unilluminated. It may be a grand conception of history or a mere aggregation of confusions. But it is there in the mind, inexorably. To borrow from Croce, when grand philosophy is ostentatiously put out at the front door of the mind, then narrow, class, provincial, and regional prejudices come in at the back door and dominate, perhaps only half-consciously, the thinking of the historian.

The supreme issue before the historian now is the determination of his attitude to the disclosures of contemporary thought. He may deliberately evade them for reasons pertaining to personal, economic, and intellectual comfort, thus joining the innumerable throng of those who might have been but were not. Or he may proceed to examine his own frame of reference, clarify it, enlarge it by acquiring knowledge of greater areas of thought and events, and give it consistency of structure by a deliberate conjecture respecting the nature or direction of the vast movements of ideas and interests called world history.

This operation will cause discomfort to individual historians but all, according to the vows of their office, are under obligation to perform it, as Henry Adams warned the members of this Association in his letter of 1894. And as Adams then said, it will have to be carried out under the scrutiny of four great tribunals for the suppression of unwelcome knowledge and opinion: the church, the state, property, and labor. Does the world move and, if so, in what direction? If he believes that the world does not move, the historian must offer the pessimism of chaos to the inquiring spirit of mankind. If it does move, does it move backward toward some old arrangement, let us say, of 1928, 1896, 1815, 1789, or 1295? Or does it move forward to some other arrangement which can be only dimly divined—a capitalist dictatorship, a proletarian dictatorship, or a collectivist democracy? The last of these is my own guess, founded on a study of long trends and on a faith in the indomitable spirit of mankind. In any case, if the historian cannot know or explain history as actuality, he helps to make history, petty or grand.

To sum up contemporary thought in historiography, any written history involves the selection of a topic and an arbitrary delimitation of its borders—cutting off connections with the universal. Within the borders arbitrarily established, there is a selection and organization of facts by the processes of thought. This selection and organization—a single act—will be controlled by the historian's frame of reference composed of things deemed necessary and of things deemed desirable. The frame may be a narrow class, sectional, national, or group conception of history, clear and frank or confused and half conscious, or it may be a large, generous conception, clarified by association with the great spirits of all ages. Whatever its nature the frame is inexorably there, in the mind. And in the frame only three broad conceptions of all history as actuality are possible. History is chaos and every attempt to interpret it otherwise is an illusion. History moves around in a kind of cycle. History moves in a line, straight or spiral, and in some direction. The historian may seek to escape these issues by silence or by a confession of avoidance or he may face them boldly, aware of the intellectual and moral perils inherent in any decision—in his act of faith.

Chapter Ten

FUNCTIONALISM
IN ARCHITECTURE

THE AUTOBIOGRAPHY
OF AN IDEA *

By Louis H. Sullivan

Louis H. Sullivan (1856–1924) attributes the arrest of Modernism to the Eclecticism of Daniel Burnham and the Chicago Fair of 1893

The Boston-born son of a prosperous Irish owner of a dancing academy, Louis Sullivan studied architecture briefly at the Massachusetts Institute of Technology and then at the classical Ecole des Beaux Arts in Paris. Influenced by the organic evolutionary theories of Darwin and Spencer, he rejected Classicism for the functional ideas of H. H. Richardson and eventually emerged with the Modernist formula: "Form Follows Function."

He joined the stream of architects who found opportunities for experimentation in the Chicago of the seventies after the Great Fire of 1871. He learned from Major William L. Jenney, who became famous for his all-steel skyscraper, and who led Sullivan to dramatize the skyscraper as "a proud and soaring thing." In 1881, Sullivan began his fruitful partnership with Denkmar Adler and designed the notable auditorium whose acoustics delighted operagoers and whose interior reflected an original version of Romanesque art. In later years came the more functional design of the Transportation Building at the World's Fair of 1893. As the father

* From Louis H. Sullivan, *The Autobiography of an Idea* (1924) 304–25. Reprinted by permission of the American Institute of Architects, Washington, D.C.

of Modernism, Sullivan was associated with a young disciple, Frank Lloyd Wright. Thus the "Chicago School" began its meteoric rise.

The following selection from *The Autobiography of an Idea* (1924) tells of the stimulating Chicago days and the blow struck to Modernism by the commercialism of Daniel Burnham, whose influence at the Fair had a decisive effect upon the vogue of a stale eclecticism.

IN CHICAGO, the progress of the building art from 1880 onward was phenomenal. The earlier days had been given over to four-inch ashlar fronts, cylinder glass, and galvanized iron cornices, with cast iron columns and lintels below; with interior construction of wood joists, posts and girders; continuous and rule-of-thumb foundations of "dimension stone." Plate glass and mirrors came from Belgium and France; rolled iron beams—rare and precious—came from Belgium; Portland cement from England. The only available American cements were "Rosendale," "Louisville" and "Utica"—called natural or hydraulic cements. Brownstone could be had from Connecticut, marble from Vermont, granite from Maine. Interior equipments such as heating, plumbing, drainage, and elevators or lifts, were to a degree, primitive. Of timber and lumber—soft and hard woods—there was an abundance. This general statement applies mainly to the business district, although there were some solid structures to be seen. And it should be noted that before the great fire, a few attempts had been made to build "fireproof" on the assumption that bare iron would resist fire. As to the residential districts, there were increasing indications of pride and display, for rich men were already being thrust up by the mass. The vast acreage and square mileage, however, consisted of frame dwellings; for, as has been said, Chicago was the greatest lumber market "in the world." Beyond these inflammable districts were the prairies and the villages.

The Middle West at that time was dominantly agricultural; wheat, corn, other grains, hogs, while cattle and sheep roamed the unfenced ranges of the Far Western plains. Lumbering was a great industry with its attendant saw mills and planing mills, and there were immense lumber yards along the south branch of the Chicago River, which on occasion made gallant bonfires. And it so happened that, as Louis [Sullivan] heard a banquet orator remark, in the spread eagle fashion of the day, Chicago had become "the center of a vast contiguous territory."

Great grain elevators gave accent to the branches of the river. There was huge slaughter at the Stock Yards, as droves of steers, hogs and sheep moved bellowing, squealing, bleating or silently anxious as they crowded the runways to their reward. The agonized look in the eyes of a steer as his nose was pulled silently down tight to the floor ring, in useless protest, the blow on the crown of the skull; an endless procession of oncoming hogs hanging single file by the heel—a pandemonium of terror—one by one reaching the man in the blood-pit; the knife pushed into a soft throat then down, a crimson gush, a turn in the trolley, an object drops into the scalding trough, thence on its way to the coterie of skilled surgeons, who manipulate with amazing celerity. Then comes the next one and the next one and the next, as they have been coming ever since, and will come. . . .

A gathering of these architects [at Chicago under Daniel Burnham] took place in February, 1891. After an examination of the site [of the World's Fair], which by this time was dreary enough in its state of raw upheaval, the company retired for active conference. John Root was not there. In faith he could not come. He had made his rendezvous the month before. Graceland was now his home. Soon above him would be reared a Celtic cross. Louis missed him sadly. Who now would take up the foils he had dropped on his way, from hands that were once so strong? There was none! The shadow of the white cloud had already fallen.

The meeting came to order. Richard Hunt, acknowledged dean of his profession, in the chair, Louis Sullivan acting as secretary. Burnham arose to make his address of welcome. He was not facile on his feet, but it soon became noticeable that he was progressively and grossly apologizing to the Eastern men for the presence of their benighted brethren of the West.

Dick Hunt interrupted: "Hell, we haven't come out here on a missionary expedition. Let's get to work." Everyone agreed. Burnham came out of his somnambulistic vagary and joined in. He was keen enough to understand that "Uncle Dick" had done him a needed favor. For Burnham learned slowly but surely, within the limits of his understanding.

A layout was submitted to the Board as a basis for discussion. It was rearranged on two axes at right angles. The buildings were disposed accordingly. By an amicable arrangement each architect was given such building as he preferred, after consultation. The meeting then adjourned.

The story of the building of the Fair is foreign to the purpose of this narrative, which is to deal with its more serious aspects, implications and results. Suffice it that Burnham performed in a masterful way, displaying remarkable executive capacity. He became open-minded, just, magnanimous. He did his great share.

The work completed, the gates thrown open 1 May, 1893, the crowds flowed in from every quarter, continued to flow throughout a fair-weather summer and a serenely beautiful October. Then came the end. The gates were closed.

These crowds were astonished. They beheld what was for them an amazing revelation of the architectural art, of which previously they in comparison had known nothing. To them it was a veritable Apocalypse, a message inspired from on high. Upon it their imagination shaped new ideals. They went away, spreading again over the land, returning to their homes, each one of them carrying in the soul the shadow of the white cloud, each of them permeated by the most subtle and slow-acting of poisons; an imperceptible miasm within the white shadow of a higher culture. A vast multitude, exposed, unprepared, they had not had time nor occasion to become immune to forms of sophistication not their own, to a higher and more dexterously insidious plausibility. Thus they departed joyously, carriers of contagion, unaware that what they had beheld and believed to be truth was to prove, in historic fact, an appalling calamity. For what they saw was not at all what they believed they saw, but an imposition of the spurious upon their eyesight, a naked exhibitionism of charlatanry in the higher feudal and domineering culture, conjoined with expert salesmanship of the materials of decay. Adventitiously, to make the stage setting complete, it happened by way of apparent but unreal contrast that the structure representing the United States Government was of an incredible vulgarity, while the building at the peak of the north axis, stationed there as a symbol of "The Great State of Illinois" matched it as a lewd exhibit of drooling imbecility and political debauchery. The distribution at the northern end of the grounds of many state and foreign headquarters relieved the sense of stark immensity. South of them, and placed on the border of a small lake, stood the Palace of the Arts, the most vitriolic of them all—the most impudently thievish. The landscape work, in its genial distribution of lagoons, wooded islands, lawns, shrubbery and plantings, did much to soften an otherwise mechanical display; while far in the southeast corner, floating in a small lagoon or harbor, were replicas of the three caravels of Columbus, and on an adjacent artificial mound a representation of the Convent of La Rabida. Otherwhere there was no evidence of Columbus and his daring deed, his sufferings, and his melancholy end. No keynote, no dramatic setting forth of that deed which, recently, has aroused some discussion as to whether the discovery of America had proven to be a blessing or a curse to the world of mankind.

Following the white cloud, even as a companion in iniquity, came the gray cloud. It overwhelmed the land with a pall of desolation. It dropped its blinding bolt. Its hurricane swept away the pyramided paper structures of speculation. Its downpour washed away fancied gains; its raindrops, loaded with a lethal toxin, fell alike upon the unjust and the just, as in retribution, demanding an atonement in human sacrifice. The thunder ceased to roll, the rain became a mist and cleared, the storm subsided, all was still. Overhead hung the gray cloud of panic from horizon to horizon. Slowly it thinned, in time it became translucent, vanished, revealing the white cloud which, in platoons, unseen, had overrun the blue. Now again shone the sun. "Prosperity" awakened from its torpor, rubbed its eyes and prepared for further follies.

It is said that history repeats itself. This is not so. What is mistaken for repetition is the recurrent feudal rhythm of exaltation and despair. Its progressive wavelike movement in action is implicit in the feudal thought, and inevitable, and so long as the feudal thought holds dominion in the minds of men, just so long and no longer will calamity follow upon the appearance of prosperity. The end is insanity, the crumbling and the passing of the race, for life is ever saying to Man: "If you wish to be destroyed I will destroy you." The white cloud is the feudal idea. The gray cloud, the nemesis contained within that idea. The feudal idea is dual, it holds to the concept of good and evil. The democratic idea is single, integral. It holds to the good alone. Its faith lies in the beneficence of its power, in its direct appeal to life. Its vision reveals an inspiring vista of accomplishment. Its common sense recognizes man as by nature sound to the core, and kindly. It as clearly sees, in the feudal scheme, a continuous warfare—as well in so-called times of peace as in sanguinary battle. It views all this as lunacy, for its own word is kindness. It bases its faith upon the heart in preference to the intellect, though knowing well the power of the latter when controlled. It knows that the intellect, alone, runs amuck, and performs unspeakable cruelties; that the heart alone is divine. For it is the heart that welcomes Life and would cherish it, would shield it against the cannibalism of the intellect.

From the height of its Columbian Ecstasy, Chicago drooped and subsided with the rest, in a common sickness, the nausea of overstimulation. This in turn passed, toward the end of the decade, and the old game began again with intensified fury, to come to a sudden halt in 1907. There are those who say this panic was artificial and deliberate, that the battle of the saber-toothed tigers and the mastodons was on.

Meanwhile the virus of the World's Fair, after a period of incubation in the architectural profession and in the population at large, especially the influential, began to show unmistakable signs of the nature of the contagion. There came a violent outbreak of the Classic and the Renaissance in the East, which slowly spread westward, contaminating all that it touched, both at its source and outward. The selling campaign of the bogus antique was remarkably well managed through skillful publicity and propaganda, by those who were first to see its commercial possibilities. The market was ripe, made so through the hebetude of the populace, big business men, and eminent educators alike. By the time the market had been saturated, all sense of reality was gone. In its place had come deep-seated illusions, hallucinations, absence of pupillary reaction to light, absence of knee-reaction—symptoms all of progressive cerebral meningitis: The blanketing of the brain. Thus Architecture died in the land of the free and the home of the brave,—in a land declaring its fervid democracy, its inventiveness, its resourcefulness, its unique daring, enterprise and progress. Thus did the virus of a culture, snobbish and alien to the land, perform its work of disintegration; and thus ever works the pallid academic mind, denying the real, exalting the fictitious and the false, incapable of adjusting itself to the flow of living things, to the reality and the pathos of man's follies, to the valiant hope that ever causes him to aspire, and again to aspire; that never lifts a hand in aid because it cannot; that turns its back upon man because that is its tradition; a culture lost in ghostly *mésalliance* with abstractions, when what the world needs is courage, common sense and human sympathy, and a moral standard that is plain, valid and livable.

The damage wrought by the World's Fair will last for half a century from its date, if not longer. It has penetrated deep into the constitution of the American mind, effecting there lesions significant of dementia.

Meanwhile the architectural generation immediately succeeding the Classic and Renaissance merchants, are seeking to secure a special immunity from the inroads of common sense, through a process of vaccination with the lymph of every known European style, period and accident, and to this all-around process, when it breaks out, is to be added the benediction of good taste. Thus we have now the abounding freedom of Eclecticism, the winning smile of taste, but no architecture. For Architecture, be it known, is dead.

"WHY THE GREAT EARTHQUAKE DID NOT DESTROY THE IMPERIAL HOTEL" *

By Frank Lloyd Wright

Frank Lloyd Wright (1869–1959) tells why the functionalist Imperial Hotel of Tokyo withstood the Great Earthquake

Frank Lloyd Wright was born in Richland Center, Wisconsin, the son of a New England preacher and musician, and began his architectural education in the Civil Engineering program of the University of Wisconsin. He became one of the famous Chicago

* "Why the Great Earthquake Did Not Destroy the Imperial Hotel," From *An Autobiography*. Copyright © 1943 by Frank Lloyd Wright. By permission of Duell, Sloan & Pearce, Inc., 212–23.

emphasis of Darwin on architecture

School as an associate of Louis Sullivan, who concentrated upon commercial buildings while Wright dealt with residences. Thus began his famous Prairie Houses, displaying the essence of functionalism in their emphasis on the organic ideal of Darwin in adapting to a physical and human environment; this meant horizontal lines, plasticity of design, and long rows of windows, Soon Wright was to discover novel uses of a humble material like concrete and fresh uses of new local materials.

Berlin was first to discover the genius of Wright and hastened to publish his designs. Tokyo, as the selection below illustrates, chose him to create the unique Imperial Hotel, which blended functionalism with Japanese traditions and craftsmanship. He tells the exciting story here of how he planned to circumvent the dread energies of chronic Japanese earthquakes. By the 1930's, Wright was proudly contrasting his "organic architecture" with the allegedly mechanistic and antidemocratic architecture of Europe. Soon he became absorbed by the problems of urbanization and proposed to eliminate the sharp line between town and country. While Bauhaus leaders criticized his romanticism and indifference to mass housing, Wright continued to rank in the vanguard of Modernist architecture.

THE "FOREIGNER" with the advent of Commodore Perry came to share Japanese joys and sorrows and soon a building was needed to shelter the "foreign" element in Tokio, the capital of Japan.

A social clearing house became necessary to official Japan, as a consequence of the new foreign interest in them, because, for one reason, no foreigner could live on the floor. The need steadily increased. At that time the Mikado took it upon himself to meet the need, and asked the Germans to build one of their characteristic national wood and plaster extravaganzas for the purpose.

That wretched marvel grew obsolete and the need of another, a great one, imperative. The Imperial household, this time, proposed to share the task of providing the new accommodation with the capitalists of the Empire, ship owners, cement manufacturers, bankers, tobacco interests, etc., and I, an "American," was chosen to do the work.

No "foreigner" yet invited to Japan had taken off his hat to Japanese traditions. When foreigners came, what they had back home came too, suitable or not. And the politely humble Japanese, duly impressed, took the offering and marveled. They tried to do likewise in their turn.

And yet, Japanese fine-art traditions are among the noblest and purest in this world, giving Chinese origins due credit.

It was my instinct not to insult them. The West has much to learn from the East—and Japan was the gateway to that great East of which I had been dreaming since I had seen my first Japanese prints—and read my first "Laotze."

But this terrible natural enemy to all building whatsoever—the temblor!

The terror of the temblor never left me while I planned the building nor while, for more than four years, I worked upon it. Nor is any one allowed to forget it—sometimes awakened at night by strange sensations as at sea, strange unearthly and yet rumbling earth-noises. Sudden shocks, subsidence—and swinging. Again shock after shock and upheaval, jolting back, and swinging. A sense of the bottom falling from beneath the building, terror of the coming moments as cracking plaster and groaning timbers indicate the whole structure may come crashing and tumbling down. There may be [a] more awful threat to human happiness than [an] earthquake—I do not know what it can be.

The Japanese turn livid, perspiration starts on them, but no other sign unless the violence becomes extreme, then—panic. I studied the temblor. Found it a wave-movement, not of sea but of earth—accompanied by terrific shocks no rigidity could withstand.

Because of the wave movements, deep foundations like long piles would oscillate and rock the structure. Therefore the foundation should be short or shallow.

foundation should be shallow

There was sixty to seventy feet of soft mud below the upper depth of eight feet of surface soil on the site. That mud seemed a merciful provision—a good cushion to relieve the terrible shocks.

Why not float the building upon it? A battle ship floats on salt water.

And why not extreme lightness combined with tenuity and flexibility instead of the great weight necessary to the greatest possible rigidity?

Why not, then, a building made as the two hands thrust together palms inward, fingers interlocking and yielding to movement—but resilient to return to original position when distortion ceased? A flexure—flexing and reflexing in any direction.

Why fight the quake?

Why not sympathize with it and out-wit it?

That was how the building began to be planned.

The most serious problem was how to get the most carrying power out of that eight feet of cheese-like soil that overlay the liquid mud. During the first year of plan making, I made borings nine inches in diameter eight feet deep and filled them with concrete. Arranged to test the concrete pins thus made. Got carloads of pig iron and loaded the pins until they would drive into the ground. Kept the test figures of loads and reactions. Took borings all over the site to find soft pockets. Water stood in the holes two feet below the surface, so the concrete had to go in quickly as the borings were completed. Later, tapered piles were driven in to *punch* the holes and pulled out—the concrete thrown directly in as soon as the pile was out of the way.

These data in hand—the foundation plan was made to push these concrete pins in, two feet on centers each way over the entire areas on which the wall footings were to spread. The strength of the whole depth of eight feet of top soil was thus brought to bear at the surface. That was simple.

But here was a compressible soil that might take a squeeze under the broad footings to add to the friction of the pins. Experiments showed the squeeze could safely be added to the friction.

This meant a settlement of the building of five inches the building itself driving the piles that much deeper. This was economy but dangerous and more complicated.

But finally the building was computed pound by pound and distributed according to "test data" to "float" below the grade of the ground surface—and it did. With some few slight variations it stayed level there.

This foundation saved hundreds of thousands of dollars over the foundations then in use in Tokio. But had the owners of the Imperial superficially known what was contemplated something might have happened to prevent it. "Rumor" nearly did prevent it. Here, however, was the desired shock-absorber, a cushion, pins and all to be uniformly loaded and put to work against the day of reckoning.

Now how to make the flexible structure instead of the foolish rigid one? Divide the building into parts.

Where the parts were necessarily more than sixty feet long,

joint these parts clear through floors, walls, footings and all, and manage the joints in the design. Wherever part met part, through joints also.

So far, good sense, and careful calculation.

But a construction was needed where floors would not be carried between walls because subterranean disturbances might move the walls and drop the floors.

Why not then carry the floors as a waiter carries his tray on upraised arm and fingers at the center—*balancing* the load. All supports centered under the floor slabs like that instead of resting the slabs on the walls at their edges as is usually the case?

This meant the cantilever, as I had found by now. The cantilever is most romantic—most free—of all principles of construction and in this case it seemed the most sensible. The waiter's tray supported by his hand at the center is a cantilever slab in principle. And so concrete cantilever slabs continuous across the building from side to side, supported in that way, became the structure of the Imperial Hotel at Tokio.

Roof tiles of Japanese buildings in upheavals have murdered countless thousands of Japanese, so a light hand-worked green copper roof was planned. Why kill any more?

The outer walls were spread wide, thick and heavy at the base, growing thinner and lighter toward the top. Whereas Tokio buildings were all top heavy. The center of gravity was kept low against the swinging movements and the slopes were made an aesthetic feature of the design. The outside cover-hangs of the cantilever slabs where they came through the walls were all lightened by ornamental perforations enriching the light and shade of the structure. The stone everywhere under foot in Tokio was a workable light lava weighing as much as green oak. It was "sacrilege" to use this common material for the aristocratic edifice. But finally it was used for the feature material and readily yielded to any sense of form the architect might choose to indicate. And the whole structure was to be set up as a double shell, two shells an exterior of slim cunning bricks, and an interior one of fluted hollow bricks raised together to a convenient height of four feet or more. These shells were to be poured solid with concrete to bind them together.

The great building thus became a jointed monolith with a mosaic surface of lava and brick. Earthquakes had always torn piping and wiring apart where laid in the structure and had flooded or charged the building. So all piping and wiring was to be laid free of construction in covered concrete trenches in the ground of the basements independent even of foundations. Mains and all pipes were of lead with wiped joints the lead bends sweeping from the trenches to be hung free in vertical pipe shafts, from which the curved lead branches were again taken off, curved, to the stacks of bath-rooms. Thus any disturbance might flex and rattle but could not break the pipes or wiring.

Last but not least there was to be an immense reservoir or pool as an architectural feature of the entrance court—connected to the water system of the hotel and conserving the roof water.

Thus the plans were made so that all architectural features were practical necessities, and, the straight line and flat plane were respectfully modified in point of style, to a building respectful to the traditions of the people to whom the building would belong. The *nature* of the design too, I wanted to make something their intensive hand methods could do well because we didn't know what machinery could be used. It was impossible to say how far we could go with that. Probably not very far.

Finally the plans were ready.

No estimates could be had.

It was all so unfamiliar, no commercial concern would touch it. Nothing left but to abandon the whole or organize to build it ourselves. The Imperial Hotel and its architect and builder.

The language was a barrier. The men and methods strange.

But the "foreign" architect with eighteen or twenty architectural students from the Japanese universities, several of whom were taken to Wisconsin during the plan-making period, and one expert "foreign" builder, Paul Mueller of Chicago, two "foreigners," all else *native,* we organized with the hotel manager, Hayashi-san, as general manager. We had already bought pottery kilns in Shizuoka and made the long slim cunning bricks of a style and size, never made before, for the outside shell. They were now ready to use.

We had also made the fluted hollow-bricks for the inside shell, the first in the Empire. We bought fine lava-quarry at Oya near Nikko for the feature-material and started a flood of dimension stone moving down to the site in Tokio—a stream that kept piling into the building for four years. The size of the hole left in the ground at Oya was about like the excavations for the Grand Central Terminal.

We had a hundred or more clever stone "choppers" beating out patterns of the building on the greenish, leopard-spotted lava, for that period.

On an average we employed about 600 men continually for four years. As a large proportion of them came from the surrounding country they lived round about in the building as we built it. With their numerous families there they were—cooking, washing, sleeping.

And we tried faithfully—sometimes frantically and often profanely—to teach them how to build it, half-way between our way and their way.

We tried the stone-planer with the stone cutters. It was soon buried beneath the chips that flew from their busy stone-axes. Tried derricks and gin-poles and hoists. They preferred to carry heavy loads and enormous stones up inclined planes on their shoulders. We tried to abolish scaffolding and teach them to lay brick from the inside. Not to be done. They lashed tapering poles together in cunning ways as for centuries and clung with prehensile toes to the framework.

How skillful they were! What craftsmen! How patient and clever. So instead of wasting them by vainly trying to make them come our way—we went with them their way. I modified many original intentions to make the most of what, I now saw was naturally theirs. The language grew less an obstruction. But curious mistakes were perpetual. It is true that the Japanese approach to any matter is a spiral. Their instinct for attack in any direction is oblique and volute. But they made up for it in gentleness and cleverness and loyalty. Yes the loyalty of the retainer to his Samurai. They soon educated us and all went pretty well.

The countenance of the building began to emerge from the seemingly hopeless confusion of the enormous area now covered by the building materials of its terraces and courts and hundreds of families. And the workmen grew more and more interested in it. It was no uncommon thing to see groups of them admiring and criticizing too as some finished portion would emerge—criticizing intelligently.

There was a warmth of appreciation and loyalty unknown in the building circles of our country. A fine thing to have experienced.

The curse of the work was the holiday. There were no Sundays but a couple of holidays every fortnight instead, and it took a day or two to recover from most of them. So the work dragged.

And the rainy season! The Japanese say it rains up from the ground as well as down from the sky—in Tokio.

We did succeed in abolishing the expensive cover-shed of tight roof and hanging mattingsides under which most buildings are built in Japan. We congratulated ourselves until we found they knew their climate better than we did. Had we protected them from the rain and burning sun the buildings would have been finished about seven months sooner—besides making all more comfortable and so more efficient.

A few more such "successes" would have been enough.

The "directors" met regularly for a couple of years and began to complain.

Rumors reached them from the English (the English love the Americans in Tokio) and "Americans" (why are "Americans" invariably so unpleasant to one another abroad) to the effect that the architect of their building was mad. In any earthquake the whole thing would tumble apart—and the whole building would sink out of sight in the mud beneath. There was room enough for it in that cushion of mud.

Where all had been pleasant enthusiasm things began to drag. The loyalty of my own office force never for a moment wavered, but manager Hayashi was daily hectored and censured.

At this crucial time it became apparent that three and a half million yen more, would be necessary to complete and furnish the work. Things looked dark.

By now a small army was working away in the lower stories of the building as it was completed. As soon as one portion was built it became a hive of frantic industry. The copper features and fixtures and roof tiles were all made there; the interior wood work and furniture—the upholstery and many other things went on in the vast interior spaces as soon as the floor slabs covered them over.

I had brought examples of good furniture from home and took them apart to teach the Japanese workmen how to make them according to the new designs which made them all part of the structure. They were fine craftsmen at this. Rug designs had gone to Pekin. The rugs were being woven there to harmonize with the interior features of the great rooms and the guest rooms.

We were about two-thirds of the way over with the building itself. The foreigners had no way of keeping track of costs or finding out much about them in detail. So things had gone on for several years.

The crash came.

The directors were called together.

Baron Okura was chairman of the board—representing, besides his own interests, the interest of the Imperial Royal Household, sixty per cent, besides ownership of the ground. There was also, Asano-san—a white-haired Samson of the shipping interests, a powerful man with shaggy white brows and piercing eyes. Murai of the tobacco interests—a peacemaker and with pleasant ways, always. Wakai, the banker, as broad as he was long with a beard that reached below the table when he stood up. Kanaka and half a dozen others.

Baron Okura had rather sponsored me from the beginning. He was in trouble now.

The meetings had been held in the old hotel building and were pleasant social affairs with refreshments.

This one was not. It was black. A long time, it had been threatening. The Baron, a black-haired youth of eighty—a remarkable man regarded as one of the astute financial powers of the Empire, sat at the head of the table. I sat on his left. On his right sat his cultivated secretary, a Harvard graduate who was interpreter. It doesn't matter where the others were. They were there and all talking at once. I answered leading questions without end. The foundations. Always the foundations—and the money. The money!

The Baron was patient and polite—for some time. His lower lip had a trick of sticking out and quivering when he became intense. This personal idiosyncrasy of his was evident now.

Suddenly he rose—leaned forward, head thrust forward, angry, hissing, pounding the table with both fists—extraordinary conduct for him.

The crowd went back and down as though blown down by the wind.

There was silence—the Baron still standing looking over toward me. Not knowing what it was all about I instinctively rose. The interpreter rose, too, and said, "The Baron says that if the 'young man' (all things are relative) will himself remain in Japan until the building is finished, the Baron will himself find the necessary money and they could all go to"—whatever the Japanese word is for the place they could go to.

Although homesick by now and sick besides I reached out my hand to the Baron. The compact was made. The meeting was over. The directors filed out red and angry to a man, instead of happy to have the responsibility lifted from them.

Was it Pericles who enacted some such role as the Baron's when the Parthenon was building?

And the building of the new Imperial went on.

But now every director became a spy. The walls had ears. Propaganda increased. My freedom was gone. I worked under greater difficulties than ever. But my little band of Japanese apprentices was loyal and we got ahead until another storm broke.

"Why not," said the directors to the Baron, "eliminate the pool and save 40,000 yen." The Baron saw sense in this and sent for me. His mind was made up. No arguments took effect. I told him via interpreters that it was the last resource against the quake. In disaster, the city water would be cut off, and the window frames being wood in the 500 foot building front along the side street where wooden buildings stood, fire could gut the structure even though it withstood the quake. I had witnessed five terrible fires in Tokio already—walls of flame nothing in any degree inflammable could withstand.

No matter. The pool must come out. No, I said, it is wrong to take it out and by such interference he would release me from my agreement and I could and would go home, with no further delay. And I left his office. But I did not leave Tokio and the pool went in to play its final part in the great drama of destruction that followed two years later.

Another year and I could go home. The Tokio climate, so moist and humid summer and winter, depressing except in fall and early spring, together with the work and anxiety were wearing me down.

But now came a terrible test that calmed troublesome fears and made the architect's position easier.

The building construction was about finished. The architect's work-room had been moved to the top of the left wing above the promenade entrance. It was nearly noon. The boys in the office, reduced to ten, were there, and workmen were about. Suddenly with no warning a gigantic jolt lifted the whole building, threw the boys down sprawling with their drawing boards. A moment's panic and hell broke loose as the wave motion began. The structure was literally in convulsions. I was knocked down by the rush of workmen and my own boys to save their own lives. It is a mercy there were not more workmen in the roof space beyond or I should have been trampled out. As I lay there I could clearly see the "ground swell" pass through the construction above as it heaved and groaned to hideous crushing and grinding noises. Several thunderous crashes sickened me but later these proved to be the falling of five tall chimneys of the old Imperial left standing alone by the recent burning of that building.

At the time it seemed as though the banquet hall section, invisible just behind the work-room, had crashed down.

Only one faithful assistant stayed through this terrible ordeal. Endo-san, loyal rightbower—white to the teeth—, perspiring. Otherwise the building was utterly deserted. We got up shaking to the knees and went together out onto the roofs. There across the street were crowds of frightened work-men. They had thrown down their tools and run for their lives, even those working in the courts. There they all stood strangely silent, pasty-faced, shaking. A strange silence too was everywhere over the city. Soon fires broke out in a dozen places—bells rang and pandemonium broke —women dragging frightened children, ran weeping and wailing along the streets below.

We had just passed through the worst quake in fifty-two years. The building was undamaged. A transit put on the foundation levels showed no deviation whatever.

The work had been proved.

Hayashi-san, when reports of the damage to the city and none to the building came in, burst into tears of gratitude. His life had barely been worth living for more than a year, so cruel were the suspicions and harassing the doubts.

The year passed. The building was now so nearly complete there was no longer pressing need for the presence of the architect.

Another wing remained to be finished but it was a duplication of the one already done and furnished. So I could go home with a good conscience. My clients, headed by the Baron, were generous, added substantial proof of appreciation to my fee, and I was "farewelled" at a champagne luncheon by the Baron and his directors; at a tea house entertainment by the building organization itself, all with unique expressions of esteem; by the workmen at another characteristic entertainment—all as usual in such matters.

The day of sailing came. To get to my car I had to pass from the rear through the new building to the front. All was deserted and I wondered. Arrived at the entrance courts, there all the workmen were, crowding the spaces, watching and waiting. Already there had been gratifying evidence of appreciation—I thought, but here was the real thing. This could have happened nowhere but in Japan. Here was the spirit of the old Japan I had tried to compliment and respect in my work.

As their architect came out they crowded round, workmen of every rank from sweepers to foremen of "the trades," laughing, weeping, wanting awkwardly to shake hands—foreign fashion. They had learned "aw-right," and mingled it now with "arigato" and "sayonara Wrieto-san."

Too much, and "Wrieto-san" broke. They followed the car down along Hibiya way to the station, running, shouting "Banzai, Wrieto-san, banzai!"

The dock at Yokohama, eighteen miles away, was reached by train, to find that sixty of the foremen had paid their own way down from Tokio to shout again and wave good-bye, while they faded from sight as the ship went down the bay. Such people! Where else in all the world would such touching warmth of kindness in faithfulness be probable or possible?

Two years later—1923—in Los Angeles. News shouted in the streets of terrible disaster. Tokio and Yokohama wiped out! The most terrible temblor of all history!

Appalling details came day after day. Nothing human it seemed could have withstood the cataclysm.

Too anxious to get any sleep, I tried to get news of the fate of the New Imperial, Shugio, Endo, Hyashi, the Baron, and the hosts of friends I had left over there. Finally, the third night, about two in the morning, the telephone bell rang. The "Examiner" wished to inform me that the Imperial Hotel was completely destroyed. My heart sank, but I laughed, "how do you know?" They read the despatch, a list of Imperial University, Imperial Theatre, Imperial Hospital, Imperial this and Imperial that. "You see," I said, "how easy it is to get the Imperial Hotel mixed with other Imperials? I am sure if anything is above ground in Tokio it is that building. If you print its destruction as 'news' you will have to retract."

Their turn to laugh and hang up the receiver.

Ten days of uncertainty and conflicting reports, for during most of that time direct communication was cut off.

Then a cablegram . . .

FRANK LLOYD WRIGHT

OLIVE HILL STUDIO RESIDENCE B 1645 VERMONT AVE

HOLLYWOOD CALIF

FOLLOWING WIRELESS RECEIVED FROM TOKIO TODAY HOTEL STANDS UNDAMAGED AS MONUMENT OF YOUR GENIUS HUNDREDS OF HOMELESS PROVIDED BY PERFECTLY MAINTAINED SERVICE CONGRATULATIONS SIGNED OKURA IMPEHO

For once good news was news, and the Baron's cablegram flashed around the world to herald the triumph of good sense.

Both the great Tokio homes of the Baron were gone. The splendid museum he gave to Tokio and all its contents destroyed. The building by the American architect, whose hand he took and whose cause he sponsored, was all he had left in Tokio—nor could love nor money now buy it or buy a share of stock in it.

When the letters began to come and nearly all the friends were found to be safe, the news most gratifying to the architect was the fact that after the first great quake was over, the dead rotting in unburied heaps, the Japanese in subsequent shocks had come in droves, dragging their children into the courts and onto the terraces of the building, praying for protection by the God that had protected that building as the wall of fire driving a great wail of human misery before it, came sweeping across the city toward the long front of the building: the hotel boys formed a bucket line to the big pool, water there the only water available anywhere, and kept the window sashes and frames on that side wet to meet the flames that came leaping across the narrow street.

The last thought for the safety of the New Imperial had taken effect.

Chapter Eleven

THE SUPREME COURT
AND CIVIL LIBERTY

DISSENT IN THE ABRAMS CASE *

By Oliver Wendell Holmes

Justice Oliver Wendell Holmes (1841–1935) in the Abrams Case defends free speech short of "a clear and imminent danger"

Dr. Oliver Wendell Holmes, Sr., the noted Boston physician and poet, was proud of his son and namesake in 1864 when he was mustered out of Civil War service a captain and a hero who had been wounded three times. Young Holmes had attended Harvard before the war and now entered its law school, practicing briefly thereafter and then turning in 1870 to a lectureship in constitutional law and the editorship of the *American Law Journal*. His most scholarly achievement was *The Common Law* (1880), which dwelt on the idea that the life of the law has not been logic but experience. The book earned him a professorship in the Harvard Law School, which he resigned after a semester to accept a justiceship (like his maternal grandfather) in the Supreme Judicial Court of Massachusetts (1882–1902).

In 1902 President Roosevelt was looking for a liberal justice whom he needed to check four conservative Supreme Court members and to uphold his antitrust policies. He chose Holmes but was taken aback somewhat by the latter's unexpected dissent in the *Northern Securities Case* in which the majority dissolved a holding company. However, the new justice came much closer to expectations in his other famous opinions, urging "judicial restraint," which meant in effect that judges must not seek to legis-

* O. W. Holmes' Dissent in *Abrams* v. *U.S.* (given completely), 250 U.S., 624.

late, and applying pragmatism to his doctrine of free speech permitting "free trade in ideas."

In his famous dissent in *Lochner* v. *New York* (1905), Holmes sharply disagreed with the majority that had nullified a ten-hour-day law for bakers as an infringement of "freedom of contract." He pointed out that this principle did not prevent school laws, Sunday laws, postal laws, and usury laws, and he attacked the extreme individualistic bias of his colleagues in the words, "The Fourteenth Amendment does not enact Mr. Herbert Spencer's Social Statics."

In the famous 1919 cases of *Schenck* v. *U.S.* and *Abrams* v. *U.S.*, Holmes developed his lasting doctrine of free speech. As the Abrams case below indicates—and the Schenck case opinion follows the same reasoning—Holmes argued as a pragmatist (although he disliked this word) that truth is a product of "free trade in ideas" and is limited only by "a clear and imminent danger." Furthermore, he returned to the theme of Lincoln's Gettysburg Address that the United States had been founded as an experiment in the equality of man, and he argued that Congress could not interfere with this test by passing any law restricting free speech. He did not think that Abrams' "silly" pamphlet presented a clear and imminent danger to the country.

With the advent in 1916 to the Supreme Court of Louis Brandeis, a man more experienced in economics and social realities, Holmes became greatly stimulated along practical lines, and the two became the great dissenters for social democracy as well as free speech during the conservative 1920's. Holmes retired in 1932 and died three years later, nearing the age of ninety-four.

᙮

THIS INDICTMENT is founded wholly upon the publication of two leaflets which I shall describe in a moment. The first count charges a conspiracy pending the war with Germany to publish abusive language about the form of government of the United States, laying the preparation and publishing of the first leaflet as overt acts. The second count charges a conspiracy pending the war to publish language intended to bring the form of government into contempt, laying the preparation and publishing of the two leaflets as overt acts. The third count alleges a conspiracy to encourage resistance to the United States in the same war and to attempt to effectuate the purpose by publishing the same leaflets. The fourth count lays a conspiracy to incite curtailment of production of things necessary to the prosecution of the war and to attempt to accomplish it by publishing the second leaflet to which I have referred.

The first of these leaflets says that the President's cowardly silence about the intervention in Russia reveals the hypocrisy of the plutocratic gang in Washington. It intimates that "German militarism combined with allied capitalism to crush the Russian revolution"—goes on that the tyrants of the world fight each other until they see a common enemy—working class enlightenment, when they combine to crush it; and that now militarism and capitalism combined, though not openly, to crush the Russian revolution. It says that there is only one enemy of the workers of the world and that is capitalism; that it is a crime for workers of America, &c., to fight the workers' republic of Russia, and ends "Awake! Awake, you Workers of the World! Revolutionists." A note adds "It is absurd to call us pro-German. We hate and despise German militarism more than do you hypocritical tyrants. We have more reasons for denouncing German militarism than has the coward of the White House."

The other leaflet, headed "Workers—Wake Up," with abusive language says that America together with the Allies will march for Russia to help the Czecho-Slovaks in their struggle against the Bolsheviki, and that this time the hypocrites shall not fool the Russian emigrants and friends of Russia in America. It tells the Russian emigrants that they now must spit in the face of the false military propaganda by which their sympathy and help to the prosecution of the war have been called forth and says that with the money they have lent or are going to lend "they will make bullets not only for the Germans but also for the Workers Soviets of Russia," and further, "Workers in the ammunition factories, you are producing bullets, bayonets, cannon, to murder not only the Germans, but also your dearest, best, who are in Russia and are fighting for freedom." It then appeals to the same Russian emigrants at some length not to consent to the "inquisitionary expedition to Russia," and says that the destruction of the Russian revolution is "the politics of the march to Russia." The leaflet winds up by saying "Workers, our reply to this barbaric intervention has to be a general strike!," and after a few words on the spirit of revolution, exhortations not to be afraid, and some usual tall talk ends "Woe unto those who will be in the way of progress. Let solidarity live! The Rebels."

No argument seems to me necessary to show that these pronunciamentos in no way attack the form of government of the United States, or that they do not support either of the first two counts. What little I have to say about the third count may be postponed until I have considered the fourth. With regard to that it seems too plain to be denied that the suggestion to workers in the ammunition factories that they are producing bullets to murder their dearest, and the further advocacy of a general strike, both in the second leaflet, do urge curtailment of production of things necessary to the prosecution of the war within the meaning of the Act of May 16, 1918, c. 75, 40 Stat. 553, amending § 3 of the earlier Act of 1917. But to make the conduct criminal that statute requires that it should be "with intent by such curtailment to cripple or hinder the United States in the prosecution of the war." It seems to me that no such intent is proved.

I am aware of course that the word intent as vaguely used in ordinary legal discussion means no more than knowledge at the time of the act that the consequences said to be intended will ensue. Even less than that will satisfy the general principle of civil and criminal liability. A man may have to pay damages, may be sent to prison, at common law might be hanged, if at the time of his act he knew facts from which common experience showed that the consequences would follow, whether he individually could foresee them or not. But, when words are used exactly, a deed is not done with intent to produce a consequence unless that consequence is the aim of the deed. It may be obvious, and obvious to the actor, that the consequence will follow, and he may be liable for it even if he regrets it, but he does not do the act with intent to produce it unless the aim to produce it is the proximate motive of the specific act, although there may be some deeper motive behind.

It seems to me that this statute must be taken to use its words in a strict and accurate sense. They would be absurd in any other. A patriot might think that we were wasting money on aeroplanes, or making more cannon of a certain kind than we needed, and might advocate curtailment with success, yet even if it turned out that the curtailment hindered and was thought by other minds to have been obviously likely to hinder the United States in the prosecution of the war, no one would hold such conduct a crime. I admit that my illustration does not answer all that might be said but it is enough to show what I think and to let me pass to a more important aspect of the case. I refer to the First Amendment to the Constitution that Congress shall make no law abridging the freedom of speech.

I never have seen any reason to doubt that the questions of law that alone were before this Court in the cases of *Schenck*, *Frohwerk* and *Debs*, 249 U. S. 47, 204, 211, were rightly decided. I do not doubt for a moment that by the same reasoning that would justify punishing persuasion to murder, the United States constitutionally may punish speech that produces or is intended to produce a clear and imminent danger that it will bring about forthwith certain substantive evils that the United States constitutionally may seek to prevent. The power undoubtedly is greater in time of war than in time of peace because war opens dangers that do not exist at other times.

But as against dangers peculiar to war, as against others, the principle of the right to free speech is always the same. It is only the present danger of immediate evil or an intent to bring it about that warrants Congress in setting a limit to the expression of opinion where private rights are not concerned. Congress certainly cannot forbid all effort to change the mind of the country. Now nobody can suppose that the surreptitious publishing of a silly leaflet by an unknown man, without more, would present any immediate danger that its opinions would hinder the success of the government arms or have any appreciable tendency to do so. Publishing those opinions for the very purpose of obstructing however, might indicate a greater danger and at any rate would have the quality of an attempt. So I assume that the second leaflet if published for the purposes alleged in the fourth count might be punishable. But it seems pretty clear to me that nothing less than that would bring these papers within the scope of this law. An actual intent in the sense that I have explained is necessary to constitute an attempt, where a further act of the same individual is required to complete the substantive crime, for reasons given in *Swift & Co.* v. *United States*, 196 U. S. 375, 396. It is necessary where the success of the attempt depends upon others because if that intent is not present the actor's aim may be accomplished without bringing about the evils sought to be checked. An intent to prevent interference with the revolution in Russia might have been satisfied without any hindrance to carrying on the war in which we were engaged.

I do not see how anyone can find the intent required by the statute in any of the defendants' words. The second leaflet is the only one that affords even a foundation for the charge, and there, without invoking the hatred of German militarism expressed in the former one, it is evident from the beginning to the end that the only object of the paper is to help Russia and stop American intervention there against the popular government—not to impede the United States in the war that it was carrying on. To say that two phrases taken literally might import a suggestion of conduct that would have interference with the war as an indirect and probably undesired effect seems to me by no means enough to show an attempt to produce that effect.

I return for a moment to the third count. That charges an intent to provoke resistance to the United States in its war with Germany. Taking the clause in the statute that deals with that in connection with the other elaborate provisions of the act, I think that resistance to the United States means some forcible act of opposition to some proceeding of the United States in pursuance of the war. I think the intent must be the specific intent that I have described and for the reasons that I have given I think that no such intent was proved or existed in fact. I also think that there is no hint at resistance to the United States as I construe the phrase.

In this case sentences of twenty years imprisonment have been imposed for the publishing of two leaflets that I believe the defendants had as much right to publish as the Government has to publish the Constitution of the United States now vainly invoked by them. Even if I am technically wrong and enough can be squeezed from these poor and puny anonymities to turn the color of legal litmus paper; I will add, even if what I think the necessary intent were shown; the most nominal punishment seems to me all that possibly could be inflicted, unless the defendants are to be made to suffer not for what the indictment alleges but for the creed that they avow—a creed that I believe to be the creed of ignorance and immaturity when honestly held, as I see no reason to doubt that it was held here, but which, although made the subject of examination at the trial, no one has a right even to consider in dealing with the charges before the Court.

Persecution for the expression of opinions seems to me perfectly logical. If you have no doubt of your premises or your power and want a certain result with all your heart you naturally express your wishes in law and sweep away all opposition. To allow opposition by speech seems to indicate that you think the speech impotent, as when a man says that he has squared the circle, or that you do not care whole-heartedly for the result, or that you doubt either your power or your premises. But when men have realized that time has upset many fighting faiths, they may come to believe even more than they believe the very foundations of their own conduct that the ultimate good desired is better reached by free trade in ideas—that the best test of truth is the power of the thought to get itself accepted in the competition of the market, and that truth is the only ground upon which their wishes safely can be carried out. That at any rate is the theory of our Constitution. It is an experiment, as all life is an experiment. Every year if not every day we have to wager our salvation upon some prophecy based upon imperfect knowledge. While that experiment is part of our system I think that we should be eternally vigilant against attempts to check the expression of opinions that we loathe and believe to be fraught with death, unless they so imminently threaten immediate interference with the lawful and pressing purposes of the law that an immediate check is required to save the country. I wholly disagree with the argument of the Government that the First Amendment left the common law as to seditious libel in force. History seems to me against the notion. I had conceived that the United States through many years had shown its repentance for the Sedition Act of 1798, by repaying fines that it imposed. Only the emergency that makes it immediately dangerous to leave the correction of evil counsels to time warrants making any exception to the sweeping command, "Congress shall make no law . . . abridging the freedom of speech." Of course I am speaking only of expressions of opinion and exhortations, which were all that were uttered here, but I regret that I cannot put into more impressive words my belief that in their conviction upon this indictment the defendants were deprived of their rights under the Constitution of the United States.

MR. JUSTICE BRANDEIS concurs with the foregoing opinion.

DISSENT IN THE DENNIS V. UNITED STATES CASE*

By William O. Douglas

Justice William O. Douglas (1898–   ), like O. W. Holmes, sees no imminent danger in American communist propaganda

Among the advanced Supreme Court liberals of the Holmes and Brandeis type is William O. Douglas, the son of a Presbyterian missionary of rural Minnesota, and a young man who worked his way through high school, Whitman College, and the Columbia Law School. He began with a law lectureship at Columbia and Yale and published studies in his specialty, bankruptcy law. President Roosevelt chose him as a member of the Securities and Exchange Commission in 1934, and he became the chairman of this key New Deal agency in 1937. Two years later, he was appointed Supreme Court justice, winning a reputation for his consistent New Deal philosophy and his brilliant opinions in civil liberties cases such as the famous case of *Dennis v. United States,* given below. The argument is similar to that given in the famous Holmes dissent in the Abrams case, and, as the long quotation included indicates, suggests the philosophy of Louis Brandeis.

I F THIS were a case where those who claimed protection under the First Amendment were teaching the techniques of sabotage, the assassination of the President, the filching of documents from public files, the planting of bombs, the art of street warfare, and the like, I would have no doubts. The freedom to speak is not absolute; the teaching of methods of terror and other seditious conduct should be beyond the pale along with obscenity and immorality. This case was argued as if those were the facts. The argument imported much seditious conduct into the record.

* W. O. Douglas, Dissent in *Dennis* v. *U.S.,* 341 U.S., 581.

That is easy and it has popular appeal, for the activities of Communists in plotting and scheming against the free world are common knowledge. But the fact is that no such evidence was introduced at the trial. There is a statute which makes a seditious conspiracy unlawful. Petitioners, however, were not charged with a "conspiracy to overthrow" the Government. They were charged with a conspiracy to form a party and groups and assemblies of people who teach and advocate the overthrow of our Government by force or violence and with a conspiracy to advocate and teach its overthrow by force and violence. It may well be that indoctrination in the techniques of terror to destroy the Government would be indictable under either statute. But the teaching which is condemned here is of a different character.

So far as the present record is concerned, what petitioners did was to organize people to teach and themselves teach the Marxist-Leninist doctrine contained chiefly in four books: Stalin, Foundations of Leninism (1924); Marx and Engels, Manifesto of the Communist Party (1848); Lenin, The State and Revolution (1917); History of the Communist Party of the Soviet Union (B.) (1939).

Those books are to Soviet Communism what Mein Kampf was to Nazism. If they are understood, the ugliness of Communism is revealed, its deceit and cunning are exposed, the nature of its activities becomes apparent, and the chances of its success less likely. That is not, of course, the reason why petitioners chose these books for their classrooms. They are fervent Communists to whom these volumes are gospel. They preached the creed with the hope that some day it would be acted upon.

The opinion of the Court does not outlaw these texts nor condemn them to the fire, as the Communists do literature offensive to their creed. But if the books themselves are not outlawed, if they can lawfully remain on library shelves, by what reasoning does their use in a classroom become a crime? It would not be a crime under the Act to introduce these books to a class, though that would be teaching what the creed of violent overthrow of the Government is. The Act, as construed, requires the element of intent—that those who teach the creed believe in it. The crime then depends not on what is taught but on who the teacher is. That is to make freedom of speech turn not on *what is said*, but on the *intent* with which it is said. Once we start down that road we enter territory dangerous to the liberties of every citizen.

There was a time in England when the concept of constructive treason flourished. Men were punished not for raising a hand against the king but for thinking murderous thoughts about him. The Framers of the Constitution were alive to that abuse and took steps to see that the practice would not flourish here. Treason was defined to require overt acts—the evolution of a plot against the country into an actual project. The present case is not one of treason. But the analogy is close when the illegality is made to turn on intent, not on the nature of the act. We then start probing men's minds for motive and purpose; they become entangled in the law not for what they did but *for what they thought;* they get convicted not for what they said but for the purpose with which they said it.

Intent, of course, often makes the difference in the law. An act otherwise excusable or carrying minor penalties may grow to an abhorrent thing if the evil intent is present. We deal here, however, not with ordinary acts but with speech, to which the Constitution has given a special sanction.

The vice of treating speech as the equivalent of overt acts of a treasonable or seditious character is emphasized by a concurring opinion, which by invoking the law of conspiracy makes speech do service for deeds which are dangerous to society. The doctrine of conspiracy has served divers and oppressive purposes and in its broad reach can be made to do great evil. But never until today has anyone seriously thought that the ancient law of conspiracy could constitutionally be used to turn speech into seditious conduct. Yet that is precisely what is suggested. I repeat that we deal here with speech alone, not with speech *plus* acts of sabotage or unlawful conduct. Not a single seditious act is charged in the indictment. To make a lawful speech unlawful because two men conceive it is to raise the law of conspiracy to appalling proportions. That course is to make a radical break with the past and to violate one of the cardinal principles of our constitutional scheme.

Free speech has occupied an exalted position because of the high service it has given our society. Its protection is essential to the very existence of a democracy. The airing of ideas releases pressures which otherwise might become destructive. When ideas compete in the market for acceptance, full and free discussion exposes the false and they gain few adherents. Full and free discussion even of ideas we hate encourages the testing of our own prejudices and preconceptions. Full and free discussion keeps a society from becoming stagnant and unprepared for the stresses and strains that work to tear all civilizations apart.

Full and free discussion has indeed been the first article of our faith. We have founded our political system on it. It has been the safeguard of every religious, political, philosophical, economic, and racial group amongst us. We have counted on it to keep us from embracing what is cheap and false; we have trusted the common sense of our people to choose the doctrine true to our genius and to reject the rest. This has been the one single outstanding tenet that has made our institutions the symbol of freedom and equality. We have deemed it more costly to liberty to suppress a despised minority than to let them vent their spleen. We have above all else feared the political censor. We have wanted a land where our people can be exposed to all the diverse creeds and cultures of the world.

There comes a time when even speech loses its constitutional immunity. Speech innocuous one year may at another time fan such destructive flames that it must be halted in the interests of the safety of the Republic. That is the meaning of the clear and present danger test. When conditions are so critical that there will be no time to avoid the evil that the speech threatens, it is time to call a halt. Otherwise, free speech which is the strength of the Nation will be the cause of its destruction.

Yet free speech is the rule, not the exception. The restraint to be constitutional must be based on more than fear, on more than passionate opposition against the speech, on more than a revolted dislike for its contents. There must be some immediate injury to society that is likely if speech is allowed. The classic statement of these conditions was made by Mr. Justice Brandeis in his concurring opinion in *Whitney* v. *California,* 274 U. S. 357, 376–377:

> Fear of serious injury cannot alone justify suppression of free speech and assembly. Men feared witches and burnt women. It is the function of speech to free men from the bondage of irrational fears. To justify suppression of free speech there must be reasonable ground to fear that serious evil will result if free speech is practiced. There must be reasonable ground to believe that the danger apprehended is imminent. There must be reasonable ground to believe that the evil to be prevented is a serious one. Every denunciation of existing law tends in some measure to increase the probability that there will be violation of it. Condona-

tion of a breach enhances the probability. Expressions of approval add to the probability. Propagation of the criminal state of mind by teaching syndicalism increases it. Advocacy of law-breaking heightens it still further. But even advocacy of violation, however reprehensible morally, is not a justification for denying free speech where the advocacy falls short of incitement and there is nothing to indicate that the advocacy would be immediately acted on. The wide difference between advocacy and incitement, between preparation and attempt, between assembling and conspiracy, must be borne in mind. In order to support a finding of clear and present danger it must be shown either that immediate serious violence was to be expected or was advocated, or that the past conduct furnished reason to believe that such advocacy was then contemplated.

Those who won our independence by revolution were not cowards. They did not fear political change. They did not exalt order at the cost of liberty. To courageous, self-reliant men, with confidence in the power of free and fearless reasoning applied through the processes of popular government, no danger flowing from speech can be deemed clear and present, unless the incidence of the evil apprehended is so imminent that it may befall before there is opportunity for full discussion. *If there be time to expose through discussion the falsehood and fallacies, to avert the evil by the processes of education, the remedy to be applied is more speech, not enforced silence.* (Italics added.)

I had assumed that the question of the clear and present danger, being so critical an issue in the case, would be a matter for submission to the jury. It was squarely held in *Pierce* v. *United States,* 252 U. S. 239, 244, to be a jury question. Mr. Justice Pitney, speaking for the Court, said, "Whether the statement contained in the pamphlet had a natural tendency to produce the forbidden consequences, as alleged, was a question to be determined not upon demurrer but by the jury at the trial." That is the only time the Court has passed on the issue. None of our other decisions is contrary. Nothing said in any of the nonjury cases has detracted from that ruling. The statement in *Pierce* v. *United States, supra,* states the law as it has been and as it should be. The Court, I think, errs when it treats the question as one of law.

Yet, whether the question is one for the Court or the jury, there should be evidence of record on the issue. This record, however, contains no evidence whatsoever showing that the acts charged, *viz.,* the teaching of the Soviet theory of revolution with the hope that it will be realized, have created any clear and present danger to the Nation. The Court, however, rules to the contrary. It says, "The formation by petitioners of such a highly organized conspiracy, with rigidly disciplined members subject to call when the leaders, these petitioners, felt that the time had come for action, coupled with the inflammable nature of world conditions, similar uprisings in other countries, and the touch-and-go nature of our relations with countries with whom petitioners were in the very least ideologically attuned, convince us that their convictions were justified on this score."

That ruling is in my view not responsive to the issue in the case. We might as well say that the speech of petitioners is outlawed because Soviet Russia and her Red Army are a threat to world peace.

The nature of Communism as a force on the world scene would, of course, be relevant to the issue of clear and present danger of petitioners' advocacy within the United States. But the primary consideration is the strength and tactical position of petitioners and their converts in this country. On that there is no evidence in the record. If we are to take judicial notice of the threat of Communists within the nation, it should not be difficult to conclude that *as a political party* they are of little consequence. Communists in this country have never made a respectable or serious showing in any election. I would doubt that there is a village, let alone a city or county or state, which the Communists could carry. Communism in the world scene is no bogeyman; but Communism as a political faction or party in this country plainly is. Communism has been so thoroughly exposed in this country that it has been crippled as a political force. Free speech has destroyed it as an effective political party. It is inconceivable that those who went up and down this country preaching the doctrine of revolution which petitioners espouse would have any success. In days of trouble and confusion, when bread lines were long, when the unemployed walked the streets, when people were starving, the advocates of a short-cut by revolution might have a chance to gain adherents. But today there are no such conditions. The country is not in despair; the people know Soviet Communism; the doctrine of Soviet revolution is exposed in all of its ugliness and the American people want none of it.

How it can be said that there is a clear and present danger that this advocacy will succeed is, therefore, a mystery. Some nations less resilient than the United States, where illiteracy is high and where democratic traditions are only budding, might have to take drastic steps and jail these men for merely speaking their creed. But in America they are miserable merchants of unwanted ideas; their wares remain unsold. The fact that their ideas are abhorrent does not make them powerful.

The political impotence of the Communists in this country does not, of course, dispose of the problem. Their numbers; their positions in industry and government; the extent to which they have in fact infiltrated the police, the armed services, transportation, stevedoring, power plants, munitions works, and other critical places—these facts all bear on the likelihood that their advocacy of the Soviet theory of revolution will endanger the Republic. But the record is silent on these facts. If we are to proceed on the basis of judicial notice, it is impossible for me to say that the Communists in this country are so potent or so strategically deployed that they must be suppressed for their speech. I could not so hold unless I were willing to conclude that the activities in recent years of committees of Congress, of the Attorney General, of labor unions, of state legislatures, and of Loyalty Boards were so futile as to leave the country on the edge of grave peril. To believe that petitioners and their following are placed in such critical positions as to endanger the Nation is to believe the incredible. It is safe to say that the followers of the creed of Soviet Communism are known to the F. B. I.; that in case of war with Russia they will be picked up overnight as were all prospective saboteurs at the commencement of World War II; that the invisible army of petitioners is the best known, the most beset, and the least thriving of any fifth column in history. Only those held by fear and panic could think otherwise.

This is my view if we are to act on the basis of judicial notice. But the mere statement of the opposing views indicates how important it is that we know the facts before we act. Neither prejudice nor hate nor senseless fear should be the basis of this solemn act. Free speech—the glory of our system of government—should not be sacrificed on anything less than plain and objective proof of danger that the evil advocated is imminent. On this record no one can say that petitioners and their converts are in such a strategic position as to have even the slightest chance of achieving their aims.

The First Amendment provides that "Congress shall make no law . . . abridging the freedom of speech." The Constitution provides no exception. This does not mean, however, that the Nation need hold its hand until it is in such weakened condition that there is no time to protect itself from incitement to revolution. Seditious conduct can always be punished. But the command of the First Amendment is so clear that we should not allow Congress to call a halt to free speech except in the extreme case of peril from the speech itself. The First Amendment makes confidence in the common sense of our people and in their maturity of judgment the great postulate of our democracy. Its philosophy is that violence is rarely, if ever, stopped by denying civil liberties to those advocating resort to force. The First Amendment reflects the philosophy of Jefferson "that it is time enough for the rightful purposes of civil government, for its officers to interfere when principles break out into overt acts against peace and good order." The political censor has no place in our public debates. Unless and until extreme and necessitous circumstances are shown, our aim should be to keep speech unfettered and to allow the processes of law to be invoked only when the provocateurs among us move from speech to action.

Vishinsky wrote in 1938 in The Law of the Soviet State, "In our state, naturally, there is and can be no place for freedom of speech, press, and so on for the foes of socialism."

Our concern should be that we accept no such standard for the United States. Our faith should be that our people will never give support to these advocates of revolution, so long as we remain loyal to the purposes for which our Nation was founded.

OPINION OF THE COURT IN BROWN V. TOPEKA*

By Earl Warren

Chief Justice Earl Warren (1891–   ) argues in Brown v. Topeka (1954) that "separate and equal" schools are inherently unequal

When President Eisenhower appointed Earl Warren as Chief Justice of the United States Supreme Court, he tapped one of California's leading progressive Republicans. Warren was born in Los Angeles, took a B.A. and a J.D. at the University of California (Berkeley), practiced law in San Francisco, and served with distinction from 1925 to 1939 as a crusading district attorney for Alameda County before becoming California's state's attorney. He proved a strong vote-getter among both parties as the progressive governor of his state, winning a reputation on the issues of civil liberties and fair employment practices as well as for his internationalist utterances.

In this famous opinion of *Brown* v. *the Board of Education of Topeka* (1954), Chief Justice Warren drew upon the observations of social scientists, some of whom stressed the effect of segregation upon the child's feeling of inferiority and hence a resulting inhibition of learning. In 1963, President Lyndon B. Johnson chose Warren to investigate all the circumstances behind the assassination of Kennedy, hoping to silence the harmful and irresponsible rumors regarding a sinister conspiracy.

IN APPROACHING this problem, we cannot turn the clock back to 1868 when the Amendment was adopted, or even to 1896 when *Plessy* v. *Ferguson* was written. We must consider public education in the light of its full development and its present

* Chief Justice Earl Warren, Opinion of the Court, 347 U.S., 492–95.

place in American life throughout the Nation. Only in this way can it be determined if segregation in public schools deprives these plaintiffs of the equal protection of the laws.

Today, education is perhaps the most important function of state and local governments. Compulsory school attendance laws and the great expenditures for education both demonstrate our recognition of the importance of education to our democratic society. It is required in the performance of our most basic public responsibilities, even service in the armed forces. It is the very foundation of good citizenship. Today it is a principal instrument in awakening the child to cultural values, in preparing him for later professional training, and in helping him to adjust normally to his environment. In these days, it is doubtful that any child may reasonably be expected to succeed in life if he is denied the opportunity of an education. Such an opportunity, where the state has undertaken to provide it, is a right which must be made available to all on equal terms.

We come then to the question presented: Does segregation of children in public schools solely on the basis of race, even though the physical facilities and other "tangible" factors may be equal, deprive the children of the minority group of equal educational opportunities? We believe that it does.

In *Sweatt* v. *Painter, supra,* in finding that a segregated law school for Negroes could not provide them equal educational opportunities, this Court relied in large part on "those qualities which are incapable of objective measurement but which make for greatness in a law school." In *McLaurin* v. *Oklahoma State Regents, supra,* the Court, in requiring that a Negro admitted to a white graduate school be treated like all other students, again resorted to intangible considerations: ". . . his ability to study, to engage in discussions and exchange views with other students, and, in general, to learn his profession." Such considerations apply with added force to children in grade and high schools. To separate them from others of similar age and qualifications solely because of their race generates a feeling of inferiority as to their status in the community that may affect their hearts and minds in a way unlikely ever to be undone. The effect of this separation on their educational opportunities was well stated by a finding in the Kansas case by a court which nevertheless felt compelled to rule against the Negro plaintiffs:

Segregation of white and colored children in public schools has a detrimental effect upon the colored children. The impact is greater when it has the sanction of the law; for the policy of separating the races is usually interpreted as denoting the inferiority of the negro group. A sense of inferiority affects the motivation of a child to learn. Segregation with the sanction of law, therefore, has a tendency to [retard] the educational and mental development of negro children and to deprive them of some of the benefits they would receive in a racial[ly] integrated school system.

Whatever may have been the extent of psychological knowledge at the time of *Plessy* v. *Ferguson*, this finding is amply supported by modern authority. Any language in *Plessy* v. *Ferguson* contrary to this finding is rejected.

We conclude that in the field of public education the doctrine of "separate but equal" has no place. Separate educational facilities are inherently unequal. Therefore, we hold that the plaintiffs and others similarly situated for whom the actions have been brought are, by reason of the segregation complained of, deprived of the equal protection of the laws guaranteed by the Fourteenth Amendment.

Chapter Twelve

CURRENT ISSUES

THE FAMOUS COMMONWEALTH CLUB ADDRESS OF SEPTEMBER, 1932 *

By Franklin D. Roosevelt

Franklin D. Roosevelt (1882–1945) in his Commonwealth Club Address calls for a New Deal to cope with an era of mature capitalism

The philosophy and assumptions of the early New Deal are outlined in the following address, which is partly attributed to Adolf Berle and others of the Brain Trust as well as to Roosevelt himself. The reader will recognize the sober assumptions of Turner's closed frontier with the end of a "safety valve" for the unemployed. There is also the much-discussed idea that America had entered the stage of "mature capitalism," which implied the end of rapid expansionism and the need for a government capable of effectively administering the existing and relatively stationary economy. This was a portent of the NRA and the AAA with its philosophy of social planning.

The ideological roots of this thinking belongs to the Progressive Movement, especially to the idea of Herbert Croly's *The Promise of American Life* (1909) and its activist counterpart, Theodore Roosevelt's New Nationalism. Both would meet the growing danger of corporate bigness through a strong regulative federal government. Yet undecided in New Deal philosophy was the future

* F. D. Roosevelt, "Campaign Address on Progressive Government," in Samuel Rosenman (ed.), *The Public Papers and Addresses of Franklin D. Roosevelt* (New York: Random House, Inc., 1938). 750–56. Reprinted by permission of Random House, Inc.

of Wilson's New Freedom and Brandeis' prescriptions to regulate competition, for the NRA virtually suspended the antitrust laws. Roosevelt's facts and arguments regarding corporate concentration by 600 firms are obviously taken from Adolf A. Berle, Jr., and Gardiner C. Means's book, *The Modern Corporation and Private Property* (1932).

A GLANCE at the situation today only too clearly indicates that equality of opportunity as we have known it no longer exists. Our industrial plant is built; the problem just now is whether under existing conditions it is not overbuilt. Our last frontier has long since been reached, and there is practically no more free land. More than half of our people do not live on the farms or on lands and cannot derive a living by cultivating their own property. There is no safety valve in the form of a Western prairie to which those thrown out of work by the Eastern economic machines can go for a new start. We are not able to invite the immigration from Europe to share our endless plenty. We are now providing a drab living for our own people.

Our system of constantly rising tariffs has at last reacted against us to the point of closing our Canadian frontier on the north, our European markets on the east, many of our Latin-American markets to the south, and a goodly proportion of our Pacific markets on the west, through the retaliatory tariffs of those countries. It has forced many of our great industrial institutions which exported their surplus production to such countries, to establish plants in such countries, within the tariff walls. This has resulted in the reduction of the operation of their American plants, and opportunity for employment.

Just as freedom to farm has ceased, so also the opportunity in business has narrowed. It still is true that men can start small enterprises, trusting to native shrewdness and ability to keep abreast of competitors; but area after area has been preempted altogether by the great corporations, and even in the fields which still have no great concerns, the small man starts under a handicap. The unfeeling statistics of the past three decades show that the independent business man is running a losing race. Perhaps he is forced to the wall; perhaps he cannot command credit;

perhaps he is "squeezed out," in Mr. Wilson's words, by highly organized corporate competitors, as your corner grocery man can tell you. Recently a careful study was made of the concentration of business in the United States. It showed that our economic life was dominated by some six hundred odd corporations who controlled two-thirds of American industry. Ten million small business men divided the other third. More striking still, it appeared that if the process of concentration goes on at the same rate, at the end of another century we shall have all American industry controlled by a dozen corporations, and run by perhaps a hundred men. Put plainly, we are steering a steady course toward economic oligarchy, if we are not there already.

Clearly, all this calls for a re-appraisal of values. A mere builder of more industrial plants, a creator of more railroad systems, an organizer of more corporations, is as likely to be a danger as a help. The day of the great promoter or the financial Titan, to whom we granted anything if only he would build, or develop, is over. Our task now is not discovery or exploitation of natural resources, or necessarily producing more goods. It is the soberer, less dramatic business of administering resources and plants already in hand, of seeking to reestablish foreign markets for our surplus production, of meeting the problem of underconsumption, of adjusting production to consumption, of distributing wealth and products more equitably, of adapting existing economic organizations to the service of the people. The day of enlightened administration has come.

Just as in older times the central Government was first a haven of refuge, and then a threat, so now in a closer economic system the central and ambitious financial unit is no longer servant of national desire, but a danger. I would draw the parallel one step farther. We did not think because national Government had become a threat in the 18th century that therefore we should abandon the principle of national Government. Nor today should we abandon the principle of strong economic units called corporations, merely because their power is susceptible of easy abuse. In other times we dealt with the problem of an unduly ambitious central Government by modifying it gradually into a constitutional democratic Government. So today we are modifying and controlling our economic units.

As I see it, the task of Government in its relation to business is to assist the development of an economic declaration of rights, an economic constitutional order. This is the common task of statesman and business man. It is the minimum requirement of a more permanently safe order of things.

Happily, the times indicate that to create such an order not only is the proper policy of Government, but it is the only line of safety for our economic structures as well. We know, now, that these economic units cannot exist unless prosperity is uniform, that is, unless purchasing power is well distributed throughout every group in the Nation. That is why even the most selfish of corporations for its own interest would be glad to see wages restored and unemployment ended and to bring the Western farmer back to his accustomed level of prosperity and to assure a permanent safety to both groups. That is why some enlightened industries themselves endeavor to limit the freedom of action of each man and business group within the industry in the common interest of all; why business men everywhere are asking a form of organization which will bring the scheme of things into balance, even though it may in some measure qualify the freedom of action of individual units within the business.

The exposition need not further be elaborated. It is brief and incomplete, but you will be able to expand it in terms of your own business or occupation without difficulty. I think everyone who has actually entered the economic struggle—which means everyone who was not born to safe wealth—knows in his own experience and his own life that we have now to apply the earlier concepts of American Government to the conditions of today.

The Declaration of Independence discusses the problem of Government in terms of a contract. Government is a relation of give and take, a contract, perforce, if we would follow the thinking out of which it grew. Under such a contract rulers were accorded power, and the people consented to that power on consideration that they be accorded certain rights. The task of statesmanship has always been the re-definition of these rights in terms of a changing and growing social order. New conditions impose new requirements upon Government and those who conduct Government.

I held, for example, in proceedings before me as Governor, the purpose of which was the removal of the Sheriff of New York, that under modern conditions it was not enough for a public official merely to evade the legal terms of official wrongdoing. He owed a positive duty as well. I said in substance that if he had acquired large sums of money, he was when accused required to explain the sources of such wealth. To that extent this wealth was colored with a public interest. I said that in financial matters, public servants should, even beyond private citizens, be held to a stern and uncompromising rectitude.

I feel that we are coming to a view through the drift of our legislation and our public thinking in the past quarter century that private economic power is, to enlarge an old phrase, a public trust as well. I hold that continued enjoyment of that power by any individual or group must depend upon the fulfillment of that trust. The men who have reached the summit of American business life know this best; happily, many of these urge the binding quality of this greater social contract.

The terms of that contract are as old as the Republic, and as new as the new economic order.

Every man has a right to life; and this means that he has also a right to make a comfortable living. He may by sloth or crime decline to exercise that right; but it may not be denied him. We have no actual famine or dearth; our industrial and agricultural mechanism can produce enough and to spare. Our Government formal and informal, political and economic, owes to everyone an avenue to possess himself of a portion of that plenty sufficient for his needs, through his own work.

Every man has a right to his own property; which means a right to be assured, to the fullest extent attainable, in the safety of his savings. By no other means can men carry the burdens of those parts of life which, in the nature of things, afford no chance of labor; childhood, sickness, old age. In all thought of property, this right is paramount; all other property rights must yield to it. If, in accord with this principle, we must restrict the operations of the speculator, the manipulator, even the financier, I believe we must accept the restriction as needful, not to hamper individualism but to protect it.

These two requirements must be satisfied, in the main, by the individuals who claim and hold control of the great industrial and financial combinations which dominate so large a part of our industrial life. They have undertaken to be, not business men, but princes of property. I am not prepared to say that the system which produces them is wrong. I am very clear that they must fearlessly and competently assume the responsibility which goes with the power. So many enlightened business men know this that the statement would be little more than a platitude, were it not for an added implication.

This implication is, briefly, that the responsible heads of finance and industry instead of acting each for himself, must work together to achieve the common end. They must, where necessary, sacrifice this or that private advantage; and in reciprocal self-denial must seek a general advantage. It is here that formal Government—political Government, if you choose—comes in. Whenever in the pursuit of this objective the lone wolf, the unethical competitor, the reckless promoter, the Ishmael or Insull whose hand is against every man's, declines to join in achieving an end recognized as being for the public welfare, and threatens to drag the industry back to a state of anarchy, the Government may properly be asked to apply restraint. Likewise, should the group ever use its collective power contrary to the public welfare, the Government must be swift to enter and protect the public interest.

The Government should assume the function of economic regulation only as a last resort, to be tried only when private initiative, inspired by high responsibility, with such assistance and balance as Government can give, has finally failed. As yet there has been no final failure, because there has been no attempt; and I decline to assume that this Nation is unable to meet the situation.

The final term of the high contract was for liberty and the pursuit of happiness. We have learned a great deal of both in the past century. We know that individual liberty and individual happiness mean nothing unless both are ordered in the sense that one man's meat is not another man's poison. We know that the old "rights of personal competency," the right to read, to think, to speak, to choose and live a mode of life, must be respected at all hazards. We know that liberty to do anything which deprives others of those elemental rights is outside the protection of any compact; and that Government in this regard is the maintenance of a balance, within which every individual may have a place if he will take it; in which every individual may find safety if he wishes it; in which every individual may attain such power as his ability permits, consistent with his assuming the accompanying responsibility.

All this is a long, slow talk. Nothing is more striking than the simple innocence of the men who insist, whenever an objective is present, on the prompt production of a patent scheme guaranteed to produce a result. Human endeavor is not so simple as that. Government includes the art of formulating a policy, and using the political technique to attain so much of that policy as will receive general support; persuading, leading, sacrificing, teaching always, because the greatest duty of a statesman is to educate. But in the matters of which I have spoken, we are learning rapidly, in a severe school. The lessons so learned must not be forgotten, even in the mental lethargy of a speculative upturn. We must build toward the time when a major depression cannot occur again; and if this means sacrificing the easy profits of inflationist booms, then let them go; and good riddance.

Faith in America, faith in our tradition of personal responsibility, faith in our institutions, faith in ourselves demand that we recognize the new terms of the old social contract. We shall fulfill them, as we fulfilled the obligation of the apparent Utopia which Jefferson imagined for us in 1776, and which Jefferson, Roosevelt and Wilson sought to bring to realization. We must do so, lest a rising tide of misery, engendered by our common failure, engulf us all. But failure is not an American habit; and in the strength of great hope we must all shoulder our common load.

INAUGURAL ADDRESS *
The New Frontier Philosophy

By John F. Kennedy

President John F. Kennedy (1917–1963) offers a new frontier of freedom and economic security

The election of an Irish-American Catholic to the White House, albeit by a margin of only one tenth of one per cent, marked the fast upward rise of the Boston Irish immigrants toward general

* John F. Kennedy, *Inaugural Address*, January 20, 1961.

acceptance. Earlier Kennedy had accomplished a perhaps more significant feat. This son of the wealthy financier and Democratic "angel," Joseph Kennedy, had defeated a scion of Puritan stock, Senator Henry Cabot Lodge, despite an Eisenhower landslide.

Kennedy had graduated from Harvard, becoming absorbed in cultural interests, writing an excellent analysis of foreign affairs in *Why England Slept* and a perceptive study of character in *Profiles in Courage*, a Pulitzer Prize-winner. He escaped the isolationist bias of his father, the New Deal ambassador to Britain, and won distinction for bravery as a commander of a P–T boat in the Solomons. His warm personality, quick wit, political ability, as well as his father's campaign financing facilitated his rise from Massachusetts congressman (1947–53) to Senator (twice elected), and then to president through his victory over Richard M. Nixon in 1960.

His presidential career is too well known to require detailed summarization. He thwarted the Soviet effort to drive the United States out of Berlin and Europe and ejected from Cuba the Russian missiles that menaced the hemisphere. Although much of his legislative program was either buried in congressional committees or defeated outright because he lacked a real working majority, he did initiate major educational reforms as well as stabilizing economic measures, which halted a wave of chronic recessions. He confirmed the New Deal welfare trend and revived the Good Neighbor policy through a $20 billion Alliance for Progress program. Noteworthy were his enthusiastic efforts ably supported by his wife to make the White House the focus of a cultural awakening. Because of its unusually felicitous expression and thought, his Inaugural Address has been frequently quoted.

V ICE PRESIDENT JOHNSON, *Mr. Speaker, Mr. Chief Justice, President Eisenhower, Vice President Nixon, President Truman, Reverend Clergy, fellow citizens:*

We observe today not a victory of party but a celebration of freedom—symbolizing an end as well as a beginning—signifying renewal as well as change. For I have sworn before you and Almighty God the same solemn oath our forebears prescribed nearly a century and three quarters ago.

The world is very different now. For man holds in his mortal hands the power to abolish all forms of human poverty and all forms of human life. And yet the same revolutionary beliefs for which our forebears fought are still at issue around the globe—

the belief that the rights of man come not from the generosity of the state but from the hand of God.

We dare not forget today that we are the heirs of that first revolution. Let the word go forth from this time and place, to friend and foe alike, that the torch has been passed to a new generation of Americans—born in this century, tempered by war, disciplined by a hard and bitter peace, proud of our ancient heritage—and unwilling to witness or permit the slow undoing of those human rights to which this nation has always been committed, and to which we are committed today at home and around the world.

Let every nation know, whether it wishes us well or ill, that we shall pay any price, bear any burden, meet any hardship, support any friend, oppose any foe to assure the survival and the success of liberty.

This much we pledge—and more.

To those old allies whose cultural and spiritual origins we share, we pledge the loyalty of faithful friends. United, there is little we cannot do in a host of cooperative ventures. Divided, there is little we can do—for we dare not meet a powerful challenge at odds and split asunder.

To those new states whom we welcome to the ranks of the free, we pledge our word that one form of colonial control shall not have passed away merely to be replaced by a far more iron tyranny. We shall not always expect to find them supporting our view. But we shall always hope to find them strongly supporting their own freedom—and to remember that, in the past, those who foolishly sought power by riding the back of the tiger ended up inside.

To those peoples in the huts and villages of half the globe struggling to break the bonds of mass misery, we pledge our best efforts to help them help themselves, for whatever period is required—not because the communists may be doing it, not because we seek their votes, but because it is right. If a free society cannot help the many who are poor, it cannot save the few who are rich.

To our sister republics south of our border, we offer a special pledge—to convert our good words into good deeds—in a new alliance for progress—to assist free men and free governments in casting off the chains of poverty. But this peaceful revolution of hope cannot become the prey of hostile powers. Let all our neighbors know that we shall join with them to oppose aggression or subversion anywhere in the Americas. And let every other power know that this Hemisphere intends to remain the master of its own house.

To that world assembly of sovereign states, the United Nations, our last best hope in an age where the instruments of war have far outpaced the instruments of peace, we renew our pledge of support—to prevent it from becoming merely a forum for invective—to strengthen its shield of the new and the weak—and to enlarge the area in which its writ may run.

Finally, to those nations who would make themselves our adversary, we offer not a pledge but a request: that both sides begin anew the quest for peace, before the dark powers of destruction unleashed by science engulf all humanity in planned or accidental self-destruction.

We dare not tempt them with weakness. For only when our arms are sufficient beyond doubt can we be certain beyond doubt that they will never be employed.

But neither can two great and powerful groups of nations take comfort from our present course—both sides overburdened by the cost of modern weapons, both rightly alarmed by the steady spread of the deadly atom, yet both racing to alter that uncertain balance of terror that stays the hand of mankind's final war.

So let us begin anew—remembering on both sides that civility is not a sign of weakness, and sincerity is always subject to proof. Let us never negotiate out of fear. But let us never fear to negotiate.

Let both sides explore what problems unite us instead of belaboring those problems which divide us.

Let both sides, for the first time, formulate serious and precise proposals for the inspection and control of arms—and bring the absolute power to destroy other nations under the absolute control of all nations.

Let both sides seek to invoke the wonders of science instead of its terrors. Together let us explore the stars, conquer the deserts, eradicate disease, tap the ocean depths and encourage the arts and commerce.

Let both sides unite to heed in all corners of the earth the command of Isaiah—to "undo the heavy burdens . . . (and) let the oppressed go free."

And if a beach-head of cooperation may push back the jungle of suspicion, let both sides join in creating a new endeavor, not a new balance of power, but a new world of law, where the strong are just and the weak secure and the peace preserved.

All this will not be finished in the first one hundred days. Nor will it be finished in the first one thousand days, nor in the life of this Administration, nor even perhaps in our lifetime on this planet. But let us begin.

In your hands, my fellow citizens, more than mine, will rest the final success or failure of our course. Since this country was founded, each generation of Americans has been summoned to give testimony to its national loyalty. The graves of young Americans who answered the call to service surround the globe.

Now the trumpet summons us again—not as a call to bear arms, though arms we need—not as a call to battle, though embattled we are—but a call to bear the burden of a long twilight struggle, year in and year out, "rejoicing in hope, patient in tribulation"—a struggle against the common enemies of man: tyranny, poverty, disease and war itself.

Can we forge against these enemies a grand and global alliance, North and South, East and West, that can assure a more fruitful life for all mankind? Will you join in that historic effort?

In the long history of the world, only a few generations have been granted the role of defending freedom in its hour of maximum danger. I do not shrink from this responsibility—I welcome it. I do not believe that any of us would exchange places with any other people or any other generation. The energy, the faith, the devotion which we bring to this endeavor will light our country and all who serve it—and the glow from that fire can truly light the world.

And so, my fellow Americans: ask not what your country can do for you—ask what you can do for your country.

My fellow citizens of the world: ask not what America will do for you, but what together we can do for the freedom of man.

Finally, whether you are citizens of America or citizens of the world, ask of us here the same high standards of strength and sacrifice which we ask of you. With a good conscience our only sure reward, with history the final judge of our deeds, let us go forth to lead the land we love, asking His blessing and His help, but knowing that here on earth God's work must truly be our own.

THE SHAME AND THE GLORY
OF THE INTELLECTUALS*

By Peter Viereck

Peter Viereck (1916–   ) assails the softness of intellectuals on communist totalitarianism

Heredity, social or biological, does not explain why Peter Viereck and his brother George of New York City became such uncompromising anti-Nazis despite the fact that their well-known father, George Sylvester Viereck, was a notorious propaganda agent not only for Kaiser Wilhelm but for Adolf Hitler. Possibly they owed something to their great-grandfather who had fled reactionary Germany with Carl Schurz and the other Forty-eighters who were indeed refugees for freedom. Still, Viereck did share his father's flair for writing poetry and vigorous political prose, even if it became impossible for him to discuss politics with his father at home. He studied at Harvard, identified himself with liberal student causes, then went on to study at Oxford. His writings reveal a first-class mind.

By 1940 he was writing that the socialism of both Hitler and Stalin were essentially alike in economics, ruthlessness, and crude materialism. He began to call for a New Conservatism within a critical traditional framework and urged direct intervention to overthrow Nazism. His severe attack on the German mentality, *Metaphysics, from the Romantics to Hitler* (1941, revised as *Metapolitics* in 1961), which explored the sickly ideology and history of the Nazi, saw the German fluctuating between a love for the police state and rational democracy. Both Viereck brothers practiced their convictions by joining the army.

With the war over, Peter Viereck was dismayed and troubled, as the selection shows, by the tolerance of intellectuals for Stalin's brand of totalitarianism and by the impact of mass culture. Once more he sought a New Conservatism, though not in the strident irresponsible manner of the followers of Senator McCarthy.

indiff.
of the intellectuals

A Specter Haunts the Communists

THE TYPICAL book titles of our age are not *The Age of Reason* (typical eighteenth-century title of Paine) but *The Age of Longing, The Age of Anxiety, The Politics of Murder, The Strategy of Terror, The Age of Terror*. Such representative book titles, with their mood of 1983 and eleven months, could only have been written in the century of which Nietzsche had prophesied: "With every growth in man's stature, he grows in depth and terribleness too. Where are the Vandals of the twentieth century?"

1984

Well, here they are. The whole intellectual life of the eighteenth-century "age of reason" was aroused to white-hot indignation over one individual miscarriage of justice: the famous Calas case. Yet in our "age of terror," the mass-murder of millions in Hitler's and Stalin's slave camps was long met with indifference and even appeasement. Why? The communazi "Vandals of the twentieth century" have emerged from both socialist and capitalist economic systems. Therefore, the "why" is found not in economics but in values, in our lack of ethical traffic lights.

Nietzsche had hoped for "a transvaluation of values." This was to lead "beyond good and evil." Instead, our devaluation of values is beneath good and evil.

Once man was considered God's image. Today he degenerates into mass-man. Then into ape. Then into a jungle beast of prey. Finally into a mere material object, from whose lard despots make soap and from whose skin the mistresses of despots make lampshades.

The way back to human dignity is for all creeds, right or left, monarchist or republican, capitalist or socialist, to treat man as an end, not a means. Man must be treated as a moral subject to revere individually, not a material object to push around in impersonal blueprints. Conservatives, liberals, parliamentary monarchists, parliamentary republicans, democratic capitalists, democratic socialists: all have in common certain values of humaneness and honest thinking. This is not true of the communazis. They—I refer to the rulers, not to their slaves—are not interested in humaneness and honest thinking to start with. They are howling in the savage outer darkness, beyond the metaphoric Roman *limes* of civilized humanity.

Man as an END.

commu- nazis.

One relativist kind of liberal "knows the price of everything and the *value* of nothing." The function of humanistic conservatism in philosophy and in literature, a function from which political action follows merely as secondary, is the rediscovery of the values of western man. I can imagine a sarcastic liberal replying: "Your kind of conservative knows the value of everything and the realistic market price of nothing."

But have we not made a mess of reality by being too realistic? This is a plea for the material necessity of more idealism, for the economic necessity of more than economics, and for a road back from *Realpolitik* and brutalization.

My mistake in past books and essays: too much fuss about labels. Most labels represent oversimplified half-truths that misunderstand each other. Distinctions between labels and -isms are real enough when properly defined. I continue to stress their importance. But I have now learnt to place greater stress on *what kind of* conservative, liberal, capitalist, or socialist you are. Freedom depends on the means you seek it with. This is never realized by the impatient, monomaniac partisans of any one of the above -isms.

The most effective single piece of revolutionary propaganda is the *Communist Manifesto* of 1848 by Marx and Engels. Its dramatic opening and closing paragraphs (capital letters and all) are today recited religiously by millions in Europe and Asia:

> A specter haunts Europe—the specter of communism. All the powers of old Europe have entered into a holy alliance in order to lay this specter: pope and tsar; Metternich and Guizot; French radicals and German police.
>
> . . . . Let the ruling classes tremble at the prospect of a communist revolution. Proletarians have nothing to lose but their chains. They have a world to win.
>
> PROLETARIANS OF ALL LANDS, UNITE!

Several things have happened since 1848. Himmler has happened, and the crematories. Korea has happened, and the misery of the forced-labor camps at Karaganda. As a direct result of these happenings, mankind is beginning to make a rediscovery. The rediscovery involves *three questions:* Do you work for your economic objectives (no matter which ones)

(1) with ethical self-restraint?
(2) within a framework of equitable universal values?

(3) with rigorous intellectual honesty?

A specter—here is freedom's Anti-Communist Manifesto to answer 1848—a specter haunts the Communists. The specter is mankind's rediscovery that these three questions *matter*. All the powers of left and right totalitarianism have entered into an unholy alliance in order to lay the specter: Commissar and Fuehrer; Mao and Perón; French Communists and German neo-Nazis. . . . Let the ruling secret police tremble at the prospect of an anticommunist revolution. Slave laborers have nothing to lose but their barbed wire. They have their soul to win back, sweeter than conquest of a world. HUMAN BEINGS OF ALL CLASSES, UNITE!

Assumptions

This book makes four assumptions. If even one of the four is wrong, then the argument that follows is wrong. If they are acceptable to the reader, then what follows follows. At least it would seem to follow in general logic, even though it may err in particular details. The four assumptions:

(1) The plain duty of every citizen, including the most ivory-tower intellectual, is to fight the totalitarian evil.

(2) The contemporary form taken by the totalitarian evil (now that its Nazi form has at least momentarily had its fangs drawn) is, above all, communism.

(3) The glory of twentieth-century liberal intellectuals is the vigor with which they took the only possible moral position towards the Nazi threat, a position betrayed by the appeasement policies of the wrong kind of anti-communists, conservatives, and capitalists.

(4) The shame of twentieth-century liberal intellectuals is their failure to expose and fight Stalinist totalitarianism with exactly the same vigor they showed against its brown-shirted version.

That American thought is getting too standardized is by now a standard observation. One qualification: often this observation is used indirectly, by men too clever to attack anti-communism directly, in order to discredit—as "standardizing"—anybody who talks back a little too indiscreetly in free debate against fellow-traveler attitudes.

Provided you keep that important qualification in mind, the dangerous increase in standardizing is undeniable. Its cause is not the present lawful prosecution of the lawbreaking members of the conspiratorial CP. The cause in part is the mechanizing trend of a mass society, with mass production of thought capsules. This being so, an independent-minded protest against standardized thinking should start first of all against the one group that ought to know better. Ought to know better because by education they at least—namely the liberal intellectuals—are relatively free from the mass magazines and mass movies and mass kultcher. To re-examine their unconscious standardizing should not be construed as "attacking" liberal intellectuals. On the contrary, to scrape the barnacles off an excellent but aging boat is never considered an attack on it.

Except by the barnacles.

"THE CRISIS IN AMERICAN PROTESTANTISM"*

By Reinhold Niebuhr

Reinhold Niebuhr (1892–   ) warns that individualist Protestant culture faces a crisis in meeting race and class issues during a collectivist age

Reinhold Niebuhr was born in Wright City, Missouri, the son of a German immigrant who served as a pastor in the Evangelist Synod Church. He graduated from Elmhurst College and the Yale Divinity School and then for thirteen years he administered to a parish of auto workers in Detroit, championing radical causes in his Bethel Evangelical Church. In 1928 he taught at the Union Theological Seminary in New York and two years later accepted a permanent post as professor of Applied Christianity. He expressed his ideas of social action as well as theology in frequent

* Reinhold Niebuhr, "The Crisis in American Protestantism," *The Christian Century* (December 4, 1963), 1498–1501. Reprinted by permission of The Christian Century Foundation.

college lectures and in his prolific writings, notably in *The Nature and Destiny of Man* (1941–43).

Like so many Protestant preachers of his generation, he admired the Christian socialism and social gospel of Walter Rauschenbusch. He was guided by a pragmatic reformism akin to that of John Dewey and William James, but his evangelical beliefs led him to stress man's sinful nature and the allegedly naive assumptions, Utopianism, and perfectibilist notions of American liberals. But this did not prevent him from embracing the outstanding liberal causes of his time. When Nazism menaced the world, he denounced the Christian pacifists and called for immediate intervention. After World War II, he became deeply concerned with the crises of the Cold War, urged the Marshall Plan, demanded the ouster of Franco from Spain, and called for aid for the refugee professional class. He reacted to the communist threat and the theories of the New Conservatism by a greater emphasis upon the neo-orthodox dogmas of original sin and stressed the limitations of liberal panaceas and the new cult of science. But he continued as ever to support the social gospel and various meliorative causes.

Martin Luther King, Jr., has told in *Stride Toward Freedom* (see pages 47–49) that he was far more indebted to Reinhold Niebuhr than to Gandhi in formulating the gospel of nonviolence that served the Negro Revolution of the 1960's. King referred to Niebuhr's book of 1932, *Moral Man and Immoral Society*. Much of Niebuhr's recent views, especially his dissatisfaction with the anachronism of a Protestant, individualist culture operating in an increasingly collectivist age, may be inferred from the accompanying selection.

Refer to p. 48

I T HAS been said that perhaps the weakness of American Protestantism reveals itself in the fact that it is "captive to the power structure."

In a sense there is not, in an open society, a single power structure. Such justice as we have achieved in a technical age has been due to a tolerable equilibrium between various power structures. We have "big business" and "big labor" and "big government," and the government is still democratic and functions under a two-party system. In his brilliant new book *The American Economic Republic* Adolf Berle argues that we have achieved a tolerable harmony and a consequent tolerable justice through an equilibrium of social forces.

The Protestant Church, because it advocates individuality cannot collectively criticise its functioning

Inconsistencies of the Protestant Ethic.

We do not have a single power structure. But we have a single culture. Yet the Protestant church, which has created this individualistic culture, is no more able to exercise a critical function over its handiwork than was the Roman church able to be critical of (or extricate itself from) the medieval feudalism which it had created. On the other hand, the Roman church, with its sense of the social substance of human existence, has been more creative in efforts to solve the modern problems of technical collectivism than has Protestantism.

indiv. v.s. collective age

The crisis of American Protestantism derives from the fact that it is inveterately individualistic in a collectivist age which must deal with the moral and social problems raised by relations between classes and races—not to speak of nations. We are individualistic. Our sense of virtue is individualistic. Has not Max Weber revealed (in *Protestantism and the Spirit of Capitalism*) that the Protestant virtues of "thrift, honesty and industry" launched the modern enterprise?

Beyond those economic virtues, however, we have had some nobler ones. We encouraged all people to love their neighbors. We made much of the fact that the New Testament admonishes us not only to love our neighbor in the sense of being responsible for his welfare, but also to sacrifice for our neighbor in the spirit of Christ. Yet in all such noble sentiments there were lacking a sense of justice and a passion to achieve just adjudication of competing rights and interests in a world of self-seeking men. We are, of course, all self-seeking: the universality of self-regard was one of the doctrines of the Reformation.

Love thy neighbor But Be self-seeking

Incidentally, one of the sources of confusion in American Protestantism is the fact that Protestants in this nation derive from two reformations rather than from one. The classical Reformation was realistic; it regarded all men as actuated by self-love. The other, which the late Rufus Jones regarded as the real Reformation, was perfectionist; it saw the Christian enterprise as an effort to transmute selfish men and nations into unselfish ones. American Protestantism, whatever its origins, has exhibited more sectarian perfectionism than Reformation realism. But whether perfectionist or realist, it has been consistently individualistic in its conception of virtue and of vice.

Throughout the period from the close of the Civil War to the end of the century, the nation rapidly industrialized, producing the social distresses consequent upon a tremendous shift of power in the economic sphere like that which characterized the industrial period in European democracy. The social distresses produced in America, as they did in Europe, a spate of social movements and revolts: the populists, the "Knights of Labor" and, finally, the American Federation of Labor.

But Protestantism was not moved by any of these revolts. Perhaps its complacency stemmed from the fact that the owners of modern industry were members of the white, Protestant, earlier immigration; while the workers, the "hewers of wood and drawers of water," were later arrivals, mainly Catholic and Jewish. In any case, the regnant social creed of Protestantism was, except for aspects espoused by a few heroic spirits, drawn from a moribund Calvinism which regarded wealth as the reward of virtue and poverty as the punishment for drunkenness or laziness. The more secular "social Darwinism" was a staunch ally of this Calvinism. Nothing in the distress of the impoverished workers and farmers could penetrate the complacency of the consistently bourgeois, Protestant conception of heaven.

The organization of labor, however, proceeded. But the culture was still so individualistic that the Supreme Court, reading the presuppositions of the culture into the Constitution, prevented by judicial injunction all action on behalf of labor. It was not until a worldwide depression arrived that an astute statesman, Franklin D. Roosevelt, belatedly persuaded a reluctant middle-class culture to establish the legal right to set collective power against collective power and thus establish that equilibrium of power in the economic sphere which is the necessary prerequisite of a tolerable justice in a technical age. The United States achieved this milestone in the third decade of the present century, long after European democracies had through gradual steps in social legislation laid the foundations of the welfare state.

Meanwhile, of course, there were critical and prophetic voices in American Protestantism which sought to bring Christian morality into terms of relevance with the burning issues of social justice. The social gospel emerged at the turn of the century. Walter Rauschenbusch wrote his *Christianity and the Social Crisis*. Washington Gladden, Richard Ely and a host of other Protestant leaders challenged the regnant individualism of American Protestantism. The Federal Council of Churches adopted a "social creed" in which the rights of the workers to organize were affirmed. Franklin Roosevelt won his first election armed with the Protestant social creed and Pope Leo XIII's historic encyclical *Rerum Novarum,* published in 1891.

Despite the great contribution of the social gospel school, it must be admitted that it never consistently analyzed the complicated relation between power and justice. Vaguely socialist and pacifist, it ultimately separated into two wings. The right wing talked of "evangelical justice" which was "given" and not "grasped." The left wing was involved in socialist and even communist speculations, and a sorry fringe of that wing finally became enmeshed in Stalinist politics.

In short, the major issues of economic and social justice were met and solved, and American industrial society came to terms with its neglected collective problems without too much aid from the Protestant churches. This judgment must not, however, be seen as detracting from the value of those services to the nation which many heroic spirits in the Protestant ministry have contributed through their witness.

Our nation has thus reached a tolerable solution of its problems of economic justice because the society was "open" enough to allow the economically weak but politically strong (armed with the ballot) to use their power to achieve economic as well as political gains. So a tolerable equilibrium of power was established, an equilibrium without which justice cannot be achieved in a world of self-seeking men, particularly when those men act collectively.

Since the church is not a social engineer we cannot demand from it a blueprint of the relation of justice to power. But the Protestant church was undoubtedly both too individualistic and too sentimental to be able to give much guidance to a nation in the throes of industrial unrest. Above all, it failed to acquaint the community with the deviousness of the human heart and with the labyrinthine depth of self-deception into which the self-seeking heart can sink. Is not the Christian gospel a good guide to the mysteries of good and evil in the human heart? Should it not make us aware of both the heights of true love and the depths of self-love of which man is capable?

The tolerable solution of the issue of economic justice has not affected the issue of racial justice. A century after their emancipation from slavery one-tenth of our population, the Negroes, the real proletarians of the American scene, still wait in vain for justice from their fellow citizens. In his classic inquiry into our racial situation published in 1948, the Swedish sociologist Gunnar Myrdal characterized the Negro's position in our Christian, democratic nation as constituting the "American dilemma." It was more than that. It was a scandal.

From the very beginning a certain degree of dishonesty entered into the relation of the idealistic young republic with the Negro. Thomas Jefferson, who wrote the brave words of the Declaration of Independence about equality and liberty being "inalienable rights," was a slaveholder. The founding fathers, who had accused King George III of profiting from the slave trade, did nothing to abolish slavery in the several states. While the Constitution allowed a certain percentage of representation for citizens "in servitude" and did not use the hated word "slavery," ironically enough slavery spread in those colonies and states in which Jeffersonian liberalism and evangelical Christianity were very strong. In fact, both were employed as ideological defenses for slavery. The Jeffersonians used the states' rights doctrines to protect their "peculiar institution." The Christians had discovered Augustine's dictum, "It is better to be a slave of man than a slave of sin." They did not acknowledge the obvious fact that slavery is the instrument of sin for the slaveowner who has arbitrary power over a fellow human being. But the fact that they defended slavery, an obvious defiance of the basic love commandment of the Christian faith, left their consciences uneasy. Therefore evangelicalism hardened into a graceless legalism in which Christians tried to prove their faith by "tithing mint, anise and cummin," by exaggerated prudery in sex behavior and extravagant sabbatarianism. The institution of slavery turned even the sweetest things sour.

The Civil War was fought on the issue of the preservation of the union, not on the issue of slavery. The Emancipation Proclamation issued by President Abraham Lincoln in order to ensure victory for the union had, in the words of a learned historian, "all the eloquence of a bill of lading." The Negro was indeed emancipated. But a decade later the Fourteenth amendment, which was supposed to give him the vote, was circumvented when, as the price for the south's support of Rutherford B. Hayes in the disputed election results of 1876, the north did not insist on enforcement of the enfranchisement. In many states even now, a century after the Civil War, the Negro must fight for the right to vote. Thus one-tenth of our population has been rendered rightless and powerless—the former because of the latter. In this world of self-seeking men the Negro, because of his powerlessness, is being defrauded of opportunity for access to housing, education and employment, as well as of every civil right in regard to which the Constitution had ensured his "equality."

Since this state of affairs has been an affront not only to democratic justice but also to Christian universalism, the Christian church should have championed the cause of these disfranchised people. The complacency of the church has, however, been as great as that of the community at large. It represents an evil in which we are all involved and which should make us sympathetic whenever we are tempted to judge the German people severely for their acquiescence in the racism espoused by the nazis. Meanwhile, the Catholic Church has been truer to the principles of Christian universalism than has Protestantism—though in making that statement one must allow for the fact that it has had no great strength in the south and that its rigor in desegregating parochial schools is a recent development.

Nothing can excuse the abject capitulation of American Protestant Christianity to perpetuation of this social injustice. Our Negro friends are right when they term the Sunday morning church hour the most segregated area of American life. There were, of course, good reasons for the Negroes to organize their own churches, and those churches have proved themselves stalwart in the present crisis. But there has been no good reason for the absence of fellowship between white and colored churches. The church has proved to be no resource in efforts to bridge the tremendous gap that yawns between the two separated nations within a single nation.

Protestantism has not supplied a cohesive and tough Christian culture to defy the racism of the American culture. There have, thank God, been some notable exceptions. Heroic parsons have lost their pulpits; many of them, though themselves southerners, have been able to find pulpits only in northern suburbs. The student movement has sought to do its part. I remember with gratitude the student interracial conferences organized three decades ago in the south by the Christian Student Federation.

In one of them a young miss confessed: "My mamma said I would vomit if I ate a meal with a Negro. I have had several meals with Negroes and have not vomited at all." But we cannot deny that we have all been remiss in cultivating a Christian universalism in the congregations, and that frequently an extravagant congregationalism has delivered Christian people from the alleged evils of clericalism only to place them in subjection to white citizens' councils.

Our failure in the cause of racial justice is the more shocking because the issues are fairly simple. They do not involve the technical details which had to be mastered when we confronted the issue of economic justice in a modern industrial society. The law of love, which demands justice, has been displayed in all its starkness—and we have failed to heed it.

If we speak of the "renewal of the church" in the light of these failings, it must become clear that renewal will not come through the fervency of our commitment to the cause of Christ. The portions of the country most scourged by racism have probably had more revivals than any other part.

The simple fact is that the evangelistic tradition in American evangelicalism accentuated the failure of a highly individualistic version of faith to come to terms with a social evil which is embedded in the mores and customs of the community. We can repent of individual derelictions and defections from general standards of decency and virtue. We can become converted. But the whole community will have to be converted from those mores and customs which defy the ultimate standards of Christian virtue. We have been too individualistic to come to terms with these social sins. The renewal of the church demanded of us now must therefore include encounter with the sins of the community.

The cause of racial justice and the position of the hapless Negro in our culture until the day of his present revolt may serve to point out the issue. The Negro revolt was sparked by an act of emancipation. The Supreme Court was the instrument of that emancipation. The Negroes appealed to the court on the ground that segregated schools violated the Bill of Rights embedded in our Constitution to ensure our citizens "equal protection of the laws." Thus a long-since forgotten right, one drawn from the social ideals of the 18th century, was used to challenge the present customs and inequalities of our culture.

While the Supreme Court ordered desegregated schools "with all deliberate speed," many states and counties have not yet heeded the court order. But the act of emancipation set up the Negro revolt, for revolutions are fed not only by resentments but also by hopes. Intervention of the law suggested that the long night of connivance with the white man's arrogance was over, for the submerged portion of our nation was thus led to protest any form of inequality, injustice or discrimination. We shall probably not experience in this century the end of this significant revolt; it will not spend itself until full justice is achieved.

Two important aspects of the Negro revolt are significant for the renewal of the churches. One is the fact that the Negro church has been renewed in the process of leading the struggle for justice. A clergyman, Martin Luther King, Jr., has become one of the leading citizens of our nation. The Negro church has had its problems; but many of them were resolved when it forgot the minutiae of creed and law, and strove for essential justice for its people.

The other important aspect of the present struggle for justice is the fact that the courts used an ancient and purer standard of justice to correct a contemporary and corrupted standard. To be sure, the court had behind it the sovereign authority of the state, while the church has no such supporting authority. But within its own community it has—or ought to have—sufficient authority to use an even older tradition than that of the 18th century to correct the impurities of our present traditions. In dealing with social evils embedded in a culture, we must challenge the culture to repent and reform. Individual conversion, the mark of an individualistic evangelicalism, can deal only with the moral corruptions which violate a general standard. It has never been successful in correcting the standard. The results of heroic individual actions among both the white and the Negro population reveal that there is always room for individual responsibility and response. But these individual acts of heroism, while displaying the freedom of the individual above and beyond the standards of his culture, gain in significance when they are directed to the evils embedded in a culture. Then they display both the individual and the social dimension of our human existence.

Among the many weaknesses of the Protestant movement, surely its indifference to the social substance of human existence is the most grievous one. In an industrial civilization and in an age of nuclear terror, the renewal of the church must certainly include full awareness of the fact that we are all involved in the virtues, the vices, the guilt and the promises of our generation. In a sense it is true that we cannot be saved unless we are all saved.

"WHAT IS HAPPENING TO THE AMERICAN FAMILY?" *

By Margaret Mead

Significance

Margaret Mead (1901–), cultural anthropologist, points out the weaknesses of the isolated mid-century American family

The Philadelphia-born Margaret Mead was reared in the home of a father who was a professor of economics at the University of Pennsylvania and a mother who was a sociologist and a pioneer in child psychology. She took undergraduate and graduate degrees at Columbia and as an anthropologist was deeply influenced by Franz Boas and Ruth Benedict of that institution. She did much of her field work in the South Pacific and wrote her thesis on "Cultural Stability in Polynesia." Professionally she was a curator of ethnology at the American Museum of Natural History. Firmly committed to the ideal of Boas and Benedict that anthropology must apply its techniques to solve contemporary social problems, she became a specialist in the study of comparative child psychology, competitive behavior among primitive peoples, and social implications of oceanic ethnology. She reached an unusually wide public because of her informal style as well as her shrewd insights into the modern family, notably in the inferences drawn from *Coming of Age in Samoa* (1928), depicting the amazing resources of the child and the communal responsibility in the Samoan family; *And Keep Your Powder Dry* (1942), comparing the American character with that of other cultures; and *Male and*

* Margaret Mead, "What Is Happening to the American Family?" *The National Conference of Social Work* (New York: Columbia University Press, 1947), 66–74. Reprinted by permission of the Columbia University Press.

Female (1949), which found a basis for an analysis of the role of the sexes by studying Polynesian societies.

Margaret Mead's preoccupation with the relationship of psychology and culture is usually clear in these books and specifically in this selection.

Baby sitter

IN CITIES like Oak Ridge the sitter is a social institution that dwarfs almost any other institution in the community. People "sit" in order to get into homes. The people who are living in dormitories and have no home life become sitters in order to lounge in an upholstered chair and look at the fire; and, on the other hand, all the people in homes are trying to get out of them, for at least one evening a week, and get a sitter in. The whole situation is a sharp reminder that the typical American family now consists of a husband and wife and one or more children living in a community where they do not know anyone, where they have no relatives, and where they have no one to depend upon to care for the children in the evening except a sitter who may be psychopathic.

We have built up the picture that in-laws, especially grandmothers, are a menace. The nurse sighs if a grandmother is around when the baby is born. The pediatrician moans when there is a grandmother on the scene. The assumption has been that the family should have no relatives to confuse the issue with their counsel. This has been our ideal for a long time, but fortunately we did not realize it. Now we are beginning to achieve our ideal, and as we do so we are, of course, becoming aware that we cannot ask that type of family to do the kind of things that a family was expected to do in the past. In this country, for instance, we have always expected the members of a family to do most of the nursing of their sick. In the old days the family even buried its own dead, but the neighbors came in and helped to wash the body of the deceased. Today, of course, no one ever sees a dead body if he can help it; we have moved the dead right out of society, and we are getting birth out fairly rapidly, into the hospitals. We are left now with what we call the "facts of life." But we still expect the family, the inexperienced young wife and the inexperienced young husband, to manage its own finances, to handle the children's education and health, to tend the sick, to care for the mildly insane and the defective, and to meet major emergencies. At the lower socio-economic levels there are social agencies to help them, and at the upper socio-economic levels a few people can still afford service, but for the rest of the country, we now expect a family to achieve alone what no society has ever expected an individual family to accomplish unaided. In effect, we call upon the individual family to do what a whole clan used to do. We put all those demands on the individual family and we make the members of that family feel inadequate if they are unable to discharge those duties.

poor & rich can get help, but the middle class can't they must make it alone.

As we realize the fragility of this small, inexperienced, unsupported, isolated family living in an unfamiliar environment, amid temporary friends and associates, our big problem is to bring in community services to provide the assistance that the larger family used to extend. We can do this much faster if we realize that the family has not suddenly lost its moral fiber, as a lot of people think. We read in the discussions about juvenile delinquency, for instance, that the family has lost its moral fiber when what it has lost is its grandmother. And that is especially true in particular groups in society. When Negro workers, for instance, come North they leave their old people down South, especially the mother's mother, who used to be an important factor in caring for the children. In the migrations to our war towns, too, the young people moved and the older people did not. The family has become smaller and more isolated and less experienced, and the husband and wife are less well adjusted to each other. That is much more true than that some mysterious thing called the "moral fiber" of the family has been lost and with it parental ties to the children.

To the extent that we continue to act as if the family were what it used to be, we compromise our capacity to understand its limitations, and also we delay the development of the community services, the education, and the counseling that we need. For instance, I believe that now Oak Ridge does have a home where children can be cared for when somebody is sick, when the mother is having a baby. It is in a community like Oak Ridge which, par excellence, has no grandmothers in it, that we develop first the services that are needed all over the country to supplement the family, to help this isolated, young family in ways that the family of the past did not need helping.

No Nursery School

— divorce

This terminability of marriage has had another serious effect. It has made women's position exceedingly insecure. Europeans think that American women are greatly spoiled, and, of course, they are. But a highly educated Polish woman remarked after she had been here a little while, "I wouldn't be an American woman for anything in the world. American women have to work to keep their husbands." We are so used to seeing in the advertisements such promises as, "If you use this kind of soap, your husband will think your hands are still soft." And if we peruse any woman's magazine, we see the endless emphasis on the fact that wives must continue to be charming enough to be rechosen every day before breakfast!

So, in addition to the strain put upon the small family that is supposed to carry its illnesses, its economic ups and downs, its psychological and spiritual pressures, there is the problem of having constantly to work at remaining a family. There is no security, even for the mother of young children. She too is faced every day, according to the advertisements, with the possibility that if she lets herself go, if she gains two more pounds, if she does not keep her stocking seams straight, she will lose her husband.

mother is faced w/ the poss. of losing her husband daily.

Several other aspects of this problem are important to social workers. One of them concerns the whole position of the homemaker. "Homemaker," you know, is really a very interesting word that seems to have been invented to describe professional home economists who marry. It is a good word, but it is not a word that we have been able to dignify successfully outside home economics. Today most of our women are homemakers. But many of them describe themselves as "just keeping house," "just staying home," "not doing anything." Of course, the better educated they are, the more they are likely to say that. If a woman has a doctorate and is a homemaker she will definitely say that she is not doing anything. She may be taking care of four children in the country and doing all the family washing, but she will still say that she is not doing anything. Half of our population, the half that is charged most intimately with family life, with its stability, with its tone, with its temper, is somehow robbed in public opinion of dignity. This is a serious situation, and the major seriousness comes, I think, from two factors. This is a country of choice, and just as we have built our marriage pattern on choice, we also build our occupation pattern on choice. The theory is that you decide at the age of eight or ten or eighty what you want to do, and then you go and do it, and if you need a little extra education, you take an extension course, but you get there. You are not bound to an occupation by your past, by your lack of education, not by what your father was, nor by what your grandfather was. You are free to choose. We have emphasized more than any other people in modern times the importance of choice.

The one group to whom we have given no choice is married women. Of course there are married women who go on with what is called a "career" if a woman has it, even though it might be a "job" if a man had it. They go on, in the face of their own and other people's disapproval, and as they work at their desks they think about the dust under the beds as no man would ever worry about the dust under a bed. They still feel that they ought to be at home brooming and tending to the dust.

[margin note: Married women have no choice as to a profession]

Perhaps we can realize the implications of such a course if we consider what it would be like if we said to a young man, "What are you going to do?" And he would say, "I am going to be a lawyer—unless I marry, of course." And we would say, "Why, what difference will that make?" He replies, "Of course, if I marry, I will have to live on a farm. I'd have to give up law." And when we ask, "Why?" he answers, "Oh, because it's good for children to be brought up on a farm." Now, if men had to consider that they could have one way of life if they did not marry, and another way of life if they did marry, and ways of life as different as being a farmer and being a lawyer, they might think twice about getting married, and they would certainly not feel that they had free choice. That is really women's position. Women in our society are still a status group; if they marry, certain sorts of behavior are expected from them. I do not at all think that most married women do not want to stay at home, but I do think that most married women would like not to have it taken quite so for granted that they should stay home. If they were given a choice, most of them would stay at home. In a recent *Fortune* survey, in answer to the question to women, "If you were born again, what sex would you like to be?" 25 percent of the women, one out of four, said, "a man." A society is not very stable when one out of four of one sex wants to be of the opposite sex, and it is not a very stable family life in which the carriers of that family life are the people who would like to have, obviously, carried it in another way.

It is serious that we have not solved the problem of choice for married women. We have presented the illusion of choice so effectively to all men that women feel deprived because they do not have it also. Of course, men do not have anything like the choice they think they do, but they think they have it, and that is what is important.

Another serious difficulty for the homemaker is that she can no longer see tangible results of what she does. In the past the housewife did a lot of canning. She made the children's clothes. She baked the bread. She did big, conspicuous things, material things that she could point to, things that the neighbors could point to. Today, if a woman in an urban home has really been successful as a mother for a week, it means that nothing tangible has happened at all. The modern woman's life, in which she gets one child here and another child there, and gets the laundry in and the laundry out, the electrician in and the plumber in, and goes shopping here and shopping there, and leaves this here and gets that from there all day long, leaves her with nothing to say at the end of the day except that she got through it. She has shifted her position from being a producer to being an integrator and organizer of consumption, and we have no standards for appreciating and judging this new role. Most American women are still up against the old standards which called for showing that something has been accomplished, and yet they can no longer boast of large numbers of children, and we have no standards of pride and self-esteem and self-respect for the homemaker which make it possible for the woman on whom family life depends to be as contented and as secure as she deserves to be.

There have been a great many attacks lately on women. Women have been attacked by the psychiatrists, who found that a lot of boys in the army were not ready to leave home. Nobody had expected that they would have to leave home so early, and our weaning system was not adjusted to the demands of the army. And since the men in this country are reared by women, the women were blamed. Most of what is good in children and most of what is bad are due to their mothers, because the mothers bring them up, and the fathers do not. To the extent that we are re-evaluating the maturity of our adolescents and the behavior of our children, we are bound to find a heavy barrage against women because we put such a heavy burden on them.

It is understandable that we should have come to lay such an excessive burden on mothers in this country. In the pioneer days of America a woman had to assume a great deal more responsibility than did the women in old and stable countries of Europe. The American pioneer man wanted a wife who was capable of providing hospitality to the settlers as they came through in the covered wagons, of fending off the Indians if necessary, staying alone for weeks, and looking after the property in his absence. Here was built up the standard of organizing, responsible, and rugged womanhood.

Then, when large numbers of non-English-speaking people began coming to this country and had to learn as adults how to live in America, the men had quite enough to do to learn how to support themselves and their families, and all the details of daily living were turned over to the women. Thus the women became the arbiters of home life and of consumption standards far more than they had been in the countries from which they had come.

So, a variety of perfectly understandable historical reasons has turned the responsibilities of parenthood over to women in this country, but not without serious consequences. One of the most far-reaching consequences is the demand that women combine motherliness with discipline. That is difficult and, to some extent, contradictory. After all, motherly behavior is responsive. You think, "The baby is hungry. I will feed him." He initiates, you go toward him. In a disciplinary, dominating type of behavior you initiate, you give the order, you tell the child to stop or to start, and he stops and he starts. In one case the mother is responsive to the child, and in the other case the mother is disciplinary and restrictive and punitive. That is a difficult combination to achieve, much more difficult than when the discipline was lodged in the father and the responsiveness in the mother. We assign both characteristics to the mother's role, and to that extent we have made women's role difficult. We have made it necessary for them to say, "mother loves you better than anyone in the world," and "you had better get 'A'!" In most European countries, a mother could love the child whether he got "A" or not, and father could discipline him on matters like school marks. There was a balance that was easier to manage than the American balance.

Furthermore, the mother has had to do all the weaning of the children. She has had to keep them at home and push them off simultaneously. It has not been a question of the father taking over the children, of schoolmasters taking over the boys, of a men's society taking over the boys. The schoolteacher is a woman too, and the mother has had to push the child off and off and off: "You are old enough to go to bed by yourself"; "You are too old to sit on mother's lap"; "You are old enough to do this and that and the other"—pushing, pushing, pushing the child away. When the person who is supposed to love him best keeps pushing a child away, there is a basic contradiction. So, we have asked American mothers to do something which is quite difficult. I think it is important, not only to realize how difficult it has been, but also to foster every attempt to get fathers into the home.

The role of the father is one on which there is genuine disagreement between American women and American men. As the 1946 *Fortune* survey showed, more American women would like their husbands to take greater part in the discipline and rearing of the children than there are American men who would like to do so. At the same time there is a trend in the contemporary American family for young fathers to do more for their children than fathers have ever done before. This is partly due to the fact that the returning veteran finds that his baby is more interesting and exciting than it might have seemed if he had been home from the time of its birth.

As we move into the five-day week, free Saturday mornings are appearing all over the country, unpre-empted by church or state or golf club. Here is a situation that should interest every person who is concerned with changing the tone or pattern of our culture. Nobody knows what a man *ought* to do on Saturday morning. Saturday morning is one fourteenth of the week; if every American father spent one fourteenth of the week with his children, the American family would present a very different picture from what we have now. We have the opportunity before a pattern freezes, before some commercialized interest gets hold of Saturday morning, to set Saturday morning up as father's morning. A large number of young fathers would like to do just that; for they have realized, partly through the separation of the war years, that if they could see more of their children, they would be able to make more of their family life. This is a promising, positive trend in American life, something that we can grasp as a means of bringing the younger fathers, particularly, into the home.

We need also a new ethic for family life. We need a new valuation of family life for the secularized people in our society. After all, we have, out of our total population, 65,000,000 church members in this country, and that is a generous count. In many denominations the census includes all the christened children regardless of their church attendance or church interest. We have an increasing number of people who are unrelated to any sort of religious sanction or to any sort of ethical judgment as to why they should do one thing rather than another, why they should stay married instead of being divorced, why they should bring up their children rather than desert them. To these people the family has no definite value, no ethical role, as it had in our older culture and as it must have in every culture if it is going to survive.

One of the values that we can give young people in schools, give people who are struggling with the question of why they should keep on with their marriage, is a sense of the importance of a family in which the father and mother respect each other and yet may disagree in the bringing up of whole individuals in a democracy. Early in the twenties Russia experimented with marriage and the family as an institution on the general theory that the family was an outworn, bourgeois institution, but they seem to have found, even with all the ideology that would have supported another position, no other way to produce responsible human beings who would grow up and marry and have children themselves. They now re-enforce the family very heavily.

We know no other way to produce whole human beings than through the family, and we know no other way to produce "democratic" human beings—the kind who can tolerate the two-party system. Toleration of the two-party system is based on the experience gained when father says "yes" and mother says "no" about the same thing. It is interesting to learn that the typical German character may be traced back to the family structure where somebody dominated, and it did not have to be father. There were families in which the mother dominated, it was the domination that was important, and the children felt safe in the resulting environment. In America we bring up children to feel safe in a world where father likes this and mother likes that, where the parents vote for different candidates, where one week mother supports the boy's desire for a bicycle and the next week father supports his plea to go fishing, where two people whom he loves and respects disagree with each other. Out of this picture grows the kind of character which can tolerate and respect disagreement. We know of no other way of producing such a character save in a family form in which women are accorded a reasonably high level of respect, the right to their own opinions, and a capacity to stand up to their husbands without quarreling and without giving the children a sense of insecurity.

People of all ages are asking today what is the relationship between their personal lives and their personal choices, and between the personal lives and personal choices of their neighbors, their clients, their patients, their students, and the great crisis that faces the human race. For this is the greatest crisis, perhaps, since a small group of prehistoric men wandered north with fire that they knew how to keep but knew not how to make. The relationship between family structure and coherent personality and citizenship, and faith in the continuance of the human race, is something which we can stress for the very young and for those who are beginning family life at a period which is fearfully unrewarding in its prospects for stability and for continuance. But if we recognize the extent to which the present situation is partly temporary and partly a function of the whole world crisis, if we tie in personal choices to the possibility of people feeling strong enough and optimistic enough to go on, and if we recognize the extent to which the family has changed, and the sort of support it needs, we may be able to develop an ethic appropriate to the new and fragile family forms that we have in this country today.

"AUTOMATION AND TECHNOLOGICAL CHANGE"*

By Walter Reuther

Walter Reuther (1907–70), AFL-CIO President, advises new policies to insure the benefits of automation to all groups

Walter Reuther was born in the militant mining center of Wheeling, West Virginia, the son and grandson of German socialists and labor leaders. He studied labor-management relations in the evening classes of Wayne University. During the depression years of 1931–32, when unionization was at a very low ebb, he was a foreman for the Ford Motor Company in the tool and die department and even worked for sixteen months in Ford's Russian plant. When John L. Lewis began his drive for industrial unionism in the mass production industries, Reuther was among the first to join the United Automobile Workers, to actively recruit members, and to use the sit-down technique to assure collective bargaining. He became so indispensable a leader in negotiating with both Ford and General Motors that in 1946 he was elected president of the UAW and Vice President of the CIO.

On the eve of World War II, he attracted national attention for his proposal that Roosevelt get his much-needed plane production by merging the facilities and manpower of the auto industry to achieve the vast output necessary. During the war, his UAW faithfully kept its No-Strike pledge, and, after the war, he was instrumental in purging the CIO of communist influence. Going far beyond the limited bread and butter objectives of Samuel Gompers, he tried to integrate union objectives with the interests of the entire community, urged that labor raises must not be the occasion for inflationary price increases, pioneered in making the "annual guaranteed wage" part of union agreements, persuaded General Motors and others to peg hourly wage rates to the changing cost of living, and secured far-reaching fringe benefits ranging from pensions to medical insurance.

He was a strong New Deal supporter and spoke frankly of a "mixed economy" in which federal participation would steadily increase. Within the NAACP executive board and within the CIO, he fought against racial discrimination. In 1952, when the unions

* From Walter Reuther, "Automation and Technological Change," *Hearings Before the Sub-Committee on Economic Stabilization . . .* 84th Congress, 1st Sess., October 17, 1955, 98–100, 112–14.

1955

felt apprehensive about President-Elect Eisenhower's conservatism, Reuther was elected president of the CIO and in 1955 president of the merged AFL-CIO.

The Reuther testimony on automation that is cited below was given on October 17, 1955, at a time when railroad management was fighting alleged "featherbedding" and eliminating (eventually by 1960) some 725,000 jobs. During these years the UAW lost 168,000 members due largely to automation, and the United Steel Workers reported a loss of 200,000 members. Public opinion polls showed that workers were very apprehensive over computer-directed mechanization that was estimated by the Department of Labor to have displaced 1.8 million workers a year. Automation was one of the chief causes for the great newspaper strikes in New York and Cleveland. It will be noted that while Reuther was very well informed as to the cumulative effects of automation, he preserved his balance and suggested how the anticipated evils could be met by wise national policies and better labor-management relations.

Automation—A Revolutionary Development

WE HAVE been told so often that automation is going to bring on the second industrial revolution that there is, perhaps, a danger we may dismiss the warning as a catch-phrase, and lose sight of the fact that, not only the technique, but the philosophy of automation is revolutionary, in the truest sense of the word. Automation does not only produce changes in the methods of manufacturing, distribution, many clerical operations, and in the structure of business organization, but the impact of those changes on our economy and our whole society bids fair to prove quite as revolutionary as were those of the first industrial revolution.

Through the application of mechanical power to machinery, and the development of new machinery to use this power, the first industrial revolution made possible a vast increase in the volume of goods produced for each man-hour of work. Succeeding technological improvements—such as the development of interchangeable parts and the creation of the assembly line which were essential to the growth of mass production industries—have led to continuous increases in labor productivity. But however much these machines were improved, they still required workers to operate and control them. In some operations, the worker's function was little more than to feed the material in, set the machine in operation and remove the finished product. In others, proper control of the machine required the exercise of the highest conceivable skills. But whether the required skill was little or great, the presence of a human being, using human judgment, was essential to the operation of the machine.

The revolutionary change produced by automation is its tendency to displace the worker entirely from the direct operation of the machine, through the use of automatic control devices. No one, as far as I know, has yet produced a fully satisfactory definition of automation, but I think John Diebold came close to expressing its essential quality when he described automation as "the integration of machines with each other into fully automatic, and, in some cases, self-regulating systems."

In other words, automation is a technique by which whole batteries of machines, in some cases almost whole factories and offices, can be operated according to predetermined automatic controls. The raw material is automatically fed in, the machine automatically processes it, the product is automatically taken away, often to be fed automatically into still another machine that carries it automatically through a further process. In some cases the machine is self-regulating—that is, it is set to turn out a product within certain tolerances as to size or other factors, and if those tolerances are exceeded, the machine itself detects the variation and automatically adjusts itself to correct it.

The revolutionary implications of this new technology can best be understood by looking at a few examples of what is actually being done through automation today, in scattered parts of the economy.

The Lathe That Replaces Its Own Tools

The application of automation ranges all the way from individual automatic machines to virtually automatic factories.

An example of the first is an automatic lathe, produced by the Sundstrand Machine Tool Co., described in American Machinist, March 14, 1955, page 117, which gages each part as it is produced and automatically resets the cutting tools to compensate for tool wear. In addition, when the cutting tools have been worn down to a certain predetermined limit, the machine automatically replaces them with sharp tools. The parts are automatically loaded onto the machine and are automatically unloaded as they are finished. These lathes can be operated for 5 to 8 hours without attention, except for an occasional check to make sure that parts are being delivered to the loading mechanism.

An Automatic Plant

A completely automatic plant is now producing mixed and ready-to-use concrete for the Cleveland Builders Supply Co. (Business Week, Apr. 16, 1955, p. 80). Operated from an electronic control panel, the plant can produce and load into ready-mix trucks any one of some 1,500 different mixing formulas that may be demanded. This plant uses no manual labor at any point in the process.

By a combination of teletype and radio, the control operator is informed as to the particular formula to be loaded into each truck as it arrives. He gets out a punched card, coded for that formula, and the automatic mechanisms take over. Specified amounts of the required materials are delivered by conveyors, in precisely the right quantities, to a mixing bin where they are automatically mixed and then loaded into the waiting truck. The control mechanisms even measure and compensate for any deficiency or excess of water in the aggregate (sand, coarse rock, slag, etc.) which goes into the mixer, and if the order calls for a dry mix, the materials are automatically routed through a dry spout.

This automatic plant has a capacity of 200 cubic yards of concrete per hour, as against 100 cubic yards per hour in the company's conventional plants.

The Automatic Broaching Machine Cuts Direct Labor Costs Drastically

An automatic two-way horizontal broaching machine for machining automobile cylinder heads has cut direct labor costs between 1949 and 1954 by more than all the technological improvements made in this process during the previous 35 years—and with an actual decline in the investment required (Instruments & Automation, January 1955, p. 111).

In 1914 the Cincinnati Milling Machine Co. would have used

162 machines, representing an investment of $243,000, to machine 108 cylinder heads per hour at a direct labor cost of 40 cents per piece. By 1949 it took six machines, representing an investment of $240,000, to turn out the same volume of production at a direct labor cost of 20 cents per piece. (The saving in man-hour requirements is much greater than indicated by these figures, when the increase in wage rates between 1914 and 1949 is taken into account.)

By 1954, however, those six machines had been replaced by a single automatic machine, representing an investment of only $230,000, for the same volume of production, and direct labor costs had been cut from 20 cents a piece in 1949 to 4 cents a piece in 1954—a reduction of 80 percent in 5 years.

Merely Change the Tape to Change the Job Run

One of the important features of automation is that it can be applied not only to long runs of identical operations, but to fairly short-run jobs where instructions given to the machines have to be changed at the end of each job. This is made possible through the use of printed tape, punch cards, etc., on which the instructions are coded, and the machine is given a new set of instructions simply by changing the tape or card.

Minneapolis-Honeywell Regulator Co., for example, reports (Wall Street Journal, April 22, 1955) the development of a precision boring machine, used in aircraft equipment production, which can bore holes with an accuracy of one-thousandth of an inch. Electronic signals from a tape move the blank metal back or forward, rotate it into position, and then turn on the boring mechanism to cut the hole exactly where it is desired. The machine is specially suited for medium-size production in lots of several hundred parts.

Running a Bank with an Electronic Computer

The use of automation is not restricted to manufacturing plants. Increasingly, so-called electronic brains are taking over the functions of office clerks, accountants, and other white-collar workers.

Stanford Research Institute has produced for the Bank of America (Fortune, October 1955, p. 131) an electronic computer

wide applicability

which will do the jobs of many employees. When a check comes to the bank, an operator merely punches into the machine the amount on the face of the check. The check itself carries a code, printed in magnetic ink, which identifies the account number. The machine scans this code to identify the account. It then refers to its "memory bank," which contains information on 32,000 separate accounts, makes sure there is enough in the account to meet the check (if there is not, a warning "overdraft" light is blinked at the operator's desk), and deducts the amount of the withdrawal from the account. The machine also checks up to make sure that there is no stop-payment order against the account. The whole operation takes approximately 1 second.

The transaction is recorded, first in a "temporary memory" bank, and is transferred later to a "permanent memory" bank. At the end of the month, the computer automatically calculates the service charge and then, connected to a high-speed printer which can print 800 characters a second, it prints the customer's complete monthly statement in less than 5 seconds. It is claimed that 9 operators and 1 such machine can replace up to 50 bookkeepers.

Similar computers are being used to make up payrolls, to prepare insurance premium notices and record payments, to prepare telephone bills, to take inventory, to control the operation of electric power generating plants, and for many similar purposes. One central computer to be installed by the Ohio Edison Co., for example, will simultaneously control the operations of 35 generators in 9 plants scattered over an area of 9,000 square miles (New York Times, August 18, 1955).

Even automation itself is being automated. One of the bottlenecks in the use of computers to which data is [fed on] punched cards has been the time required to have the information punched on the cards by trained operators. Now the Burroughs Corp. has produced for the First National City Bank of New York (Wall Street Journal, June 17, 1955) an electronic device which "reads" the serial numbers on travelers' checks and reproduces them on punched cards at a rate of 7,200 checks per hour, doing the work of 10 highly skilled operators.

The great variety of applications shown in these few examples illustrates one of the most significant features of the new technology—its wide applicability. That is the real quality that makes automation a genuinely revolutionary force in our economy, rather than just another technological improvement.

It is technically possible to apply the feedback principle of automation, and the servomechanisms which implement it, to virtually every situation where human control of industrial processes is now used. The growing flood of new uses of automation indicates how quickly the economics of its application are being worked out.

Even Routine Technology Is Accelerating   Reason

One of the factors which has been responsible for the steadily increasing rate of productivity since World War II has been the enormous increase in research expenditures both by industry and by Government. Alfred North Whitehead, the British philosopher, once said, "The greatest invention of the 19th century was the invention of the art of inventing." We might add that one of the great developments of the 20th century has been to change inventing from an art to a standard business procedure. The research department is now a fixture in every important corporation, while the needs of government, especially in national defense, have added to the numbers of research workers, many of whose discoveries are readily applied to industry.

As a result, the flow of what may be considered routine technological innovations—new production methods, new materials and machines applicable only to specific processes or industries, and improvements in work flow—has been greatly accelerated. Harlow Curtice, president of General Motors, noted recently that "new products, new processes are coming off the drawing boards of the engineers and out of the laboratories of the scientists at ever faster pace. . . ."

For the most part, it is the large companies that will be in the best financial position to scrap old equipment and old plants, and replace them with new automated machines and automated plants, thus increasing still more the margin of efficiency which they enjoy over their smaller competitors.

It is possible that relatively low-priced electronic computers will be available for smaller firms. It is also possible that some types of multiple-purpose automated equipment will be available for medium-sized plants whose products are mixed. But in industries where a great volume of identical products are made—as in the automobile industry—the required output for profitable operations may be so great, and the cost of the equipment may be so high, as to make it difficult, if not impossible, for small firms to purchase automated machines.

Government policy should be aimed at assisting small business firms to maintain their existence. A generally liberal credit policy —with low interest rates—is an essential part of such programs to enable small businesses to obtain funds for investment in expensive automatic machinery. Long-term Government loans, at low interest rates, for industrial and commercial expansion, should be made available to small- and medium-sized firms. Government procurement policies should aim at getting work on Government contracts to smaller businesses. The antitrust division of the Justice Department should be instructed to be more vigilant than it has been in the recent past in the effort to eliminate monopolistic practices in industry.

Automation may bring with it the danger that big firms will grow even bigger, while small- and medium-sized competitors are squeezed against the wall. The danger must be minimized by Government policies and actions to assist small business and prevent trends toward monopoly.

Suggested Policies

Automation has been hailed as the "second industrial revolution." But no radical change in technology can take place without parallel changes in the economic structure.

It is within our power to see to it that these economic and social changes take place in an orderly and evolutionary manner —toward improved standards of living and social welfare, an extension of leisure and new horizons of individual opportunities for educational and cultural achievements. Such evolutionary changes in the coming decade will require forethought, planning, and guidance. If we permit the new technology to follow its own blind course, directed only by the selfish interests of those who would utilize it for their own immediate profit, our free society may be subjected to dangerous disruption in a world beset by international tensions.

We cannot permit any weakening of our national strength nor any undermining of our social fabric. The Communists are only too willing to assist in such an endeavor. We should take advantage of the rising productivity that automation makes possible to increase our national strength and improve living standards at the same time.

High levels of employment and rapid economic growth must be achieved in the period ahead. But those goals can be attained only through growing markets that will expand rapidly, along with the economy's rising productivity. A positive Government effort is required to provide the expanding markets that are the basis for economic growth.

Organized labor is doing its part, through collective bargaining for higher wages, extended vacations and holidays, guaranteed wage plans, improved pension and health-welfare plans. There is no need to defend these social gains won by unions for millions of working people; they stand on their own merits, and rising profits, generally, indicate that business has been able to pay for them. But the power of big corporations to administer prices has tended to dilute some of the benefits of these improvements.

A national approach is needed to help make certain that the benefits of automation will be shared among all groups in the population. A congressional inquiry into the price policies of giant corporations, for example, is long overdue—to place the spotlight of public attention on the failure of the dominant corporations to pass on to consumers the benefits of rising productivity.

There is need, too, for a more equitable distribution of the tax burden, an adequate unemployment compensation system, improved social-security benefits, a higher legal minimum wage and reduced legal workweek, protection of farm income, improved educational facilities, financial aid to students, and an extended program of hospital and road construction, and natural resources and development.

Continued Study Is Essential

We in the CIO do not pretend to have the answers to all the problems posed by automation. We are quite sure, in fact, that no one can have all the answers at present. Not nearly enough is known yet about the current achievements of automation, the planned progress of automation, or the precise impact that automation will have on productivity, on employment, and on the national economy.

Index

INDEX